Switching Sides

SWITCHING SIDES

*How a Generation of Historians
Lost Sympathy for the Victims of the
Salem Witch Hunt*

TONY FELS

Johns Hopkins University Press

Baltimore

Johns Hopkins University Press
2715 North Charles Street
Baltimore, Maryland 21218-4363
www.press.jhu.edu

Library of Congress Cataloging-in-Publication Data

Names: Fels, Tony, 1949– author.
Title: Switching sides : how a generation of historians lost sympathy
for the victims of the Salem witch hunt / Tony Fels.
Description: Baltimore : Johns Hopkins University Press, 2018. |
Includes bibliographical references and index.
Identifiers: LCCN 2017016625| ISBN 9781421424378 (pbk. : alk. paper) |
ISBN 9781421424385 (electronic) | ISBN 1421424371 (pbk. : alk. paper) |
ISBN 142142438X (electronic)
Subjects: LCSH: Witchcraft—Massachusetts—Salem—
History—19th century. | Trials (Witchcraft)—Massachusetts—
Salem—History—19th century.
Classification: LCC BF1576 .F45 2017 | DDC 133.4/3097445—dc23
LC record available at https://lccn.loc.gov/2017016625

A catalog record for this book is available from the British Library.

Special discounts are available for bulk purchases of this book.
For more information, please contact Special Sales at 410-516-6936
or specialsales@press.jhu.edu.

Johns Hopkins University Press uses environmentally friendly book
materials, including recycled text paper that is composed of at least
30 percent post-consumer waste, whenever possible.

But what, the reader may ask, does causal attribution have to do with ethics or moral sensibility? Everything, for they are two sides of the same coin. To be an agent is to be causally efficacious, a producer of intended consequences. To hold people responsible is to presume that they are causally efficacious agents and therefore capable (within limits) of choosing which consequences to produce. Judgments of praise, blame, responsibility, liability, courage, cowardice, originality, deliberateness, and spontaneity are just a few of the quintessentially ethical qualities that ride piggyback on perceptions of cause and effect.

—Thomas L. Haskell, *Objectivity Is Not Neutrality*

Contents

Figures

Preface

The following pages offer an essay in historical interpretation. Historians call this facet of their interests by one of the few technical terms of their trade, "historiography." Literally the study of historical writing, "historiography" emphasizes not the events of the past and their causes—the standard subject matter of the discipline of history—but rather how historians construct their narratives and explanations of these events. The aim of all historical analysis is to uncover the truth about the past, but since the complexity of most human developments, especially as they recede in time, typically defies the grasp of any single, subsequent scholar or even of any one scholarly era, it becomes useful to notice the selectivity process and assumptions of value underlying each attempt to retell the historical record. This added focus on the interpretative act in the writing of history promotes a deeper understanding of human history itself, because it encourages thinking about the past from multiple angles and also because it calls attention to the ways in which the study of history serves the needs, legitimate or otherwise, of later generations.

My fascination with historiography began along with my earliest interest in history. I can still remember my excitement when my high-school United States history teacher introduced our class to the debate over the meaning of the mid-nineteenth-century "Jacksonian movement." One leading historian had characterized the Jacksonian Democrats as champions of "the working man," while another had seen the very same politicians as spokesmen for a rising middle class. (Later historians would see Andrew Jackson and his white, male followers principally through the lens of the racial prejudices these men held toward American Indians, African Americans, and Chinese immigrants. And there would be still other interpretations.) From that moment on, I was about equally drawn to learning about the causal relationships of the past as I was to considering the vantage points of the historians from whose works we come to know those relationships. Most of my later academic colleagues would speak about how happy they could be, alone in an archive, immersed in old, yellowed documents that illuminated the past. For me the greatest intellectual thrill came from seeing how the understanding of an era, an empire, a war, or an institution took shape and changed under the influence of scholarly minds.

I cannot remember exactly how I first became engaged by the subject of the Salem witch hunt. However, when early in my university career I had the chance to teach the historical methods course for our undergraduate majors, I decided to refashion it away from the traditional approach of acquainting students with snippets of the "great historians" (from Herodotus forward) in favor of an exercise that would demonstrate how contemporary historians actually operate. This meant showing how, when one chooses a subject from the past to investigate, one usually begins by acquiring an awareness of the ways that previous historians have conceptualized the field. I picked the Salem witch hunt of 1692 for the class to study. Not only were the documentary sources for students' later research projects readily available but the subject matter had generated a wide range of conflicting historical interpretations. For the first part of the course, students read a selection of books and articles, all telling the Salem story in dramatically different ways. Teaching this course over a period of years deepened my own curiosity about the Salem literature and raised a number of historiographical questions, the pursuit of which has formed the substance of this book.

There is also a political dimension to the argument that ensues, as will be readily apparent to readers. For many of the years that I was teaching about Salem, I entertained only a vague sense that something was missing from the principal contemporary accounts. All seemed to slight, to one degree or another, the religious element in the witch hunt. For a social panic to occur among such deeply religious people as the Puritans of New England—a fear based on the perceived threat of hidden supernatural attack—it seemed clear that religious beliefs would have to occupy a central place in any satisfactory explanation. Yet authors of the leading Salem works over the past forty-five years called first upon economic, sociological, psychological, gender-based, ethnic, and political factors to explain the witch hunt. Why, I wondered, had the religious dimension of the events taken a back seat in these accounts?

And then, by chance, developments transpired at my university and within my department that produced a mini–"witch hunt" of its own, this one based on a modern, secular belief system with characteristics of utopian intolerance similar to those associated with the ideals held by the Puritans. Moreover, these events came with many of the social correlates common to witchcraft accusations of the past: a close community with a history of personal grievances, charismatic indi-

viduals who instigate the process, perceived misfortune without easily understood explanations, and a reservoir of guilt inhibiting the ability of people to
stand up to the scapegoating that results. Since historians often study scapegoating in many historical settings, I now wondered why most of my colleagues failed
to recognize this particular form of the phenomenon when it happened in our
very midst. This question led in turn to my realization that a rather unified ideological outlook that had become dominant in the academic world could explain
both the myopia of my own colleagues and the deficiencies in the works of the
Salem historians. It was not simply the religious element of the witch hunt that
had faded from view in the recent Salem literature but the fundamental recognition that a terrible injustice had taken place. My study thus became a deeper criticism of the ideological foundations of an entire scholarly era.

The book that follows began as a prospective article, and in many respects it
still bears the markings of a single, long essay. There is one sustained argument
throughout, tracing and accounting for the sharp shift in interpretation of the
Salem witch hunt that occurred from the post–World War II period through the
development of the scholarly era that began in the late 1960s. The uneven length of
the chapters reflects the fact that the principal historical works I consider treat the
Salem events in different degrees of depth. Some of these works even look away
from Salem in order to turn their studies into ones of witchcraft accusation in
general. That Mary Beth Norton's *In the Devil's Snare* receives the most extensive
critical attention marks the recognition that, in my view, her book has supplanted
Paul Boyer and Stephen Nissenbaum's *Salem Possessed* in providing the leading
academic interpretation of the witch hunt, even if many historians might say she
has exaggerated her case. In my conclusion I note the very recent emergence of an
alternative strain of interpretation to Norton's, one that stands a good chance of
bringing to a close the scholarly era that is the subject of this book.

In terms of form, *Switching Sides* proceeds along two tracks. There is a concise narrative built around an analysis of the five most significant works in the
Salem scholarship of the past seven decades. One can readily ascertain the book's
argument by reading this text alone. There is a second track, however, consisting
of extensive notes to the text. The notes serve two purposes. First, as in all scholarly writings, they supply documentation for the statements of fact and judgment
that appear in the text, adding qualifications where needed and providing wider
contexts of understanding to help illuminate the subjects under discussion. Second,
for a work of historiography like this, the notes allow for the inclusion of references to the very large number of less well-known scholarly books and articles
about Salem (over one hundred in all), without obscuring the main lines of my

story. While the notes may attract the special attention of scholars of witch hunting, they have been written in an accessible fashion meant to invite all readers to regard them as an extension of the main text. The division between text and notes is simply a structural device designed to present a large and complex subject in comprehensible form.

Because of the book's brevity, I have allowed its argument to unfold along with its presentation of evidence rather than provide a detailed introduction summarizing its perspective. In general, I prefer this approach. Readers impatient to know where the book is headed may wish to jump to the conclusion, where I review the main points of my argument and draw out their scholarly and political implications. While the focus of my study remains fixed on the movement of ideas concerning Salem over the last seventy years, I hope readers also come away from this book with a sound, summary knowledge of what is currently understood about the causes and leading features of the 1692 witch hunt itself.

Acknowledgments

Over ten years in the making, this book owes a great deal to the help, both general and specific, provided me by the staff of Gleeson Library at the University of San Francisco (USF). Among the many helpful staff members at the library, I particularly want to thank Joseph Campi (Coordinator for Interlibrary Loan) and Janet Carmona (Evening/Weekend Circulation/Reserves Coordinator) for their special support. At USF I am also indebted to John Pinelli, Executive Director of the College of Arts and Sciences, and to the joint university and faculty association Faculty Development Fund for financing some of the final steps in the book's production. Cheryl Czekala, the History Department's program assistant, has always provided expert logistical support. An early version of the book's argument was presented to a History Department colloquium for faculty and students in April 2008.

For supplying particular research materials, thanks go to Janet Bloom of the William L. Clements Library at the University of Michigan and to Candace Falk of the Emma Goldman Papers Project, Berkeley, California. Robert Cronan, of Lucidity Information Design, LLC, did a wonderful job in working with me to turn my sketches for the book's seven figures into visually appealing electronic files of graphic art.

In refining and improving the book's argument and ideas, I have benefited enormously from the careful reading of the manuscript by scholarly colleagues and friends Michael Kazin, Richard S. Taylor, and Andrew Heinze. Helpful reflections on my project also came from colleagues and friends Elliot Neaman, Dorothy Sue Cobble, Kim Voss, and Bruce Redwine. Richard Taylor did me the additional favor of going through the entire manuscript with the fine eye of a copyeditor, offering innumerable suggestions for improving the argument's clarity and strength. The book reads far better than it would otherwise as a result of his generous efforts.

A special note of appreciation goes to historian Michael Zuckerman, who stepped in at a critical stage of the manuscript's later development and helped push it forward toward publication. Although he retained significant disagreements with the book's argument, he believed strongly in its quality and importance as a scholarly contribution, a distinction drawn too infrequently by today's ideologically driven academics and publishers. I am equally grateful to Elizabeth Demers, senior acquisitions editor at Johns Hopkins University Press, and the press's editorial and advisory boards, for choosing to add my book to their list. Helpful suggestions in my journey to find a publisher were also made by Fredrika J. Teute, Philip Leventhal, and Russell A. Berman.

I wish to call attention to the outstanding scholarly resources that previous historians and editors have produced to support the modern study of the Salem witch hunt. Of greatest benefit to my research were the anthologies that Paul Boyer and Stephen Nissenbaum compiled in the 1970s—the three-volume *Salem Witchcraft Papers* and the single-volume *Salem-Village Witchcraft*—and the still more comprehensive and magnificently annotated *Records of the Salem Witch-Hunt*, put together by a team led by Bernard Rosenthal in 2009. Other important sources, found in both older volumes and on new Internet sites, provide essential pieces to the Salem puzzle. All of these sources are named in the notes and bibliography. Although my book speaks critically of a number of prior historical interpretations, I have never forgotten that its own insights, whatever their value, stand on a foundation constructed by the sincere and meticulous work of a great many earlier scholars.

Finally, I want to thank my wife, Debbie Poryes, for believing in the significance of this work at every stage in its development. She too read the entire manuscript and contributed to its strengths through countless conversations.

Switching Sides

Introduction

For educated Americans living during the post–World War II era, the Salem witch hunt of 1692 offered one of the rare touchstones from the colonial era that was both widely known and broadly understood in terms of its historical significance. With public opinion shaped especially by Arthur Miller's popular play, *The Crucible*, first produced in 1953, the Salem events stood for a terrifying episode in mass hysteria, in which twenty people were executed for alleged crimes of which they were completely innocent. At Salem village, a small farming community in eastern Massachusetts, a group of mostly young, female accusers, suffering from severe physical and mental afflictions, began to name local people as their tormentors. They charged that these "witches" had entered into a pact with Satan to lure the God-fearing people of the Puritan colony away from their churches and into an upside-down world of blasphemy and immorality. The panic continued for nine months, stretching from January 1692, when the first two girls—nine-year-old Betty Parris and her cousin, eleven-year-old Abigail Williams, both living in the household of the Salem village minister, Samuel Parris—showed symptoms of catatonia, uncontrolled anger, and convulsions, through September, when the last of the trials and executions took place. By its end, over 150 people from communities across Essex County had been jailed on charges of witchcraft, 42 confessed to the crime and named other suspects, and at least 5, dying in prison, joined those executed in the episode's lethal outcome.[1]

This rough understanding of the events of 1692, disseminated initially by Miller's play and by Marion L. Starkey's *The Devil in Massachusetts* (1949), the principal historical work on which Miller based his drama, has probably remained the way most Americans comprehend the Salem witch hunt. Amateur and professional theater groups still perform *The Crucible*, which has also been successfully adapted for film. In 1992 the town of Salem, today the leading tourist destination for those interested in remembering what began three centuries ago in the town's adjoining village (now known as Danvers), commemorated the tercentenary of the witch hunt by building a monument to those who were executed. The monument takes the form of a small park surrounded by stone benches, each one austerely dedicated to a different victim. "Rebecca Nurse, Hanged, July 19, 1692," reads one. Inscribed in the stone threshold to the park are the pleas of innocence submitted to the magistrates at the trials. Two of these proclaim, "I am wholly innocent of such wickedness," and "I can deny it to my dying day." In its coverage of the tercentenary, *Newsweek* noted the participation of Amnesty International and the commemoration's "emphasis on human rights and the role of the individual conscience in times of terror."[2]

However, in the nation's colleges and universities for the past four and a half decades—beginning around 1969—the leading academic monographs on the subject of colonial witchcraft have taught the story of Salem in a startlingly different way. These works mostly ignore the victims of the witch hunt, occasionally even expressing hostility toward them, and either write sympathetically about the accusers or else shift the reader's attention away from the 1692 panic itself. In these accounts the role of courageous individuals standing up to mass prejudice moves out of view. Instead, social conflict among groups takes center stage, even to the point of seeming to justify the witch hunt.

With most of its primary sources—pretrial examination records, trial depositions, and contemporary accounts by ministers and laymen—increasingly available in published and online forms, the Salem witch hunt has attracted the attention of a great many serious historians since the 1960s.[3] But four works, Paul Boyer and Stephen Nissenbaum's *Salem Possessed: The Social Origins of Witchcraft* (1974), John Putnam Demos's *Entertaining Satan: Witchcraft and the Culture of Early New England* (1982), Carol F. Karlsen's *The Devil in the Shape of a Woman: Witchcraft in Colonial New England* (1987), and Mary Beth Norton's *In the Devil's Snare: The Salem Witchcraft Crisis of 1692* (2002), stand apart from the rest as the most influential books on the topic. A survey of thirteen leading United States history college textbooks finds that the arguments of these monographs dominate the textbooks' explanations of the Salem witch hunt, and references to the same four works comprise three-quarters of all citations to scholarship on Salem or witchcraft in their related bibliographies.[4] When in 2008 the prestigious *William and Mary Quarterly* decided to devote an entire issue to a forum on the subject of *Salem Possessed* forty years later, the journal invited five responses to the three main articles about the book; four of the five responses came from Demos, Karlsen, Norton, and Boyer and Nissenbaum themselves. Thoughtful articles about Salem written for more popular audiences equally reveal the influence of these works. One article in *Smithsonian* in 1992 mentioned exclusively Boyer and Nissenbaum, Demos, and Karlsen. The four-page *Newsweek* article that covered the tercentenary of the witch hunt presented the arguments of Boyer and Nissenbaum and Karlsen but no others. And the publication of Norton's book in 2002 was greeted by reviews in a host of mainstream periodicals.[5]

These four books have achieved their strong reputations for good reason. All reflect deep and broad knowledge of the source materials, including original documents that sometimes span as many as one hundred years of colonial history and numerous secondary accounts of Salem written by historical commentators over the past two centuries. All present forceful arguments and often elegant narratives that capture their readers' historical imagination. All stimulate ethical considerations in the minds of their modern audience without forgetting the historian's first task of conveying the past in its marked differences from the present. In short, these are exemplary histories that have greatly augmented the world's knowledge of witch hunting in seventeenth-century America. And yet, precisely because they are such outstanding representatives of a generation's work on this subject, these four books acutely reveal the analytical biases and moral deficiencies of their scholarly era.[6]

During the witch hunt it was common for the accusers to base some of their charges against individual suspects on information conveyed to the accusers through visitations by the spirits of the dead, often dead children, who were said to have revealed the identity of their "murderers," the alleged witches. Although the dead in all likelihood do not live on in this fashion, they certainly do persist in the memories of the living and in the significance their life actions may hold for subsequent generations. Perhaps, then, it may be suggested that the spirits of the dead victims of the Salem witch hunt now cry out from their own graves, demanding a reckoning with the most recent round of Salem scholarship.[7]

CHAPTER 1

Starkey's *Devil in Massachusetts* and the Post–World War II Consensus

In order to identify the biases in scholarship on the Salem witch hunt after the 1960s, one must begin by recapturing the outlook post–World War II Americans held toward the subject. No historical work did more to shape this view than Marion Starkey's *The Devil in Massachusetts: A Modern Enquiry into the Salem Witch Trials*. Because Arthur Miller's play has so firmly associated Salem in the popular mind with the cruel excesses of the anti-communist crusade led by Joseph McCarthy in the 1950s, it is worth emphasizing that Starkey's contemporary reference point lay elsewhere. McCarthyism (without yet the Wisconsin senator in the lead) was only just emerging during the years 1947–48 when Starkey was writing her book. She rather had in mind the terrible persecutions of millions of innocent people by Nazis and Communists in Europe during the 1930s and 1940s. Salem's great value, in Starkey's view, was that it provided a local case study through which to grasp "intimations of history on a grander scale." For, as she wrote in her preface, once you become intimately acquainted with Salem's victims "as the people who live next door"—"a decent grandmother grown too hard of hearing to understand a crucial question from the jurors [Rebecca Nurse], a rakish, pipe-smoking female tramp [Sarah Good], a plain farmer who thought only to save his wife from molestation [John Procter], a lame old man whose toothless gums did not deny expression to a very salty vocabulary [George Jacobs Sr.]"—"a remarkable thing happens; you discover that if you really know the few, you are on your way to understanding the millions."[1]

The urge to hunt "witches," Starkey made clear, had not vanished at all from the western world: "It has been revived on a colossal scale by replacing the medieval idea of malefic witchcraft by pseudo-scientific concepts like 'race,' 'nationality,' and by substituting for theological dissension a whole complex of warring ideologies. Accordingly the story of 1692 is of far more than antiquarian interest; it is an allegory of our times." If these linkages to Starkey's own day sound somewhat oblique, she clarified them by occasional references to the frenzy whipped up by "a Hitler," judges clinging to "the party line," and Massachusetts admirably putting an end to its hysteria "without waiting for the dubious assistance of an army of occupation." The American lynch mob, whose deadly reign in the South had not yet fully run its course by the 1930s and 1940s, presented Starkey, who was born in 1902, with another modern analogy to help her readers understand what had happened at Salem, but the recent history of European radical movements and the frightful regimes they placed in power offered the principal backdrop for her study.[2]

In reconstructing the 1692 witch hunt for her postwar audience, Starkey's strength lay in her narrative ability to portray vividly the social psychological process by which fear overtakes people and an entire community becomes ready to abandon rational judgment and ethical restraint in a drive to purify itself of unseen danger. Her treatment of Martha Cory's pretrial examination offers an excellent case in point. Cory symbolized the tough, realistic, yet still devout Puritan woman, according to Starkey, whom the adolescent accusers resented for her unwillingness to coddle the young. After Cory had been named as a witch by twelve-year-old Ann Putnam, she at first adopted a defiant posture, proclaiming that she did not believe in witchcraft. But at her examination, a public event held in the village meetinghouse and attended by the afflicted girls and as many as three hundred community members, most spilling outside, Cory was soon worn down. Rather than asking her how she pleaded, the chief magistrate, John Hathorne, simply asked why she tormented the girls. When she denied that she did so, the girls screamed in agony. When Cory shifted her feet, the girls' feet jerked as well. When she bit her lip, the girls announced that Cory's specter (or invisible spirit) had bitten their lips, too, and they showed the magistrates their blood. One girl shouted out that she saw the Devil whispering in Cory's ear. An older woman in the crowd suffered a searing pain in her bowels and threw her shoe at the suspect in return. Others claimed to hear the drumbeat of the Devil out on the church lawn, summoning the witches of the area to come take the blood-red sacrament. Amid this pandemonium, the rest of the people in the meetinghouse sat quivering on their benches, awestruck at these displays of apparent diabolical intervention. When the questioning was over and she was led away to prison, Cory cried out to the magistrates, "You can't prove me a witch!" "But such a statement was beside the point," Starkey wrote with great force. "What she couldn't prove, what no one at all accused of such a thing could prove, was that she wasn't."[3]

Such hopeless irrationality, Starkey showed, led the Massachusetts authorities to bypass certain traditional procedures, cautions, and prohibitions associated with witchcraft investigations in the English-speaking world. One way that the Salem witch hunt was unusual among witchcraft prosecutions was that those who confessed to the crime of bewitching their neighbors were never executed. They survived partly by accident, owing to a delay in establishing formal trial proceedings. (The first person to confess, Rev. Samuel Parris's slave, Tituba, did so on March 1, while the first trial did not take place until June 2.) Mainly, however, confessors were preserved so they could remain available to name additional witches in what was thought right from the start to be a far-flung Satanic conspiracy. In addition, Puritans believed in redemption through a process of heartfelt renunciation of one's sins and temptations, and this principle competed against the biblical injunction to "not suffer a witch to live." Regardless of the reasons, the pattern soon became evident to the accused: confession was a likely, if only temporary, way to save one's life, even as it equally served to corroborate the seeming truth of the accusations, thus intensifying and widening the panic. Before the witch hunt ended, a great many of the accused had confessed.[4]

The twenty who went to their deaths in 1692, however, refused to take this route, and Starkey highlighted their heroism. In addition to Martha Cory's defiance, Starkey devoted separate chapters to seventy-year-old Rebecca Nurse's quiet insistence that she was a pious church member who would never bewitch anyone, at least not consciously; to the farmer and tavern owner John Procter's efforts to assemble a petition of supporters from throughout the county to attest to his innocence, though it was to no avail; to the former Salem village minister George Burroughs's impressive speech and moving recitation of the Lord's Prayer at the gallows, causing doubts to creep into the minds of those assembled, before Cotton Mather, one of the leading Boston ministers, intervened to persuade the crowd to let the execution go forward; and to Mary Esty's eloquent plea, just before her hanging, "not for my own life, for I know I must die and my appointed time is set, but . . . that no more Innocent Blood be shed . . . [for] by my own Innocency I know you are in the wrong way." It was precisely the conscientious acts of these individuals, stemming from their refusal to "belie themselves" before God, that Starkey aimed to showcase in her history, believing that they represented the best in Puritanism and a beacon of light for humanity in a dark time.[5]

Along with her descriptions of these martyrs, Starkey allotted considerable pages to the core group of accusers, a collection of about twelve young women, most in their late teens, two as young as eleven and twelve, and several in their twenties or thirties. (The mother-daughter pair of Ann Putnam Sr. and Jr. alone was responsible for many of the early accusations.) Here Starkey employed adolescent psychology and the psychoanalytic theory of hysteria to account for their behavior—this is what constituted the "modern enquiry" of her subtitle—even if there is little detail to her analysis beyond the simple assertion that hysteria results from sexual repression, to which single, teenaged girls, and especially those living in the disciplined, work-centered, and holiday-less world of Puritan New England, would be especially prone. To early twenty-first-century readers, these passages are apt to be the least satisfying (if not outright offensive) aspect of her book. Although the general notion of what would today be termed psychosomatic illness certainly fits the reported experience of most of Salem's afflicted accusers, the gender-specific connotations carried by the very old diagnosis "hysteria," still in use by psychologists of the postwar period, could not escape their two-thousand-year-old association with female inferiority. Thus, in spite of her attempt to provide a serious, scientific explanation for the behavior of the accusers, Starkey herself fell back on a number of gratuitous slurs, referring to the young women at times as a "sorority" of "crazed little girls," a "pack of bobby-soxers" (she acknowledged this one was anachronistic) subject to the "storms of oncoming puberty," or asking of the male magistrates, "Had they no daughters or sisters that they should not know how silly a female can be in the silly season of her teens, to what lengths she can go in her craving for attention?" Such observations have confused some of Starkey's readers. Was she implying that the accusers might not have been suffering from genuine physical and mental distress—something quite apparent to eyewitnesses, whose descriptions of the contorted bodies of the afflicted have survived to this day—but rather were faking their conditions in order to gain "attention"?[6]

Starkey certainly meant to place her emphasis on the genuineness of the "hysterical" symptoms—why else bring Freud's ideas into the center of her study? But in order to be more persuasive (even to herself), she needed to have supplied much more material about the strength of Puritan religious beliefs, including the New Englanders' sense of certainty that in the afterlife physical terrors awaited the souls of those who had turned against the Lord. Salem village in the seventeenth century was not so very different from the more obviously cloistered setting of a convent or monastery, where an ascetic, penitential ethos could produce, in the words of one historian, an "awe-filled sense that one can never sufficiently humble oneself before God." Without an adequate appreciation of the mental world of such thoroughly religious people as the Puritans, it is only too easy for the voice of modern cynicism to intrude, insisting that nothing more than simple fraud and gullibility lay at the roots of the witch hunt. That viewpoint had entered the historiography of Salem at the time of the Enlightenment and has never been very far from the common understanding of its causes ever since.[7]

What actually appears to have generated the initial psychosomatic symptoms in the young accusers, as Starkey noted, was guilt and fear over having engaged in such forbidden, Devil-associated practices as fortune-telling about the future course their lives would take. Starkey did not make explicit the next step in the process, but the accusers then projected a likely impulse for self-punishment—that at the same time deflected blame away from themselves—onto those individuals (the accused "witches") presumed to have the power, granted by Satan, to pinch, choke, and otherwise inflict harm on them. As for the names selected to be targeted, these were influenced by long-standing suspicions, hatreds, and envies held by the adults close to the afflicted young people, what Starkey called Salem's "web of spite." The accusations gained force and spread in the community due to the ardent desire of ordinary people to find an explanation for all sorts of everyday misfortunes, ranging from the inability of cows to give milk to such heartbreaking losses as the deaths of infants, children, and spouses. There was little that was fraudulent or consciously conspiratorial in this deadly form of group therapy.[8]

The ambiguities in Starkey's treatment of the female accusers were too much a part of her own day's prejudices to be noticed at the time, and they did not get in the way of her book's enthusiastic reception in intellectual circles.[9] Historian Edmund Morgan, who had just published his first book, *The Puritan Family: Religion and Domestic Relations in Seventeenth-Century New England* (1944), wrote in the *American Historical Review* that "Miss Starkey is probably as thoroughly versed in the sources of the Salem episode as anyone has ever been" and commended the book as the best account of the witch hunt that had yet been written. Morgan recognized that the courage shown by the condemned "witches" (as well as that demonstrated by some of the magistrates and jurors who later repented for their complicity in the injustices) constituted "the moral of the book." And he drew the same political implications from the story that Starkey herself had identified when he likened the Salem trials, "with their apparatus of secret torture, phony confessions, exposures of alleged accomplices, irregular procedures, and admission of inadmissible evidence," to the ongoing Communist show trials in Eastern Europe and Salem's public hysteria to "the recurrent red scares in this country."[10]

British novelist and essayist Aldous Huxley, by then living in the United States, was also drawn to Starkey's account. He called it "a small historical classic" in an introduction he wrote for the 1963 edition of her book. Having recently produced his own part-historical, part-philosophical study of an incidence of group demonic possession that occurred in a seventeenth-century French nunnery and that also resulted in the execution of a scapegoat, *The Devils of Loudun* (1952), Huxley had little trouble recognizing in the Salem events the same combustible mixture of what he termed "magical belief," local grievance, and religious absolutism. Huxley's points of political reference were the same as well. "In medieval and early modern Christendom," he had written in *Devils*, "the situation of sorcerers [i.e., witches] and their clients was almost precisely analogous to that of Jews under Hitler, capitalists under Stalin, Communists and fellow travelers in the United States. . . . Death was the penalty meted out to these metaphysical Quislings of the past and, in most parts of the contemporary world, death is the penalty which awaits the political and secular devil-worshipers known here as Reds, there as Reactionaries." Huxley had also written an epilogue to *Devils* in which he decried the perils of "crowd delirium" and other attempts at what he termed "downward [or, destructive] self-transcendence." In his introduction to Starkey's work, he again called attention to the universal value in studying witch hunts of the past, concluding that her book "made it possible for us to understand those dark, those truly diabolic forces which lurk in the recesses of the human mind, ready, whenever history gives them their opportunity, to break out into the open."[11]

Thus, out of the ideological catastrophes of the first half of the twentieth century, a resurgent and defiant liberalism had emerged in postwar America that both shaped the historical understanding of the Salem witch hunt and made it a compelling topic of interest.[12] Arthur Miller stood slightly to the left of this consensus, but his 1953 play, *The Crucible*, portrayed the witch hunt in virtually identical terms to Starkey's. Probably because of the strong resemblances between the two works, including in the overall sense of drama that Starkey imparted to her narrative—she wrote in her preface, "I have tried to uncover the classic dramatic form of the story itself, for here is real 'Greek tragedy,' with a beginning, a middle, and an end"—Miller was hesitant for a long time to acknowledge the earlier book's influence, doing so for the first time, it appears, only thirty-four years later in his autobiography. During the 1950s Miller spoke only about how he had traveled to the Essex County courthouse and combed through manuscript records of the trials to find his story. In truth, it would have taken him far longer than the seven days he allotted for his stay there to have succeeded in this manner.[13]

Yet none of this personal subterfuge takes away from the power of Miller's play, which manages to condense the story of a yearlong, county-wide panic into a gripping, two-hour drama surrounding a distant but loving couple, John and Elizabeth Procter, whose intimate lives are menaced by the enveloping hysteria of the witchcraft accusations. At the play's end John is forced to reveal his infidelity in a failed attempt to discredit his wife's accuser, their former servant, Abigail Williams, who had been spurned by Procter following an earlier sexual encounter. Then, despite the tearful reconciliation of the couple's complicated marriage (for Elizabeth has sinned, too, in her own way), John goes to his death rather than betray his own good name and the names of his equally innocent friends by confessing to the false charge of having joined the Devil's league. Miller thus brought home to his audience in a most poignant and personal way exactly how much courage it took for individuals to stand up for truth (symbolized by the sanctity of their "names") against the tide of fear and false witness. Writing about *The Crucible* four years after it was first produced, Miller said, "I wished . . . to write a play that . . . would show that the sin of public terror is that it divests man of conscience, of himself." The following year, he added, "The form, the shape, the meaning of *The Crucible* were all compounded out of the faith of those who were hanged. . . . They were asked to deny their belief in a God of all men [in favor of] . . . a god each individual could manipulate to his interests." Starkey had emphasized just this central point in her own book.[14]

If Miller's play thus mainly added the immediacy of a theatrical performance to Starkey's history—and even weakened her analysis of the accusers' motivations by reducing them nearly exclusively to fraud and calculation in the service of petty vengeance and material gain—*The Crucible* nevertheless called attention to a critical dimension in the social psychology of "public terror" that Starkey had touched on but not given the emphasis it deserved. This was the role played by guilt in the witch hunt, not the guilt of the initial accusers for their illicit fortune-telling activities (which had already been made plain in Starkey's account) but the guilt that lay dormant in the average person in the Puritan community, a guilt waiting to be activated and manipulated by the prime movers in a panic. Miller could only conceive of such guilt in sexual terms. This limitation accounts for his most striking departures from the historical record in order to create the plot of his play: raising the age of Abigail Williams from eleven to seventeen, lowering John Procter's age from sixty to mid-thirties, and positing a sexual liaison between the two during a time—wholly made up, it appears—when Williams was said to have lived in the Procters' house as a servant. This situation of "broken faith" in a marriage, so close to home for Miller, whose own marriage was in the process of dissolution during the early 1950s, gave the playwright the emotional material to create a drama, set three centuries earlier, that would ring true to his audiences in the present.[15]

Miller's insight, however, was exactly right, minus the sexual element. Most people, and especially Puritans trying strenuously to live up to a godly ideal that even their own intelligent faith told them no human being could achieve, are silently aware of how they fall short of their community's own moral standards. For the Puritans, every idle wish to surpass someone else or see one's rivals fall was apt to cause a suspicion that one had, just perhaps, invited Satan in. With this dreadful image came guilt that stood ready, under conditions of heightened fear, to be expiated by a confession or externalized onto a scapegoat. What was at stake, Miller recognized, was the powerful need of the individual to belong to a community, a need that severely tests the call of individual conscience, especially when that community defines its morality, as the Puritans did, in such uncompromising terms.[16]

Politically, as is well known, the modern-day manipulators of the "public terror" that Miller had immediately in mind when he wrote *The Crucible* were the anti-communist demagogues of the House Committee on Un-American Activities and, more broadly, of the McCarthy movement. These politicians also demanded public confessions and the naming of other names from those who felt the guilt of having broken faith with American ideals when they had—perhaps innocently enough, given the context of the Great Depression—embraced communism in their youth. Beneath his loathing for these Red hunters lay an even more profound fear of the return of fascism, a fear stemming from the deep imprint on Miller's Jewish identity made by the vicious, anti-Semitic record of the Nazis and their allies. Indeed, the shadow of fascism, as Miller's leading biographer has explained, structured the major themes of his life and work at this time. Yet even in *The Crucible*, in one of the lengthy historical asides that provide background material for the printed version of Act 1, Miller offers a grudging inclusion of communist tyranny in his survey of threats to individual conscience. Much later in life he could point proudly to the applicability of his play to the terror faced by Chinese intellectuals during the Cultural Revolution. Here, in other words, was the same triad of ideological evils—fascism, communism, and extreme anti-communism—that stood everywhere in the background of the postwar understanding of the Salem witch hunt. Never fully a "joiner" of any cause, including the Communist Party, despite his strong and long-lasting emotional ties to Marxism and the Soviet Union, Miller remained enough the alienated individual to allow his dramatic talent in *The Crucible* to bring Starkey's liberal themes to millions.[17]

❦

It is hard not to see Starkey's influence, finally, in that most unlikely of places, the work of the greatest scholar of Puritanism in the postwar era, Perry Miller. The second volume of Miller's intellectual history, *The New England Mind*, came out in the same year, 1953, that *The Crucible* was first produced. No scholar did more to free the Puritans from the scorn of their descendants, bringing to Americans who had experienced the shocks of economic collapse, menacing world dictatorships, and war a new appreciation for the achievements of the Puritan endeavor, especially its ability to sustain believers in persevering with guarded hopefulness in the face of enormous challenges and without any facile assurance that they could fathom the ways of God. Perry Miller was not one to credit other historians in his work, so closely did he stick to the primary texts in allowing the movement of a region's ideas to unfold before his readers' eyes. Thus it is impossible to know what he thought of *The Devil in Massachusetts*. However, whether by gentle influence (he would have needed little more than this) or by convergence of thought and sentiment, he regarded the Salem witch hunt in much the same terms as did the journalist-turned-historian Starkey. This convergence bears emphasizing because two sentences early in the chapter Miller devoted to Salem have been taken out of context in a number of post-1960s works on the witch hunt to suggest that Miller dismissed the entire panic of 1692 as unimportant and irrelevant to the course of history in colonial New England. Nothing could be further from the truth, as a careful reading of the chapter and related pages shows. And nothing so misunderstands Perry Miller's method as to believe that a sentence or two could capture his judgment of so complex an affair as the witch hunt, for he often proceeds in zigzag fashion, offering statement followed by qualification followed by further qualification followed by restatement, in an intimate, moral, and often polemical engagement with the ideas of his historical subjects.[18]

Throughout the chapter on Salem, Perry Miller's sympathies lay fully with the innocent victims of the mass fear, which he called variously "the madness," a "mania," a "stampede," and a "saturnalia," during which "every man's life lay at the mercy of any accuser, brother looked sidewise at brother, and the friend of many years' standing became a bad security risk." Like Starkey, he quoted Mary Esty's poignant appeal to save the lives of those innocent men and women who would be tried after her. He decried the logic of the witchcraft court, justices, and juries that accepted without due caution the veracity of spectral evidence, just "as juries have been known to act upon a settled pre-conviction that no white woman can possibly offer sexual provocation to a Negro." And he expressed his profound disappointment with Increase Mather, the colony's preeminent Puritan minister, who could have "stood in American history with a Zenger or a Lovejoy"— John Peter Zenger, the eighteenth-century champion of free speech, and Elijah Lovejoy, the martyred abolitionist who was killed by a mob in the 1830s—had he spoken what he knew to be true and repudiated the court instead of producing in *Cases of Conscience* (October 1692) an ambiguously worded criticism that ended up no better than "a miserable species of double-talk." Miller thus spoke directly to Americans of the mid-twentieth century, citing moral and political benchmarks in the nation's liberal tradition to help them comprehend what had occurred in 1692.[19]

As an intellectual historian, Perry Miller approached the Salem witch hunt through the writing produced by participants in the year's events: former Salem village minister Deodat Lawson's public sermon of March 24; Rev. Cotton Mather's May 31 letter to trial judge John Richards; the June 15 advisory *Return* of the colony's leading ministers to Gov. William Phips; Cotton Mather's August 17 letter to Massachusetts Council member John Foster; Rev. Increase Mather's pivotal *Cases of Conscience* of October 3 (which Miller credited, despite its equivocation, with causing the governor to replace the witch-hunting court with a new one); Boston merchant and scientist Thomas Brattle's hard-hitting letter of October 8, attacking the trials; Cotton Mather's retrospective defense of the proceedings in his October 15 *Wonders of the Invisible World*; Rev. Samuel Willard's critical dialogue between "S" (most likely signifying Salem) and "B" (most likely signifying Boston) of mid-October; and Rev. John Hale's soul-searching *Modest Enquiry into the Nature of Witchcraft* of 1698. Starkey, too, had analyzed each of these important documents, plus some others, including Samuel Parris's crucial March 27 sermon on John 6:70, "Have not I chosen you twelve, and one of you is a Devil?" which rationalized the discovery of witches even among the "saints" of the local congregation. For Miller (as for Starkey) the point of this investigation was to address the key question, present in the historiography of Salem from the beginning, of how much Puritanism itself should be blamed for the panic.

In Miller's subtle hands (but no less in Starkey's), the answer to this question paid due respect to the many worries about the proceedings that the leading ministers expressed, especially surrounding the difficult problem of how to evaluate spectral evidence in the absence of a confession. Few doubted that Satan had the power, granted by God, to torment people through the "specters," or ethereal likenesses, of those whom the Evil One had enlisted in his cause, but did that mean that if an afflicted individual identified a particular specter, the corresponding person was necessarily guilty of witchcraft? In other words, could the Devil impersonate only those who were guilty (people who had consciously agreed to serve the Antichrist) or could he also appear in the guise of the innocent (people who had entered into no such pact)?[20] Though somewhat ambiguous on this critical point, learned Protestant opinion in England and New England leaned to the latter position, which meant that great care needed to be taken in the process of examination and trial to determine through empirical, corroborating evidence if spectral torment was genuine. Such corroborating evidence included signs of extraordinary, "diabolical" abilities or disabilities in the suspect (for example, an ability to foretell future events or an inability to recite the Lord's Prayer); close correlations between the suspect's curses and the accuser's subsequent misfortune; discovery of effigy puppets in the suspect's possession; and the presence of "witch marks" or "witches' teats" on the bodies of the accused (places where the Devil had, respectively, indicated one of his followers with a visible sign, or created an abnormal growth on which a witch's animal "familiars," or accomplices, could nourish themselves on the witch's blood). All such latter evidence was subject to circular reasoning, to be sure, but less so than apparitions visible only to the afflicted. During the witch hunt, at least three local ministers (Parris, Hale from neighboring Beverly, and Nicholas Noyes from the town of Salem), along with virtually all of the examining magistrates and trial judges, including the chief justice, Deputy Governor William Stoughton, held to the belief that if an identified specter bit, pinched, strangled, or convulsed an individual, a guilty suspect lay behind the attack, although they sought corroborating proof as well. Meanwhile, the colony's leading ministers, including Increase and Cotton Mather (father and son), Samuel Willard, and some others, in effect, knew better, but, as Perry Miller makes clear, their words of caution were uttered too late and too privately and were too hemmed in by qualifications aimed at ingratiating themselves with their friends among the justices.

In large part, as Miller states, "the [colony's leading] ministers were in a quandary of their own making." Both Mathers had spent the better part of the 1680s trying to convince their countrymen that God still worked supernatural wonders, especially terrible wonders, among his chosen people. They pointed to gruesome Indian attacks; sickness and crop failures; factional discord; the revocation of Massachusetts's original, self-governing colonial charter in 1684 in favor of autocratic rule (temporary, as it turned out); and *witchcraft*. This was the tried and true method of the jeremiad, the longstanding hortatory device used by the ministers to keep their followers believing that New England held a special place in the providential design for human redemption. It worked not because the Puritan leadership hoodwinked the population but because most New Englanders really were strong Calvinists. And so, when in 1688 a case of apparent witchcraft against four children, well publicized by Cotton Mather, occurred in Boston, resulting in the execution of one woman, and then four years later word of the Salem afflictions spread, there was little in the intellectual arsenal of the colony's leadership to put down the public outcry before it had gathered a momentum of its own.[21]

In the end Miller found Puritan leaders wanting, none more so than Cotton Mather. Like his father, Mather knew what had gone wrong but convinced himself that most of those executed had been guilty, while justifying the entire disaster—Miller called this step "both appealing and repulsive"—as one of God's special trials for his covenanted people. Starkey had not gone quite this far in her criticisms of the minister. Miller was kinder to Brattle and Willard for their stronger attacks on the proceedings, but, as he pointed out, even Brattle waited to deliver his critique until early October, after the tide had begun to turn against the panic, and Willard had earlier endorsed Reverend Lawson's March sermon, calling on the local magistrates to prosecute real witches with vigor. Miller might have added that Willard's later critique of the witch hunt, which appeared in mid-October, was issued anonymously.

In short, the hysteria swept all, eminent and lowly, enthusiastic and skeptical, along with its murderous wave. Created to no small degree by Puritanism's own all-encompassing belief in the supernatural, together with its stringent standard of conduct that few could meet, the witch hunt, Miller argued, contributed to nothing less than the dismantling of the covenant theology—linking humanity to God—that constituted the very foundation of Puritan faith. Once confession and repentance became insincere while fidelity to one's conscience led to punishment, the terms of the contract between God and humankind were broken. "The whole edifice of the New England mind," Miller wrote of the aftermath of the witch hunt, "rocked at the very thought that it might be based, not upon a cosmic design of the covenant, but merely upon fallible founders." More generous interpretations of Protestant faith, both Enlightenment based and evangelical, now lay in the immediate future.[22]

CHAPTER 2

Boyer and Nissenbaum's *Salem Possessed* and the Anti-capitalist Critique

To move into the accounts of Salem that began to appear after the 1960s is to encounter a very different interpretive world. No longer does the history of the witch hunt seem to provoke existential dilemmas concerning the individual's relationship to society, authority, or God. No longer lurking in the background are such morally pertinent questions as, what would you have done if you had lived in colonial Massachusetts in 1692? Or, who was to blame for the deaths of twenty innocent people? Instead, a focus on groups supplants an interest in the actions of individuals, the social functions of witchcraft accusation become more important than the mass psychology of witch hunting, and the panic that gripped Salem village and its surrounding communities in 1692 itself recedes from center stage. Along the way, sympathy for victims like Martha Cory, Rebecca Nurse, John Procter, and George Burroughs fades, until it is sometimes no longer clear that these people *were* the victims.

An early hint that the story handed down by Marion Starkey, Arthur Miller, and Perry Miller was in for revision came in introductory remarks John Demos supplied to his first publication on the subject of colonial witchcraft, an article that would later be expanded into an important book. It was "faintly embarrass-ing," Demos wrote in 1970, for historians to return to the subject, both because the "overworked" Salem witch hunt played only a minor role in the colonial history of the region and, more pointedly, because "the historiography of Salem can be viewed, in large measure, as an unending effort to *judge* the participants—

and above all, to affix blame." This unfortunate focus, Demos asserted, was not likely to yield fruitful results. "Will such a debate ever be finally settled?" he asked. "Are its partisan terms and moral tone appropriate to historical scholarship?" Demos thought the answer to both these questions was no, and on this basis he embarked on what he thought would be a more promising inquiry into the anthropology and psychology of colonial witchcraft accusations without a specific interest in Salem at all.[1]

Demos aimed his dismissal of the judgmental tendency in Salem historiography at Starkey and a number of nineteenth- and early twentieth-century historians who had preceded her, but he included in this criticism a book that had just appeared, *Witchcraft at Salem* (1969), by Chadwick Hansen. This book, too, proved a harbinger of things to come. Hansen's choice of wording for his title—"witchcraft" rather than "witch hunt"—was deliberate, because he maintained that at least some of the executed individuals at Salem, perhaps as many as eight of the twenty, were guilty of practicing witchcraft. Hansen took pains to combat what he called the "standard" interpretation of the 1692 witch hunt: fanatical Puritan ministers, seeking to safeguard their prestige in the colony, had worked up a fraudulent group of accusers and their gullible followers into a frenzy that took the lives of innocent people who represented no threat to anyone. This interpretation had indeed been the leading view *before* Starkey's book came out, but both Starkey's and Perry Miller's work had made it clear that the local Puritan community and its elected magistrates, not the colony's prominent ministers, were the prime movers in the witch hunt; that the afflicted accusers suffered from genuine distress of psychosomatic origins; and that the top ministers in Massachusetts could be faulted chiefly for their failure to provide the strong leadership that might have brought reason and restraint to the community's fears. Curiously, Hansen wished to make much the same set of points, but, misconstruing the contributions of his immediate predecessors, he chose to do so by arguing along different lines. When traditional societies (including colonial New England) believe in the efficacy of witchcraft, Hansen asserted, not only can some people truly fall ill if they think they have been bewitched—he again advanced hysteria as the modern explanation—but others may legitimately be judged guilty if they have attempted to do harm through supernatural means. In other words, it was likely there really had been a threat to the Salem community in the form of intentional witchcraft, even though an irrational witch hunt soon took over, sweeping up innocent people in its net along with the guilty. The leading ministers, and especially Cotton Mather, in Hansen's view, tried their best to corral the runaway process but were ignored.[2]

In theory, the possibility that witchcraft had been practiced at Salem was not unreasonable. There was plenty of evidence that seventeenth-century New Englanders occasionally resorted to magical techniques for purposes of healing, divining the future, or warding off misfortune. But was there also evidence of individuals using image magic or some other occult means to place curses on neighbors and, equally necessary for witchcraft to be present, of accepting the help of the Devil to do so? The problem with Hansen's argument was that he lacked persuasive evidence of any such activity. His strongest case, that against Bridget Bishop, came down to testimony offered on the day of her trial by two men she had employed seven years earlier to demolish a portion of a house in which she had formerly lived. The men told of discovering at that time rag puppets bearing outward-pointing pins in the cellar wall of the building. What Hansen failed to tell his readers was that the "two men" were father and son, that the son was just eight years old at the time of the recalled incident, and that this same family, the Blys, had clashed (exactly when is not clear from the original evidence) with the Bishops over the sale of a sow, all pertinent facts casting doubt on what was already highly indirect evidence for the practice of witchcraft at the time of the Salem panic. Even if the Blys were telling the truth, it is more likely that the effigies they discovered were tokens of countermagic *aimed at* Bridget Bishop, who had first been formally accused of witchcraft in 1680, rather than devices used by her to harm others. The rest of Hansen's case against Bishop consisted of depositions—nearly all heartfelt, to be sure—by individuals, including the afflicted girls from Salem village and a number of men, relating past incidents in which they believed Bishop had sent her specter to torment them or in one case to cause a boy to become sick.[3] In two other instances (concerning accused "witches" Wilmot Redd and Sarah Good), Hansen offered no greater evidence for probable witchcraft than verbal curses uttered by the suspects in anger toward people with whom they were in conflict.[4]

The insufficiencies of his evidence aside, Hansen also showed little sympathy for those whom he regarded as probable witches, most of whom were either poor, uneducated, or considered troublesome by neighbors and local officials. In one striking example, Hansen described a scene at the hanging of eight accused witches on September 22, quoting from Boston cloth merchant Robert Calef's eyewitness account that, following the execution, Salem town minister Nicholas Noyes had turned to the bodies and commented how sad it was "to see eight firebrands of Hell hanging there." Hansen added, "One of them was a witch, and deserved Noyes' comment—Wilmot 'Mammy' Redd, the Marblehead woman who had cursed Mrs. Simms, wishing upon her 'the distemper of the dry bellyache.'" Hansen was similarly contemptuous of Sarah Good, whom he accused of "malice" and "deceit" when she was simply trying to fend off the badgering questions of Magistrate Hathorne in any way she could, including by naming her fellow accused Sarah Osburn as a witch. Hansen also accepted at face value all the negative testimony about George Burroughs, dismissing the former minister's desperate attempt to save himself before his hanging by flawlessly reciting the Lord's Prayer as "something of a trick." (It was a common seventeenth-century belief that witches would not be able to speak the word of God without stumbling.) At the same time, Hansen betrayed favoritism toward the respectable members of Massachusetts society, assuming the innocence of such well-to-do suspects as Rebecca Nurse, Mary Esty, and Elizabeth Procter, often in the face of evidence similar to that brought against his "guilty" suspects. He was so protective of Cotton Mather's reputation as to call the minister's sharpest contemporary critic, Robert Calef, "insolent" on two occasions.[5]

Displaying such apparent leanings toward the elite of colonial society while showing disdain for that society's more vulnerable members, *Witchcraft at Salem* was not likely to have become a popular text just when the new radicalism of the 1960s was starting to influence academic life, even if the book's evidence for the practice of witchcraft had been stronger. Hansen shifted sympathies away from the witch hunt's victims but without identifying a new social group that could plausibly be portrayed as enough of an underdog to take their place, a step that Paul Boyer and Stephen Nissenbaum would soon accomplish so successfully. Yet Hansen's book and Demos's article indicated the two main directions that scholarship on colonial witchcraft would now take. Where Salem remained the focus, as it did for Hansen and would continue to do so for Boyer and Nissenbaum and then for Norton, historians would seek to identify the threat to society that could account for, and even implicitly justify, the witch hunt. Otherwise, as in the case of Demos's article and the later books by Demos and Karlsen, investigations would leave Salem behind and search for patterns of witchcraft accusation across all of seventeenth-century New England.[6]

The first major work in this new scholarship, *Salem Possessed: The Social Origins of Witchcraft*, by Paul Boyer and Stephen Nissenbaum, appeared in 1974 and quickly became the single most influential monograph about the witch hunt. Adopting the sociological techniques of the "new social history," which rose to prominence in the historical profession in the 1960s as a way to write "history from the bottom up" (perspectives that focused first on common people), Boyer and Nissenbaum removed the narrative of the events of 1692 almost entirely from their study. These developments appeared solely in the prologue, entitled "What Happened in 1692," which mentioned by name—and only in passing—just ten of the accused witches. Readers met five of the famous victims again in the book's final chapter (with just two brief, earlier references), where the authors presented biographical sketches that omitted the courageous responses of these individuals to their persecution. Next to go were the afflicted girls and young women, for as Boyer and Nissenbaum fairly pointed out, if the adults of Salem village had not listened to and even encouraged these accusers, no arrests or prosecutions would have gone forward. The afflicted young people might simply have been disciplined, and the whole episode would have ended before it got started. With these powerful preparatory moves, Boyer and Nissenbaum made plain they had no intention of adding a new installment to what they termed the "dramatic set piece" that the history of the witch hunt had become. Instead, the authors directed their readers' attention to the adult householders of the community and asked, what was peculiar about Salem that could have produced such an unusual and tragic outcome?[7]

The book's six central chapters delivered an answer to this question in the form of a carefully constructed socioeconomic analysis. The authors attempted to show that the village had long been subject to intense factionalism, which pitted a slight majority of farmers living on the poorer lands of its west side against a slightly smaller group of farmers and tradespeople living on the more productive lands of the village's eastern side. The latter group also maintained closer economic and personal ties to the adjoining town of Salem, a rapidly growing commercial center, second only in wealth to Boston in the colony. The western farmers, predominantly middling to poor in their taxable wealth, tended to be the more stalwart Puritans. They belonged to the village church in far greater numbers than their eastern neighbors and supported its two most recent ministers, Deodat Lawson and then Samuel Parris, in whose parsonage the first young Salem girls showed signs of affliction. The eastern farmers and tradespeople, by contrast, included most of the village's richer families, along with some middling and poor. The church members among these people tended to belong to the church in Salem town, even if they sometimes worshipped with their neighbors in the village meetinghouse. There they had been partial to the two earlier ministers in the village, James Bayley and then George Burroughs, the latter of whom would become one of the most prominent victims of the witch hunt. At the head of each faction stood one of the two leading extended families and landholders in the village, the Putnams (for the westerners) and the Porters (for the easterners). Drawing on a residential map of Salem village in 1692 compiled by the nineteenth-century historian Charles W. Upham, Boyer and Nissenbaum linked their factional picture to the witch hunt by showing that a disproportionate number of the accusers lived on the western side of the village while those accused of witchcraft and their defenders came disproportionately from the eastern side.[8]

As the authors explained this pattern of factional conflict, they could not suppress their sympathies for the struggling farmers on the village's western side. *Salem Possessed* portrayed these families, including the well-to-do but declining Putnams, as hardworking and honest but sometimes bumbling farmers who always seemed to get outsmarted economically by the more devious, slick-minded people to the east. Characterizing the Putnam clan's support for Rev. Samuel Parris, Boyer and Nissenbaum wrote, "The Putnam approach was bluff, direct, and obvious. They worked for their man through the established channels: as Village Committeemen, as deacons, as church elders. . . . The Porters, by contrast, were behind-the-scenes men. Except when their enemies flushed them into the open, they left few marks." Describing a petition that Israel Porter organized in defense of the accused witch Rebecca Nurse, which the authors conceded to be an emotionally moving document, they commented that its style "is not the rough-hewn prose of a sturdy peasant; it is the studied product of a sophisticated and urbane intelligence." To be studied, sophisticated, and urbane is not good, it becomes clear, because these are the attributes associated with the merchant class of Salem town, a place that impressed a London visitor with "the 'many fine houses' he saw there. If this," the authors added, "was how the Town impressed an English cosmopolite, how must it have struck the farmers of Salem Village?" Even the minister, Samuel Parris, who certainly played a leading role in launching the witch hunt, was portrayed as a sympathetic, if often paranoid, victim of circumstances stemming from commercial opportunities that went awry—including being shortchanged in his father's will—and had begun back in his original home in England. The root of the conflict between the two factions of Salem village, the authors explained, lay in the resentments the western farmers felt over their own failings and their eastern neighbors' successes, disparities produced when "a subsistence, peasant-based economy was being subverted by mercantile capitalism." Citing one of Cotton Mather's sermons, which condemned the new shifts in upward and downward mobility that seemed to be undermining the stable Puritan commonwealth, Boyer and Nissenbaum wrote, "The feeling that Mather articulated in this 1689 sermon was one shared by many people in Salem Village three years later [i.e., in 1692]: the social order was being profoundly shaken by a superhuman force which had lured all too many into active complicity with it. We have chosen to construe this force as emergent mercantile capitalism. Mather, and Salem Village, called it witchcraft."[9]

If the witches of Salem thus served as surrogates for the new capitalist order, symbols of a way of life in which "private will" would be asserted over the "public good," then just how sympathetic could a young reader in a university in the 1970s be to the victims of the witch hunt? Boyer and Nissenbaum certainly never defended the execution of innocent people. Indeed, they expressed shock at the lethal outcome of the witch hunt on the rare occasions when they mentioned it. Yet they again placed the witch hunters in a sympathetic light when they likened them in their preface to the antiwar protesters of the 1960s and the African American urban rioters of the same decade, whose anger and frustration sometimes led to outbreaks of terrible violence. "The decade of Watts and of Vietnam helped us realize," the authors wrote, "that the sometimes violent roles men play in 'history' are not necessarily a measure of their personal decency or lack of it. These perceptions deepened our sense of the ambiguities inherent in the events we were studying, as we watched Salem Villagers for whom we had developed real sympathy driven to instigate the deaths of their own neighbors." Later in the book they returned to the same moral puzzle, admitting, "Oddly enough, it has been through our sense of 'collaborating' with Parris and the Putnams in their effort to delineate the larger contours of their world, and our sympathy, at least on the level of metaphor, with certain of their perceptions, that we have come to feel a curious bond with the 'witch hunters' of 1692."[10] Significantly, Boyer and Nissenbaum placed the phrase "witch hunters" in quotation marks here, a sign that they could not quite bring themselves to affix such a pejorative label to the perpetrators of the hangings, even though it accurately reflected the latter's actions. Like Hansen before them, they preferred to use the term "witchcraft" or "witchcraft episode" in place of "witch hunt" throughout their study. Reflecting the positive value placed on crowd behavior by such pioneers in the new social history as the British Marxist historians George Rudé and E. P. Thompson, Boyer and Nissenbaum in *Salem Possessed* could not conceive of the common people of Salem village as anything other than fundamentally well-meaning folks who simply had allowed their justifiable anger to get out of hand.[11]

Because the anti-capitalist argument of *Salem Possessed* struck such an immediate chord with so many of its academic readers, the book at the time escaped the extended critical examination that it deserved. Brief responses over the next three decades typically did note that Boyer and Nissenbaum's factional thesis contained some "ragged" edges. Some of the 1692 participants failed to play their expected roles according to their socioeconomic position, and the book's local focus fell short of accounting for the geographical breadth of the witch hunt throughout Essex County. The number of accusations emanating from the neighboring town of Andover, for example, surpassed the combined totals from Salem village and town as the panic spread to that community just west of Salem village from mid-July to early September, although the initial group of accusers remained the same. But as for explaining the origins of the witch hunt and its dynamics within Salem itself, the argument of *Salem Possessed* won wide acceptance. Only beginning in 2006 would Boyer and Nissenbaum's study come under sustained criticism, the timing of which I take up in my concluding chapter. Yet all of the criticisms prior to that date and even the more penetrating ones of the new century, with which I concur, failed to identify fully the structural weaknesses in so beguiling a perspective.[12]

Problems for the argument of *Salem Possessed* begin with the recognition that the longstanding and consistent factionalism that the authors allege affected Salem village from the mid-1670s until the late-1690s turns out to have been far shorter-lived and much less consistent than they claim. According to the book, the Putnam-led faction of western farmers is said to have opposed the village's first two ministers, supported the two subsequent ministers, and then taken the lead in the witch hunt. The Porter-led faction of eastern farmers and trades people is said to have supported the village's first two ministers and opposed the next two ministers, before becoming targets of the witch hunters or defenders of the accused. But the question of support for the first minister, James Bayley (in office 1672–80), in fact split the wide-ranging Putnam clan: two important Putnam men (Nathaniel and his son, John "Jr.") opposed Bayley, while three (Capt. John [a frequent designation for John Sr.], Thomas Sr., and Thomas Jr.) defended him. Thomas Jr., and his wife, Ann Carr Putnam, whose household in 1692 would accuse more individuals of witchcraft than any other, were probably among Bayley's strongest supporters, since Ann's older sister, Mary Carr, was Bayley's wife. Ann had come with her sister to Salem from Salisbury when Mary had married the minister or soon after. Other names found on petitions for and against Bayley similarly display a strong intermixing of later allegiances during the witch hunt.[13]

For the second minister, George Burroughs (in office 1681–83), there is scant evidence concerning his supporters and opponents. All that is known is that Capt. John Putnam brought suit against Burroughs for failure to repay a personal debt, and six villagers posted bail for the minister, four of whom had earlier signed a pro-Bayley petition while two had not. Two of these four, Nathaniel Ingersoll, a landowner and the village innkeeper, and John Buxton, a substantial farmer—contrary to the expectations of Boyer and Nissenbaum's argument for pro-Bayley and pro-Burroughs men—would later play forceful roles, along with Rev. Samuel Parris and Thomas Putnam Jr., in support of the witch hunt. George Burroughs abruptly left Salem village in spring 1683 to return to Maine before the full three years of his probationary contract with the village had ended. The reasons why he left are not explored in *Salem Possessed*, but the authors suggest that the five-member Salem Village Committee, which in April 1683 filed a petition in Essex County court to compel Burroughs to return to Salem either to complete his term or to settle his accounts with the village, was working in tandem with Capt. John Putnam's suit against the minister. If so, this convergence, bringing together Capt. John Putnam with his two brothers (Thomas Sr., and Nathaniel), who sat on the village committee with him, and the two other committee members (Thomas Fuller Sr. and Daniel Andrew), was likely episodic, for of this group of five seemingly anti-Burroughs men, only one (Capt. John Putnam) would be strongly identified with the later witch hunters, and two (Nathaniel Putnam and Thomas Fuller Sr.) only loosely so. Thomas Putnam Sr., died in 1686, while Daniel Andrew became one of those accused of witchcraft, only evading prosecution by going into hiding. Thus, the personal alignments concerning the treatment of Burroughs while he was a minister in Salem village, whether on the pro-Burroughs or anti-Burroughs side, are not nearly as predictable as the authors assert. Yet at this point in their presentation, looking backward to the Bayley and Burroughs disputes and forward to the antagonists of 1692, Boyer and Nissenbaum conclude with little justification, "Ministers came and went, but the basic lines of factional divisions in Salem Village were hardening year by year."[14]

Only by late in the third year (1686) of the tenure of the village's third minister, Deodat Lawson (in office 1684–88), does something closer to the lines of conflict that would emerge during the witch hunt start to become visible. A fairly unified nucleus of Putnam men and allies, including Capt. John Putnam, Thomas Putnam Jr., William Sibley, and Thomas Flint, appears to have taken the lead in a petition to the magistrates and the mother church in Salem town to have Reverend Lawson ordained. This was the formal step needed to turn the village congregation into a true and autonomous Puritan church, the goal toward which most of the villagers had been aiming since the early 1670s. These four men were all members of the Salem Village Committee for that year, all had been former supporters of Reverend Bayley (contrary to Boyer and Nissenbaum's argument), and three would become supporters of the witch hunt. (William Sibley appears to have died before 1692.) By this point, Thomas Putnam Sr. was dead, while

Nathaniel Putnam, a leader in the earlier move to oust Bayley, may have stepped
back from his involvement in the village's religious affairs (his name never appears
among the many Salemites connected with the effort to bring Lawson to the village), leaving the Putnam clan less divided than in previous years. Still, one
important future opponent of the witch hunt, John Tarbell, a son-in-law of the
later-executed Rebecca Nurse and also a member of the village committee in
1686, joined in the effort to have Lawson ordained.[15]

Meanwhile, four men (Joseph Hutchinson, Daniel Andrew, Joseph Porter,
and Job Swinnerton), all major landowners in the village, came forward to block
Lawson's ordination, and none would later become a prominent supporter of the
witch hunt. Again, however, details mar any picture of continuous factionalism.
The four had divided evenly in the earlier Bayley conflict, with Hutchinson and
Swinnerton opposed to the first minister and Andrew and Porter in favor. Hutchinson did go along with the witch hunt at first but seems to have withdrawn his
support soon after the first three women (Tituba, Sarah Good, and Sarah Osburn)
were accused, possibly when Rebecca Nurse was arrested. He later signed a petition in Nurse's defense. Of the other three Lawson opponents, Daniel Andrew,
as noted earlier, became a target of the witch hunt, while Joseph Porter remained
silent, so far as the historical record reveals, throughout 1692, and Swinnerton
had died before the panic began.

Exactly what caused these men to oppose Lawson's ordination is also not fully
clear. It seems likely they did not oppose it in principle but rather sought to hold
it hostage, in effect, to the achievement of other ends related to the workings
of the village and church. All, in fact, had participated in the various committees
that had worked to invite the minister to the village just a couple years earlier.
The detailed statement issued in February 1687 by the Salem town and church
authorities in turning down the petition for Lawson's ordination suggested that
the current disagreements among the villagers, while rancorous enough to cause
a delay in the process of forming a true church in Salem village, were "not in
themselves of sufficient weight to obstruct so great a work." These disagreements
stemmed from an ongoing dispute about the disposition of land surrounding the
meetinghouse (it had originally been granted to the village by Joseph Hutchinson)
and complaints over what some said was the partisan way in which the villagers'
decisions were made and registered in the village book of record. The town officials urged the villagers to cultivate greater peace and harmony in their community and then proceed "with all convenient speed to go on with your intended
ordination." Evidently, the villagers met this challenge. When Lawson decided
to leave the parish during the winter of 1687–88, household heads from all sides

of the previous disputes came together to locate a new minister (Samuel Parris), saw him ordained without argument in November 1689, and continued working together on numerous committees to improve the physical state of their church and to advance the cause of ultimate independence from Salem town. A new conflict over the terms of Reverend Parris's "maintenance" (means of support) would erupt in 1691, but on the eve of the witch hunt, it would be an exaggeration to characterize Salem village, disputatious as it could be, as a community riven by longstanding factions.[16]

In fact, Boyer and Nissenbaum foster the illusion of continuous and consistent village factions *independent of the events of 1692* by adopting a strategy in two early chapters of presenting the history of Salem town and village from 1639 through 1697, with the developments of the year 1692 left out completely! This makes the "factions" appear to be the independent variable, driving whatever might occur during any of the intervening years, 1692 included. Even more problematic is the authors' use of two key petitions—one calling for the removal of Reverend Parris and a second defending him—dating from 1695, to supply the names (84 on the first petition, 105 on the second) for all of the quantitative investigations (into church membership, household income, and place of residence) used to characterize the two social factions said to have been in operation from as early as the mid-1670s. (Throughout the book the two sides are referred to as the "pro-Parris" and "anti-Parris" factions.) Boyer and Nissenbaum amplify this problem by often resorting to data and events that postdate the witch hunt in order to add substance to their explanation for the witch hunt itself. For example, they freely utilize a number of Parris's post-1692 sermons in their analysis of his preoccupations. Even more strikingly, they emphasize the perceived insult suffered by Thomas Putnam Jr. when his stepmother (Mary Veren Putnam) died in 1695, leaving the remainder of her deceased husband's estate to their son, Joseph, rather than providing portions to Thomas Jr. and his siblings from his father's earlier marriage. The authors suggest that Ann Carr Putnam (Thomas Jr.'s wife) likely accused Rebecca Nurse of witchcraft (in 1692) as a more vulnerable substitute for Mary Veren. All of these discrepancies and analytical problems raise the critical question of whether indeed the "factions" caused the witch hunt, as the authors contend, or whether the witch hunt caused the (later) factions.[17]

Many important participants thought that the latter was closer to the truth. Three members of the extended Nurse family (Rebecca's son Samuel Nurse, son-in-law John Tarbell, and brother-in-law Peter Cloyce), together with Thomas Wilkins, one of Bray Wilkins's sons, all members of the village church, took the lead in calling for Parris's removal beginning in late 1692. They persisted until they succeeded in forcing him out in 1697, and they continually cited the events of 1692 as the source of their discontent. It is no surprise that these men took this action and described it in these terms. The first three had lost not only their beloved matriarch, Rebecca Towne Nurse, but also Rebecca's younger sister, Mary Towne Esty, in the witch hunt, while Thomas Wilkins lost his eldest daughter Margaret's husband, John Willard. Peter Cloyce also came close to seeing his wife Sarah, the youngest of the three Towne sisters, executed. She had been arrested for witchcraft soon after Rebecca was named, spent months (perhaps close to a year) confined under the pitiless conditions of the colony's jails—suspects were often kept in chains to prevent, it was believed, their specters from doing harm to others—but managed to escape trial for reasons that are still unclear. Significantly, when describing these four men's actions from 1693 to 1697, Boyer and Nissenbaum never identify them as close relatives of the witch hunt's victims. Rather, because the authors place their discussion of these years at the end of their two-chapter, witch-hunt-less narrative of events, they portray these villagers' campaign to expel Reverend Parris as if it grew simply out of the community's longstanding factional divide. Yet there is no evidence that any of these four leading anti-Parris spokesmen opposed the minister prior to the witch hunt. On the contrary, they appear in the records of the village church covering the period 1689–91 to be as active as any other members.[18]

Even Parris's leading supporters after the witch hunt indicated a similar understanding of the rift in the village as having been caused by the passions of 1692. In December 1692, Nathaniel Putnam, Capt. John Putnam, and Jonathan Walcott submitted to the county court a petition on behalf of the church to force the Salem Village Committee to collect taxes for Reverend Parris's maintenance. In the petition these men spoke of the committee's neglect of its legal duty as a case of a disenchanted few enlisting the support of "others who heretofore could not by an[y] means join with them" as a result of the "tribulation" of the current year.[19]

Boyer and Nissenbaum, however, argue that these interpretations by the participants were mistaken because they overlooked the rise in October 1691 of a unanimous group of "anti-Parris men" to leadership in the village committee, which immediately decided to curtail collection of the funds for the minister's livelihood. To Boyer and Nissenbaum, it was this action—"the *coup* of October 1691," they call it—as much as any other, that precipitated the witch hunt, provoking Parris and his allies to strike back at their factional enemies, using what the authors term the "archaic strategy" of witchcraft accusation. The phrase "archaic strategy," which had only recently been made popular by the works of British Marxist historian Eric Hobsbawm, invoked a romantic appeal to early forms of anti-capitalist resistance. But here again, as in the authors' telling of the disputes over the three earlier Salem ministers, Boyer and Nissenbaum imputed too much unity and continuity to the actions of the "two sides," a distortion suggested by the authors' use of such overtly and misplaced political rhetoric. The victors in the village committee election of 1691 did not seek a new regime in Salem village (probably not even a new minister), and witchcraft accusations in general throughout the western world in the late seventeenth century were neither chiefly political nor yet, sadly, out of date.[20]

The five individuals elected to the village committee in October 1691 were Joseph Hutchinson, Joseph Porter, Daniel Andrew, Francis Nurse (Rebecca's husband), and Joseph Putnam (the twenty-three-year-old son of Thomas Putnam Sr. by his second wife, Mary Veren). The actions of the committee in deciding to hold off on collecting the minister's taxes are best understood as a power play designed to force discussion of a contentious issue that had apparently only recently come to light for many Salemites. As part of the arrangements for bringing Samuel Parris to Salem village, a number of villagers, including Nathaniel Putnam, Capt. John Putnam, Jonathan Walcott, Thomas Flint, and Nathaniel Ingersoll, had acted semi-surreptitiously in the name of the inhabitants to grant the house and land of the village parsonage to Parris and his heirs, a move in violation of a 1681 decision by the village to provide only temporary usage of the ministry property to whoever occupied the minister's post. The people who had taken this step had also, at the same secret or at least poorly attended meeting (held on October 10, 1689), rescinded the 1681 decision that would have stood in their way. As best can be determined from the surviving records, it appears that the householders represented by the men elected to the village committee in October 1691 had only gradually learned of this transaction starting in the fall of 1690, and from this point forward, doubts began to be raised about the terms of Parris's maintenance. This questioning culminated in the village committee's decision to couple the threat of withholding tax collection to the announcement of a meeting, called for December 1, 1691, to reconsider these controversial aspects of the initial agreement struck with Reverend Parris.[21]

The December meeting never took place, perhaps because by December 1, Parris had made known to the village committee his intention to have the church file suit in Essex County Court to compel the committee to do its job of requiring the residents to support their minister. No doubt Parris would have prevailed on this point, since the committee had clearly exceeded its authority. Indeed, the minister did prevail a year or so later when, after the witch hunt had ended, the church followed through with its threatened lawsuit, and the court ruled in its favor. Eventually, the village committee would receive some satisfaction of its own toward reversing the transfer of title to the village parsonage, for in the 1697 settlement that removed Parris from the village ministry, title to the parsonage was returned to Salem's inhabitants. In any case, in late 1691 and early 1692 the conflict remained a standoff, and as the weeks went forward, it appears that it even lost some of its intensity.

One finds in the village and church records the supposed antagonists working together to advance common interests. On January 8 and January 28, 1692, when Betty Parris and Abigail Williams would have just been starting to act strangely, two village subcommittees, both composed of the same group of six men—Nathaniel Putnam, Capt. John Putnam, Thomas Flint, Francis Nurse, Joseph Hutchinson, and Joseph Porter—were "voted by a general concurrence" of the inhabitants to continue the important goal of pursuing greater autonomy from Salem town. On March 1, 1692, by which time the first three women had been accused of witchcraft, "a general meeting of the inhabitants of Salem Village" delegated Capt. John Putnam and his son Jonathan to represent the village's interests vis-à-vis the town in court, while it chose Daniel Andrew to speak on behalf of the village to the town's officials. Meanwhile, within the church the later witch-hunt opponent Thomas Wilkins had been delegated, along with Nathaniel Putnam and Thomas Putnam Jr., to present to the county court the church's petition to stop the village committee from blocking collection of the minister's tax. There is also no evidence at this time that any of Francis Nurse's six close relatives who were village church members (the three men noted earlier and their wives) or Joseph Hutchinson's wife, Lydia Buxton Hutchinson, another local church member, showed any disaffection from their minister. Nor is there anything to indicate that any of these future opponents of the witch hunt had trepidations about Samuel Parris when he had first arrived in the village. Indeed, another Nurse relative (his son-in-law, Thomas Preston, not a church member), along with Joseph Hutchinson himself, would participate in the first charges leveled against the women suspected of witchcraft. In short, there was no "coup" in October 1691, and as the accusations of witchcraft issued forth in the spring months of 1692, there was little to relate them to the immediate events in the recent history of the village.[22]

In the end a picture of the witch hunt emerges from the data assembled in *Salem Possessed* and its collateral volume of documents, *Salem-Village Witchcraft*, not of two socioeconomic factions facing off against one another but rather of multiple lines of conflict that ran along paths of family alliances and enmities, often reinforced but sometimes undercut by ties of marriage and remarriage in these large, extended clans. This accounts for the fact that Putnams, Wilkinses, Walcotts, Ingersolls, Holtons, Buxtons, and Flints together accounted for the lion's share of the witch hunt's accusations (at least before its later Andover phase). No analogous group of leading families comprised a similarly interlocking network of victims, although Boyer and Nissenbaum attempt to construct one centered on the Porter clan, specifically around Israel Porter, a wealthy landowner and merchant in Salem village and longstanding political official in Salem town. The Porter connection is important to the authors' economic argument because of the family's strong commercial ties to Salem town. But the attempt to make Israel Porter the phantom center—Boyer and Nissenbaum acknowledge that Porter himself was never accused, despite his having organized a petition in support of the jailed Rebecca Nurse—of a circle of witch-hunt victims is unpersuasive, as the relationships shown in figures 1–3 illustrate. Figure 1 reproduces *Salem Possessed*'s hypothetical network of accused witches, built around their connections to Israel Porter. However, once one removes from this network the linkages that postdate the origins of the witch hunt (figure 2), the connections to Porter are quite skimpy. Porter's presence as an explanatory factor in the charges against the suspects then disappears completely if one arranges the linkages in their chronological order of accusation, placing the actual accusers—members of the Thomas Putnam Jr. family—at the center of the constellation, where they belong (figure 3).

Witches were believed to run in families—not through heredity but through training—and the accusations of 1692 make this principle evident again and again. Elizabeth Bassett Procter and her Bassett relatives were not accused because they were connected to John Procter, as shown in Boyer and Nissenbaum's supposed network, but rather John Procter and his wife's Bassett relatives were all accused because they were connected to Elizabeth Procter, who had been named first by Ann Putnam Jr. (in fact as early as March 6, just after the first three suspects), probably due to the prior reputation of her grandmother, Ann Burt, for witchcraft. Similarly, Daniel Andrew was probably not accused because he was Israel Porter's brother-in-law (or had been elected to the Salem Village Committee in 1691 or to Salem town's board of selectmen in March 1692, as Boyer and Nissenbaum also suggest) but rather because his sister, Rebecca Andrew Jacobs, was the daughter-in-law of George Jacobs Sr. (Boyer and Nissenbaum omit him entirely from their network), who again had been named before anyone else in the Jacobs family grouping. There is no reason to think that Israel Porter had anything to do with any of the accused people shown in Boyer and Nissenbaum's original chart.[23]

Some antagonisms that could lead to accusations of witchcraft may have stemmed, at least in part, from particular tensions over land or other economic

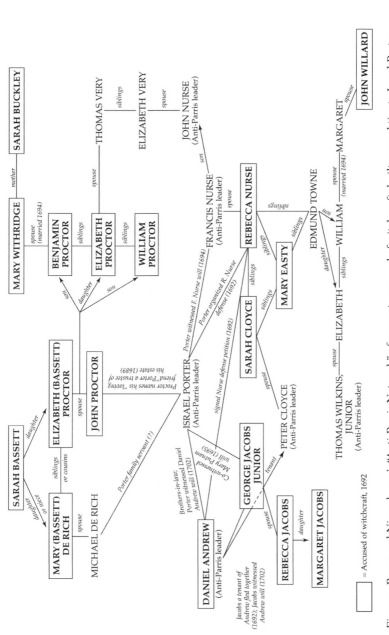

Figure 1. Boyer and Nissenbaum's "Anti-Parris Network" of suspects accused of witchcraft, built around ties to Israel Porter. *Source: Salem Possessed: The Social Origins of Witchcraft*, by Paul Boyer and Stephen Nissenbaum, Cambridge, MA: Harvard University Press, Copyright © 1974 by the President and Fellows of Harvard College, 184.

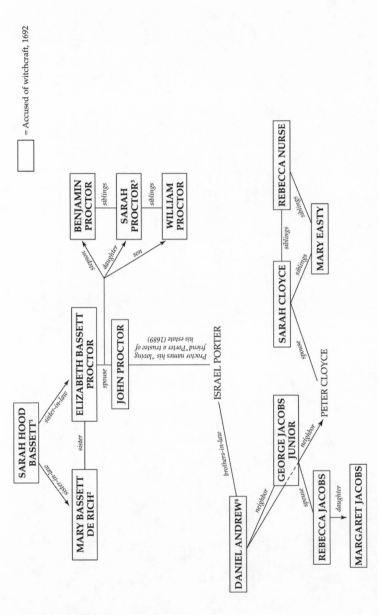

Figure 2. Boyer and Nissenbaum's "Anti-Parris Network," restricted to shown pre–witch-hunt relationships. *Notes*: 1. The full name and corrected relationships of Sarah Hood Bassett have been substituted for the original "Sarah Bassett." 2. Mary De Rich's husband, Michael De Rich, has been removed, because the original chart established only a relationship to Israel Porter's father, not Israel Porter. After the elder Porter's death in 1676, De Rich appears to have begun working for John Buxton (*RFQCE*, 5:346, 428; 7:160). 3. Sixteen-year-old Sarah Proctor was the one accused of witchcraft; her older stepsister Elizabeth was never accused. 4. I have found no evidence that Daniel Andrew was the landlord to George Jacobs Jr. or Peter Cloyce. *Salem Possessed* cited (183n4) Upham's *Salem Witchcraft* frontispiece for this information, but Upham states only that the land surrounding their houses was "owned, in 1692, by Daniel Andrew and Peter Cloyce" (1:xxvi). *Source*: Modification of data from figure 1.

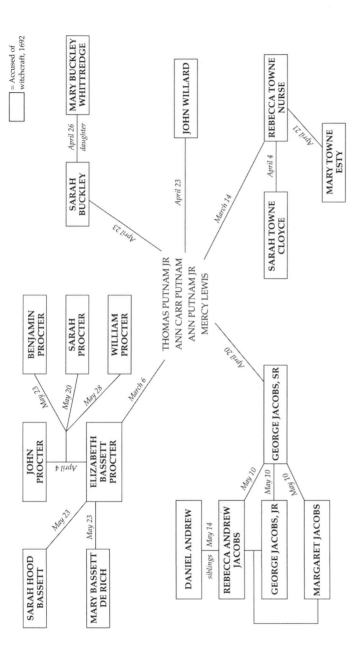

Figure 3; Boyer and Nissenbaum's network of suspects accused of witchcraft, rearranged in chronological order of accusation, built around the accusing family of Thomas Putnam Jr. *Notes*: Dates shown are the earliest recorded mention of accusation. For all unlabeled personal relationships, see figure 2. In this figure, unlike figures 1 and 2, I revert to the spellings of names used throughout my book. *Sources*: For E. Procter, see Norton, *In the Devil's Snare*, 30; J. Procter, Norton, *In the Devil's Snare*, 71; S. H. Bassett, *SWP*, 1:77; M. B. De Rich, *Records*, #198; B. Procter, *SWP*, 2:655; S. Procter, *SWP*, 2:692–694; W. Procter, *Records*, #221; S. Buckley, *SWP*, 1:148; M. Whittredge, *SWP*, 1:320; G. Jacobs Sr, Norton, *In the Devil's Snare*, 132; R. Jacobs, *Records*, #135; G. Jacobs Jr, *SWP*, 2:476; M. Jacobs, Norton, *In the Devil's Snare*, 158–159; D. Andrew, *Records*, #151; R. Nurse, Norton, *In the Devil's Snare*, 47; S. Cloyce, Norton, *In the Devil's Snare*, 73; M. Esty, *Records*, #79; J. Willard, *SWP*, 3:850.

resentments. Here lies a kernel of truth in Boyer and Nissenbaum's economic interpretation. For example, the accusations brought against the Towne sisters (Rebecca Nurse, Mary Esty, and Sarah Cloyce), Elizabeth How, Sarah Wilds, and Sarah Wilds Bishop may have reflected the fact that these women were the daughters, daughters-in-law, sisters, or wives of Topsfield men (John, Jacob, and Joseph Towne, Isaac Esty Sr., John How, and William Wilds) with whom the Putnams had come into conflict over lands that fell ambiguously within the jurisdictions of Salem village and its neighboring community to the north. But these past disputes likely generated only a portion of the emotions behind even these particular accusations. More potent in the case of the Towne sisters may well have been the longstanding reputation of their mother, Joanna Towne, for witchcraft, while both Elizabeth How and Sarah Wilds had also long been suspected of witchcraft by their Topsfield and Ipswich neighbors for reasons having nothing to do with the disputed land claims. In any case, competition over land ownership can hardly be characterized in terms of opposition to the spread of merchant capitalism, which is probably why Boyer and Nissenbaum do not highlight the record of this strife.[24] To make their strongest claims that conflicting attitudes about commerce lay at the heart of the "factional" divide producing the witch hunt, the authors end up relying on a contrasting economic picture of "pro-Parris" decline versus "anti-Parris" prosperity, as well as on their residential map locating a preponderance of the accusers on the poorer, interior side of the village and most of the accused and their defenders on the village's more resource-laden, town side. Both of these final building blocks in the authors' argument, however, have been successfully challenged or seriously weakened by recent research.

While still accepting Boyer and Nissenbaum's construction of two continuous factions based on the petition lists (for and against the minister) from 1695, Richard Latner reexamined the authors' single "snapshot" of the two sides' comparative economic standing based on mean tax assessments for 1695, which had shown the minister's supporters at about two-thirds the level of prosperity attained by the minister's opponents. By adding data from village tax-assessment lists created in 1681, 1690, 1694, and 1700 to the one from 1695, Latner was able to show a trend in the two groups' comparative standing over time. It turns out that 1695 was an atypical year in these assessments, the year of greatest disparity between the groups. In 1681 the householders who would later (in 1695) rally behind Reverend Parris stood at about 80 percent of the level of wealth (using medians) of the future opponents of the minister, but by 1690 these same "pro-Parris" householders had made up the difference entirely and stood at parity with their future antagonists. Thus it is incorrect to say that the faction Boyer and Nissenbaum identified as the witch hunters were an economically "declining" group in the decade leading up to the witch hunt. By 1694 and 1695, the pro-Parris group's economic position did slide downward to a low point of two-thirds of their opponents' assessable wealth, but it then rebounded to reach approximate parity again in 1700. "The tax rolls do not support the claim that the pro-Parris group lashed out in resentment in 1692 against those who represented the superior forces of modernization," Latner concludes. "If any group had reason to complain, it was the minister's opponents."[25]

Since Boyer and Nissenbaum used the same sample of names (signers of the two 1695 ministerial petitions) to determine both the taxable wealth and residential locations of the two sides in the witch hunt, it follows from the antagonists' rough parity in taxable wealth that there must not have been significant implications for economic success, contrary to the authors' stated assumption, in the topographical differences between the eastern and western sides of Salem village, at least not during the closing decades of the seventeenth century. What then should be made of the peculiar geographic distribution that *Salem Possessed* displayed in its striking map of the residences of accusers and accused, together with the latter's defenders? (See figure 4 for a reproduction of this map.)[26] In a strong challenge to the book's most famous graphic, Benjamin C. Ray has attempted to show that due to a few mistakes, the arbitrary categorizing of certain participants, and many omissions, Boyer and Nissenbaum greatly exaggerated the east-west divide between the two sides in the witch hunt. Ray "corrected" the book's map by adding a net sum of thirty-four accusers, most of whom lived on the village's eastern side, and a net sum of three accused, all of whom lived on the village's western side. The result (reproduced in figure 5) presents an image of accusers and accused as much more evenly distributed throughout the village. "Twenty-eight accusers appear on the eastern side of the east-west line and forty on the western side," Ray wrote in summary of his findings. "The east-west distribution of accused witches is less even, but there are enough in the west so that the situation is not one-sided. Clearly, accusers and accused did not live on opposite sides of the village as Boyer and Nissenbaum stated." And yet, Ray's analysis is not entirely satisfying, partly because the logic behind some of his modifications is not always persuasive, but mainly because even with these changes, something remains of Boyer and Nissenbaum's uneven distribution that Ray seems ready to gloss over. (In Boyer and Nissenbaum's map, 94% of accusers [33 of 35] resided on the western side, and 77% of accused witches [17 of 22] lived on the eastern side. With Ray's modifications, 59% of accusers [40 of 68] resided on the western side, and 68% of the accused [17 of 25] lived on the eastern side.)[27]

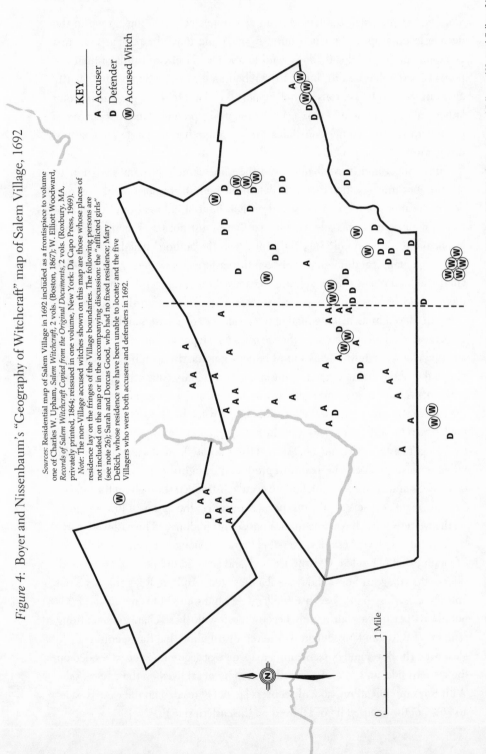

Figure 4: Boyer and Nissenbaum's "Geography of Witchcraft" map of Salem Village, 1692

Sources: Residential map of Salem Village in 1692 included as a frontispiece to volume one of Charles W. Upham, *Salem Witchcraft,* 2 vols. (Boston, 1867); W. Elliott Woodward, *Records of Salem Witchcraft Copied from the Original Documents,* 2 vols. (Roxbury, MA, privately printed, 1864; reissued in one volume, New York: Da Capo Press, 1969).

Note: The non-Village accused witches shown on this map are those whose places of residence lay on the fringes of the Village boundaries. The following persons are not included on the map or in the accompanying discussion: the "afflicted girls" (see note 26); Sarah and Dorcas Good, who had no fixed residence; Mary DeRich, whose residence we have been unable to locate; and the five Villagers who were both accusers and defenders in 1692.

KEY

A Accuser
D Defender
Ⓦ Accused Witch

FIGURE 5: Benjamin C. Ray's "Geography of Witchcraft Accusations in 1692 Salem Village," modifying Boyer and Nissenbaum's original map

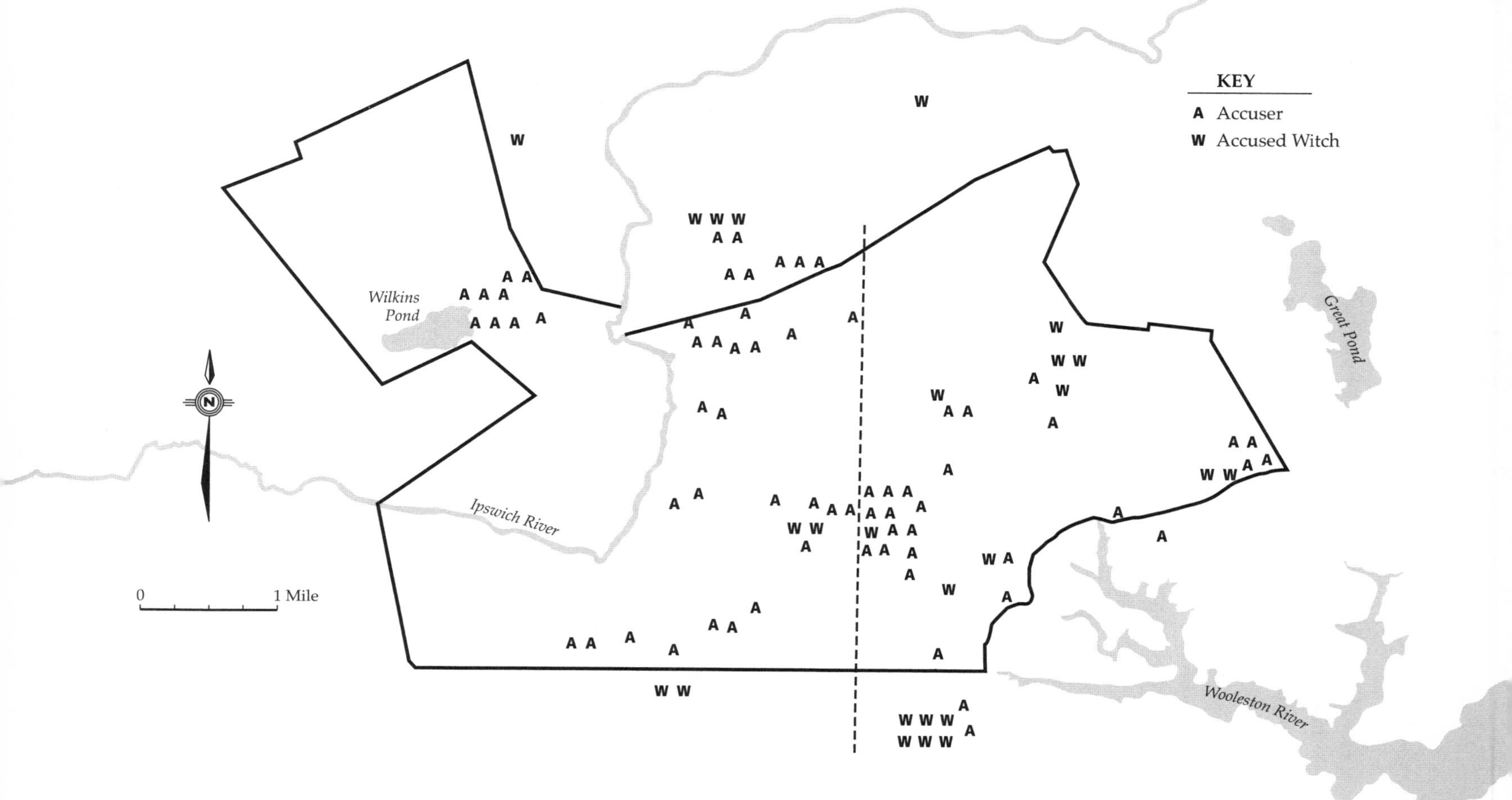

KEY
A Accuser
W Accused Witch

Great Pond

Woolston River

Ipswich River

Wilkins Pond

1 Mile

0

N

Source: Benjamin C. Ray, "The Geography of Witchcraft Accusations in 1692 Salem Village," *William and Mary Quarterly*, 3rd ser., 65, no. 3 (July 2008): 469.

The problem of what is left over from Boyer and Nissenbaum's map is solved, however, if we return to the recognition that, given the presence of strong religious beliefs, witchcraft accusations traveled foremost along family lines (for both accusers and accused) and stemmed primarily from personal grievances and fears. What Boyer and Nissenbaum took as representing a more fundamental socioeconomic cleavage was really the geographic patterning that resulted from contiguous lands being held by extended families, whose members tended to live near one another. Large landholdings held by a family's first generation were typically subdivided for its sons, grandsons, and in-laws. Thus their antagonists lived some distance away. When Ann Carr Putnam accused Rebecca Towne Nurse of bewitching to death three babies that her sister, Mary Carr Bayley, had lost in childbirth, did she make this charge because she had absorbed the stories of her Putnam in-laws about the way they thought the Towne family had treated the Putnams over their disputed lands; or because Rebecca's mother, Joanna Towne, had once been accused of witchcraft; or perhaps because Ann believed Rebecca looked down on her in daily affairs, reflected in the elderly Nurse's refusal to transfer her membership from the Salem town church to the village church, unlike most of the rest of the Nurse clan; or for all of these and perhaps additional reasons? We do not know the answer to this question, but the charge quickly established a geographic divide between the wide-ranging Putnam holdings on the western side of the village and those of the many Nurses to the east. Similarly, Salem villager Sarah Osburn's vulnerability to accusation likely stemmed from the fact that after she remarried (under somewhat scandalous circumstances), she successfully obstructed the will of her deceased husband, which had directed that their considerable estate be transferred eventually to their two sons, nephews of John Putnam Sr. Osburn's property happened to lie within the eastern half of the village.

The accusations against John Willard, to take one more example, proceeded from his having run afoul of his wife's extended family, the Wilkins clan, which owned most of the land in the northwest corner of Salem village. The Wilkinses believed that Willard had abused his wife, and he stood accused by at least twelve (probably quite a few more) members of their extended family. They alleged that he had bewitched to death the young wife of his own wife's cousin; had caused the patriarch of the clan, Bray Wilkins, to suffer a painful urinary disorder; and had taken the life of Bray's seventeen-year-old grandson who, it was said, had stated publicly that he wished Willard to hang. Yet Bray's son, Thomas Wilkins, whose daughter was married to Willard, stood by him, estranging himself in the process from the rest of his extended family, Reverend Parris, and the Putnams, who had actually been the first to accuse Willard, charging that he had killed Ann Jr.'s little sister. The Wilkinses' charges against Willard account for the presence of eleven accusers on the western side of Boyer and Nissenbaum's map, living near to just one accused witch and a single defender.

One could go on and on detailing such personal vignettes and geographic placements. So often behind these accusations stood the reputations of the accused for prior acts of witchcraft or for having descended from women (and occasionally men) who held such reputations. Martha Cory, Rebecca Nurse, Bridget Bishop, Elizabeth Procter, Alice Parker, and Ann Pudeator, six of the seven women from Salem village or town who were executed, all fit this characterization, to which group we might add John Procter and Giles Cory through marriage. My own modified version of Boyer and Nissenbaum's map, displaying the leading accusers and accused in the vicinity of Salem village by family grouping (figure 6), shows that what remains of the witch hunt's geographical divide (after most of Ray's corrections are accepted) can best be explained simply by the location of extended family residences.[28]

By focusing so heavily on the supposed economic roots of antagonism between Salem village and Salem town, not only did Boyer and Nissenbaum obscure these more personal, emotion-laden sources of conflict, but they ironically overlooked what was probably an even more important point of difference between the village and town as far as the witch hunt was concerned. Readers learn from *Salem Possessed* how the orthodox Puritanism of Reverend Parris appealed to many of the farmers in the village, but nowhere in the book do the authors disclose that under the three-decades-old leadership of Rev. John Higginson, the church in Salem town (where the accused Rebecca Nurse, Giles Cory, Sarah Buckley, and probably the Procters held membership) had become one of the most liberal in the entire colony. The Salem town church accepted as early as the 1660s the so-called Halfway Covenant, which created a second tier of membership for full church members' children who had been baptized, were morally upstanding, but had not themselves testified to a conversion experience. (This status enabled these people to have their own children baptized.) The church later made further innovations in admission to the sacraments of baptism and communion that were designed to bring into its fold as many town residents as possible. By 1692 something like 80 percent of Massachusetts churches had embraced the Halfway Covenant, but the Salem village church, where Samuel Parris preached an uncompromising spiritual warfare between the forces of God and those of the Devil—always one way of expressing the ardent hope among Puritans for the coming millennium—stood with the 20 percent that had not.[29]

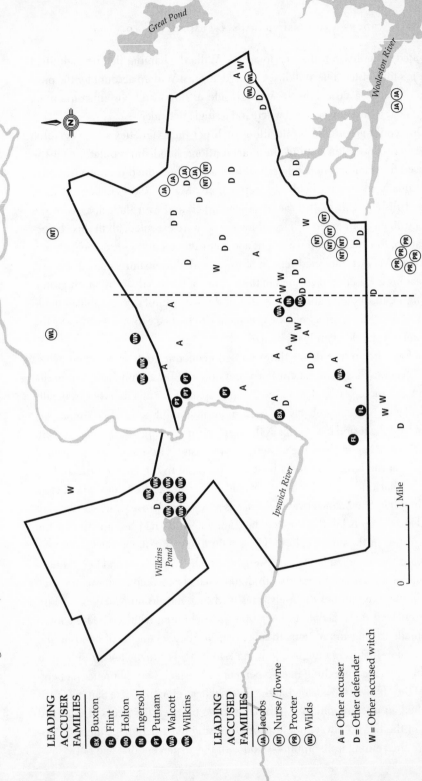

Figure 6: Boyer and Nissenbaum's "Geography of Witchcraft" data, with family groups highlighted

LEADING ACCUSER FAMILIES
- **BX** = Buxton
- **FL** = Flint
- **HO** = Holton
- **IN** = Ingersoll
- **PT** = Putnam
- **WA** = Walcott
- **WK** = Wilkins

LEADING ACCUSED FAMILIES
- **JA** = Jacobs
- **NT** = Nurse/Towne
- **PR** = Procter
- **WL** = Wilds

A = Other accuser
D = Other defender
W = Other accused witch

Notes: Extended family names have been assigned to the data points shown in figure 4 by correlating the data points with the lists of accusers, accused, and defenders presented in Boyer and Nissenbaum, ed. *Salem-Village Witchcraft*, 375–382, and with the households shown on the residential map appearing in Upham, *Salem Witchcraft* 1:xv–xxvii, plus map insert. The household names of all but two of Boyer and Nissenbaum's ninety data points (two accusers) could be identified. A complete list of each data point and associated household name appears in appendix 1. Documentation for extended family members not readily apparent from the list in appendix 1 may be found in note 28. I have added to figure 6 four data points not appearing in figure 4 – the accused witches Sarah Wilds (WL) and Mary Esty (NT) just north of Salem village, and George Jacobs, Sr. (JA) and Margaret Jacobs (JA) just south of the village – because they are in line with the rules governing the rest of Boyer and Nissenbaum's data and they help illustrate the significance of family ties in the witch hunt. *Source:* Modification of data from figure 4

The Salem town church owed its postmillennial progressivism in large measure to its substantial merchant class, for along with their aggressive pursuit of self-interest, the merchants brought an expanding appreciation for religious tolerance and individual freedom. Yet there were still some religious conservatives among the merchants of Salem. One was John Hathorne, who, as one of the three magistrates in the town (which legally encompassed the village under its jurisdiction), became the leading examiner of the accused witches. During the year of the witch hunt, the special witchcraft court would include conservative Puritans like Hathorne; the Boston merchant John Richards, who forced the Mathers to delay instituting the Halfway Covenant at their Second Church; the Boston merchant Samuel Sewall, whose famous diary recorded his spiritual strivings amid the growing temptations of the world; and the Dorchester magistrate and lieutenant governor William Stoughton, who had also long opposed the Halfway Covenant. In their capacity as specially appointed judges, these men, all Massachusetts Council members, would try and convict twenty-seven people of witchcraft, sending twenty to their deaths. With its vivid sense of Satan's devious ability to disrupt the godly in their endeavors, the religious outlook of these men, shared by Reverend Parris, the Thomas Putnam Jr. family, and their neighbors among the frightened people of Salem village, provided the ideological underpinnings for the persecutions that ensued.[30]

An Aside

Investigations into the Practice of Actual Witchcraft in Seventeenth-Century New England

As noted near the beginning of chapter 2, two main directions of scholarship followed on Hansen's and Demos's work of 1969–70. One aimed at identifying an external threat that could explain the Salem witch hunt, while the other looked past Salem toward describing general patterns of witchcraft accusation in seventeenth-century New England. At the same time, a third scholarly vector, less consequential than the other two, picked up from Hansen's interest in actual witchcraft. Shedding Hansen's attitude of hostility toward Salem's "real witches," this line of inquiry proceeded to investigate occult religious forms among the common people of New England, expecting to find witchcraft among them. Indeed, the historians pursuing this idea were, like Boyer and Nissenbaum, broadly influenced by the new radical desire to write history "from the bottom up" and by the tendency of like-minded historians of the European past to view popular forms of religion sympathetically and as distinct from what were taken to be more repressive forms of elite faith. Problems would soon arise, however, in assimilating witchcraft into a wider, positive stream of lay, non-Christian practices. If witches really aimed to do harm to their neighbors, then how could their actions be viewed sympathetically? And what if the common people turned out to use all means at their disposal, techniques of countermagic along with Christian persecution, to do harm to outcasts whom they were quick to regard as "witches"?[1]

Efforts to study the popular persistence of occult religiosity received an enormous boost from the publication in 1971 of the British historian Keith Thomas's important study of religious change in sixteenth- and seventeenth-century

England, *Religion and the Decline of Magic*. Strikingly, however, while Thomas provided persuasive evidence of "cunning men" and "wise women" utilizing magic to help clients in such diverse endeavors as healing from illness, discovering stolen property, winning at cards, prevailing in a law suit, escaping arrest, protecting against accidents or witchcraft, succeeding in love, finding buried treasure, and discerning the future, his 148-page section titled "Witchcraft" offered scant evidence that witchcraft itself (magic employed to do harm to others, with or without the explicit invocation of the Devil) was practiced at all. Thomas noted the recovery of "cursing tablets" (stones, meant to be buried underground, bearing magical symbols along with a written curse aimed at an individual) that dated back to the mid-sixteenth century, but one gets the sense that few had been found. An older study, George Lyman Kittredge's *Witchcraft in Old and New England* (1929), which Thomas cited, referenced just three instances of cursing tablets being recovered, in addition to the single instance Thomas repeated in his own account. Kittredge provides no details, so it is hard to evaluate his claims. In any case, he called this practice "a learned species of magic to which educated Englishmen resorted now and then in the sixteenth and seventeenth centuries," so it could not have been very widespread.[2]

Thomas similarly stated that magic employing effigies made of wax or clay, into which pins would be stuck, was "extensively practiced," but his only examples came from records of political figures who were attacked in this manner by angry subjects or from accusations made in witchcraft trials, always a suspect source. Kittredge, whom Thomas again cited for corroboration concerning these effigies, chiefly offered cases, often sounding more literary than historical, from the annals of English royalty and the many murder plots that swirled around them.[3] The rest of Thomas's evidence boiled down to verbal expressions of anger uttered by people, typically poor and without the means to pursue grievances through legal channels, against those whom they had good reason to believe had injured them—what had traditionally been known as the "beggar's curse." In fact, the great weight of the discussion in *Religion and the Decline of Magic*— and in this lies its strength—went to show that the problem of "witchcraft" in the early modern period is best understood as the existence of *witch-belief*, a term Thomas ended up using far more than witchcraft itself. Confirmed by the occasional boastings of village outsiders and more tragically by the confessions of disturbed, guilt-ridden, or intimidated individuals brought to trial, the belief in witchcraft remained powerfully present in English society until the final decades of the seventeenth century. But always, Thomas wrote, "society . . . forced the role of the witch upon its victims."[4]

Historians who have endeavored to find witchcraft practiced in colonial America have fared no better, despite intermittent claims to the contrary. In his 1979 article, "Magic, Astrology, and the Early American Religious Heritage, 1600–1760," Jon Butler detailed the existence in colonial America of astrological books and almanacs, a few individuals willing to dispense occult advice, and traces of magical remedies to cure illness or ward off misfortune. But when he came to the practice of witchcraft, Butler relied chiefly on endorsing Hansen's findings in *Witchcraft at Salem*. The rest of his evidence documented only the belief in witchcraft or the practice of countermagic aimed at thwarting the presumed actions of witches. Yet he asserted, "Despite the problem of finding evidence that does not descend from courts or Christian ministers, the present essay is designed to demonstrate that historians can, in fact, uncover actual occult practices, including witchcraft." In his later book, *Awash in a Sea of Faith: Christianizing the American People* (1990), Butler presented data almost identical to that used in the earlier article, again including Hansen's findings, but he now qualified his earlier claim to have identified the practice of witchcraft, at least for the Salem witch hunt. "Despite the problem of finding evidence that does not descend from the courts or Christian ministers," he wrote in 1990, "a sufficient range of evidence—legal, clerical, and literary—now seems to demonstrate that such practices did indeed occur, though it will never tell us whether the individuals accused at Salem engaged in witchcraft or in more benign occult activity."[5]

At first glance Richard Weisman's *Witchcraft, Magic, and Religion in 17th-Century Massachusetts* (1984) also appeared to accept the existence of practicing witches in colonial Massachusetts. Strongly influenced by Thomas's work, Weisman's study took for granted that the English repertoire of magical practices, including witchcraft, must have accompanied the Puritan migration to New England. His book made much—too much for New England, where the laity was so thoroughly influenced by Calvinist ideas—of the distinction, emphasized by Thomas, between the common people's understanding of magic-inspired *maleficia* (evil deeds accomplished through occult means alone) and the Puritan leadership's religious emphasis on the witch's pact with Satan. And his study sometimes allowed a suspect's reputation for witchcraft to be confused with evidence of its practice. However, not only did Weisman fail to document any examples of actual witchcraft (as distinct from acts of divination, protective countermagic, and occult healing), but it became clear as his study progressed that his emphasis, like Thomas's, fell on the prevalence of the *belief* in witchcraft, not its practice. Proceeding from an interest in the sociology of deviance, Weisman's account ended up arguing that "witches" were produced as scapegoats by communities under stress, whether in the pre-Salem accusations by the everyday problems of seventeenth-century village life, or in the Essex County witch hunt of 1692 in response, he believed, to greater threats (the Massachusetts charter's recent revocation and the resumption in 1689 of attacks by Native Americans).[6]

David D. Hall's work on the subject of popular religion in colonial New England, especially his book, *Worlds of Wonder, Days of Judgment: Popular Religious Belief in Early New England* (1990), brought this line of research to a near-conclusion. While earlier willing to entertain the possibility that Hansen's "controversial" hypothesis of witches at Salem could be true, by the time he wrote *Worlds of Wonder,* Hall omitted witchcraft from among his examples of occult practices in Puritan New England. A year later he stated directly that he disagreed with Hansen about the existence of witches in the Salem panic. Instead, Hall found evidence in seventeenth-century New England only of fortune-tellers, occult healers, and advisers in the techniques of countermagic. Even for these "cunning men and women," the number of individuals involved was probably small, Hall believed, because conscientious Puritans condemned all such people as trafficking with the Devil and, paradoxically, because many of their remedies (for example, nailing an upside-down horseshoe outside the door to protect against witchcraft) were widely known through oral tradition and printed almanacs and utilized on occasion by pious and less pious people alike.[7]

However, the absence of practicing witches, Hall pointed out, did not diminish the spread of a deep belief in witchcraft, fostered by a prescientific mentality that infused the natural world with supernatural forces and moral imperatives, allowing misfortunes or provocations of all sorts to be explained by a presumed evildoer's conscious manipulation of those forces, with Satan's help. At most, a "witch" in this society was someone who might, quite off-handedly, have predicted some dire aspect of the future that turned out to be true; suggested a cure that failed to work; invoked the common curse, "the Devil take you"; or, as Hall wrote in an earlier article, been "perhaps not unwilling to play on rumors of [her or his] occult powers." But always the witch was the product of other people's beliefs and accusations, so often fed by the suspect's prior reputation and by stereotypical descriptions handed down through verbal lore and printed texts, ranging from sermons to sensational pamphlets. Well-publicized confessions added to the stock of these beliefs, as is poignantly illustrated in the case Hall cited of Mary Parsons of Springfield, Massachusetts, around 1650. Parsons fantasized that she had entered into a covenant with the Devil so she could see her deceased child again. Not surprisingly, therefore, Hall's book and articles spoke far more often of "witch hunting" than of "witchcraft." In one of his later articles on the subject, Hall helpfully concluded, "Witch-hunting was not about witchcraft in our usual sense of the term. Its source was a fearfulness among ordinary people."[8]

Otherwise a valuable book, Richard Godbeer's *The Devil's Dominion: Magic and Religion in Early New England* (1992) then took an analytical step backward in maintaining, again with Hansen's *Witchcraft at Salem*, which it cited favorably, that there really had been witches in colonial New England, including some uncovered by the Salem witch hunt. In particular, Godbeer maintained that a substantial number of New Englanders used image magic, effigies that ranged from crude rolls of knotted rags to more elaborately formed puppets or dolls, to harm the targets of their malevolence. But in nearly all the instances he cited, the evidence comes from witchcraft confessions, statements that elsewhere contain outlandish fantasies of Devil-inspired activities. Take the case of Mary Lacey Sr., of Andover, who confessed to being a witch in July 1692. Based on her confession, Godbeer suggested that Lacey would roll up a rag or cloth, imagine it to represent a person, and then injure the person by manipulating the rag. But in the same confession, Mary Lacey also said she had ridden on a pole with another witch to Salem village, had been carried in the Devil's arms to Newbury Falls to witness him baptize Rebecca Nurse and other witches there, and had afflicted another Andover resident, Timothy Swan, using an iron spindle and perhaps a tobacco pipe. Each of these elements in her confession represented one piece of a common set of stereotyped responses assumed to represent the activities of a witch (in the context of the particulars of 1692), and it makes little sense to credit any one element (the use of rag puppets) with greater truth than the others. No doubt Mary Lacey Sr. believed her own confession at that point in time, but there is no reason why readers should today.[9]

In his later writings, Godbeer drew back, though not completely, from this position. In *Escaping Salem: The Other Witch Hunt of 1692* (2005), a close study of the trial for witchcraft of two western Connecticut women, Elizabeth Clawson and Mercy Disborough, Godbeer at no point suggests that either woman attempted to harm her neighbors through occult practices. Both are portrayed as victims of popular beliefs, although there is one ambiguous paragraph, reminiscent of his treatment of witchcraft in *The Devil's Dominion*, that blurs the distinction between the general belief in witchcraft and the actual practice of it. That lingering ambiguity persists in Godbeer's more recent treatment of the subject, *The Salem Witch Hunt: A Brief History with Documents* (2011), which again implies not only that New Englanders believed in the efficacy of witchcraft but that some likely practiced it through image magic. Godbeer includes in this volume three documents said to illustrate this practice, but all are suspect. The first comes from an accusation made as part of a confession in the midst of the Salem panic—Sarah Churchill's charge against Ann Pudeator that the latter stuck thorns in images of three young Salemites. This was the same Sarah Churchill who on another occasion tearfully confessed to a friend that she had "bel[ied] herself and others" in her testimony to the magistrates. The other two documents repeat evidence Hansen used to build a case for witchcraft against Bridget Bishop: the deposition, discussed in chapter 2, from two members of the Bly family; and a second deposition from a tailor (Samuel Shattuck), who already believed that Bishop had bewitched his son. In this testimony the tailor claimed that since Bishop had once asked him to dye sleeves and pieces of lace that seemed to him too short for any human use, these articles of clothing must have been meant to dress an effigy. These documents work well as evidence for the widespread belief in witchcraft but not for its practice.[10]

The scholarly search for witches in seventeenth-century New England thus reached a dead end. It uncovered no such people carrying forth an independent tradition of occult practice aimed at harming others. But this entire line of research and especially the contradictions that emerged from its findings were nevertheless revealing of the outlook of most post-1960s historians toward witch hunting. Unlike Hansen, these historians had no desire to blame the "witches," if they could find any. On the contrary, these scholars stood ready to welcome witches, as practitioners of one strain of popular religion, into the company of "cunning men" and "wise women," who carried out a variety of mostly benign, if not always effective, rituals. At the same time, the existence of occult figures who sometimes mixed "black magic" with "white" could help explain why the otherwise good people of seventeenth-century New England might on occasion be provoked into a rage against this sort of seeming danger, as they had been at Salem in 1692. Hence the tendency persisted among a number of scholars to hold onto the existence of witchcraft, despite the lack of evidence to support such a conclusion. Meanwhile, Puritanism, as a stringent expression of elite religion imposed on the common people, could be held accountable for witchcraft's suppression, together with that of all other forms of magic. In this way, the ordinary people of colonial New England retained their innocence.[11]

This line of inquiry, like the more influential ones documented in this book, thus reflected a subtle shift in scholarly sympathies from the accused to the accusers in terms of identifying "the victims" during the era of witch hunting. There was little need to direct attention to the murderous potential of popular scapegoating, so long as witch hunting could be attributed to malevolent provocations by a few antisocial individuals (the "witches"), along with the fearsome effects of learned Puritan preaching. One may hope that Hall's work, which had never joined in positing such a pronounced split between elite and popular religion in Puritan New England and which quickly rejected the likelihood of discovering practicing witches, will in the long run succeed in returning the designation of victimhood to the accused, where it belongs.[12]

CHAPTER 3

Demos's *Entertaining Satan* and the Functionalist Perspective

In 1982, John Demos came out with the extended study of witchcraft accusations he had promised in his 1970 article. *Entertaining Satan: Witchcraft and the Culture of Early New England* was a major scholarly achievement, well worthy of the prestigious Bancroft Prize it received in 1983 for distinguished work in American history. Across five hundred densely worded but elegantly written pages, Demos brought to life the intricacies of personal and social conflict that lay behind the charge of witchcraft leveled so commonly by some New Englanders against others. Along with four substantial chapters of sociological and psychological analysis, the book offered as its high point eight brilliant case studies that set forth in all their necessary detail the situations that faced seven people (six women and one man) accused of witchcraft and one teenaged girl suffering from the afflictions of diabolical possession. If one of these case studies may be elevated above the rest, the story of Elizabeth Garlick, accused of witchcraft in the Puritan-founded Long Island community of Easthampton during the 1650s, presents a dazzling piece of historical reconstruction. The reader gets to walk up the single muddy road of this hamlet, viewing its roughly sixteen house lots on either side, gazing outward toward the farm fields that surrounded the main road, while noticing the cows, hogs, sheep, goats, and horses that each household kept in its barn or on its land. One learns where each of these families had lived previously in Old and New England. In this setting the antagonism between the approximately fifty-year-old Garlick and nine other village inhabitants (six women and three men) unfolds, leading to her trial and acquittal for witchcraft.[1]

True to his promise, Demos took as his field of study the entire range of witch-craft accusations emerging out of colonial New England from the 1640s through the end of the seventeenth century, with the "overworked" Salem episode left out. His database, Demos explained in his introduction, comprised 93 indictments for witchcraft (50 from Massachusetts, 43 from Connecticut), out of which 16 defendants were found guilty and executed. Had he included Salem, these totals would have reached 234 indictments with 36 executed. The choice to omit Sa-lem amounts to more than numbers, however, even with noting that its inclusion would have more than doubled the size of the phenomenon under study. By re-moving from consideration what Demos himself calls the "witch hunt" of 1692—as well as the other colonial instance of mass hysteria connected to the fear of witchcraft, the panic that overtook Hartford, Connecticut, and its surrounding towns in 1662, which produced fourteen indictments and four likely executions—*Entertaining Satan* was able to shape to its own purposes the very subject of its inquiry. Again, among the major works of scholarship in this era, the term "witchcraft" largely replaced "witch hunt," a decision certainly made easier by placing Salem and Hartford outside the study's bounds. In addition, in not one of the book's eight case studies did the accusation of witchcraft lead to an execu-tion. As examples of cases disconnected from any true panic over the danger witches were thought to present to a community, the selection of this sample may have made sense, since such isolated prosecutions allowed judicial officials to show greater scrutiny and restraint than they did in cases brought forth in the midst of a scare. But such a selection underplayed the prospect of what was so terrifying to the accused about the charge of witchcraft—that they might lose their lives. Most significantly, the omission of Salem from the scope of his study enabled Demos to develop his argument that witchcraft accusations served a variety of useful functions in these small, personal communities, a perspective he acknowledged would be harder to support in cases of full-blown witch hunts. All in all, the choice to leave Salem out of the picture was a little like deciding to study the history of European anti-Semitism without the pogroms or the history of white supremacy in the American South without the lynchings.[2]

If the omission of Salem thus predisposed *Entertaining Satan* to produce a more benign view of witchcraft accusations than would otherwise have been the case, one must still ask how the book's examination of these non-Salem in-stances colored the sympathies of its readers. The answer is complex because the book's analysis proceeds along two broad tracks, sociological (or anthropological) and psychological, with two arguments advanced on each track. But in all cases the dominant vantage point taken is that of the accusers rather than of those accused of witchcraft, which is why in this account the "victims"—a term that appears frequently—are the babies believed to have been killed through supernatural means or the farmer's cow that abruptly stopped giving milk, rather than the accused "witches" themselves. Demos wants to learn what motivated these accusations and why they represented a "continuous presence" in the communities of seventeenth-century New England.[3]

Functionalist theory provides Demos with his first answer. The people accused of witchcraft, he finds, were typically women, aged forty to sixty, married but with few or no children, of low to moderate social status, and exhibiting abrasive or stubborn character traits that often had previously involved them in domestic disputes or even petty crimes. Conflicts may have developed between such a person and a neighbor over a range of possible interactions; often the accused had asked the accuser for a favor, or sought to be hired, or tried to assist with a sick child, each request tendered perhaps without the deference the other party thought due, and the accuser had rebuffed her. After tensions escalated into threats or curses, the accuser suffered some misfortune. With the accumulation of these incidents over years, to which were added gossiped reports of similar encounters with other neighbors, accusers advanced charges of witchcraft to local magistrates to bring before a grand jury that would consider an indictment. Drawing on anthropological models, Demos asserts that charges and prosecutions of these sorts served useful purposes in their local communities. They resolved conflicts between people that could not otherwise have been easily settled, they sharpened the moral boundaries of the community by defining what sorts of behavior were considered proper and improper, and they strengthened the community's inner bonds by purging it (if the prosecution were successful) of its most immediate—he does not add, "if exaggerated"—danger. Nowhere does Demos applaud this kind of community behavior; however, except for the rare note of qualification, the great weight of his discussion falls on the side of explaining how normal, ordinary, and sensible these actions seemed and how even the accused "witches" to a surprising degree colluded in them.[4]

Concerning Ipswich resident Rachel Clinton, whose life Demos describes sensitively as spiraling downward for years before she was accused of witchcraft in 1692 (a charge apparently unrelated to the Salem witch hunt), he concludes, "With Rachel, victim and victimizer were two halves of the same whole. Simply put: events combined against her, depriving her of wealth and dignity, and she responded out of a deep, angry despair. But was there *more* than mere 'response' on Rachel's part? Was there also some veiled complicity—such as one often finds in habitual victims?" Of John Godfrey of Haverhill, whose penchant for conflict brought him to court (as both plaintiff and defendant) at least once each year between 1658 and 1675, three of those times to answer charges of witchcraft, Demos observes,

> The blunt, assertive style, the appearance of envious and vengeful motive; indeed, the unrestrained expression of a whole aggressive side: in all this Godfrey epitomized the character which New Englanders expected in their "witches." . . . In another sense [apart from reflecting conflict], however, "witches" and their accusers interacted on a deeply reciprocal basis; disturbances and disharmony were themselves an epiphenomenon, the paradoxical sign of an inner bond. Here, too, Godfrey's case is instructive. Even in moments of bitter antagonism he and his peers were inextricably joined. Theirs was a relationship of functional dependence, with implicit gains for each side.

For Elizabeth Morse, a sad, marginal figure in Newbury when, as an elderly woman, she was accused of witchcraft in 1679, Demos approaches the end of this vignette by noting her husband's plea to the court: "As to rumors of some great wickedness in our house, which should cause the devil so to trouble us, our conscience is clear of the knowledge of any such thing, more than our common frailties." But then the historian adds, " 'Common frailties' or 'great wickedness'? That, of course, was the vital question. The accused gave one answer; the accusers and victims, another." Why conclude on such a note of ambiguity, of neutrality, when nothing in the entire account of the Morses suggests any reason to doubt William Morse's assessment? Summarizing this part of his argument, Demos writes that accusers and accused "met halfway" in their respective behaviors. "In this respect (among others) the principals on all sides in witch trials were joined by deep, though unacknowledged, bonds of psychic complicity." The problem here is not that Demos gives credence to a belief in witchcraft; he does not. And it is proper for him, as a historian, to show just how groups of people made sense of their world, no matter how repellant their actions may seem to us today. But in his strenuous efforts to avoid casting judgment (to recall the phrasing from his 1970 article), Demos ends up being so even-handed as to make the scapegoats in these situations seem equally responsible for their plight as their persecutors.[5]

Demos's functionalist interpretation of witch hunting was somewhat peculiar for the time period in which he wrote. While there was much encouragement, beginning in the early 1970s, to "blur disciplinary genres," allowing historians and anthropologists to borrow from one another's methods, Demos chose to adopt an older anthropological model that was just then being abandoned by most practicing ethnographers. Significantly, the functionalist approach had been pursued in the middle decades of the twentieth century as a humane way for social scientists to make sense of beliefs—like those in witchcraft—they encountered in traditional societies that might at first glance appear backward and abhorrent to modern Western minds. By demonstrating how witchcraft accusations organized personal conflict in such a way as to increase social cohesion and reduce individual anxiety, an earlier generation of anthropologists had in effect shown how rational traditional societies really were—no less so in their own way than modern societies. Under the influence of the radicalism in thought that took hold in the late 1960s, however, anthropologists increasingly turned against the assumptions of functionalism in favor of a sharper identification with the outlooks expressed by native informants in the field. The functionalist approach was criticized for its unstated reliance on the concept of social equilibrium, as if traditional societies remained static while Western societies alone could generate the spark of dynamic social change. Functionalism equally appeared to denigrate the "manifest" reasons indigenous people gave for their own actions, compared to the hidden, "latent" explanations that only a trained social scientist could identify. Even more jarring was a dawning sense that the ethnographer, together with his or her theories, could not escape the subjectivity of the Western mind—infiltrated as well by the long history of colonialism—as he or she attempted to take in and interpret the data of the people and regions under study. By the late twentieth century, these ideas would greatly limit field study by Western anthropologists in places of the world far from their homes, but already in the early 1980s, when Demos was writing, anthropology had shifted in a more cognitive, symbolic direction, attempting to make sense of the constructs of thought and action expressed by traditional people chiefly in terms of their own internal logic.[6]

Demos's choice to apply a functionalist approach to the witchcraft accusations in seventeenth-century New England, though less radical in direction than where the discipline of anthropology was then heading, may still be understood as a step in keeping with the radical spirit of the times within American universities and within the field of history in particular. It fit well with the turn toward writing history "from the bottom up," precisely because, as in all anthropological approaches, the functionalist perspective took as its point of departure the actions and beliefs of common people. The functionalist ethnographies of witchcraft that Demos cited as models in his book and earlier article situated their studies in small, village communities in sub-Saharan Africa or, as in the case of Clyde Kluckhohn's *Navaho Witchcraft* (1944), which may have provided the closest prototype for *Entertaining Satan*, in the local, indigenous communities of the

American Southwest. The anthropologists' fundamental empathy for the people they were studying comes across in these works, as does Demos's for the Puritans who populated the small towns of seventeenth-century New England.

But there was more than just empathy in this approach. There was also the attraction of a romantic posture that wished to hold up these distant, exotic societies as markers of something valuable that was missing from the modern, more bureaucratized life of the West. As Mary Douglas put it, referring specifically to the functionalist witchcraft studies of African groups produced by mid-century British anthropologists, "their enthusiasm for native cultures led them to take up a theoretical position which treated conflict as benign in primitive society, a position they would not [have] extend[ed] to their own society." It helped, she added pointedly, that under the British colonial regimes, the worst violence of witch hunting within these indigenous groups had been suppressed. In the American anthropologist Kluckhohn's study, the reader similarly learns that witchcraft accusations or the threat of them (which for the Navajos were directed chiefly at men) helped channel the Navajos' aggressive impulses in ways that pierced the pretensions of leaders, the well-to-do, and prominent ritual "singers"; helped maintain respect for siblings and the elderly; and inhibited acts of adultery. There is passing mention of the fact that presumed witches could be executed in "violently sadistic" fashion, but the monograph stays focused on the benefits accruing to the wider community, not on the people who might have suffered as a result of these accusations. For historians in the 1970s and 1980s, the study of "worlds we have lost" served an equally romantic purpose. For Demos, whose seventeenth-century Puritans occupied the place of the Navajos for Kluckhohn, it also helped to have removed the Salem case, where twenty people had met violent deaths, so as to allow the witch-hunting instances under study to remain more obscure and far milder in outcome.[7]

To his functionalist explanation for why witchcraft accusations were so prevalent in seventeenth-century New England, Demos added a second, related sociological argument. Here he borrowed a theory advanced by British historians to explain witch hunting in England, one that influenced Boyer and Nissenbaum's *Salem Possessed* as well. This explanation, shaped by some of the same works in functionalist anthropology that Demos had consulted, held that people accused of witchcraft served as scapegoats for tensions produced as a traditional, communal society gave way before the rise of the new market economy. The British historians (Keith Thomas and Alan Macfarlane were the leading ones) characterized the conflict between the two competing sets of social ethics involved in this transition as "neighborliness versus individualism." But an interesting irony in terms of sympathies developed when this theory crossed the Atlantic. In English history the accused came overwhelmingly from the bottom levels of traditional society. They were the dependent poor, destitute widows, the disabled, or the incompetent—people whose requests for the customary charity set off feelings of guilt in the new market-oriented individualists, causing the latter to reject their entreaties and turn on them as "witches" in order to salve their own consciences. Such an anti-capitalist explanation placed British historical accounts clearly on the side of the accused, the representatives of a passing order that appeared more charitable and humane than its successor. But in colonial New England, where the victims of witch hunting were not dependents but often people of quite moderate and occasionally even substantial means, the same anti-capitalist explanation, as Boyer and Nissenbaum found in the case of Salem, put one on the side of the accusers, who in both regions of the British empire were typically only middling farmers or tradespeople themselves.

Demos escaped some of this moral predicament by omitting from his study the Salem witch hunt, which caught up a greater proportion of well-to-do suspects in its net than did the more isolated incidents of witchcraft accusation studied in *Entertaining Satan*. Demos also located the dilemma of "neighborliness versus individualism" within the minds of all New Englanders (Boyer and Nissenbaum on occasion tried to do the same but with less success), making sense of their accusations against certain aggressive people in their midst as unconscious attempts to excise their own acquisitive or individualistic impulses. Still, the reader does not come away from *Entertaining Satan* with any great reservoir of sympathy for the objects of these projections. Not only does Demos, in an aside, endorse Boyer and Nissenbaum's explanation for the Salem witch hunt based on socioeconomic factions (i.e., the less successful versus the more successful), but his own extensive descriptions of the accusers, with their multiple ties to one another and lives so enmeshed in the daily goings-on of their villages, make *them* out to be the neighborly ones, more so than the eccentric, "grasping," and often isolated accused. Again, it is the accusers who are portrayed with greater understanding than the accused.[8]

Entertaining Satan advances two psychological arguments as well. Both serve to explain what Demos says lies at "the heart of the story." Witchcraft accusations, he asserts, "are everywhere similar: they express a tendency to 'project,' to 'scapegoat,' to extrude and expel that which individuals (or groups) define as bad." As virtually all of his case studies reveal, the main thing that accusers defined as bad was the emotion of anger, anger felt in an immediate sense toward the accused for one perceived provocation or another. Since that unacceptable emotion could not be acknowledged, it needed to be projected back onto the accused, resulting in imagined attacks (the "witchcraft") on the accuser's body, close relations, or possessions. If the accusation led to a successful prosecution, the accuser would gain the psychic satisfaction of retaliating against the accused, while feeling personally blameless.

These assumptions—which seem reasonable to me—lead Demos to raise a critical question: What was the ultimate source of that anger, a source that could account not just for the irritation produced by the immediate affront from the accused "witch" but for the wellspring of unacceptable emotion that fueled the charge of witchcraft hurled back at her and the palpable fear of her retribution? In his first answer to this question, Demos finds that source in the characteristics of Puritan upbringing. Puritan parents aimed to instill a strong sense of self-discipline in their children in order to turn them into adults who would seek to obey God's will and place the good of the commonwealth above their own personal interests. This meant sharply suppressing the developing sense of self in their young children, especially through the use of shaming at the ages of two and three. Signs of anger and conflict were frowned upon from the earliest years in favor of demonstrations of contentment and harmony. Given this early training, Puritans found themselves, despite their vaunted purposefulness and effectiveness in the world, "vulnerable in their core sense of self," particularly to any provocation that might set off submerged aggression, and this made them especially receptive to the logic of witchcraft projection.[9]

Had Demos stuck to this promising explanation, it might have led him to emphasize further the role played by Puritanism as a religious and cultural system in the generation of witch hunting. Instead, he moved toward his second and favored answer to the question posed above. Drawing specifically on psychoanalytic theory, Demos insists that at bottom what motivated the accusers was not simply a residuum of anger formed through overly strict childrearing practices but repressed "narcissistic rage" that harkened back to the withdrawal of maternal support in infancy. Everything, in his view, points in this direction, especially the symptoms of supernatural affliction: the painful attacks on the body (the bites, pricks, pinches, all projections of "infantile sadism"), the defiance of authority figures along with a dependency on them, the exhibitionist need for an audience (reflecting the "grandiosity" of the narcissistic self)—in general, love and need intermixed with rage and resentment. So, too, does most of the lore of witchcraft come to rest on mothers, implicating women of midlife above all other social categories, assigning to them animal "familiars" as horrid accomplices that nourished themselves on the "witch's teat," and focusing so much of their supposed deadly mischief on infants and children. Even the three groups that Demos identifies as those accounting for the bulk of accusers (adolescent girls, men in young adulthood, and other women of midlife) can best be explained, he claims, by their special sensitivities toward mothers. For adolescent girls, he cites the need to pull away from maternal attachment in preparation for finding a husband; for young men, the need to fend off threats to their newly established autonomy; and for other middle-aged women, the need to quell insecurities that came with menopause in a society that so fully identified a woman's role with childbearing. Whatever the value of these mostly unprovable propositions—the data for which are often more susceptible to religious explanations—they had the effect of shifting the weight of Demos's psychological argument onto a universal plane and away from an understanding of witch hunting as a Puritan phenomenon. Along the way these propositions returned the reader's sympathies to the accusers, since all people must deal with the same problem of infant loss of maternal attachment.[10]

But witch hunting was not universal in seventeenth-century America or, for that matter, in seventeenth-century England. It occurred with far greater frequency in the Puritan colonies of New England than it did in the Anglican-dominated colonies to the south of this region, just as it broke out with much greater ferocity in the Puritan stronghold of East Anglia than in the rest of England.[11] In the end a failure to pursue the Puritan connection was a major blind spot in Demos's account, just as it had been for Boyer and Nissenbaum's earlier study. Puritanism was not completely ignored in *Entertaining Satan*, since Demos noted its potential to produce a form of strict childrearing that was particularly hostile toward signs of aggression, and he also identified (as had Boyer and Nissenbaum) the Puritans' emphasis on communal harmony and Christian love as a source of the difficulty New Englanders had in accepting individualistic striving in themselves and others. But Puritanism as a compelling religious force that brought powerful beliefs in the supernatural to bear on nearly all aspects of daily life and organized these beliefs along sharply dualistic lines of good and evil—*this* Puritanism barely appears in Demos's book, yet it probably affected all participants in the drama of witch hunting more than any other single factor. Toward the close of his study, Demos supplies a revealing quotation about such providential beliefs from an account of early seventeenth-century Connecticut, written some years later, by the son of one of the colony's first pastors. The writer was talking about the fear of wolves in those early days and wrestling with his feelings of hatred for these animals. "The noise of their howlings was enough to curdle the blood of the stoutest, and I have never seen the man that did not shiver at the sound of a pack of 'em," this fellow remembered. "When I do [hear that sound even now], I feel again the young hatred rising in my blood, and it is not a sin because God made 'em to be hated." Much the same could be said of Puritan beliefs about witches.[12]

Demos, however, allows Puritanism to have done nothing more than to have "amplified" the fundamental impulse for generating witchcraft accusations, which for him originates in the "premodern village," with its distinctly personal quality of life. Yet this subject constituted another blind spot for him, as again it had earlier for Boyer and Nissenbaum. Despite a few qualifications to the contrary, the local community with its dense set of face-to-face relationships emerges from Demos's account mainly as a positive place, in keeping with its "functional" means of conflict resolution and its ethic of "neighborliness." Demos creatively evokes its tenor of life by asking the reader to "imagine: The bricklayer who rebuilds your chimney is also the constable who brings you a summons to court, an occupant of the next bench in the meetinghouse, the owner of a share adjacent to one of yours in the 'upland' meadow, a rival for water-rights to the stream that flows behind that meadow, a fellow-member of the local 'train band' (i.e. militia), an occasional companion at the local 'ordinary,' . . . And so on. Do the two of you enjoy your shared experiences? Not necessarily. Do you know each other well? Most certainly." By contrast, for us today, he writes, "our institutions are many in number and various in operation; and we deal with them separately, one for this reason, another for that. Of course, they confront us with people—but people who are performing 'roles,' *and who are otherwise unknown to us.* In the usual course of events such dealings are decidedly *impersonal*" (emphasis in the original). Neither form of social organization is explicitly favored over the other in the text, but within the entire context of the book's presentation, this passage and others sound a note of nostalgia for pre-capitalist life. Without conveying how lethal Puritanism could be to those whom it demonized and without underscoring how unwelcoming the New England town could feel to those who failed to conform to its standards of behavior, *Entertaining Satan* left itself little room to encourage readers to sympathize with the victims of witchcraft accusation.[13]

CHAPTER 4

Karlsen's *Devil in the Shape of a Woman* and Feminist Interpretations

When Carol F. Karlsen's book, *The Devil in the Shape of a Woman: Witchcraft in Colonial New England*, came out in 1987, it quickly rose to rival *Salem Possessed* for adoption in university classrooms, and for good reason. A product of the new wave of feminist scholarship that began in the 1970s and 1980s, Karlsen's study announced itself with a simple assertion that carried great weight. "The story of witchcraft is primarily the story of women," Karlsen wrote on the second page of her preface. In fact, she pointed out, 78 percent of all people accused of witchcraft across one hundred years of colonial New England's history were female, a proportion, incidentally, that mirrors almost exactly the 80 percent figure commonly given for the female share of victims in early modern European witch hunting. Moreover, roughly half the men accused of witchcraft during these years were either related to or closely connected with female suspects. How could this most basic of all associations have been missed?[1]

Actually, the relationship of women to witch hunts had not been entirely overlooked. While Boyer and Nissenbaum mostly ignored the issue, Demos addressed it squarely, noting the prevalence of women among the accused (in the same proportion that Karlsen cited) and highlighting the role that women aged forty to sixty played as symbols of motherhood in his psychoanalytically informed argument for why this group received the brunt of witchcraft accusations. But Demos, together with nearly all recent historians writing on the subject before Karlsen, made a point of stating that neither the concept of patriarchy nor that of misogyny would go far toward elucidating the phenomenon of witch hunting. After all, these historians pointed out, women manifestly placed themselves within the ranks of the accusers, often standing at the forefront; male dominance was taken for granted in seventeenth-century America; and the crime of witchcraft itself was not defined by Puritan leaders or the average New Englander as specific to women. Among the post–World War II writers, the treatment of women as a group within the story of the Salem witch hunt had been even skimpier. Starkey belittled the afflicted accusers of Salem village as silly, teenaged girls, although she championed as individuals some of the panic's female martyrs. Arthur Miller felt no awkwardness about making the hero of *The Crucible* one of the executed men, John Procter. The subject of gender never entered Perry Miller's discussion of Salem. In contrast to all of these authors, Karlsen placed attitudes of hostility and resentment to women, leading to "systematic violence" against them, at the center of her interpretation. Karlsen thus gave gender in the persecution of "witches" an emphasis it had long deserved.[2]

Based on an examination of 344 persons accused of witchcraft in New England between 1620 and 1725 (78% of whom were female), Karlsen develops a portrait of the characteristics that made a woman vulnerable to the charge. Like Demos before her, she notes that most women accused of witchcraft were over age forty and married. But unlike Demos, Karlsen stresses that women over sixty were just as vulnerable to accusation (and sometimes even more vulnerable to conviction) as were women at midlife, and that women above the age of thirty and living apart from husbands (whether divorced, widowed, deserted, or never married)— "women alone," she calls them—were more vulnerable still than those who were currently married. In part these differences reflect methodological variations in the works of the two historians (and there are pluses and minuses to be said about each of their sets of analytical decisions), but the emphasis Karlsen gives to the particulars of her demographic findings points toward a new interpretation of why women were targeted in witchcraft accusation: they functioned not so much as symbols of maternal power, as Demos pictured them, but as living examples of women who failed to fulfill the twin roles meant for them to play in Puritan New England: bearers of children and "helpmeets" (helpmates) to their husbands.[3]

Karlsen goes on to define other ways in which women accused of witchcraft typically broke with conventional patterns of feminine behavior. Many had strong, assertive personalities and may have dared to express discontent with their station in life, to respond with anger when a neighbor mistreated them, to avoid regular church attendance, or to engage in sexual activities outside of marriage. In all these ways and more, "witches" were presumed to exhibit a shameful degree of pride that stood as the opposite of what Puritan society expected from women. For "it was not just pride that most fundamentally distinguished witches from other people," Karlsen pointedly observes, "it was female pride in particular." But even while noting these character traits, Karlsen cautions her readers to remember that nearly all such descriptions of the personalities of the accused come down to us through surviving trial depositions taken from the mouths of their accusers and, just as important, that most characterizations of the "disagreeable" nature of the accused stemmed from situations of conflict. To take the case of Sarah Good (from among many examples she provides), Karlsen helpfully explains that during the summer of 1692 when seventeen-year-old Mercy Short accused Good of bewitching her by "bestow[ing] some ill words upon her," Good's curse had followed upon Short's insulting behavior. (The quote is from Cotton Mather, who related the incident.) Mercy Short had thrown wood shavings into the cell in which Sarah Good was incarcerated as a sign of disgust. As Karlsen puts it, "It was in some cases not the witch's ire that generated the accusation, but the accusation that generated her ire."[4]

Of all the ways that accused women departed from the norms of feminine behavior in seventeenth-century New England, the one Karlsen most emphasizes lay in the economic sphere. Most of these women, she claims, lacked either a brother or a son, and as a consequence they threatened to disrupt—and many did disrupt—the common expectation of land inheritance from father to son. Katherine Harrison of Wethersfield, Connecticut, for example, stood trial for witchcraft in the late 1660s soon after the death of her husband, who had left his sizable estate to her and their three daughters. (The couple had no sons.) A jury convicted her, but the Connecticut magistrates overruled the sentence of execution in favor of banishing her from the colony. Susannah North Martin, of Amesbury, Massachusetts, who would be executed in the Salem witch hunt, had earlier engaged in a failed four-year litigation to gain what she felt was her rightful portion of her father's inheritance. Martin had sons by this point (the early 1670s), but she and her sister, who joined in the lawsuit, were the sole surviving children of Richard North when he died in 1668, and their stepmother, whose wishes prevailed in the case, had alternate plans for the estate. Martha Allen Carrier of Andover, Massachusetts, also executed in the Salem witch hunt, came under intense suspicion of witchcraft when her destitute family (including her husband Thomas and their five children) contracted smallpox in late 1690, and it quickly spread to wipe out nearly all the men in her extended family: her father, both her brothers, one brother-in-law, and two nephews, all from prosperous wings of the clan. These vignettes, along with other descriptions of family inheritance patterns, form a central chapter entitled, "The Economic Basis of Witchcraft," and illustrate Karlsen's contention that "inheriting or potentially inheriting women" were particularly vulnerable to the charge of witchcraft because they "stood in the way of the orderly transmission of property from one generation of males to another."[5]

Karlsen probably exaggerates the importance of this part of her argument. The family portraits she offers, not to mention accounts of the same people found in other sources, provide evidence of noneconomic grounds for suspicion of witchcraft by these women that often appears more compelling. Katherine Harrison, for example, was known for her outspokenness in situations of conflict with neighbors, her unusual skills at spinning and healing, her intelligence (shown by predicting future events), and her longstanding connections to the liberal faction of Puritans in the Hartford area, some of whose members had come under attack for witchcraft during the 1650s and again in the panic of 1662–64. She might even have been the daughter of a woman executed for witchcraft at Hartford in 1654. Susannah Martin was first brought to trial on charges of witchcraft in 1669, two years before she and her sister initiated legal action on behalf of their inheritance. Neighbors already believed Martin had once vanished into thin air, invisibly attacked a woman with a pricking sensation that traveled up the victim's body from her legs to her throat, and caused another man to lose his way in the woods before tossing him into a pit that had never existed in that place before. In addition, it was said she had had at least two children before marriage, one of whom she had killed when the child was still an infant. Martha Carrier, who had lived in the nearby town of Billerica before returning to her native Andover, was also known to have had a child with her husband before they were married. In Billerica she had already come under suspicion for witchcraft when, after a dispute with a neighbor, two of his sows went missing. One turned up dead near the Carriers' house, the neighbor said, with its ears cut off. Her sister, Mary Allen Toothaker, and Mary's husband, Roger, who also lived in Billerica, were similarly charged and imprisoned for witchcraft during the Salem panic, suggesting a family connection as well in the accusing of the two Allen sisters and their immediate relatives. (Roger Toothaker died in prison.) When smallpox followed the Carriers to Andover, the town seems to have blamed Martha Carrier even before her male relatives succumbed to the epidemic.[6]

More generally, as an analytical tool, Karlsen's category of women lacking *either* a brother *or* son raises doubts. It creates a broad subgroup of people comprising women who, as one critic observed, might only hold title to property (or threaten to do so) for a short period of time before another male, if only a son-in-law, would take over the inheritance. Karlsen believes that even a brief disruption in male-to-male land transfers would have been perceived as threatening to the young men of colonial New England, owing to mounting population pressures on landed inheritances, but it is hard to see how such resentments alone would lead to fears of Satanic intervention. An actual or potential female inheritance might better be regarded as simply one possible factor among many—not the prime factor—that could cause a woman to stand out in a community and place her in jeopardy of being thought a witch.[7]

Given how forcefully Karlsen proclaims the innocence of these female scapegoats within the male-dominated society of Puritan New England, one might imagine that in terms of its sympathies her work belongs better with the post–World War II era scholarship on Salem than with that of her contemporaries working after the 1960s. But the question of how *The Devil in the Shape of a Woman* shapes the feelings of its readers toward witchcraft prosecutions and especially toward the Salem witch hunt yields a more complicated answer. Notice first how Karlsen, like Demos, directs readers' attention away from the events of 1692 in eastern Massachusetts, focusing instead on witchcraft accusations over a one-hundred-year period (1620–1725) and across all of New England. Unlike Demos, Karlsen does include the victims of the Salem witch hunt within her database of 344 accused individuals, but in this way the Salem victims still disappear into a broad group of persecuted people. When she brings into her text some of the famous martyrs from 1692—Sarah Good, Martha Cory, Rebecca Nurse, or Martha Carrier, for instance—they serve only as examples of underlying sociological patterns that Karlsen uses to explain why, at any point in time, certain categories of women and not others were likely to be accused. Most curiously, the term "witch hunt" rarely appears in the book, a characteristic that links Karlsen's study with those of her scholarly generation. Even the book's subtitle, "Witchcraft in Colonial New England," where "Witch *Hunting* in Colonial New England" would actually have fit her interpretation better, recalls the usage of the same misleading term, "witchcraft," in the titles of Hansen's, Boyer and Nissenbaum's, and Demos's works.

Instead of "witch hunt," Karlsen prefers the term "outbreak" to denote a witch hunting panic. Along with the two well-established panics begun at Salem village in 1692 and at Hartford in 1662, she includes under this heading a much smaller scare affecting the area around Fairfield, Connecticut, also in 1692. But she employs this term solely as an analytical device to disaggregate her database in order to highlight differences in her findings between "outbreak" and "non-outbreak" cases. Moreover, it turns out that the findings from the outbreak cases are the peculiar ones that need to be separated from the rest so as not to dilute the main patterns that Karlsen wishes to emphasize in the "normal," non-outbreak cases. We learn, for example, that at Salem more men were accused of witchcraft than was usually the case, more women under age forty were rounded up than was customary, and a disproportionately large number of single women came under attack as well. Salem, in short, becomes somewhat of a distraction from the main subject of Karlsen's book, the unrelenting persecution of women as witches throughout the history of colonial New England. The critical phenomenon of a social panic, fed by uncontrolled fear and guilt, trampling rationality and caution underfoot thus drops out of the picture entirely. As a result, the two events responsible for two-thirds of all executions for witchcraft in colonial New England—the Salem panic, where twenty were killed, and the Hartford panic, where probably four were hanged—are lost in this study of witch hunting.[8]

Deemphasizing the largest witch crazes in her account also enables Karlsen to omit from her sympathies any of the male victims of witch hunting, since seven of the eight men executed for witchcraft in New England (out of the thirty-six people executed in all) perished at Salem or Hartford. None of these men merits more than a mention or two in Karlsen's book, and most of these quick characterizations are negative, as when the author notes that John Procter, George Jacobs Sr., and George Burroughs were all accused of abusing either their female servants or their wives. Moreover, Karlsen does not remind readers at these points, as she does elsewhere when charges against female suspects are discussed, to regard the truth of such accusations with caution. The only man to receive a substantial biographical vignette of his own is John Godfrey, who was acquitted of witchcraft in a 1669 trial but about whom suspicions lingered. Karlsen selects his case to show how men, when acquitted of the crime, typically faired far better than did acquitted women, against whom the local community sometimes exacted a frightful "justice" of its own.[9]

Even more problematic is Karlsen's decision to focus solely on men when she devotes an entire chapter to those accusers who were not thrown into a state of trancelike affliction, those whom she calls the "non-possessed accusers." Demos's close study of the social situations giving rise to witchcraft accusations presented a very different picture of this group. In his account, nonpossessed women joined rather equally with nonpossessed men in raising suspicions of witchcraft against feared members of their towns, even if men typically took the lead in advancing formal legal proceedings and offering depositions. "When a husband and wife were victimized together by some sort of witchcraft," Demos wrote in his first article on the subject, "it was the former who would normally come forward to testify." Committees of women also routinely played critical roles in examining a female suspect's body for "witches' teats," places where the "witch's" animal familiars were thought to receive nourishment. Karlsen's own tally of the nonpossessed accusers, a statistic derived from unidentified sources, finds that only one-third of them were female, but even if this lower proportion (one-third, compared to Demos's one-half) turns out to be accurate, it is still misleading to leave women out of the discussion of the nonpossessed people who brought charges against the accused. Karlsen appears to take this liberty because it fits with her argument that these male colonists, especially as the first century of settlement wore on, resented the increased economic and sexual power that the accused women had acquired or were threatening to acquire for themselves. Together with her neglect of men who were victimized in witchcraft prosecutions, the result of Karlsen's omission of women in her discussion of nonpossessed accusers is to convey a more sharply polarized picture of men versus women in the drama of witch hunting than was actually the case.[10]

Her interpretation based on gender conflict becomes still more distorted when Karlsen turns in her final chapter to the "possessed accusers," the young women whose extreme physical afflictions, including wild contortions of the body and frightening dialogues with the Devil, often set off a witch hunt.[11] This chapter is the most powerful in the book, because here with these young women in pain, even more than with the older women who lost their lives, lie Karlsen's deepest sympathies. She begins this part of her discussion by showing that these individuals disproportionately occupied positions of low status in their local communities. Many were servants in the homes of prosperous or at least well-placed families, and a surprising number, especially during the Salem witch hunt, had been orphaned or half-orphaned by Indian attacks on their parents' settlements in Maine, after which the surviving family members had retreated southward to the towns of Essex County. These young women, Karlsen believes, held little in the way of future prospects, yet they often found themselves in pious homes, even clerical households, where they were being taught to accept their stations in life and to be grateful to God for deliverance from what surely might have been worse situations.

Those who became possessed, Karlsen surmises, were the willful ones who wrestled with the constraints on women's roles in Puritan society as they anticipated adulthood for themselves. She portrays them as psychologically torn. They envied the assertive, outspoken, and sometimes well-positioned women in their communities who were tainted with the suspicion of witchcraft, while simultaneously shrinking back in horror at such feelings. Were they destined to become community outcasts as well? In their possessed states, they could temporarily act out the part of an angry, blasphemous witch; when they returned to their senses, they could name one of the community's female scapegoats as their tormentor and seducer, projecting their own desires onto a vulnerable target. "Possession, then," Karlsen writes insightfully, "was a dramatic religious ritual through which young females publicly enacted their struggle to avoid internalizing the evil of witchcraft." It was a process designed "to convince young women that the danger lay outside them, not within."[12]

Behind it all, for Karlsen, lay the condition of dependence on men that these young women and all Puritan women faced. Karlsen chooses to highlight in her chapter on the possessed accusers not the experience of the afflicted Salemites but rather that of sixteen-year-old Elizabeth Knapp, who when she became possessed in 1671, was living as a servant in the home of the young minister Samuel Willard and his family in the town of Groton, Massachusetts. Knapp's torments, recorded carefully by Willard in a diary, went on for three months. They included fits of roaring and screaming, periods of catatonic speechlessness when her tongue was drawn up tightly to the roof of her mouth, and other times when Satan spoke coarsely through her, hurling insults at Willard. The minister tried his best to counter the Devil's presence with prayer, and he encouraged Knapp to show remorse for her discontent with her lowly social position, the sin that had evidently invited Satan in with his promises of riches, leisure, and travel. Summarizing this episode, Karlsen explicitly draws out its social lessons in terms of patriarchy.

> Elizabeth Knapp was a young woman who had accepted the Puritan explanation for her troubles, who deeply appreciated Willard's concern for her plight and his dedication to freeing her from the demons that held her in their power. But she had cause to resent him. He was a young, well-off Harvard-educated minister whose life was full of promise; she was a young woman with little schooling and little prospect of anything but service to others, whether as a servant, daughter, or wife. He spent most of his time reading, writing, and traveling; she had never been taught to write, seldom left Groton, and spent her time sweeping his house, caring for his children, carrying in his wood, keeping his fires burning—all so he could continue his work in peace and comfort. . . . Only when taken over by the Prince of Evil could she express the full force of her feelings—her *desire for* the independence and power embodied in the symbol of the witch and her rage at the man who taught her that independence and power were the ultimate female evils.

After a passage like this one, where can the modern reader's sympathies turn except to Elizabeth Knapp? And if Knapp goes on to name someone in the community as a witch, which she did on two occasions during her ordeal, can we blame her? In the end these afflicted young women become the heroes of Karlsen's account, even more so than the accused witches, whose defiant statements of their innocence are nowhere recorded in *The Devil in the Shape of a Woman*. Karlsen hails the possessed women for their "subversion" of the system of witch-craft belief, because ultimately at Salem they stood the colonial region's power structure on its head, using the diabolical power granted them—the only power they had—to name as witches more and more unlikely suspects, including prosperous men and the wives of established figures, until those in authority were forced to bring the trials and all future witchcraft prosecutions to an end.[13]

The problem with this interpretation is not that one should be bereft of feel-ings for these possessed young people. Samuel Willard, too, felt much sympathy for his servant, Elizabeth Knapp. The problem is that framing the anguish of the afflicted so thoroughly in terms of female dependence on men—a predica-ment with powerful modern resonances—obscures the terrifying implications of its expression for the lives of the named witchcraft suspects, and it directs atten-tion away from alternate explanations for this suffering. It is easy to sympathize with Elizabeth Knapp because nobody died as a result of her witchcraft accusa-tions. That this did not happen was largely due to the intervention of her master and minister, Samuel Willard, who prevented her accusations from gaining sup-port in Groton by taking steps to discredit them. Because of Willard's close involve-ment in Elizabeth Knapp's distress, her afflictions remained a case of "possession" and did not become one of "witchcraft." The afflicted at Salem, by contrast, caused lethal damage to countless people in their surrounding communities. It would seem much harder to sympathize with them, yet Karlsen goes so far as to encour-age readers to do so by crediting Salem's possessed with unconsciously bringing about the end of witch hunting through their excessive accusations. What an odd misplacement of ethical praise, especially given the presence at Salem of real heroes among the accused (most of whom were female), those who refused to confess to a crime they had not committed. Moreover, it was the accumulation of these heroic denials, far more than the sheer number of accusations, that did so much to discredit witch hunting after Salem.[14]

In truth, New England's possessed were not always young, and most did not occupy positions of servitude. Karlsen herself found that about half of all pos-sessed individuals were over the age of twenty and one quarter over thirty. About a third were either married or widowed. (Fourteen percent were male, mostly children.) Even during the Salem witch hunt, when an unusually large propor-tion of the possessed had lost one or both parents and were living in the homes of other families, Ann Putnam Jr.—the twelve-year-old daughter of Thomas Jr., and

Ann Carr Putnam, living with her parents in one of the most well-established households in Salem village—probably cried out the single greatest number of "witches" during the entire panic. The elder Ann Putnam, who also suffered from possessed states of mind, brought additional names to the roster of the accused. Neither Ann Putnam Jr. nor her mother was an orphan or a servant. Nor was Mary Walcott or Susannah Sheldon, two of the other most active possessed accusers during the Salem panic.[15]

It is worth remembering, too, that Puritan families not uncommonly placed their teenaged children in the homes of other families, where the tasks they were expected to perform as servants or apprentices made them more like other young adults in the household than outsiders bound by an indenture.[16] Elizabeth Knapp's parents, Karlsen neglects to say, lived in the same town as the Willards—Groton— where her father was a successful landowner and a town selectman, although her mother likely suffered from mental illness. At Salem in the 1690s, virtually all of the possessed servants also had family living nearby or else were related to the families into whose homes they were placed. Mary Warren, the Procters' servant, had a mother, stepfather, and sister living in Salem town. Elizabeth Hubbard (the only instance of an accuser where an indenture is mentioned) was the great-niece of the wife of the village's doctor, William Griggs, with whom she lived. Sarah Churchill, who resided as a servant in the home of George Jacobs Sr., had a father still living and was related to the Walcott, Putnam, and Ingersoll families of the village. Mercy Lewis, Thomas Jr. and Ann Carr Putnam's servant, had both a married sister and an aunt and uncle living in Salem village, as well as more distant village relatives in the Cloyce family. Called a servant in some secondary accounts of the witch hunt, Abigail Williams was always referred to in the primary sources as Samuel Parris's niece or "kins-woman." In many of these cases, there was some family problem (most often the death or incapacity of the mother) that caused a female child to be placed as a maidservant or apprentice in the home of another, usually related family, but this status was neither rare nor especially stigmatized in a society accustomed to the markings of hierarchy.[17]

The later lives of some of these servants equally bear out this generalization. Just three years after the time of her possession, Elizabeth Knapp married a man who seems to have been an average yeoman farmer, with whom she had at least six children. For the next twenty-five years, they resided in Groton, where Knapp lived out what John Demos calls a quite unextraordinary life, considering her former notoriety as a possessed teenager. The possessed young servants of Salem showed greater trauma in their later years, but still Sarah Churchill at age thirty-seven, seventeen years after the Salem events, married a Maine weaver and claimed at least a portion of her inheritance from her wealthy maternal grandfather. Elizabeth Hubbard, age seventeen in 1692, moved to Gloucester after the panic, married a man from that town at age thirty-six, and had four children with him. Mercy Lewis moved to Greenland, New Hampshire, to live near an aunt. There she was tried for fornication but then married the man who had likely fathered her child, and the family later moved to Boston. Nothing is known about the post-Salem lives of Mary Warren or Abigail Williams.[18]

Common to all or most of these possessed young people is a factor that Karlsen mentions but slights in her explanation of their inner conflicts: they were being brought up in pious, Puritan homes. As such, they were particularly subject to the sorts of spiritual doubts and self-recriminations to which the Puritan faith leant itself. This factor also unites the young possessed with the older people who suffered from similar torments. All likely endured the same feelings of guilt for not measuring up, in one way or another, to their own, culturally conditioned standards of godly behavior, and all—or nearly all—succumbed to the temptation to externalize their perceived failings onto a scapegoat. Some portion of those self-recriminations may have owed something to discontent with the particular ways that life opportunities for women in Puritan New England were hemmed in by social constraints, while other portions may have denoted an especially sensitive spiritual nature, transient youthful rebelliousness, mental instability, or simply the suggestive power of peers. Nevertheless, the main determinant in triggering these possessions was no doubt religious in nature.[19]

Karlsen does not neglect Puritanism in her study, but her treatment of the religious factor in witch hunting remains a weakness that recalls the earlier works of Boyer and Nissenbaum and Demos. She does describe how the Puritan movement ideologically elevated the position of women to a "necessary good" from the "necessary evil" of pre-Reformation Christianity, turning women into wifely "helpmeets" in support of their husbands' developing sense of inner rectitude. After this valuable first step in understanding why women's behavior became so important to the Puritans, however, Karlsen too quickly leaves Puritanism behind. Even her observation that many of the male suspects at Salem stood accused of verbally or physically abusing their wives or servants would have been better explained by linking these charges to the perceptions—and possible distortions—of pious accusers, strenuously aiming to uphold new standards of nonviolent, loving hierarchy, rather than to an unstated assumption of timeless, male domination. Karlsen instead drops her inquiry into Puritanism's responsibility for witch hunting in favor of concentrating on a continuous substratum of Christian belief in the inferiority and dangerousness of women, which she identifies as providing the chief justification for persecuting women as witches. Karlsen traces the essence of this ancient and abiding belief to the biblical stories of Eve, which blame her more than Adam for humanity's fall from grace because her excessive pride, rebelliousness, and gullibility made her the easier target for Satan's seductive ways. There is not much more one needs to know, in Karlsen's account, about how religion helped create a culture open to attacking women as witches. In this way Puritanism is collapsed into Christianity, and Christianity in turn falls back onto patriarchy.[20]

Founded in an era of male domination—and all eras before today's would have to be characterized in this way—Christianity, like all the world's major religions, contains myths, rituals, and organizational practices shot through with patriarchal principles. But women were not persecuted as witches uniformly across Christianity's two-thousand-year history. Puritanism, like the kindred forms of Christian practice that emerged with the Protestant and Catholic Reformations, brought a renewed intensity to Christian faith, including a particularly vivid sense of the supernatural world and a sharp dualism in its moral demands, that made the early modern period in Euro-American history a time of heightened witch hunting. An awareness of this critical religious component is missing from A Devil in the Shape of a Woman, even if Cotton Mather is treated to numerous and mostly deserved slaps in the face. In the final analysis Karlsen turns witch hunting in colonial New England into simply another chapter in the long story of women's oppression. As she notes fatalistically near the end of her study, "new ways would be found in the eighteenth century to keep most women in their place." There is something to be said for this perspective, but it fails to identify the deepest lessons that the Salem witch hunt stands to teach, ones applicable to any group of people unjustly persecuted.[21]

CHAPTER 5

Norton's *In the Devil's Snare* and Racial Approaches I

If Demos's and Karlsen's books on witchcraft downplayed the importance of the Salem witch hunt, either omitting it altogether or subsuming it into a larger story, Mary Beth Norton's *In the Devil's Snare: The Salem Witchcraft Crisis of 1692*, published in 2002, carried forward the line of inquiry begun earlier by Boyer and Nissenbaum (and before them by Hansen) in searching for a threat to society that could explain the Salem panic. Norton found this threat not, as had Boyer and Nissenbaum, in the rise of merchant capitalism nor, as had Hansen, in the practice of actual witchcraft, but rather in the reverberations of racial conflict between colonial New Englanders and the Wabanaki people, a loose confederation of Native American bands living all around the Puritans' northern settlements. Again, however, as with her predecessors, Norton's efforts at arguing for an external cause of the Salem panic led her along a path that would mute the devastating results of the witch hunt, inviting her readers to remove their sympathies from its victims and to lodge them elsewhere.[1]

That racial themes should enter interpretations of the Salem witch hunt for the post-1960s academic generation should come as little surprise. Along with its heightened interests in the origins of capitalism, the social and cultural lives of common people, and power relationships between women and men, this cohort of scholars, many of whom had witnessed and sometimes participated in the civil rights revolution of the mid-twentieth century, took as one of its primary goals exploring the varied ways in which racial concepts and confrontations pervaded the long history of the United States. At the same time, America's involvement in the Vietnam War raised related questions about how the nation's history resembled the colonial records of European powers in its own relationships with indigenous people in North America and other populations around the globe. In the case of Salem, some details in the accepted accounts of how the panic began provided an early focus for considering potential racial factors. Living along with his wife, children, and niece in the village parsonage, Salem minister Samuel Parris owned two slaves, Tituba and Indian John, who were probably married. Tituba was one of the first three women accused of witchcraft. While the other two, Sarah Good and Sarah Osburn, both denied the charge (although Good implicated Osburn in her own denial), Tituba on March 1 became the first person to confess to the crime. Convincing to local magistrates and ministers in its plausible description of meetings with Satan and his human followers, including the two Sarahs of Salem village, Tituba's confession fueled the initial expansion of the witch hunt by suggesting that a wide conspiracy was afoot. She mentioned the involvement of "a tal[l] man of Boston" and at least six additional witches who had signed the Devil's book but whose names she could not make out.[2]

This much is known for sure. But along with these facts came two additional assertions concerning Tituba's role in generating the witch hunt, one wholly made up and the other based on an enigmatic reference in the accounts of participants. The first placed Tituba in the position of leading a fortune-telling circle of young followers, including her accusers, based on the slave's knowledge of the occult gained during her early years in the West Indies—"fragments of something like voodoo remembered from the Barbados," in Starkey's phrasing. It was said that these experiments had been the practices that had caused the young people to take fright in the first place. The second assertion claimed that Tituba and her husband, Indian John, at the direction of a neighbor, Mary Sibley, probably in mid-February, had baked a "witch cake," using the urine of the possessed children, Betty Parris and Abigail Williams, as a means of countermagic to discover who was tormenting them. (Presumably the "witch" would be drawn to the product.) Samuel Parris himself declared in late March that this action of "going to the Devil for help against the Devil"—by which he meant relying on countermagic, rather than God, to do battle with magic—was responsible for the full unleashing of witchcraft in the community.[3]

Chadwick Hansen was the first among the new generation of scholars to call attention to the racial biases in these accounts. Writing in the mid-1970s, Hansen was not quite ready to debunk as a fabrication the image of Tituba as head of a fortune-telling circle—that step would have to await Bernard Rosenthal's even more penetrating research on the subject in the 1990s. But he was able to point out that the only references in the primary sources to magical practices, including forms of divination, employed at Salem prior to the witch hunt referred to demonstrably English ones and that none of these references mentioned Tituba. As for the witch cake, it, too, represented a common form of English countermagic used to discover the identity of a witch, and in any case it had been known since the 1850s, when Samuel Parris's church records from the period were first published, that the Puritan woman Mary Sibley had been responsible for suggesting its application. Yet none of these facts had prevented an elaborate tradition from being built up around Tituba as the instigator of the witch hunt through her alleged magical practices. Central to this tradition was Tituba's nonwhite race. The primary sources all referred to Tituba and her husband as "Indian," and it was fairly well established from at least as early as the 1760s that both had come originally from "New Spain." Parris had probably purchased them in Barbados, where the future minister resided in the 1670s before moving permanently to New England. As Hansen showed, *these* ethnic origins were not sufficiently stigmatized to suit a culprit on which a nineteenth- and early twentieth-century, white American public could place the blame (along with Puritanism in general, that is) for the Salem witch hunt. Thus, a process of "blackening" Tituba's race set in, beginning with Henry Wadsworth Longfellow's verse drama, *Giles Corey of the Salem Farms* (1868), which made Tituba half Indian and half African. In this way, a derogatory depiction of a superstitious, lazy, and excitable slave, witlessly starting a major social catastrophe, developed over a one-hundred-year period in literary and historical accounts of the witch hunt. By the time this image was included in Arthur Miller's *The Crucible*, Tituba had been rendered as exclusively black. To Hansen, the racial metamorphosis of Tituba signified just how powerful the prejudice of white Americans could be, influencing not only overt racists of the late nineteenth century (he cited one of that period's leading historians, John Fiske) but even well-meaning intellectuals of recent times, like Miller.[4]

But there was more to this part of the story. The 1990s brought to publication a flurry of new work on Tituba, the most important of which was an article by Bernard Rosenthal. Rosenthal recognized that the altered figure of Tituba in the historiography of Salem represented not simply, or even principally, a sign of white prejudice but rather—quite the opposite—a token of romantic protest against the Puritan and European foundations of the United States. This had been true from the beginning of her being imagined as the leader of an occult circle of Salem girls and young women. Rosenthal was able to trace this image back to a short story by British writer Elizabeth Gaskell, "Lois the Witch" (1859), whose depiction of the character "Nattee, the old Indian servant," reads almost exactly like the description of Tituba that Marion Starkey would later incorporate into her history of the witch hunt. Remarkably, as Rosenthal demonstrated, this act of cultural transmission seems to have occurred indirectly via the single most influential nineteenth-century history of the Salem panic, Charles W. Upham's two-volume *Salem Witchcraft* (1867), which melded Gaskell's portrait of Native American sorcery with what little had been reported about Tituba in the primary sources to produce a representation that would endure up through Starkey's account and Arthur Miller's play. In many renditions Tituba comes across as a woman of covert power or unrepressed energy (whether spiritual or sexual), a figure whose instigation of the witch hunt constituted an act little short of revenge for how Puritan society mistreated those in lowly positions—servants of her race (whether Indian or African), and children and adolescents. This tendency to view Tituba as an avenger, Rosenthal noted, has only become more prominent in literary products based on the Salem events in recent decades.[5]

Significantly, the same might be said of the recent historical works about Tituba, with important implications for the way in which they shift the sympathies of modern readers from the victims of the Salem witch hunt to one of the panic's most famous accusers. Even Rosenthal himself yielded to this temptation in his book-length treatment of the Salem events, *Salem Story: Reading the Witch Trials of 1692* (1993). He devoted a first chapter, revealingly entitled "Dark Eve," to exonerating Tituba from the charge of having been the woman of color who brought the evil of the witch hunt into the New England world, certainly a valuable contribution that quashed once and for all the legend of her occult leadership at Salem. But he went too far. Rosenthal minimized the importance of Tituba's startling and detailed confession for the progression of the witch hunt, and he also hinted that in telling the magistrates what they wanted to hear, the bondswoman was not simply acting in the best way she could to survive the ordeal but was also "us[ing] her plight to take revenge against the society that had enslaved her."[6]

Other historians of the 1990s also used Tituba's race sympathetically as a means of countering her longstanding denigration by asserting that she and her husband were, if not actual practitioners of some form of indigenous spirituality, perceived as such by their Puritan masters. Ignoring the fact that the witch-cake episode had been set in motion by a white Puritan woman and conformed to English patterns of countermagic, John McWilliams, for example, claimed that the Salem village community associated this incident, through Tituba and Indian John's involvement, with the "diabolical" practices of the shamans of the

Puritans' feared Algonquian neighbors. Once Tituba confessed, he wrote, "the associations of race and *maleficium* [witchcraft] became overpoweringly strong. The accuser [Tituba had at first named Sarah Good and Sarah Osburn before confessing herself] quickly became the accused." Similarly, in summarizing Indian John's successful evasion of accusation by becoming one of the afflicted accusers—even, in the historian's words, "converting the whipping scars of slavery into [supposed] witch marks"—McWilliams asserted that the male servant's afflictions were given special credence because Puritans assumed that a Native American would bring unusual insight into the Devil's ways. But no evidence exists for any of these assertions, not even for the claim that the scars Indian John exhibited came from whippings rather than from accidents or other injuries. Anyone, regardless of race, who had confessed to witchcraft would have been regarded as dangerous, and Tituba's confession was offered in such a way as to engender some sympathy in its listeners, which helps explain why she was never brought to trial, much less executed. As for Indian John's behavior, it closely resembled that of the other afflicted, perhaps with just a slightly higher admixture of feigned torment, as befit his peculiar vulnerability stemming from his connection to Tituba. There is again no reason to single out his race in explaining his role in the panic.[7]

Elaine G. Breslaw went one step further than McWilliams in arguing that Tituba really did inject an indigenous spiritual component into the events that launched the witch hunt, almost returning full circle to the traditional, mythologized portrait of the female slave's responsibility for the panic, except now with her actions regarded in positive, racial terms! Breslaw's research, reported in her book, *Tituba, Reluctant Witch of Salem: Devilish Indians and Puritan Fantasies* (1996), made the important contribution of identifying Tituba's origins with far greater precision than anyone had accomplished before. Based on extensive digging in Barbadian archives and reasoning persuasively from her knowledge of the enslavement of Amerindian peoples by the English planters in the West Indies, Breslaw was able to trace Tituba's life back to her likely birth into an Arawak band from the Orinoco River region of today's Venezuela. Breslaw then followed her until, as a teenager, she was likely purchased to be a house slave by Samuel Parris in 1678 or 1679 during his time in Barbados. Like Rosenthal, Breslaw dismissed the legend of Tituba leading a fortune-telling circle of Salem girls and young women. In fact, she wrote, there is no evidence of Tituba's involvement in any form of conjuring or occult practice prior to 1692. Moreover, it seems that Tituba was a quite acculturated member of the Parris household and the Puritan community. She and her husband lived inside the parsonage, not in separate quarters, she ate with the family and joined in its daily prayers and Bible teachings, and she may have learned to read. Her confession was made in roughly standard English sentences appropriate to her likely level of education, differing from the later Salem confession of another Barbadian slave of African origins, known as Candy, who had apparently come to New England and perhaps to a position of household servitude much more recently than Tituba. Tituba's confession also touched on familiar themes of English witchcraft lore: being forced to sign the Devil's book, noting the various animal forms (a hog, a black dog, a red rat, a black cat, a wolf, a yellow bird, a hairy imp) into which the Devil could transform himself, riding through the air on sticks or poles, and being promised riches if she would serve Satan for six years and acknowledge him as god. None of this should be surprising, since Tituba had likely been living under the close guidance of an English mistress or master since she was a girl of about eight, some eighteen years before the Salem panic began, and in a Puritan minister's household for most of this time.[8]

Yet despite all this evidence of Tituba's acculturation, Breslaw wants to have the slave bring a distinctively Amerindian influence into the early stages of the Salem panic. The historian begins with the doubtful assumption, also found in McWilliams's work, that Mary Sibley turned to Parris's servants to make the witch cake because they were Native American. The more likely explanation is that they would have been the logical people to ask simply because they were servants in the Parris household, with easy access to Betty Parris's and Abigail Williams's urine, a point Breslaw ends up conceding. The author places the greatest weight of her argument, however, on elements in Tituba's confession that she finds reminiscent of themes in Arawak demonology. But none of these correspondences is persuasive, if only because nearly all closely resemble analogous aspects of English demonology, and Breslaw is forced to acknowledge that the magistrates did not take note of anything alien in Tituba's lengthy confession.[9]

Breslaw's insistence that Tituba brought "her own" spirituality into her confession rests especially on two misleading propositions. The first is her assertion that the Arawaks, unlike the English, selected their witches from outside their local communities: hence, Tituba's naming of at least one witch from Boston. But Breslaw goes on to explain that "outsider" status for the Arawaks probably meant outside one's clan. New Englanders similarly almost never accused a blood relative of witchcraft. The second is the claim that Tituba's identification of the Devil in one of his guises as a man in a black coat with white hair reflected the Arawak vision of evil inhering in a particular person as opposed to being a disembodied spiritual force. But for the Puritans, Satan was no less capable of embodiment in the form of particular human beings or animals, including within English witch lore as "a foule, ugly man with a white beard." Breslaw emphasizes these two elements of supposed Amerindian religion in Tituba's confession as a way of portraying the slave's responsibility for widening the witch hunt beyond the confines of Salem village and beyond its customary targeting of poor, female suspects. The author then embraces Tituba's reputed responsibility for enlarging the panic to threaten the well-to-do members of the colony in much the same way that Carol Karlsen credited the powerful accusations of Salem's possessed female servants. Both sets of charges, in their authors' telling, produced such a destructive result that they led to the ultimately beneficial effect of ending witchcraft prosecutions for good. Tituba emerges from Breslaw's account as a "sophisticated manipulat[or]" of her situation rather than its "passive victim," using her indigenous cultural background if not exactly as an avenger—determined to bring down the entire Puritan, colonial enterprise along with her own unjust persecution—then at least as an agent of violent social reform.[10]

Why is it not enough to credit Tituba simply with the survival instinct of anyone similarly placed? She likely referenced Boston in her confession because she had lived there with the Parris family before coming to Salem. She probably mentioned the Devil appearing in the guise of a man because Satan himself was always regarded as male. In expanding the circle of the Devil's accomplices from three to ten, as Breslaw notes, Tituba must have intuited that there would be protection in prolonging the search for witches. Most of all, as reading the preserved transcriptions of her confession in their original question-and-answer form makes clear, Tituba was tentatively feeling her way forward at every step, following out the lines of thought in her examiners' leading questions, often repeating their words at the start of her own sentences. She needed to provide enough substance to corroborate the sort of conspiracy the magistrates were looking for—something big enough to account for the bewitchment of what had grown already to four young people by the end of February—while still seeking to protect herself. She accomplished the latter goal by insisting again and again what an unwilling follower of Satan she was and how she would never have hurt anyone unless forced to do so by the Devil's violent threats, perhaps half-consciously alluding to her master, who, she later said, had beaten her to force a confession. That she ended up convincing her listeners that she was as much a victim of Satan's malevolence as one of his henchmen is plenty testament to her resourcefulness under the most terrifying and overwhelming circumstances. The importance of her confession notwithstanding, what followed in the witch hunt was surely not of her making and especially not a result of her race, which appears to have been mostly irrelevant to the Puritans, for whom the world was divided between the godly and the unregenerate.[11]

When Mary Beth Norton set out to place the witch hunt in the context of warfare between the Puritans and their northern Algonquian neighbors, she thus inherited a formidable legacy of recent academic work offering a racial understanding of Tituba's role in the events. Would Norton's study follow in its path by turning the Wabanakis into a kind of Tituba writ large, an avenging force capable of mounting such a serious physical threat to the Puritan colony as to induce the colossal and seemingly well-deserved psychic crisis that we have come to know as the Salem witch hunt? Some earlier scholars of the post-1960s generation who had looked at the Puritan-Wabanaki relationship in connection with the Salem witch hunt had implied just this sort of interpretation. Writing, respectively, in the 1970s, 1980s, and 1990s and drawing on a Freudian strain of thought derived from studies in American literary criticism, Richard Slotkin, James E. Kences, and John McWilliams each indicted the Puritans for hypocritical dealings with Indians, in which the English had countered their own, forbidden attractions toward Native American life with a determination to eradicate the source of their temptation. When Indian retaliation, according to these historians, produced English war refugees, who soon enough would be accusing other Puritans of witchcraft, there was little cause to sympathize with the victims of this persecution; the Puritans were now simply on the receiving end of the violence they themselves had initiated.[12] At first glance, it is possible to take Norton's book in this way as well. But a close reading of her study yields a far more surprising result that returns us once again, like Boyer and Nissenbaum's and Demos's work before hers, to the relative innocence of the local Puritan community in the witch-hunting panic.[13]

Despite scholarly criticisms, many justifiable, that quickly greeted the central argument of *In the Devil's Snare*, Norton's book has by now probably overtaken Boyer and Nissenbaum's *Salem Possessed* in providing the leading explanation for the Salem witch hunt. It has acquired this influence for good reason, delivering the single most important study of the subject since Marion Starkey's *The Devil in Massachusetts*, a book to which it may be usefully compared. Like Starkey's account, Norton's work thoroughly grounds itself in the chronology of events taking place during 1692, allowing the structure of narrative to dominate its presentation, a strategy essential for conveying the social psychology of an unfolding panic. As a result, readers come away with a chilling sense of the victims' helplessness in the face of the witch hunt's galloping fears and accusations, fueled by the vicious yet unconscious circularity of the empirical tests employed to demonstrate the guilt of the accused. Regrettably, the author fails to emphasize this defining feature of the crisis, but it is nonetheless present throughout her account. Without detracting from her narrative, Norton also manages to include some of the most lucid discussions of the Puritans' complicated ideas about witchcraft in the Salem literature. She reveals, for example, how doubts about the perplexing phenomenon of spectral torment entered into the deliberations and actions of the colony's justices and ministers from the witch hunt's beginning to its end. One only wishes again that she had given these religious ideas the full explanatory weight they deserve. No less valuable is the author's detailed attention to the personal and familial ties among the participants. Drawing extensively on genealogical records and studies by talented antiquarians, Norton's account demonstrates how witchcraft accusations again and again fed on the prior reputations of the accused (or their maternal relatives), longstanding suspicions, and personal resentments. Norton followed Starkey in this line of interpretation as well, bettering her predecessor's account by filling in virtually everything that is now known about these intimate relationships but, alas, losing sight along the way of the centrality of these interpersonal antagonisms to the story that was so evident in Starkey's work. If it is impossible to cite these considerable strengths in Norton's book without at the same time noting their corresponding weaknesses, this is because In the Devil's Snare was after something it regarded as much bigger: identifying the witch hunt's mostly hidden, underlying cause. In pursuit of this quest, Norton offered a new, essentially political explanation for the Salem events, and everything else was subordinated to this end.[14]

The central contention of Norton's study proceeds along two interrelated lines of argument. First, she claims that the witch hunt arose against a backdrop of fears held by Essex County residents concerning the imminence of Indian raids, which had resumed in 1688 after a ten-year lull. Attacks in that year on settlements in neighboring New Hampshire and Maine signaled the start within months of a full-fledged war between England and France that engulfed their respective colonial settlements (always larger for the English) and their Native American allies (always more numerous for the French). This conflict, known among the English colonists as King William's War, would not end until 1699. In such an environment of anxious watchfulness, especially for those who had earlier suffered trauma at the hands of the Wabanakis, "witches" came to serve as stand-ins for Indians, an association made all the easier for a Puritan people whose ministers inveighed against these two threats to the godly as twin columns in the Devil's army. Second, Norton asserts that these fears were enabled to grow

into a witchcraft panic of unprecedented proportions because the political leaders of the Massachusetts colony, who functioned also as the examining magistrates and trial judges during the witch hunt, sought to deflect attention from
their own failure to extinguish the Indian danger to the north. Better to have the
colony's population mobilized against Satan's "invisible" allies (the witches),
these leaders intuited, than asking nagging questions about why Satan's "visible"
allies (the Wabanakis, with the support of French "Papists") had been permitted
to mount such a devastating and continuing challenge. It is helpful to examine
each of these propositions separately, while at the same time observing how both
lines of argument condition the sympathies of Norton's readers relative to the
witch hunt's victims.

Most of the critical scholarly reaction to *In the Devil's Snare* centered on the
exaggeration in Norton's first claim—that the accusers in the Salem witch hunt
were motivated chiefly or at bottom by fear of Indian attack. Critics conceded in
general terms the plausibility of the connection, pointing out that the context of
the northern war had occupied a limited, supporting place among the probable
causes of the Salem events in most historical treatments.[15] The problem was that
Norton took this one factor and elevated it into the preeminent reason why the
witch hunt reached the epic proportions that it did. "Had the Second Indian War
[i.e., King William's War] on the northeastern frontier somehow been avoided,"
she writes in one of her concluding formulations, "the Essex County witchcraft
crisis of 1692 would not have occurred." A few people—Sarah Good, Sarah
Osburn, maybe even Elizabeth Procter, Martha Cory, and Rebecca Nurse—might
still have been accused, she maintains, but most of these women would likely
have been acquitted, judging by the past practices of Massachusetts magistrates.
It was the population's sense of vulnerability to Indian attack that turned these
first, local, "routine" charges into a cascade of over one hundred accusations and
confessions, many involving individuals with strong ties to the frontier communities in New Hampshire and Maine.[16] Most reviewers disagreed. They noted
that only two of the twenty executed in the panic, George Burroughs and Ann
Pudeator, had ever lived in the northern frontier, and of these, only Burroughs
had a strong, recent connection to the area. Three of the principal accusers (Mercy
Lewis, Susannah Sheldon, and Sarah Churchill) and two important confessor-
accusers (Abigail Hobbs and her mother, Deliverance Hobbs) had resided in
Maine during times of prior Indian attack, but that still left more than half of all
the accusers, including such leading figures as Ann Putnam Jr., Mary Walcott,
Abigail Williams, Elizabeth Hubbard, Ann Putnam Sr., Mary Warren, and
Elizabeth Booth with no direct ties to the frontier. These critics might have

added that Susannah Sheldon joined the ranks of the accusers only in late April and Sarah Churchill in early May. Together with Mercy Lewis, these three were responsible for a little over twenty accusations, while Putnam Jr., Walcott, Williams, Hubbard, and Warren collectively advanced about eighty accusations.[17]

Reviewers also pointed to Norton's questionable inferences in support of her argument. Where Norton saw the ominous imprint of imagined Indian attack when the afflicted girls cried out that the witches' specters "tore me all to pieces" or threatened to "roast me on a spit," other scholars pointed out that such imagery of torture could be found in the literature and oral traditions of English witchcraft and Reformation-era Protestant martyrdom. Moreover, the afflicted employed phrases of more obviously European provenance, like "racked me all to pieces." Was Tituba accused of witchcraft because she was an Indian, or did she get named simply because she was a vulnerable servant? Were the specters that tormented the people of Essex County described as "black" because that color was sometimes used interchangeably with "tawny" by the Puritans to describe the Wabanakis, or were these apparitions dark simply because so much of the Devil's domain was traditionally pictured by the English as black in color? Similar questions arose about the "drum beat" and "trumpet sound" of Satan's forces heard drilling on the field near Samuel Parris's parsonage by the afflicted. Were these martial images occasioned by the fear of French and Indian attack, or did they arise from the familiar stock of emblems Puritans drew upon to characterize the great conflict between the "armies" of the Devil and the Lord? In a juxtaposition that seemed particularly far-fetched, Norton linked the June 11, 1692, Indian attack on the southern Maine community of Wells to the witch hunt's first execution, the hanging of Bridget Bishop, which had occurred just one day earlier. Of this "conjunction," Norton asks, "Did anyone view the attack as revenge for Goody Bishop's execution?" She replies, "It would have been easy for New Englanders to reach such a conclusion," although she admits that "no such reasoning is recorded in surviving documents." Critics were rightly unpersuaded by this linkage. Indeed, Salemites had plenty of local reasons in the days following the hanging to believe they were now safer because they had rid their community of a woman who had wrought supernatural mischief on her neighbors for over twenty years. After Bishop's death, Norton reported a little later on, "afflictions in Salem Village ceased almost entirely for two full weeks."[18]

There are many more instances of such dubious inferences in Norton's book. Take, for example, the case against northern Essex County resident Susannah Martin, who was hanged on July 19. Norton highlights the deposition of Martin's Salisbury neighbor Joseph Ring as "differ[ing] dramatically" from the rest of the more typical accusations of witchcraft made out against her, which alleged threatening nocturnal appearances, vengeful predictions, and attacks on neighbors' animals. Ring had served in the militia company that arrived too late to save the British Fort Loyal at Falmouth, Maine, in May 1690. Over two hundred English settlers were slaughtered at the end of that siege when they were deceived into believing they could surrender safely to their Wabanaki and French attackers. In Norton's interpretation, Ring was haunted for the next two years by visions of "'a company of several other creaturs' of 'hidious shapes' who made 'dreadful noyse' as they rode together on horseback along Essex County roads . . . and 'threatned to tear him in peeces.'" It seems clear to her that these specters from the invisible world of witchcraft "revealed their alliance with the same Wabanakis who had destroyed Fort Loyal" and created "Ring's obsession with the threat the French and Indians posed to northern New England and to him personally." The connection in his testimony to Susannah Martin was only tangential, according to Norton, with Martin's specter having appeared to Ring solely at some of the "mery meeting[s]" that the company of witches had forced him to attend.[19]

Yet an examination of the full texts, not provided in Norton's book, of Ring's two depositions, both given on May 13, 1692, presents a different picture. The first deposition tells of a spectral incident that placed the twenty-seven-year-old Ring, against his will, in the company of three witches: Thomas Hardy (a fellow militia man from the same 1690 mission, to whom Ring owed a gambling debt), the sixty-seven-year-old Susannah Martin, and another, unidentified woman. Ring watched the three witches drink cider in front of a fire for most of the night, after which Martin "made a noyse and turned into the shape of a blak hoge and went away and so did the other: t[w]o p[er]sons go away." The second deposition relates a series of incidents in which Ring was overtaken while traveling from one Essex County town to another by the spectral "company" that Norton described above. While the first of three references to this group notes the presence of Hardy and "several other creaturs," together with "the dreadfull noyse & hideous shapes of these creaturs and firebale [fireball]" that Norton took as lingering scars of Ring's frontier service, the other two references make clear that the company consisted of "people on horseback" or "a company of horses with men & women upon them." Wabanakis did not fight on horseback, and their warriors certainly did not include women. In these three references, Hardy is the only identified witch, and he is clearly after the debt that Ring owed him. It was Hardy who, in one of these incidents, came on horseback "to this deponent as before & demanded his: 2s[hillings]: of him and thretned to tear him in peeces." In the final spectral episode of his second deposition, Ring was again taken to witches' meetings, where feasting and dancing went on. Susannah Martin was present at these meetings, as was the Devil, who asked Ring to sign his book and promised him "all delectable things . . . but he refusing it woold usualy end with most dreadfull shapes noyses & screching that almost scared him out of his witts." Here the characteristics that Norton associates with Indian attack are attached to one of the most familiar depictions of Satan in Euro-American demonology (a man who tempts his subjects with material rewards), just as earlier in the deposition the threat of being torn in pieces came from the specter of Ring's militia mate, Hardy, not from one of the wild, unidentified "creatures."

In sum, while Joseph Ring's dreamlike imaginings are surely susceptible to a range of interpretations, conventional images of witchcraft predominate. There are no direct references to Indian warfare. Guilt and fear over his unpaid debt or perhaps over the illicit game of shuffleboard that gave rise to the debt, referenced in the magistrate's comment written on the back of the second deposition, would seem to go a long way toward explaining Ring's particular projections. Since Hardy was the source of Ring's anxiety and Martin was the local woman whose reputation already marked her in the eyes of her community as a likely witch, it follows that Ring might imagine the two as associates in supernatural evildoing.[20]

Joseph Ring's testimony against Susannah Martin provides Norton with one questionable though small building block in the construction of her case, but weightier elements in her argument betray shaky foundations as well. Three in particular have escaped the critical analysis they deserve: her attempt to undermine the widely held belief that forbidden experiments with fortune-telling likely provoked the initial afflictions in the girls and young women at Salem, her insistence that the critical turning point in the witch hunt came with Maine refugee Abigail Hobbs's confession on April 19, and her elevation of Mercy Lewis to the position of leader among the accusers.

Every treatment of the Salem witch hunt states that nobody knows for certain what prompted Betty Parris and Abigail Williams to suffer their initial torments. These afflictions spread quickly to Ann Putnam Jr. and Elizabeth Hubbard, the servant of the village doctor, and then a couple weeks later to Mercy Lewis, the servant living in Ann Putnam's household, and Mary Walcott, Ann's cousin. The girls and young women blamed their severe distresses on the malevolent acts of witches, and nearly all members of their community, except most of the accused, concurred. While understanding the ensuing witch hunt does not hinge on uncovering what caused the first accusers to take sick, modern accounts have tried to identify some action or agent as the instigator.[21] Based on several observations found in the contemporary sources, a consensus has developed around the likelihood of fortune-telling of some sort—no longer with Tituba in the lead or even as a participant, and not even in any organized group form—as the guilt-inducing activity that started the lethal stone rolling. For Norton, this consensus presents an obstacle to convincing readers that they should look first to the war in Maine, not to Puritan beliefs, for an explanation of the ensuing panic. But her attempts to discredit the fortune-telling theory by minimizing the value of the contemporary sources come up short.

She begins by dismissing Cotton Mather's observations on this subject by characterizing them as "a vague comment" and leaving it at that. No portion of his text appears, nor even a footnote to the work where these observations may be found, Mather's 1697 biography of the Massachusetts governor, William Phips. The relevant passage, however, offers far more than a vague comment.

> Now the Arrival of Sir *William Phips* to the Government of *New-England*, was at a time when . . . Scores of poor People had newly fallen under a prodigious *Possession of Devils*, which it was then generally thought had been by *Witchcrafts* introduced. It is to be confessed and bewailed, that many Inhabitants of *New-England*, and Young People especially, had been led away with little *Sorceries*, wherein they *did secretly those things that were not right against the Lord their God*; they would often cure Hurts with *Spells*, and practise detestable Conjurations with *Sieves*, and *Keys*, and *Pease*, and *Nails*, and *Horseshoes*, and other Implements, to learn the things for which they had a forbidden and impious Curiosity. . . . Although these *Diabolical Divinations* are more ordinarily committed perhaps all over the *whole* World, than they are in the Country of *New-England*, yet, that being a Country Devoted unto the Worship and Service of the Lord JESUS CHRIST above the *rest of the World, He* signalized his Vengeance against these Wickednesses, with such extraordinary Dispensations as have not been often seen in other places [italics in original].

While Mather's retrospective judgment about what had unleashed the Devil in eastern Massachusetts in 1692—he was ready by 1697 to define the result more as "possession" than as "witchcraft"—served wider religious purposes and omitted the names of any individuals from Salem or any other town in Essex County, the Boston minister's attribution of "such extraordinary Dispensations" to the fortune-telling activities of "Young People" was actually quite clear and specific.[22]

Disregarding Mather's commentary, Norton directs most of her attention to questioning the significance historians have accorded a passage in another retrospective account of the witch hunt's origins, Rev. John Hale's *Modest Enquiry into the Nature of Witchcraft*, composed in 1697–98. Hale ministered to the church in Beverly, Salem village's neighboring town to the east, and was present in the village at the outset of the crisis. The critical passage about fortune-telling consists of two short paragraphs in which Hale recounts how "one of the Afflicted persons, who" by using an egg and glass, tried to learn something about her future husband but turned up the frightful likeness of a coffin. He goes on to say how "another, [whom] I was called to pray with," had tried the same technique, confessed, repented, and was released from Satan's bonds. Norton says that Hale's second woman might not have been part of the 1692 events at all or, if she were, might not have been an afflicted accuser but rather one of the accused witches, one of whom confessed separately to the magistrates that once, years earlier, she had experimented with fortune-telling. Norton adds that Hale placed these two paragraphs in the final third of his 175-page book rather than with the main narrative of the early Salem events, which occupied the first forty pages; she considers this placement a sign that Hale must have regarded this material "as irrelevant to the development of the crisis." She concludes that "careful scholars today should regard it as equally irrelevant."[23]

But these textual judgments again appear misguided. Hale's two paragraphs begin with a sentence that Norton omits: "I fear some young persons through a vain curiosity to know their future condition, have tampered with the Devils tools, so far that thereby one door was opened to Satan to play those pranks; *Anno* 1692. I knew one of the Afflicted persons, who . . ." (italics in original). That first sentence not only makes a general assertion about how fortune-telling by "young persons" in 1692 opened the door to Satan's mischief, but it also, by use of the plural "young persons," appears to set up both paragraphs, with their two examples, as a unified commentary on the Salem events. (These two paragraphs together also conclude a chapter.) Moreover, the last two-thirds of Hale's book are not unrelated to the first four chapters covering the details of the witch hunt's early developments. Hale wrote this important and humane text in an attempt to answer the question of what had gone wrong at Salem, where, as he now realized, the lives of many innocent people had been taken. He had supported the witch hunt nearly to the end, and at the time of writing his *Enquiry* he still believed in witches. Hale's method of proceeding in the body of the work was to assemble, not in any scrupulous order, examples and reasoning from all relevant sources. He examined the 1692 events, other Massachusetts and English witchcraft cases, and passages from the Bible, all to help his readers avoid a repeat of the Salem mistakes without falling into the opposite error of failing to prosecute real witches when they appeared in the future. The instances of fortune-telling described in the two paragraphs cited by Norton are not the sole examples of events Hale included from the 1692 witch hunt in the latter part of his book. I counted six others.[24]

That Hale did not linger over or call special attention to the actions that may have set off the first Salem afflictions reflected an assumption common to all the participants: there was always plenty of sinfulness in the Puritan communities to explain why God, in his unfathomable wisdom, might decide at any particular moment to "lengthen the Chain of the Roaring Lion [Satan]," as ex-Salem village minister Deodat Lawson put it, just enough to chastise his people. Lawson, also present at the start of the witch hunt, and Boston merchant Thomas Brattle, who commented in October 1692 about the afflicted in Andover, offered still further evidence that some Puritans, especially young girls, not uncommonly engaged in forbidden fortune-telling. Both noted that contemporaries believed there was a connection between that activity and the outbreak of what they took to be witchcraft. A psychosomatic reaction to guilt over fortune-telling is still the best guess about what started the panic.[25]

Like Hale, Norton does not linger over the question of what activity gave rise to the initial afflictions. For her, the critical problem that needs to be explained is why what began as a relatively routine witchcraft scare grew to such enormous proportions. In arguing for the influence of the Indian war as the answer, much hinges on her identification of Abigail Hobbs's confession as the turning point. "Abigail Hobbs's statement on April 19," Norton writes, "set off a chain of events that within thirty-six hours explicitly linked the witches' and the Wabanakis' assaults against New England. As a result, witchcraft complaints exploded, expanding both geographically and numerically. During the next seven weeks, fifty-four people were formally accused of being witches, a sharp increase from the ten who had been complained against in the seven weeks prior to April 17." The last sentence is slightly misleading, because on April 18 four more individuals, including Abigail Hobbs herself, had been added to the list of accused. Still, the contrast between fifty-four and fourteen is sharp enough to require an explanation. A little later on, Norton asserts even more pointedly, "Before the end of April [beginning on April 21], fifteen new complaints were filed—thus doubling the number of accused witches [which had reached fourteen by April 19] in just ten days." We may assess the significance of Norton's argument for this turning point by first examining her statistical claims and then working backward through her reasoning to see how she again overstates her case. A moment of importance in the unfolding of the witch hunt did occur on April 19 and 20, but it had little to do with Maine or the Wabanakis.[26]

A number of historians before Norton have sought to identify "turning points" in the Salem witch hunt. For Carol Karlsen and, implicitly, for Marion Starkey, that moment arrived on March 21 with the examination of Martha Cory, when it became clear to all participants that there could be no successful defense against the magistrates' circular questioning and the crowd's boisterous intervention. For Elaine Breslaw, Tituba's earlier confession had created the point of no return, because it gestured in the direction of a widespread, Satanic conspiracy while corroborating the seeming truth of the initial accusations. For Bernard Rosenthal, the pivotal time came with John Procter's examination on April 11; by including a man (and one of some social standing) within the circle of the Devil's agents, this legal proceeding indicated an unusually menacing outbreak of witchcraft. Each of these "turning points" has merit (as does Norton's, although not in the way she asserts), because the witch hunt proceeded in the form of a wave— actually, two successive waves—with many points on the rising path of the curve inducing those that followed.[27]

If we graph this wave of social terror, showing the incidence of formal accusations at weekly intervals, the trajectory of the witch hunt becomes visible (figure 7). Based on this picture, we can say that there were really two distinct phases of witch fear that took hold in Essex County during 1692. Just when the first scare (centered in Salem village) seemed to be coming to an end—likely due to the execution of Bridget Bishop on June 10, followed by the convictions of five more people (Sarah Good, Rebecca Nurse, Susannah Martin, Sarah Wilds, and Elizabeth How) on June 29–July 2—a second phase (centered in neighboring Andover) took hold. Probably not too much should be made of the distinction between the two waves, since the original group of Salem accusers offered their services as "witch finders" to the new set of afflicted accusers in Andover, thus conferring legitimacy on the latter's charges and furthering them along. Meanwhile, the many confessions that quickly emerged from Andover only served at first to confirm the validity of the earlier accusations and convictions from Salem. The 1692 witch hunt is thus best thought of as a single epidemic of fear, punctuated by a breathing spell of about four weeks in the middle. By early September, the unprecedented number of confessions coming out of Andover would cross a threshold into disbelief and contribute to the doubts that now brought the entire panic to an end.[28]

Within this larger statistical pattern, how do Norton's claims hold up for the immediate weeks surrounding Abigail Hobbs's confession on April 19? Norton's rough numbers are accurate enough, as a quick glance at figure 7 suggests, but her reasoning is faulty. Fourteen-year-old Abigail Hobbs occupies a pivotal place for Norton, not only or even principally because she was the second person (after

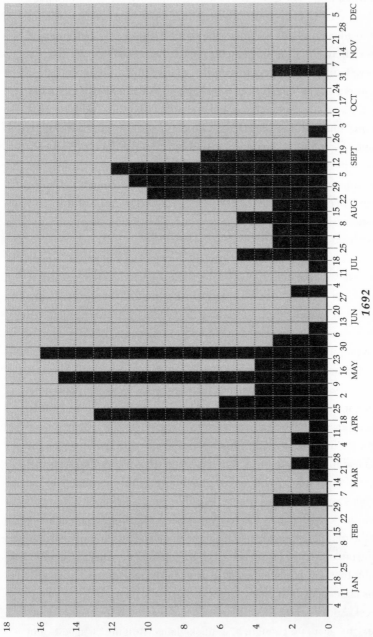

Figure 7. Accused suspects in Salem witch hunt, by date of first formal legal action (in weeks). *Notes:* Each bar represents the number of suspects accused in the week beginning on Monday (the dates displayed along the bottom of the graph) and ending on Sunday just before the start of the next week. Almost no legal actions were taken on Sundays, the Puritan Sabbath. Legal actions include, in descending order of frequency: arrest warrant, complaint, examination, testimony, statement, deposition, and other. A table showing each of the 138 suspects included in this figure, together with their dates and type of legal action, appears in appendix 2. *Source: Records*, pp. 101–124.

Tituba on March 1) to confess to the crime of witchcraft but because she was the first person to bring an association with Maine into the unfolding panic.[29] As a child of about six or seven in 1683, Abigail, together with her siblings, was probably taken by her parents to live in Falmouth, Maine, when that part of the northeastern frontier was being repopulated by English settlers in the years between the two big Indian conflicts, King Philip's War (1675–78) and King William's War. Norton did some fine historical sleuthing to place the Hobbs family in Falmouth from about 1683 to 1688, making Abigail a likely childhood neighbor of Mercy Lewis, five years her elder. The Lewis family had also returned to the northern Maine community during approximately the same years, and there is no reason to doubt Norton's strong guesswork that the girls knew one another. There is reason to doubt, however, Norton's contentions that Hobbs's April 19 confession highlighted the relevance of Maine in the developing witchcraft panic and that *for this reason* her words led to a dramatic increase in the number of accusations. "Significantly," Norton writes, summarizing the confession, "Abigail Hobbs had met the devil—in the shape of a 'black man'—on the Maine frontier about four years earlier, or just a few months before the Wabanakis renewed their attacks on the English settlements. Furthermore, she encountered Satan in the woods (the Indians' domain) near her residence in Falmouth, one of the Indians' chief targets in both the first and second wars. Those who heard her confession readily grasped the connection between Satan and the Wabanakis."[30]

But if we look at the fifteen people newly accused during the final ten days of April (April 21 to April 30), it turns out that just one had genuine ties to Maine and the northern war—George Burroughs, the ex-Salem village minister, who had moved to Falmouth with his wife and children in 1683. The accusation against Burroughs and his subsequent arrest indeed played a critical role in the witch hunt. (I return to this development below.) The only two other people among the fifteen with even tangential ties to the war were Mary and Philip English, a wealthy couple from Salem town. Although Philip English's substantial merchant business included sending ships up the Maine coast to catch fish for sale across the Atlantic, there is no evidence that his Maine connections played any role in bringing him or his wife under suspicion. More likely reasons included his French background—which Norton plays up, although few New Englanders of French descent found themselves among the accused over the course of 1692—his Anglican leanings, and his aggressive business dealings, which elicited some of the only concrete complaints in the formal testimony against him, apart from the spectral imaginings of the afflicted Salem women and a Marblehead man. An even more likely reason for suspicion was that his wife, Mary Hollingsworth English, who was accused nine days before her husband, carried the taint of her mother's reputation, which included an accusation of witchcraft years earlier. All twelve of the other individuals accused in the immediate wake of Abigail Hobbs's confession followed the usual local patterns: they were either people long suspected of witchcraft, relatives of others thought to be witches, or else parties to long-running disputes with the families of the accusers.[31]

Even Abigail Hobbs's father, William, and her stepmother, Deliverance, who were also accused on April 21, may be better identified with local doings in the town of Topsfield (just north of Salem village), to which the family seems to have returned in 1689, than with their time in Maine. The limited testimony recorded against William mentions only his failure to attend church and a boundary dispute with a Topsfield neighbor. Deliverance, who under examination on April 22 followed her daughter in becoming the third adult (or teenager) to confess to the crime of witchcraft, said nothing at all in her confession about Maine, where she may have been born and raised. She stated that she had signed the Devil's book a few days before (in Topsfield), described him in formulaic fashion as "a tall black man, with an high-croun'd hat," and named two prior suspects, Salemite Sarah Osburn and Topsfield resident Sarah Wilds, as her associates in sticking pins in the images of children in order to hurt them.

If we now glance forward through the first days of June, by which time, Norton tells us, thirty-nine additional people had been accused since Abigail Hobbs's confession, just three more could be said to have had any ties to "the Eastward" or to New England's French and Indian adversaries. These three were Salem town resident Ann Pudeator, who left Falmouth in the early 1670s and whose charges had nothing to do with Maine; John Alden, a prominent Boston merchant who served as an official emissary to the French in Canada on several occasions; and John Flood (or Floyd), from Rumney Marsh, outside of Boston, who commanded the colonial militia units stationed in Portsmouth, New Hampshire, during the northern war. In sum, out of all those accused of witchcraft from April 21 through May 30 (54 individuals), only Burroughs, Alden, and Flood held relationships to the frontier important enough to merit further examination.[32]

How could Norton have so exaggerated the influence of Abigail Hobbs's confession? She did so by conflating two events: Hobbs's actual confession, which placed no special weight on Maine, and the far more important occurrence on the following day, April 20, when Ann Putnam Jr. described for the first time a frightening spectral appearance by the ex-Salem village minister, George Burroughs, who happened to live in Falmouth, Maine, during some of the same years as the Hobbs family. Putnam named Burroughs as the ringleader of Satan's agents, "the wheel within a wheel," in the words that Ann's father used in his letter written the next day to the Salem magistrates to describe the source of his daughter's torments. Identifying Burroughs as the leader of the witches in all likelihood really did open the floodgates to many of the new accusations that we have just examined. Now the wide conspiracy that Tituba had hinted at had found a weighty enough figure to place at its head, one with the qualifications, as a minister, both to deliver perverse sacraments to the sorts of people community members had long suspected to be witches and to lure even such seemingly devout individuals as Martha Cory and Rebecca Nurse into Satan's rival "church." Here was another true turning point in the Salem witch hunt.[33]

Abigail Hobbs's confession, the day before, certainly contributed to the gathering momentum of the witch hunt, too, simply by providing the panic's second confession. Confessions in witchcraft cases were always considered the best of all evidence; everything else remained technically a mere "presumption." A confession offered proof that a real witch had been uncovered, lending credence to all other accusations. Beyond the simple fact of her confession, however, the content of Hobbs's statement provided little that went beyond conventional formulations. She said she saw the Devil in the forms of dogs, cats, and men. He had appeared to her first about three or four years previously at Casco Bay (where the community of Falmouth was located), and only in response to the magistrates' leading question, "Where, in the house, or in the woods?" did she reply, innocuously, given the ubiquity of woods throughout all of New England at this time, "In the woods," adding, "In the day." Hobbs's reference to "a black man" came only later in her confession, when she was describing a recent visit ("About a fortnight agoe") from the Devil to her home in Topsfield. Each time the Devil contacted her, he offered the standard bargain: "he would give me fine things" and "fine clothes," she said, if she signed his book and agreed to "hurt folks" and otherwise serve him, along with associates like Sarah Good, for a period of years. It thus seems an unsupportable leap from the text of Hobbs's confession to assert, as Norton does, that Abigail "had met the devil—in the shape of a 'black man'—on the Maine frontier . . . in the woods (the Indians' domain) near her residence in Falmouth, one of the Indians' chief targets in both the first and second wars," and to extrapolate from this strained rendering that "those who heard her confession readily grasped the connection between Satan and the Wabanakis."[34]

Perhaps sensing the thinness of the Maine connections in Abigail Hobbs's confession alone, Norton attempts to shore up the argument for her "turning point" by emphasizing a portion of Ann Putnam's April 20 vision that linked

Burroughs's specter to events in the ongoing northern war. According to Putnam, the specter disclosed that Burroughs had killed Rev. Deodat Lawson's child
(back in Salem village) because Lawson served as preacher to the soldiers on an
expedition against the Wabanakis led by Edmund Andros, governor of the short-
lived Dominion of New England, during the winter of 1688–89. Furthermore,
the specter claimed that Burroughs had bewitched to death many of the soldiers
on that same expedition. The young girl added that it was Burroughs who had
made Abigail Hobbs a witch (presumably in Maine) and that he had continued
making other witches since then. That was the extent of the Maine-related ac-
complishments in Burroughs's large Satanic resumé, which included, as Ann
Putnam also disclosed on April 20, the murder of his first two wives as well as
Reverend Lawson's wife. Subsequent accusations would add that he mistreated
his wives before their deaths, neglected family prayer and his children's baptism,
possessed "preternatural" physical strength, and was able to discern the unvoiced
thoughts of others. Indeed, people in Salem village and Salem town had been
gossiping about Burroughs for years. It surely did not help his defense against the
new witchcraft accusation that those people included the Salem magistrate and
examiner John Hathorne, whose ex-sister-in-law, Sarah Ruck Hathorne, had become Burroughs's second wife (John Ruck, Sarah's father, would serve as foreman
of the grand jury during the witchcraft trials), and a number of Putnams, who
had witnessed firsthand what they regarded as Burroughs's verbal abuse of his
first wife during his tenure as the village's minister.[35]

For Norton, the Maine charges against Burroughs stand out because of their
tie to the northern war and, as we will see shortly, to the antipathies she is subtly
developing toward those New Englanders, like Burroughs, John Flood, and John
Alden, who either were perceived to be or really were "soft" on the Indians in that
conflict. Norton even speculates that Ann Putnam believed Burroughs to have
used witchcraft against Lawson's child because he himself wanted to be the
minister on Andros's expedition. For Cotton Mather, however, reviewing the
case against Burroughs in early October 1692 in order to justify his execution
(which had been carried out on August 19), the Maine actions occupied no place
at all. Mather attributed the spectral killing of Deodat Lawson's wife and daughter to Burroughs's spite toward Lawson for the latter's having succeeded him in the
post of village minister, and Mather omitted entirely from his seven-page account
the accusation that Burroughs had bewitched Andros's soldiers. The charges
against Burroughs for his alleged acts of witchcraft in Maine, in short, do not appear to have been critical to the minister's conviction or to the expansion of the
witch hunt. But they *are* critical to Norton's argument for the influence of the north-

ern war on the panic, and for this purpose she adds one last hypothetical ingredient to her discussion of the turning point of April 19–20: she says that it was the Putnams' servant Mercy Lewis, another Maine refugee, who induced Ann Putnam Jr. to name the minister.[36]

Like Abigail Hobbs, Mercy Lewis and her family returned to Falmouth, Maine, in the mid-1680s, but unlike the Hobbses (so far as is known), the extended Lewis family had already suffered enormous losses at the hands of Indian raiders during King Philip's War a decade earlier. When Lewis was about three years old, as Norton relates toward the beginning of her book, the Wabanakis attacked Falmouth, killing her paternal grandparents, two uncles, and one aunt, and they took as captives another of her aunts and many of her cousins, some of whom died in the ordeal. With eleven men losing their lives and twenty-three women and children either killed or captured, the raid traumatized the English community as a whole. The survivors retreated to a nearby island, and the settlement was quickly abandoned, with Mercy Lewis and her parents probably moving to Salem town. When the Lewises arrived back to Falmouth around 1683, Mercy, now about ten years old, became the neighbor not only of Abigail Hobbs but also of George Burroughs. Together with his second wife and children, Burroughs had returned to Falmouth at about the same time to become the town's minister, a position he had occupied from 1674 to 1676, before the earlier Indian attack. Falmouth was struck again by the Wabanakis in September 1689, soon after the start of King William's War, and this time Mercy's parents were probably killed. Norton believes, plausibly, that the sixteen-year-old girl may then have lived briefly with Burroughs and his family before moving back to Essex County. (Norton further imagines, implausibly, that during the months she lived in the Burroughs household, Lewis may have heard the minister express resentment toward Reverend Lawson for having been selected as Governor Andros's expeditionary chaplain.) Lewis appears to have entered Thomas Putnam Jr.'s Salem village household as a servant in 1690, while Burroughs himself left Falmouth in the same year to become minister in the southern Maine community of Wells, where he was arrested on May 2, 1692.[37]

Given Lewis's traumatic experiences in Maine and her personal knowledge of Burroughs in Falmouth, it makes sense, as Norton hypothesizes, that Lewis might have jumped at the chance—unconsciously through her "witchcraft" afflictions—to blame a survivor of the Indian attacks that wiped out nearly her entire family. Thus she might have been the one to put the Maine charges against Burroughs in Ann Putnam Jr.'s ear and perhaps also to have suggested that it was Burroughs who had inducted Abigail Hobbs into the Devil's league. Even if true, these conjectures cannot bear the weight Norton allots them for placing the ex-Salem village minister at the center of the witch hunt, making him the "wheel within a wheel." As already noted, many of the prime movers among the adults in the witch hunt had plenty of their own reasons to suspect Burroughs of evildoing, reasons equally likely to have found their way via family gossip into the imagination of Ann Putnam Jr.

There are other grounds for doubting Norton's suggested pathway of transmission for the Burroughs accusation. If Mercy Lewis was the one who particularly wished to see the minister accused, why did she not initiate the charge, or at least quickly echo Ann Putnam Jr.'s accusation? In fact, it was Abigail Williams who, on the morning after Putnam's vision, became the second afflicted girl visited by Burroughs's specter. The apparition again confessed that he had killed the three women in question and added a boast about being able to hold up a gun with one hand in a way that no man could do. Not until two weeks later did Mercy Lewis report her own tortures at the hands of George Burroughs's specter. Neither Maine nor Indians figured in this report of witchery, which proceeded along traditional, religious lines. Lewis related that Burroughs's specter tormented her dreadfully in order to get her to sign his book and agree not to testify against him at his upcoming examination. At the same time, the minister's ghost tempted her with the Devil's promises, just as Satan had tempted Jesus. "Mr Burroughs caried me up to an exceeding high mountain," Lewis recounted, paraphrasing the Gospels (Matthew or Luke), "and shewed me all the kingdoms of the earth and tould me that he would give them all to me if I would writ in his book." The apparition also acknowledged to Lewis that he had bewitched another member of the Putnam clan, Ann Jr.'s second cousin. If indeed Lewis was the one to feed Ann Putnam Jr. the accusation that the minister had used his supernatural powers to undercut the colony's war efforts against the Wabanakis, even this specific charge would have added just one more particular to a long list of fantasies and innuendos against which no man could defend himself.[38]

Yet Norton enlarges Lewis's role still further. Mercy Lewis emerges at just this point in the narrative as the leader among the afflicted young women and remains so for the remainder of Norton's book. This element in Norton's study is striking because it contradicts most histories of the witch hunt, which have always focused on Ann Putnam Jr., as the key accuser. At issue is not so much the number of people named. One reliable count posits Ann as the lead accuser, giving twenty-one names, followed by Elizabeth Hubbard giving twenty, Mary Walcott sixteen, Mary Warren fourteen, Mercy Lewis eleven, Susannah Sheldon ten, and Abigail Williams nine.[39] The deeper problem may be to identify which members of the core group enjoyed the greatest credibility or initiated accusations against new individuals. Ann Jr. was only twelve years of age and thus technically fell below the required age of fourteen for testifying in capital felony cases, yet the special Massachusetts witchcraft court accepted her depositions and those of eleven-year-old Abigail Williams, perhaps even purposely obscuring the two girls' ages by omitting them from the documents. This fact suggests that Ann Jr.'s reported visions and related accusations were well respected by the examining magistrates and local community. No doubt it helped Ann Jr.'s credibility that she was not a servant but rather the daughter of a leading Salem village family, whose head, Thomas Putnam Jr., the eldest of the eight third-generation Putnam men, played the strongest supportive role of any adult (apart from the magistrates) in the witch hunt. He signed numerous complaints made out against the accused during the first (Salem-based) phase of the panic and was often joined in these legal acts by a number of his male Putnam relatives or close friends and neighbors. Ann Putnam Jr.'s mother, Ann Carr Putnam, also suffered afflictions that she attributed to witchcraft, becoming an important accuser herself of three village residents—Martha Cory, Rebecca Nurse, and John Willard—all of whom would be executed. Of the twenty persons put to death in the Salem witch hunt, Ann Putnam Jr.'s name appears in the surviving records as an accuser of seventeen, while Mercy Lewis's name appears as an accuser of thirteen. There is thus little doubt that despite her age, Ann Putnam Jr.'s testimony was strongly believed, probably somewhat more so than any of the other afflicted young women.[40]

But could Mercy Lewis still have been the more powerful instigator behind Ann Putnam Jr.'s spectral visions and accusations, as Norton suggests? At age nineteen Lewis would have been naturally stronger and perhaps more self-confident than the considerably younger daughter of her master and mistress. Norton emphasizes this age difference, often referring to Putnam and Abigail Williams (Betty Parris was removed from the scene by her parents in early March) as "children," "little girls," or "little children," while reserving "teenagers," "girls," "young women," or "young people" for the older adolescent members of the afflicted group. (There were also a few boys and young men among the afflicted.) To Norton, the "little girls" bore little responsibility for the witch hunt, and she offers a four-page concluding section, entitled "Interpreting the Behavior of the 'Afflicted Girls' and Assessing Responsibility for the Crisis," that remarkably never once mentions Ann Putnam Jr., while including the names of virtually every other important accuser! At stake, for Norton, here as throughout *In the Devil's Snare*, is the connection to the northern war. If Mercy Lewis can be shown to be the hidden ringleader among the afflicted, then, as with the author's attempt to discredit fortune-telling at the panic's start and her Maine-centered reasoning behind the naming of George Burroughs, then the witch hunt as a whole may be plausibly linked to the traumas resulting from frontier violence.[41]

Norton's efforts, however, again fall short. Mercy Lewis did take the lead in some instances. She seems to have single-handedly, as Norton puts it, reversed a move in the middle of May to free Mary Esty, one of the accused sisters of Rebecca Nurse. Lewis, with her teeth clamped shut, descended into nearly two days of severe and continuous fits, so frightening those around her that they thought she might die. Esty was promptly returned to jail, so that, it was believed, her specter would no longer be free to torment the teenager. Yet Ann Putnam Jr. played a similarly important role in the death of Giles Cory in mid-September. When Cory refused to go along with the legal technicality of agreeing to be tried, the magistrates decided to subject him to the punishment of placing heavy weights on his chest until he changed his mind. On the night before he was to undergo this (ultimately fatal) ordeal, Ann suffered her own severe torments. In the words of her father, who reported the incident the next day to one of the trial judges, she was attacked "by Witches . . . [t]hreatning that she should be Pressed to Death, before Giles Cory." During these afflictions, Ann was visited by the ghost of a young, male servant who had died seventeen years earlier soon after a savage beating at the hands of Cory, his master. The ghost told her, "It must be done to him as he has done to me." According to Ann's father, her vision now reminded "all people" in Salem of this forgotten incident and reconciled the community (and perhaps the magistrates) to Cory's fate. In another example, Norton made much of Lewis's leadership in declaring that the afflicted girls, including Ann Jr., had been mistaken in charging Topsfield resident Nehemiah Abbott Jr. with witchcraft, but in a different case it was Ann who persisted in successfully accusing Sarah Cloyce, another of Rebecca Nurse's sisters, of spectral attacks, even when Mercy Lewis failed to join in.[42]

Ann Jr. also identified Deliverance Hobbs when the latter was first brought in for examination prior to her confession, even though none of the other girls could or would do so. She likely instigated, Norton acknowledges, the accusations against Salisbury resident Mary Bradbury and at her trial offered crucial testimony linking Bradbury to the early death of Ann's uncle John Carr, also from Salisbury. And, Norton mentions, Ann Jr. was probably the one who shocked John Alden— and doubtless the rest of the assembly—in the middle of his examination by exclaiming, "There stands Aldin, a bold fellow with his Hat on before the Judges, he sells Powder and Shot to the Indians and French, and lies with the Indian Squaes [squaws], and has Indian Papooses." Still other examples show cases in which Mary Walcott, Mary Warren, Elizabeth Hubbard, Susannah Sheldon, Sarah Churchill, and the less-known Elizabeth Booth each took the lead in accusing particular suspects. The most persuasive conclusion to be drawn from the data found in most accounts of the witch hunt, Norton's included, is that there was no ringleader among the accusers. The core group of accusers suffered afflictions and generated charges of witchcraft over an eight-month period without benefit of formal coordination or internal hierarchy and yet with acute sensitivity to what was happening to one another.[43]

CHAPTER 6

Norton's *In the Devil's Snare*
and Racial Approaches II

As we have seen, Norton greatly exaggerated the effect of the northern war on the chronology and magnitude of accusations in the Salem witch hunt. It would be a mistake, however, to leave our examination of her argument at that. To do so would overlook the persuasiveness of her contention, once it is reduced in scope, that posttraumatic reactions to Indian violence might indeed have led a minority of accusers to join in the panic. A closer look at this part and the rest of her argument also lays bare the sympathies and moral messages that emerge from Norton's overall treatment of the Salem events. To discover these important dimensions of her book, we must return to its text.

Critics of *In the Devil's Snare* were quick to call attention to the strained connection, noted in the previous chapter, that Norton drew between Bridget Bishop's hanging on June 10, 1692, and the Wabanaki attack on Wells, Maine, the next day. These critics were correct to do so, but more significant still is to notice how the author describes the raid on Wells just before she asks her rhetorical question, "Did anyone view the attack as revenge for Goody Bishop's execution?" The vividness of her depiction of Indian cruelty in warfare points to a unique contribution of Norton's work.

The enemy assaulted both the ships and the garrison, but could take neither, despite a two-day-long battle that continued into Sunday night. Eventually, they burned the town and killed all the livestock they could find, while terming the garrison's defenders cowards for refusing to come out to fight. Cotton

Mather later wrote that in their frustration the Wabanakis "fell to Threatning and Raging, like so many Defeated Devils." They took a captive from the town "out of Gun-Shot," torturing him "in a manner very Diabolical" in the sight of the horrified people in the garrison. "They Stripped him, they Scalped him alive, and after a Castration . . . they Slit him with Knives, between his Fingers and his Toes; They made cruel Gashes in the most Fleshy parts of his body, and stuck the Gashes with Firebrands, which were afterwards found Sticking in the wounds." Thus, concluded Mather, "they Butchered One poor Englishman, with all the Fury that they would have spent upon them all."

One can readily imagine that young frontier witnesses to brutality of this sort might have been forever scarred by what they had seen and heard, resulting in displaced forms of expression later on. Just as interesting are the feelings of horror that such a description is apt to generate in modern readers. Coming on page 211 of her book, this passage is far from the first that is likely to elicit revulsion toward the way traditional Indian people waged war and, as we will see, toward certain colonial New Englanders thought to have aided them in these actions.[1]

In fact, Norton structures her study in such a manner that its emotional center of gravity lies amid the settlements on the northern frontier rather than in Salem village or even Essex County, a strategy that shapes its readers' sympathies toward the witch hunt in significant ways. Maine and New Hampshire are ever present in the narrative. A description of the terrifying attack by the Wabanakis on York, Maine, on January 25, 1692, brackets the first chapter, which covers the opening six weeks of the witch hunt up through Tituba's confession. On the first page, we read how, "About noon, in heavy snow . . . 'the Inhabitants were in their unguarded Houses, here and there scattered, Quiet and Secure,'" when "about 150 Indians, led by Madockawando, a headman of the Penobscot band of the Wabanakis, took York completely by surprise." By the time the attack was over, most of the town was burned, one hundred people had been taken captive, and close to fifty lay dead, including the community's minister, Shubael Dummer, whose body was left naked and mutilated. The chapter's last page continues this story, based on accounts from some of the York captives who had been ransomed about a month later: "That Mrs Dumer died in about 10 dayes after she was taken that 5 or 6 were kill'd in their march most children that were unable to travel & soe burthensome to them." Chapter 2 carries the narrative of the witch hunt forward from the naming of Martha Cory through Abigail Hobbs's confession, but it is broken up in the middle, when Mercy Lewis is introduced by a retrospective account of the Indian attack on Falmouth on August 11, 1676, that destroyed most of Lewis's extended family.

Chapter 3 devotes itself entirely to the history of English-Wabanaki relations, focusing especially on the two great conflicts, the one that took place in the mid-1670s and the other that began in 1688. Significantly, Norton calls these conflicts the First Indian War and the Second Indian War, eschewing their more conventional designations, King Philip's War and King William's War, because, she insists, that is how they were known to the Maine settlers. This chapter offers some of the book's most gripping pages, reflected in the chapter's title, "Pannick at the Eastward." Norton thus appropriates a term ("panic") so often applied to the Salem witch hunt itself and assigns it to the dire situation facing the English settlers in the Northeast. It is *their* panic that Norton conveys in the first instance, not the panic confronting innocent victims of mass scapegoating, such as Martha Cory or Rebecca Nurse. Like the other scholars of her generation, Norton refers to the Salem events as the "witchcraft crisis," never as the "witch hunt." Each of the book's remaining five chapters, which continue to trace the developments in the witch hunt, closes with the text of an original document from the frontier. These letters from local officials or petitions from settlers warn of imminent danger and plead with the authorities in Boston or London to do more to suppress the Indian threat. When each of the four other northern war refugees (Abigail Hobbs, Susannah Sheldon, Mercy Short, and Sarah Churchill) enters the circle of accusers, Norton repeats what she did in the case of Mercy Lewis, inserting into the events unfolding in Essex County retrospective descriptions of the ordeals these young accusers faced as children on the frontier.[2]

Given the past experiences of these young people, it is hard not to sympathize with them. Norton has no definite information about any traumatic family losses that Abigail Hobbs may have suffered, but the author writes that Susannah Sheldon was just under two when she "must have witnessed both her uncle Arthur's death agonies and her aunt's and mother's consequent grief" following a 1675 assault by the Wabanakis on the fairly isolated Maine settlement of Dunstan. The Sheldons lived nearby in the fortified town of Black Point, which was abandoned the following year. The family returned in the early 1680s and remained until 1688, when the resumption of fighting forced them to move again, this time to Salem village. Psychic wounds from the family's earlier loss may have been reopened when Susannah's oldest brother was killed in 1690 as a militia volunteer in Maine. The next year her father died of causes unrelated to the frontier, just four months before Susannah began suffering afflictions that she attributed to witchcraft at the hands of Philip English and others.[3]

Mercy Short, although she played only a small role in the Salem witch hunt, suffered a far more devastating experience as a war captive following a Wabanaki raid on Salmon Falls, New Hampshire, in March 1690. Norton offers this description:

> Her parents and three of her siblings died in the attack, while she and six or seven other brothers and sisters were carried off into Canada by their Indian captors. On that long, difficult trek through the forests in the late winter of 1690, she witnessed the torture and death of Robert Rogers, . . . one of the Salmon Falls prisoners, who tried but failed to escape his Wabanaki captors. He was stripped naked, tied to a stake, and partially burned. Then the Indians pulled the fire away from him and "Danc'd about him, and at every Turn, they did with their knives cut collops of his Flesh, from his Naked Limbs, and throw them with his Blood into his Face." . . . The Wabanakis made Rogers's death by fire and dismemberment an explicit object lesson for Mercy and other captives. After they "bound him to the Stake," they "brought the rest of the Prisoners, with their Arms tied to each other, so setting them round the Fire," . . . but they could not even shed a tear, "lest it should, upon that provocation, be next their own Turn, to be so Barbarously Sacrificed." [The internal quotations come from Cotton Mather's account, probably based on Mercy Short's own descriptions.]

Short, who was about fifteen at the time of this incident, witnessed additional atrocities dealt out to children and teenagers on the march to Canada. Ransomed eight months later, she was returned to Boston and became a servant, probably to the wealthy widow Margaret Thacher. Short's only known involvement with the witch hunt, apart from rumors that she accused her new mistress, came after encountering the suspect Sarah Good at the Boston jail and eliciting an epithet from her in response to having thrown wood shavings into Good's cell. "That Sarah Good's curse led to her being tormented by 'Invisible Furies,' is thus hardly surprising," Norton concludes with reason, after presenting Mercy Short's traumatic experience as a war captive.[4]

Sarah Churchill's case resembled more closely that of Susannah Sheldon. Churchill began her accusations in early May 1692, when she seems to have quickly shifted from initially being afflicted to becoming a confessor and then returning to the role of an afflicted accuser, much as Mary Warren, John Procter's servant, had done. Churchill recalls Warren in other ways, since she, too, was a servant who accused her master, the elderly George Jacobs Sr. (and others), of witchcraft. Jacobs would be executed along with Procter, George Burroughs, John Willard, and Martha Carrier on August 19. Norton introduces Churchill, like the other war-refugee accusers, with a look backward to her childhood experiences in

Maine. Sarah was eight years old in September 1676, when the Wabanakis attacked the community of Saco, where she was living with her parents and with the
well-to-do family of her maternal grandparents, the Bonythons, residing nearby.
About fifty people—fifteen men and thirty-five women and children—fled to
one of the garrisoned houses in the town. As Norton tells the story, "The Wabanakis
surrounded the house and, 'Creeping deckt with ffearns and boughs,' began to
shoot at any movement they saw inside. They wounded several men . . . but
otherwise made little progress in their aim of capturing the garrison." The warriors tried constructing a flaming vehicle, using the wheels of an old cart, to set
the house on fire, but the makeshift mechanism got stuck in the mud. Failing to
burn the settlers out of the house, "the Wabanakis continued to shoot at it all
night, then finally marched away the next morning, Sunday, September 19. Although everyone in the house survived, their fortuitous escape from a terrible
death" caused the Churchills and the Bonythons to move shortly thereafter to
Marblehead in Essex County.

Nothing else is known about the next sixteen years in Sarah Churchill's life.
Her mother died at some point, while her father lived on until 1710. Sarah had by
1692 moved to Salem village, where her mother's sister had married into the extended Ingersoll family and where Sarah became a servant in the household of
George Jacobs Sr. Leaving aside the question of whether the frightening 1675
Indian attack might really explain Churchill's later propensity to believe she
had fallen victim to witchcraft—neither her case nor Sheldon's is as persuasive as
Mercy Lewis's or Mercy Short's—Norton reveals her sympathies for these war-
refugee accusers when she concludes her treatment of Churchill with words that
recall Carol Karlsen's affecting description of the possessed teenager Elizabeth
Knapp. "Wartime losses," Norton writes, "had accordingly transformed the granddaughter of one of the wealthiest and most distinguished men in Maine [John
Bonython] into an unmarried maidservant in a backwater village. She had good
reason to resent her fate and to blame both the Wabanakis and inept colonial
leaders for her unenviable existence." Norton shares with Karlsen a feminist ad-
miration for the young, female accusers because they were able, if only briefly, to
turn the tables on the male officials in the colony and essentially dictate policy
for some six months during the height of the witch hunt. "As daughters and servants who occupied the lower ranks of household hierarchies," she observes,
"their normal role was to be seen and not heard, to tend to others' needs, and to
acquiesce in all tasks required of them. Yet during the crisis others tended to *them*,
and magistrates and clergymen heeded *their* words," Norton adds with emphasis.
But there is a subtle difference in the two historians' leanings, as Norton's desig-

nation of Mercy Lewis as leader among the afflicted accusers indicates. While Karlsen's account invites readers to feel for the young witchcraft accusers because they were female and seemingly trapped in servitude, Norton's book encourages sympathy for these accusers chiefly because so many were survivors.[5]

The problem with Norton's perspective is not that we should lack empathy for the war-refugee accusers, who found themselves placed as children in a hostile environment through no decisions of their own making, but rather that the author shows little recognition that these refugees' residual fears and anger, while understandable, should later express themselves in such displaced form and with such tragic consequences for a new set of innocent victims. Missing from Norton's account are any comparably affecting descriptions of what it must have felt like to be Sarah Good, George Jacobs Sr., George Burroughs, or Susannah Martin, or what tolls their executions must have taken on their surviving family members. Missing, too, is a balanced treatment of the settler families from which these accusers came, a social group that Norton paints in rather heroic colors.

Achieving such balance, significantly, would not have required holding back on the vivid depictions of Wabanaki warfare that Norton supplies. She deserves credit for providing accurate accounts of the Wabanakis' use of torture on war captives, their targeting of women and children along with men in their attacks, and their practice of desecrating the bodies of their enemy dead—all combat techniques commonly employed by native fighters of that era. Most historians of the post-1960s generation skip over the sadistic details of these military efforts to intimidate adversaries, or else they attempt to explain them away as aspects of traditional "ritual" or spirituality or yet again as retribution for atrocities committed by the Euro-Americans. In fact, fighting styles of seventeenth-century Native Americans and British colonials differed sharply in the degree of cruelty that was considered permissible. This distinction in *norms*—there were always exceptions and violations of the respective rules of war on both sides—goes a long way toward explaining why the newcomers to North America felt so ready to justify displacing the people who were already living there and why the epithets "barbarians" and "savages" fell so easily from the lips of New Englanders when they spoke about Indian people. Norton acutely conveys this clash of cultures when she describes one of the Wabanaki attacks that opened frontier hostilities in the mid-1670s, the raid on the Wakely farm outside of Falmouth. She draws on Falmouth militia lieutenant George Ingersoll's description of what he found the next day.

> The elderly Thomas Wakely and his wife were dead, "neer halfe burnt," lying "halfe in, & halfe out of the house." Their adult son had been shot and "his

head dashed in pieces"; their daughter-in-law, "bigg with Child," had been scalped; and two of their grandchildren had "their heads dashed in pieces, & laid by one another with their bellys to the ground, & an Oake plank laid upon their backs." New Englanders were well acquainted with death, but not this sort of death. . . . Ingersoll's vivid description revealed that he and his small militia contingent had found the carnage at the Wakely farmstead truly horrifying. English settlers in northern New England had never experienced the like before.

Identifying the horror and fear that English families in Maine and New Hampshire felt concerning the prospect of Native American attack is necessary to Norton's argument about the posttraumatic effects such violence could produce in survivors. It is also essential for any genuine understanding of the settlers' political outlook.[6]

Yet there was another side to this story as well, which Norton turns in a peculiar direction. Norton is far too skilled a historian to have failed to record the context of provocations coming from the English colonial venture that helped bring on armed conflicts in the Northeast. A superficial reader might almost think that she shares in the perspective of some of her scholarly predecessors, who placed the Salem witch hunt in the context of the Indian wars as a means of reducing it to a well-deserved punishment for the Puritan colony's mistreatment of its indigenous neighbors. Toward the beginning of her chapter on the two wars, Norton describes how one of the leading English fur traders and provincial officials in Maine, Richard Waldron, had made himself hated by the Wabanakis both for "sharp dealing," perhaps even cheating them in trade, and for engineering in the midst of King Philip's War two captures of Indian men, women, and children through deceit. In the larger of these two instances, somewhere between 200 and 350 Wabanakis were sent to Boston, where seven or eight fighting men were executed for violence committed against the English. Another 200, probably mostly women and children, were sold into slavery overseas. Norton includes in her account of these "reprehensible acts" a letter sent by a group of Wabanaki headmen to Boston late in the first war, blaming all the killings on Waldron's dishonesty. When in the midst of the second war, Norton relates that Waldron suffered death by torture at the hands of Wabanakis, readers may feel that justice was served.

Norton also makes mention of an act of sadistic play by some English "sailors," who seem to have purposely overturned a canoe containing the wife and young child of the Saco River band's leader, Squando, causing the child to drown. This action helped spark the Saco band's entrance into the first war. The author includes in her account as well a murderous incident of vigilantism that took place in the Essex County fishing port of Marblehead, just east of Salem town, in the summer of 1677. There, a mob of women grabbed two Indian prisoners being brought down to Massachusetts to answer for earlier attacks on English fishing vessels and the capture of fishermen off the Maine coast. As an eyewitness of the event reported, "[The women] laid violent hands upon the captives, some stoning us in the meantime, because we would protect them, others seizing them by the hair, got full possession of them, nor was there any way left by which we could rescue them. Then with stones, billets of wood, and what else they might, they made an end of these Indians. We were kept at such distance that we could not see them till they were dead, and then we found them with their heads off and gone, and their flesh in a manner pulled from their bones."[7]

But in describing these and other provocations from the English side, Norton develops a dubious dichotomy in which the "settlers" or "longtime settlers" of the Northeast remain relatively innocent, while guilt is consistently laid at the doorstep of the "authorities in Boston." She mitigates, for example, Richard Waldron's worst deed (tricking over two hundred Wabanakis into capture and eventual slavery) by emphasizing that he acted "under orders he received from Boston to capture all the Indians at his trading post." She also notes that he protected a small number of Indians and their families from this fate, while urging the Massachusetts authorities to distinguish between hostile and peaceable people among the prisoners. Not incidentally for her emerging argument about official complicity in the witch hunt, Norton adds parenthetically that the commander of the 130-man militia unit sent from Boston to help Waldron carry out this assignment was William Hathorne, younger brother of the later Salem magistrate and witchcraft examiner.

Norton's account of the Englishmen who drowned Squando's child also subtly exonerates the frontier settlers by describing the culprits as "sailors." That sounds like an apt synonym for the term "Seamen," used by Puritan minister William Hubbard in his *History of the Indian Wars in New England* (1677), the source she cites for the incident. But "sailors" implies that the guilty parties were Massachusetts men temporarily located in Maine waters, while it is more likely that they were local fishermen, perhaps from one of the offshore islands, who had a reputation for engaging in hostile and provocative acts toward neighboring Indians. Norton even supplies some mitigating, hypothetical context to the Marblehead riot, suggesting that the women who carried out the attack on the two Indian prisoners may have been "among the many refugees who had flocked into

Essex County from Maine the previous year. Under those circumstances—if they were indeed widows and bereaved mothers from the frontier—their vicious treatment of the Wabanakis exemplified their fury at the destruction of their homes and families."[8]

More broadly, Norton portrays the settlers of Maine and New Hampshire—fishermen, farmers, raisers of livestock, fur traders, and sawmill operators who resided in coastal communities—as people who had long been able to live at peace with the Wabanakis, who themselves farmed, hunted, and fished in the interior river valleys. Misguided policies coming from Boston toward native people, as Norton puts it, elicited the settlers' disapproval. "Frontier dwellers," she writes, "accurately predicted the consequences of Waldron's deceit," as they anticipated the retaliatory Indian raids on several Maine settlements in the two months that followed the incident. She also relates how Thomas Gardner, the leading fur trader at the far northern English outpost of Pemaquid, had complained to the Massachusetts governor about the preemptive policy of demanding that the Wabanakis living on the Kennebec River turn over their guns at the start of King Philip's War in southern New England. He was arrested and tried for treason, though acquitted.

Indeed, the northern settlers, in Norton's telling, strongly suspected the Massachusetts colonial officials of duplicity. These officials talked tough, the settlers believed, but meanwhile they supported wealthy metropolitan merchants (especially from Boston and Salem) who profited through trade with the Wabanakis, including the sale of guns and the purchase of contested land titles, thus adding to the Indian threat. On several occasions northeastern settlers angrily criticized the Dominion of New England regime under Edmund Andros (1686 to April 1689) and the restored Massachusetts government that followed Andros's ouster (April 1689, through 1692 and beyond) for aiding and abetting the enemy. "To residents of the frontier, of course, what mattered was not *who* [i.e., which regime] was trading arms and ammunition to the French and the Indians," Norton comments pointedly, "but simply the allegations that such trade was commonplace. For the people of Maine and New Hampshire, mercantile profits or possible diplomatic advantages paled in comparison to the threat to their families and communities posed by armed Wabanakis" (italics in original).[9]

Norton's analysis is useful in understanding how many, even most, frontier dwellers may have assessed their political position, but she errs in adopting their position as her own. In fact, English-Wabanaki relations were both more destructive and less conspiratorial than Norton claims. Settlers, too, not just Boston officials, provoked native people with reckless policies. The preemptive decision criticized by Thomas Gardner to disarm the Kennebec River band had come not from Boston but from another local fur trader, Sylvanus Davis, then living at the Kennebec settlement. Other historical accounts of seventeenth-century Maine make clear that frontier dwellers—sometimes on their own, sometimes as part of larger ventures sponsored by Massachusetts residents—were expanding their land holdings into the interior, often in violation of prior agreements made with local Wabanaki bands. And, as Norton acknowledges in a footnote, Maine residents also could be found selling guns to Indians.[10]

Meanwhile, policies originating in Boston or London that many local settlers found self-serving and confining often would have made frontier life safer for them had they been carried out. Settlers wanted things both ways: they demanded outside protection but wanted neither to pay for it nor to abide by the accompanying restrictions. Norton takes the settlers' side, for example, in giving short shrift to the complaints of the Massachusetts Council during the second war that the settlers sometimes brought Indian attacks on themselves by failing to consolidate their living quarters around garrisoned buildings and to maintain adequate vigilance, but the councilors were probably correct in these assessments. Similarly, she endorses the view of northeastern residents who characterized Governor Andros's 1688–89 expedition to northern Maine as a failure. This was the expedition that later gave rise to Ann Putnam Jr.'s charges that George Burroughs had bewitched its soldiers to death and that John Alden, a merchant sea captain who had accompanied Andros, had sold powder and shot to the Indians and slept with Indian women. Andros permitted guns to be sold to the Wabanakis after first burning their food stores, a decision intentionally designed to strike a livable balance with New England's adversaries, allowing native people to hunt for food in the winter while still projecting a strong military presence in defense of the English colonies. The policy seems to have had the desired effect, as Wabanaki raids on frontier settlements resumed only after the governor had been deposed. Andros's six-hundred-man armed expedition was thus not the failure that Maine residents believed it to be. Everything connected with Andros, in any case, became subject to negative reappraisal after he was overthrown.

The same reasoning applies to the later expedition led by William Phips, the Maine-born future governor of Massachusetts, against the French backers of the Wabanakis. That campaign during the spring of 1690 succeeded in taking the French outpost at Port Royal, Acadia, before it failed to deliver its intended coup de grace at Quebec. A parallel land campaign aimed at Montreal from New York was also stymied. There is no reason to join the settlers in deriding these endeavors as "grandiose strategies" that relegated defense of the northeastern settlements to "a distant second" in priorities, as Norton does. Nor is there cause for her to comment snidely, as the settlers may have, that when Massachusetts sent a successful militia force under the command of the seasoned King Philip's War veteran Benjamin Church to defend Falmouth in September 1689, "For once, the governor and council reacted effectively." The Massachusetts government was probably correct in focusing on the larger imperial rivalry between England and France, along with taking steps to fortify local garrisons in the Northeast. Had the 1690 Canadian campaigns fully succeeded, they might have forced the Wabanakis to pull back on their raids in New Hampshire and Maine far sooner than they did, for it would not be until French power in Canada was extinguished by the British in 1763 that Indian attacks on these northern settlements ended for good.[11]

Norton's siding with the settlers in their antagonism toward the ruling elite of Massachusetts during the wars with the Wabanakis explains the remaining part of her argument about the causes of the Salem witch hunt. If the war-refugee accusers (with Mercy Lewis in the lead) become the hidden heroes in her interpretation, those who failed adequately to defend the frontier or who allowed the Wabanakis to go on fighting become her villains, a group that includes both the magistrates in charge of the witch hunt and several of its victims. As for the magistrates, Norton asserts, with virtually no evidence to sustain her claim, that the officials who carried out the initial examinations of the accused or who later served as the trial judges—the leading ones were John Hathorne, Jonathan Corwin, and William Stoughton—"quickly became invested in believing in the reputed witches' guilt, in large part because they needed to believe that they themselves were *not* guilty of causing New England's current woes [i.e., its wartime disasters]" (italics in the original). Stoughton, she asserts, "had unaccountably failed to effect a key hostage exchange at Casco in the fall of 1688, thus bungling possibly the last chance to avert the bloodshed that followed." Hathorne and Corwin "had most likely caused the devastating losses of Fort Loyal and Falmouth" by recommending a reduction in the fort's militia defenses on May 15, 1690. Other trial judges, including Salem merchant Bartholomew Gedney and Boston merchant Samuel Sewall, "had promoted and encouraged the catastrophic [expeditionary] attempt on Quebec, perhaps as much for anticipated profits from plunder as for the colony's welfare." "If the devil was operating in their world with impunity," Norton writes in her conclusion, "then the Massachusetts leaders' lack of success in combating the Indians could be explained without reference to their own failings."[12]

But there was nothing "unaccountabl[e]" about Stoughton's role in the missed hostage exchange of September 1688. Planned hostage exchanges frequently went awry, owing to poor communications and fundamental distrust between the two parties. More to the point, Norton offers no evidence that Stoughton or anyone else regarded this lost opportunity as an important failure or critical starting point for the years of fighting that would ensue. As for Hathorne and Corwin, the two had been sent by the Massachusetts Council in late April 1690 to New Hampshire and Maine to determine what should be done next in defense of the Northeast. They were also to recommend the return to Massachusetts of militiamen who were either unable to serve any longer or who were not absolutely needed. These directions reflected another political vector in the progress of the war that Norton underplays in her account: Essex County families only reluctantly consented to have their men serve on the northern frontier, for fear both of casualties and of weakening the defense of their own towns. The people of northern Massachusetts and the settlers of the far Northeast thus did not share a concert of interests against the colony's governing elite, as Norton implies. And so, when Hathorne and Corwin made their recommendations on April 30 and May 1, the two magistrates principally advised the local settlers to stay close to their garrisons and to heighten their vigilance against any surprise attack. They also reported back to the council how minimally defended the Maine coast was north of the settlement at Wells, even after the council had sent 120 new men northward in early April. That is all that is known about Hathorne and Corwin's specific role in the events that soon followed.[13]

On May 15, a militia unit of sixty Massachusetts soldiers withdrew from Fort Loyal, leaving just the local militia to guard the garrison at Falmouth. The next day a fighting force of perhaps four to five hundred Wabanakis and seventy French soldiers attacked the town and fort. Some two hundred English people perished in the attack, a few were captured and marched to Quebec, and the town was burned to the ground. No doubt the loss stunned New England, as Norton observes. She adds in a note, "it seems that [militia leader Simon] Willard's men wanted to be relieved. The council, however, could have replaced them with other troops rather than simply withdrawing them and leaving Falmouth to be defended only by local militiamen." Fair enough, as hindsight demonstrated, although one wonders how successfully Fort Loyal could have been defended against such odds, even with sixty additional Massachusetts militiamen. But to jump from these facts to the conclusion that Hathorne and Corwin "had most likely caused the devastating losses of Fort Loyal and Falmouth, and so all of Maine north of Wells, by recommending the withdrawal of Captain Simon

Willard's militiamen" departs grossly from the evidence at hand and ignores the absence of any support for the idea that the magistrates themselves would have thought this way.

That Gedney, Sewall, and the other members of the Massachusetts Council who later became judges in the witchcraft trials supported preparations for the 1690 expedition to Quebec probably strengthened rather than weakened their position in the eyes of most New Englanders, even after this war plan later failed in meeting its objective. Such large military undertakings in that era were typically financed by a combination of public tax revenues and private investment hoping for returns in plunder. This expedition and the earlier one to capture Port Royal, however, were paid for through public funds alone, so Norton's assertion about the self-serving nature of these campaigns for the Massachusetts elite is not justi-fied. In any case, she herself concedes that the typical response in the region to the mission's failure was to attribute it, in the words of Massachusetts governor Simon Bradstreet, to the "awfull Frowne of God."[14]

In short, there is no evidence that the governing elite of Massachusetts, in-cluding the men who would soon take the lead in prosecuting those accused at Salem, regarded itself as a source of the suffering brought on by the Wabanaki attacks on the northern settlements. Far too many years of blindness to their own role in causing conflict between colonial settlers and the Indian people living around them, reinforced by their abiding belief in the all-encompassing provi-dence of God, insulated the leaders of Massachusetts from any such sense of responsibility, even if the Maine settlers slipped easily into blaming these figures for prolonging the war. As a consequence, it appears far-fetched for Norton to posit any need for these officials to deflect attention from their wartime policies, much less to turn this doubtful proposition into their motivation to embrace and abet the witch hunt.

In fact, the political leaders' own religious beliefs and past practices as guard-ians of domestic order provide ample insight into their likely motivations at Salem. All were convinced that witches operated as agents of Satan's power. Few seem to have cultivated the subtlety of belief that allowed some of the colony's leading ministers to ponder whether the Devil's store of tricks might include the spectral ability to impersonate innocent people, and even for these ministers such doubts and worries came only slowly as the witch hunt proceeded. William Stoughton, lieutenant governor of Massachusetts and chief justice of the witch-craft court, held particularly conservative ideas on the subject. All the way up through the end of the Salem events, Stoughton "expressed himself very hardly of [i.e., strongly about] the accused [servant] woman at Groton [Elizabeth Knapp, in 1671], as tho' he believed her to be a witch to this day," Thomas Brattle commented incredulously in October 1692. Most other educated New Englanders had long followed the lead of Rev. Samuel Willard, Knapp's master and minister at the time, in regarding the young woman's condition as an instance of possession, not witchcraft. Stoughton, Gedney, and Wait Winthrop, three of the Salem judges and all members of the Massachusetts Council, had probably served a few years earlier as judges in the most sensational, recent witchcraft case in Massachusetts, the 1688 conviction of Goodwife Glover, an Irish washerwoman's mother executed for bewitching the three children of a Boston family. Hathorne and Corwin, too, as Salem magistrates—the former since 1684, the latter since 1689—would have already had some experience by 1692 in examining numerous people accused of crimes. Hathorne had ordered Bridget Bishop jailed in 1687 while she was awaiting trial on a charge of theft, and both men likely had heard about an earlier accusation of witchcraft brought against her in 1680. Hathorne in particular was known for his conservative religious principles.[15]

While it is true that most Massachusetts witchcraft trials since the 1650s had resulted in acquittals or sentences short of death, it is also true that prior to 1692 there had never been such a dramatic outbreak of afflictions attributed to witchcraft. Never before had such severe physical symptoms affected so many vulnerable young people, with confessions seeming to corroborate the causes. The surprise and shock expressed by members of the Massachusetts elite in reaction to these torments attested to the genuineness and strength of their response, which could cut across usual social alignments and even sever longstanding friendships. "'Twas awfull to see how the afflicted persons were agitated," commented later trial judge Samuel Sewall when he first witnessed an examination of the accused in April. In late May, Thomas Newton, the man who would serve as the first official prosecutor in the trials, wrote of his experience at another examination that he had "beheld strange things scarce credible but to the spectators." When fellow merchant John Alden was accused of witchcraft, Norton notes, quoting from an anonymous record of Alden's examination, and he "appealed to all that ever knew him, if they ever suspected him to be such a person," Bartholomew Gedney distanced himself from his friend and former business associate. Gedney replied, "that he had known Aldin many Years, and had been at Sea with him, and always look'd upon him to be an honest Man, but now he did see cause to alter his judgment."[16]

Given the apparent demonstration of Satan's powers, the clamorous support the accusers received from the crowd, and the fear that accusations might be turned against anyone who cast doubt on the ongoing process, why is it necessary to look for a hidden political motivation to explain how the colony's governing officials assumed their natural position of leadership in the witch hunt? To do so caters to a populist desire to blame the witch hunt on an allegedly corrupt elite, when in reality New England's Puritan society, governed by probably one of the least corrupt regimes in the seventeenth-century world, was quite united, from top to bottom, behind the drive to rid its community of what it took to be the menace of witchcraft. One cannot even identify any strong correlation within the elite between subtle distinctions in religious affiliation and support for the witch hunt. Taking Boston's three Puritan churches as an index of the range in Puritan belief, one may locate the strongest support perhaps in the Mathers' Second Church, the "centrist" congregation most heavily identified with the politicized work of reforming society. Support diminished ever so slightly at the two "extremes" of the Puritan spectrum, the liberal, Enlightenment-leaning Third Church and the conservative, dissenting-minded First Church, representing the two Protestant tendencies (rationalism and sectarianism, respectively) that one hundred years later would come together to bring separation of church and state to a new nation. At the height of the Salem panic, however, the political implications of these religious distinctions remained muted, to say the least. Yet for Norton, if the governing elite can shoulder most of the blame, then the people she calls the "ordinary Essex folk" (conflating them with the northeastern settlers), can retain their innocence, simply engaging in their "gossip" about local witches, as if such storytelling remained harmless until taken up by deceitful officials.[17]

Norton further conveys the impression of innocence on the part of local communities, whether in Essex County or on the Maine frontier, in the Salem witch hunt by a curious ambiguity that pervades her treatment of the accusations against the three individuals with genuine connections to the Indian wars in the Northeast: John Flood, John Alden, and George Burroughs. In telling the stories of these men, Norton adopts formulations that withhold sympathy from these victims of the panic and that edge perilously close to justifying the charges brought against them.

A resident of the Suffolk County town of Rumney Marsh, John Flood (or, Floyd, in many accounts, including Norton's) captained a militia unit throughout the early years of King William's War. (He had also served as an officer in the earlier King Philip's War.) Due to a loss of records, all that is known about the charges of witchcraft against him is that they surfaced in late May 1692, based on complaints by "Mary Walcott[,] Abigail Williams & the rest." Perhaps nothing can be learned about any local motivations for the complaints, but without addressing that possibility Norton proceeds to describe events from Flood's military service that could explain the accusations. At the outset of her discussion, she unfairly impugns his military record by noting that his men mutinied in April 1689 at the Saco River, "deserting their post and marching toward Boston, evidently in the hope of winning redress of their grievances." She offers no further details, implying that the mutiny had to do with Flood's leadership, when in fact Massachusetts soldiers were abandoning their units all across the Northeast at that moment in the drama that touched off the successful rebellion against the unpopular Andros regime. There is even reason to believe that Flood and his men left the fighting arena together at that time.[18]

Back commanding his unit, now based in Portsmouth, New Hampshire, in May 1690, Flood, in Norton's words, "left the town [of Exeter] undefended while they [Flood and his soldiers] sallied forth to destroy some Indian cornfields. Not only did the Wabanakis attack the town in his absence, they also assaulted Floyd and his men on their return from the sortie." What justifies Norton's construction, "left the town undefended while they sallied forth," which implies a reckless, impulsive gesture? Nothing at all in the historical record, as it suggests little more than shrewdness on the part of Flood's Indian adversaries to account for their success. When Flood failed in an attempt to rally his men to keep up the fight after the Wabanakis had engaged them and inflicted significant casualties, Norton calls his action "futile persistence on the battlefield," siding with those who left the unit either during the battle or soon after.[19] A year and a half later when Flood's company arrived at York, Maine, in the aftermath of the surprise Indian raid on that town that left nearly fifty settlers dead and another one hundred captured, "once again," Norton observes, "New Englanders thought that Floyd had neglected his duty." Some angry settlers probably did hold this view, but Norton thoroughly blurs the boundary between their perspective and her own when she writes the following summary of Flood's predicament facing the charge of witchcraft in 1692: "He had effectively defended neither Exeter nor York, yet his men had nevertheless suffered terrible losses and they seemingly had no respect for his leadership. His dereliction appeared to have caused numerous deaths of fighting men and civilians. Many men and women were accused of witchcraft in 1692 for far less serious offenses than John Floyd's." "Dereliction"? "Offenses"? His actions might only be seen as "dereliction" or "offenses" in the eyes of frightened settlers, unhappy militia families, or war-refugee accusers looking for a scapegoat. Norton's ambiguous phrasing (she does not say "perceived dereliction" or place "offenses" in quotation marks) leaves the impression that Flood had really committed certain acts deserving of popular retribution.[20]

The witchcraft accusations against John Alden earn their target even less sympathy from Norton's account than that shown for John Flood. While both men shared controversial war records in the Northeast, Alden alone could claim membership in the colonial elite of Massachusetts. As such, Alden symbolizes for Norton the twin forces of evil at work ("softness" or incompetence toward the Wabanakis and corrupt elitism at home), leading the innocent people of New England astray and into the witch hunt. The son of John and Priscilla Alden, one of Plymouth colony's first families, Captain Alden was in his sixties, having achieved the reputation of a highly successful merchant sailor, when he was accused of witchcraft in May 1692. Alden maintained extensive trading interests in animal skins, timber, and other products along the North Atlantic coast. His business extended from southern Maine, where the Phillips family, his in-laws, had extensive holdings in the Saco River area, up through the lands of Acadia (also known as Nova Scotia) that kept changing hands between the English and the French. Except for the years when the two rival European powers were at war—and sometimes even during those years—trade carried on by Boston- and Salem-based merchants like Alden with the European settler communities and with the villages of native peoples (principally Wabanakis) proved valuable toward keeping the region peaceful while making profits for the businessmen involved.

Since he was trusted by all parties in the Northeast, Alden was perfectly positioned to carry out official functions for the government of Massachusetts when conflict broke out. Indeed, he made no fewer than sixteen trips, Norton tells us, from Boston to the Northeast during the period from October 1688 to April 1692, bringing militiamen or supplies to English garrisons, arranging prisoner swaps, and signing truces. More controversially, he sold guns and food on occasion to Wabanaki bands and their French backers. Alden did so first under orders from Andros in 1688–89 and then after April 1689 with the knowledge—if not the overt assent, for political reasons—of the restored colonial administration. This practice became the target of hostile rumors and criticism by militiamen in Essex County and probably some settler families in New Hampshire and Maine, who claimed that Alden was thereby committing treason.[21]

Here again, Norton blurs boundaries in her account, implying that the claims against Alden held objective truth. Her evidence comes almost exclusively from Alden's enemies, with nothing to balance her account that might shed light on his own thinking. For example, she describes some of his frontier actions as "appear[ing] less benign," or "len[ding] themselves to sinister interpretations," without clarifying to whom they appeared so or exploring alternate ways of understanding the merchant's activities. Norton relies extensively on the affidavit of a

returned militiaman, Mark Emerson, who had been held prisoner by the Wabanakis and the French, and who, she acknowledges, had reason to resent Alden for
failing to ransom him on one occasion. But the bigger problem with her use of
this evidence lies in the fact that Emerson's statement became public through
the work of a known pro-Andros figure in Boston, Samuel Ravenscroft, whose
aim, in the polemics that circulated around Boston and London in the years following the coup of April 1689, was to discredit the merchant elite tied to the restored Massachusetts government. Norton never identifies Ravenscroft, yet she
quotes from his "added information" as if it were a simple addendum to Emerson's
statement. It was Ravenscroft who made the most inflammatory charge—that
Alden carried on "Trade to assist our Enemies to Kill our Friends"—whereas
Emerson had simply described Alden's role in keeping the French and Indian
communities alive: "The Last winter & spring both French & Indians were
forced to eate their Doggs, & some of their Captives, for having noe Powder nor
shott could not kill a Fowle." With the arrival of Alden's boat, Emerson went
on, the Boston merchant "brought them all supplys, as Powder & shott, Rum,
Tobbaccoe, and Bread, with other Necessaries, or they had all perished. . . . The
Indians have a saying that Mr Alden is a good Man, & loves Indians very well for
Beaver, & hath been with them often, since the Warr to their Great Relief."

Emerson's testimony sheds light on tactics, hardly treasonous, to place the
goals of peace and prosperity above those of conflict and territorial gain, at least
in the short run. Moreover, during the time period referred to in Emerson's statement, the area of the far Northeast remained more French and Wabanaki than
English, despite the nominal victory at Port Royal by the English in May 1690.
Thus the strategy of continuing to deal with the English colonists' two adversaries
over the following year (before the French retook Port Royal) made much sense
for maintaining the shaky truce of those months.[22] The complexity of Alden's
role is lost from Norton's account when she equates Emerson's affidavit with Ravenscroft's addendum and links both statements to Ann Putnam Jr.'s outburst at
Alden's witchcraft examination, accusing him of selling ammunition to the
French and Indians and having intimate relations with Native American women.
All three assertions represented partial truths, at best. Similarly, when Norton
writes categorically that "Emerson surely told the truth" or that the Essex militiamen who once refused to sail with Alden "had been absolutely correct in their
assessment of their potential captain's current intentions and past activities [i.e.,
to trade with the French]," or, finally, that the Massachusetts government "did not
wish to consider bringing charges of trading with the enemy against John Alden
[because he was] a member of the colony's elite and a friend, fellow congregant,

and business associate of many of them," Norton obscures all ways of understanding Alden's actions except the way to which the most embittered members
of war-torn New England would have held. Yet these were the very people who
entertained charges of witchcraft against him.

In light of how knowledge of the Salem witch hunt was applied by many post–
World War II Americans to grasp the meaning of the anticommunist hysteria of
the late 1940s and 1950s, it is hard not to make an analogy between John Alden
and Alger Hiss, one of the leading targets of the later era's "red hunters." Like
Alden, Hiss was accused of treason (spying for the Russians), and again like Alden, Hiss's vulnerability in the political environment of the times stemmed from
his membership in America's elite. Yet in Norton's treatment of John Alden, we
find a witch-hunt scholar, in effect, on the side of "Hiss's" accusers. How far the
understanding of Salem has traveled from the works of Marion Starkey and Arthur
Miller! The analogy is not exact, because Hiss, most historians agree, lied about
his past Communist affiliations and probably lied in his denial of spying for the
Soviet Union, while the Salem victims went to their deaths (or escaped from jail
in Alden's case) holding to the truth. But the deeper point to make about both
sets of persecutions is to recognize how in times of fear-driven intolerance, no
room exists for subtlety in explaining the context for one's actions. As in the public outcry against Alger Hiss, Norton's book removes this same subtlety from its
presentation of John Alden's record.[23]

Neither John Flood nor John Alden lost his life in the events of 1692, but
George Burroughs did. Considering the charge that the ex-Salem minister served
as the leader of the "witches," Norton's treatment of Burroughs, which covers many
pages in her book, contributes even more than her accounts of the other two
men toward shaping the overall sentiments of her readers concerning the victims
of the witch hunt. Her approach, however, is similar. In the same way that she
handles the war records of Flood and Alden, Norton discusses Burroughs's actions in Maine with ambiguous language that obscures the boundary separating
the perspective of the war-refugee accusers from her own.

Readers learn from Norton's summary of the First and Second Indian Wars
that Burroughs was living in Falmouth when the Wabanakis attacked the town
in August 1676 and again in September 1689. On the first occasion, Mercy Lewis,
then just about three years old, lost many members of her extended family; on
the second, the now teenaged Lewis may have lost her last remaining parent.
After each raid, Lewis, Burroughs, and surviving residents (all after the first attack,
many or most after the second) evacuated the settlement. Norton writes of these
developments,

That George Burroughs had indeed spectrally allied himself to Satan and the Wabanakis might well have appeared likely to anyone who contemplated his uncanny ability to survive the attacks on Falmouth in August 1676 and September 1689, followed by his remarkably prescient decision to leave the Casco Bay region sometime in the winter of 1689–1690, mere months before both Falmouth and Black Point fell to the Wabanakis in May 1690. When nearly all the defenders of Fort Loyal were killed by the French and Indians, George Burroughs was no longer there. He had moved south to the relative safety of Wells.

Actually, Burroughs's survival and his decisions to move were neither "uncanny" nor "remarkably prescient." His actions paralleled those of numerous Falmouth settlers, although by 1692 Mercy Lewis may have come to see them in this negative light, refracted through the pain of her own losses and her resentment toward someone who had suffered far less than she. But Lewis's name never appears in the paragraph containing the sentences quoted above to remind the reader that such an interpretation of the minister's fate would have been peculiar, perhaps even pathological, and would not have simply "appeared likely to anyone." Even when Norton does link Lewis's name to the first accusation of witchcraft brought against Burroughs (by Ann Putnam Jr.), as she does two pages later, she again presents the relationship between accuser and accused not simply from Lewis's likely perspective but as if this skewed perspective contained self-evident truth. "And who more likely to initiate his accusation than Mercy Lewis," Norton writes, "a young woman who knew him well, and most of whose family had been killed in the attacks he so remarkably escaped unscathed?" By means of passages like these—incidentally, turning into a truth her previously stated hunch that it was Lewis who had put Ann Putnam Jr. up to naming the minister as a witch— Norton implies that Burroughs was a shifty, sinister figure who, perhaps through some actual contacts with the native people of Maine, knew in advance what to expect from the Indians. This implication in turn lends credibility to the related accusation that the minister had somehow undermined the efforts of the English soldiers in one of their northeastern campaigns or at least desired to do so. In truth, there is no evidence at all that Burroughs held especially conciliatory views toward the Wabanakis, and Norton includes data in her book demonstrating his participation in repelling the Indian raid at Falmouth in September 1689, and suggesting his similar response at Wells nearly two years later.[24]

Norton similarly predisposes her readers to withhold sympathy from Burroughs by conjecturing that he aligned himself with Maine's political elite, comprised chiefly, she says, of recent, moneyed arrivals from Massachusetts, rather than with the region's hard-working, "old settler" families. In this populist-tinged view, the elite also embraced those who failed in their relations with the Wabanakis, whether through coddling, reckless provocations, or incompetent leadership, while the older English residents had known how to coexist successfully with their Native American neighbors. There are multiple problems with this formulation, not the least of which is that the evidence tying Burroughs to Maine's elite stands on the shakiest of foundations.

Little is known about Burroughs's friendships or alliances in Maine and practically nothing about his earlier stint there (1674–76), except that the town of Falmouth granted him two hundred acres of adjoining land to induce him to serve as the settlement's minister. When Burroughs returned to Maine in 1683, his attachment to Falmouth quickly became more precarious. He lost most of his original holdings in the town's reorganization following its repopulation by English settlers, which apparently did not pose a problem for the minister, for he readily agreed to build a house for his family next to the church, retaining just a few acres of farmland on the town's outskirts. But the town's residents, probably for reasons of poverty, had trouble paying his salary. And so, at least as early as 1686 and probably during the year before, he began exploring the possibility of moving to the nearby community of Black Point, where that town's leading citizen, Joshua Scottow, donated ten acres for his use as the town's minister. On this land Burroughs quickly began to plant some crops. While his family appears to have remained in Falmouth, the minister seems to have tended alternately to the congregations in both communities from 1686 until the winter of 1689–90, when he left that part of Maine for the more southerly town of Wells.[25]

Norton wants her readers to believe that Burroughs sided with two of Falmouth's leaders, Edward Tyng and Sylvanus Davis, along with Black Point's Scottow, "all of whom," she states, "arrived in Maine during or after King Philip's War" and who served as local officials during the mid-1680s' royalist Andros administration. Along with being a local magistrate, Tyng was also a member of the Massachusetts Council. As representatives of the imperial governor's regime in Maine, these officials were responsible for executing its New England–wide policy of requiring existing landholders to resubmit their claims to property in the name of the king. This policy enabled the regime's officials to make money through new fees charged in the process, and it opened the door to contests over property rights that most landholders would have considered settled. Naturally, this policy was roundly hated throughout New England, although less so in Maine, where land titles had been more contested than elsewhere and many, perhaps most, property holders believed the new requirement might even provide greater security for their claims. At Falmouth, Robert Lawrence, "whose family," Norton observes, "had deep roots in the area," spearheaded the opposition to this policy, and he and Davis had previously fought in court over some of their own conflicting claims.

But where did Burroughs stand in these controversies? Norton's chief piece of evidence is the *absence* of the minister's name on a petition submitted by residents in Falmouth to the new, provisional government in Boston one month after Andros was overthrown, calling for Tyng and Davis to be replaced. Norton writes that "the conspicuous absence of the signature of George Burroughs" from the petition "implies that he took the side of those three men [Tyng, Davis, and another of their allies] in the heated dispute." More likely explanations would be that Burroughs was in Black Point when the petition was gathered or that, as minister of Falmouth's sole congregation, he chose to stay neutral in the conflict. The text of the petition provides a tiny piece of evidence that Burroughs was not personally close with Davis and that the petitioners themselves thought well of Burroughs; it complained that Davis had charged excessive rates for the new land patents and that he had refused to "'subscribe to pay to our ministear sence Sir Edmond [Andros] came.'"[26]

Norton also attempts to place Burroughs on the opposite side of the Lawrence family by citing a fragment of one of Abigail Hobbs's later examinations, conducted on May 12, 1692. On this occasion Hobbs claimed that the minister had directed her, when she was a girl in Falmouth, to bewitch Mary Lawrence (the likely daughter of Robert Lawrence and his wife Mary) to death because "he was angry with that family." Taking Hobbs's testimony practically at face value, Norton observes, "The resulting antagonisms [between Robert Lawrence on the one hand and Burroughs, Tyng, and Davis on the other] must have been fierce indeed for a girl as young as Abigail Hobbs to be aware of them." This reading seems far-fetched, since Hobbs never mentioned Burroughs at all, much less any of his relationships in Falmouth, in her initial confession, given on April 19, 1692. She probably knew little about him when their paths had crossed in Maine years before; Hobbs was between six and eleven years of age at that time. One way of fitting her May 12 testimony into Norton's general interpretation would be to assume that Hobbs learned of the purported antagonism between Burroughs and the Lawrence family during the month she spent in jail before answering the magistrates' later questions (on May 12), at which time she confessed to killing Mary Lawrence at Burroughs's instigation. Jailing the suspects and confessors together during the witch hunt enabled them to overhear and talk with one another, permitting their stories concerning the invisible world of witchcraft to converge over time. Yet even this scenario seems unlikely, since no independent evidence exists to support the notion that a hostile relationship between Burroughs and the Lawrences might have been a topic of jailhouse conversation or that such a relationship even existed.

The most plausible explanation for Hobbs's claim that she had bewitched Mary Lawrence is that she harbored a guilty conscience for unkind thoughts or mean behavior toward neighboring children at Falmouth, of whom Lawrence may have been one. Her confession on May 12 centered on harming "Boys and Girls" and included the exchange, "Q. Was you angry with them yourself? A. Yes, tho I don't know why now." Earlier in the same examination Hobbs had explained her bewitchment of Lawrence in personal terms: "Q. what provoked you, had she [Lawrence] displeased you? A. Yes by some words she spoke of mee." By the time of this confession, Hobbs had brought the name of Burroughs into everything she now related, reflecting the minister's prominence in the spectral accusations and confessions that followed Ann Putnam Jr.'s first naming of him on April 20. Hobbs's confession about killing Mary Lawrence, therefore, would seem to reveal nothing about Burroughs's actual relationship to the Lawrence family. It is even possible that the Falmouth minister kept on good terms with the family. In a brief testimony, concerning Burroughs's purported "supernatural strength," given to the witchcraft court on August 3, just before the start of the minister's trial, the militia captain Simon Willard, Rev. Samuel Willard's brother, reported an incident in which he and Burroughs had been present at the Falmouth house of Robert Lawrence. Willard recalled that "Mr Lawrance was commending Mr George Borroughs his strength: saying that we none of us could doe what he could doe: for s'd he Mr Borroughs can hold out this gun with one hand." The scene between Lawrence and Burroughs sounded quite jovial.[27]

That leaves Joshua Scottow, with whom there is at least some proof that Burroughs had a personal relationship. The aging Scottow, a wealthy Boston merchant, had begun buying land around Black Point in the 1660s, moving there in 1671—quite a bit before Norton's "dividing line" of King Philip's War. Perhaps one can go so far as to suggest, as Norton does, that Scottow served as Burroughs's patron during the mid-1680s, seeking to lure the minister from Falmouth to his own community. Yet Norton is unduly harsh in her treatment of Scottow. In a one-sided manner, she tells the story of the Wabanaki raid on Black Point and neighboring Dunstan during King Philip's War, during which the war-refugee accuser Susannah Sheldon's two uncles (Andrew and Arthur Alger) were killed. Norton places in her text one contemporary's opinion (of whether the Algers could have been rescued) impugning Scottow's conduct as the community's militia captain, but she relegates to a footnote a more forgiving account of his actions that seems just as valid. Norton is more even-handed in another controversy surrounding Scottow's military record during the same extended raid, conceding that two conflicting accounts are likely to be reconciled in Scottow's favor. Yet in the end she still appears to side with those residents, including the Sheldons, who held "the hated Scottow" responsible for many of the settlers' losses in the October 1675 attacks. Scottow was cleared of wrongdoing in three later trials before Massachusetts justices (one was William Stoughton) over his conduct; about this, Norton writes, "Captain Scottow emerged victorious from these legal battles, much to the disgust of the frontier dwellers." She leaves it at that, implying that the "high-status" Maine resident, as she calls him, pulled strings to get off easy. She never mentions Scottow's many local backers, who petitioned and testified on his behalf. Nor does she allow that some of his controversial actions as militia captain likely stemmed from his view that prudence required concentrating the community's defensive forces at his own garrisoned compound rather than spreading them too thinly among the settlers' more isolated farmsteads (like the Algers')—reflecting a broader dispute about settlement patterns that colonial officials and many Maine residents fought over for the better part of the seventeenth century. Political factionalism also entered into the contentions generated by Scottow's militia actions. During the 1670s it was not yet clear whether the province of Maine would remain under the control of Massachusetts (as some, including Scottow, favored) or whether it might be taken over by royalist authorities based in New York or London (as many of Scottow's opponents desired).[28]

George Burroughs, who resided in Falmouth from mid-1674 until mid-1676, played no part in any of these earlier Black Point disputes, and he may have been unacquainted with Scottow during the time of King Philip's War. Norton is surely on strong grounds to argue that families like the Sheldons, who returned to Black Point, as did Scottow, in the early 1680s and had their own reasons to dislike the former militia captain, might well have been predisposed to distrust Burroughs later in that decade when the minister arrived in the community under Scottow's sponsorship. It is equally reasonable to explain Susannah Sheldon's later participation in the Salem witch hunt, including her own accusations of witchcraft against Burroughs, as a partial response to her family's tragic history in Maine seventeen years earlier. But Norton goes beyond making this point about the possible motivations of an accuser. Her excessively negative portrayal of Scottow suggests that Burroughs somehow deserved the later witchcraft charges brought against him because he allowed himself to make common cause with an elite figure who was out of touch with the common people of the region. In truth, however, no firm line separated the "common people" of Maine from the region's elite (the Massachusetts governor during the witch hunt, William Phips, had been born in 1651 to a middling settler family on Maine's remote Kennebec River), its farmers from its traders (most were both), its older residents from its newer ones (many of the latter married into families of the former), and those leaders (always few in number) who engaged the Wabanakis with intelligence and restraint from those who did not. In any case, whatever bond Burroughs may have developed with Scottow, which seems likely to have resulted from their shared, conservative religious inclinations more than anything else, cannot have been very strong. When Scottow came to Boston during the witch hunt, he took time to pray on John Alden's behalf but did nothing to indicate support for the jailed minister he had once tried to bring to Black Point.[29]

Through ambiguities in language and subtle biases in her account, Norton thus allows herself to slip into the shoes of the war-refugee accusers. "Other afflicted accusers [besides Mercy Lewis], especially those with ties to the frontier," she writes in her conclusion, "then started to identify as witches men like John Alden and John Floyd, whose actions during the war suggested that they had joined Burroughs in an alliance with malevolent spirits"—as if the meaning of Alden's and Flood's "actions during the war" were self-evident. Four sentences later, still referring to Flood, Alden, and Burroughs, Norton observes, "Residents of the northeastern frontier believed their region's leaders had betrayed them, and they readily conflated visible traitors with invisible attackers." "Visible traitors" in whose eyes? She never adds, only in their own. And then, in one of the strangest paragraphs in the book, Norton takes one further step in the direction of uniting her two arguments—that the witch hunt grew out of the scars of the Indian wars and out of the failure of the Massachusetts elite to defend the frontier—by imagining that at the height of their power, the accusers served, if only temporarily, as a positive substitute for the colony's failed leadership.

> In other ways as well the accusers took on "official" duties in the invisible world. They solved crimes, disclosing who had committed murders both recently and in years past. They spied on the enemy, warning their fellow settlers of the militant witch conspiracy by reporting the musters of the spectral militias and by describing the nature of the meetings the conspirators attended. (If only the vulnerable outposts of Salmon Falls and Falmouth had received similar timely warnings of Wabanaki assaults!) By their adamant refusal to join the witches and their revelations about the conspiracy, they were defending

New England against some of the most powerful enemies the region had ever faced. In fact, one might contend that the youthful female "magistrates" were defending New England far more effectively than had their male counterparts in the visible world during the previous few years.[30]

What a revealing fantasy! The accusers depicted as just slightly misguided heroes defending New England. In fact, the accusers and their many frightened supporters sent innocent people to their deaths for "murders" that were purely imagined. Far from pointing toward an effective defense of the frontier, the accusers and their supporters, both powerful and lowly, perpetuated the blind belief that toughness alone was all that was needed to pacify northern New England. And beneath it all lay the violation of truth, though it was involuntary, in the accusers' and their supporters' resort to scapegoating. No study of the Salem witch hunt is likely to surpass In the Devil's Snare for its insight into the minds of those Salem accusers who had lived through the trauma of Indian attacks on the northern frontier. But like the mythical Icarus, who caught fire when he flew too close to the sun, Norton has merged her own perspective with that of the war-refugee accusers, producing an account that exaggerates the importance of the Indian wars in the witch hunt, turns victimizers into victims, and obscures the deepest sources of tragedy in the episode.

Conclusion

From 1969 up through the present, the leading scholarly books addressing the subject of colonial American witch hunting have expressed a subtle hostility or at best an indifference toward the victims of its largest, single incidence. Either by locating the causes of the Salem witch hunt in underlying economic changes or political developments that exonerated the common people of New England and sometimes their leaders, or by subsuming the Salem events into broader treatments of patterns in seventeenth-century witchcraft accusation, the four principal studies of these persecutions turned their backs on the more than twenty innocent individuals who lost their lives in the panic. In place of such figures as Rebecca Nurse, Mary Esty, and John Procter, who claimed center stage in post–World War II accounts of Salem for their heroism in standing up to popular and official intolerance, the post-1960s generation of scholars took for its heroes, even if slightly tainted by their actions, the Puritan farmers of Salem village, the ordinary residents of Essex County and New England's northeastern frontier, and the young afflicted women (including the slave Tituba, who may be seen as both victim and victimizer) who did most of the accusing. By any measure, this interpretive shift—in effect, switching sides in the sentiments expressed toward the episode—constitutes a remarkable turn of events.

The five authors whose books have formed the centerpiece of this study—Paul Boyer, Stephen Nissenbaum, John Demos, Carol Karlsen, and Mary Beth Norton—all came of age amid the political turbulence of the 1960s and early 1970s. All but Karlsen completed their graduate studies between the years 1966 and 1970, with Karlsen following suit in 1980. It has not been my intention to learn anything about the political lives of these historians but rather to focus solely on their books about American witch hunting. Yet the common denominator of altered sympathies toward the Salem participants displayed in these works, when compared to the sensitivities shown toward the same participants by the previous generation of Salem scholars, suggests a common, political source. That source would appear to be the radicalism of the New Left, which was just beginning to leave its imprint on universities during the mid-1960s and the residual influence of which grew over the succeeding decades, as ex-activists and sympathizers found professional homes within academic departments.[1]

Central to the development of the New Left was its angry dismissal of mid-twentieth-century American liberalism. To New Leftists, the achievements of the civil rights movement only masked a deeper vein of racial prejudice in the white American population; the government's war policy in Vietnam revealed its stated goal of anticommunism to be an excuse for the real aim of imperialist domination; the Democrats' celebrated War on Poverty accomplished little to equalize the distribution of wealth, leaving the powerful corporations firmly in control; and the gains made by women to enter jobs and other spheres of life previously monopolized by men appeared superficial next to the enduring structures of patriarchy. In this climate of opinion, such fundamental liberal values as individual rights, due process, the rational pursuit of truth, tolerance for differing views, and respect for the rule of law came to be regarded disdainfully either as unimportant or, worse, as hypocritical covers for the exercise of power and privilege by the few.[2] It is no wonder, therefore, that the very aspects of the Salem witch hunt—its rampant disregard for truth and its sacrifice of the individual to the group—that seemed crucial to identify for an earlier intellectual generation, one that had witnessed the horrifying experience of tyrannies based on mass ideological movements, should recede from view for a new scholarly generation that wished to ally itself with "the people" and found itself once again attracted to utopian ideologies. In the case of Salem, "the people" were conceived variously as the farmers, the local community, female servants, frontier settlers, or even—for some historians, though not for Norton—the neighboring Wabanakis. Meanwhile, the hyper-strenuous religious ideology of Puritanism received relatively uncritical treatment. It is not that the post-1960s scholars deliberately set out to tell a new story about Salem. Like all qualified historians, they proceeded where they thought the evidence and arguments of primary and secondary sources took them. But like players with a Ouija board, their fingers could not help but move the planchette toward the letters that spelled out their convictions.[3]

Of course, intellectuals of the previous generation like Marion Starkey, Arthur Miller, and Perry Miller were equally products of their times. Moreover, it is possible to see the shift in sympathies concerning the events of 1692 as part of a larger oscillation between two longstanding positions in the historiography of witch hunting, one that has arisen among students of European and American outbreaks. These two positions have been traditionally identified by their affiliation with either the outlook of Enlightenment rationalism or of the romanticism that followed in its wake. The so-called rationalists have recognized that the tendency to find personal scapegoats ("witches") for a wide variety of typically domestic misfortunes has been a near constant in human history, but, they argued, it was only when a powerful set of "irrational" religious ideas, linking the contrasting absolutes of good versus evil, or God versus the Devil, to the challenges of everyday life took hold, as it did in Europe during the late Medieval and early modern periods, that witch hunting on a massive scale resulted. Religious extremism, in other words, transformed a phenomenon of small-scale victimization into a lethal drive to purify an entire community or society of its internal "enemies." The so-called romantics, by contrast, have emphasized just how normal, how ordinary, witch hunting in all its manifestations really was. Accusations of witchcraft, in this view, arose from the bottom of society, amid the tensions and conflicts of face-to-face village relationships, as people struggled to make sense out of the manifest unfairness of life, using for their tools the near-universal belief in a world of spirits and supernatural forces. Anthropologists of the early and middle twentieth century gave a forceful boost to the romantic position, based on their functionalist studies of witchcraft in traditional, non-European societies, but the American historian George Lyman Kittredge captured the strength of this position best with reference to Salem, when he wrote in 1929: "The Salem outbreak was not due to Puritanism; it is not assignable to any peculiar temper on the part of our New England ancestors; it is no sign of exceptional bigotry or abnormal superstition. Our forefathers believed in witchcraft, not because they were Puritans, not because they were Colonials, not because they were New Englanders,—but because they were men of their time. They shared the feelings and beliefs of the best hearts and wisest heads of the seventeenth century. What more can be asked of them?"[4]

It was precisely to counter this view of the "ordinariness" of the Salem witch hunt that Starkey, armed with insights derived from living through the 1930s and 1940s, returned to the "rationalist" position with her powerful invocation of the sheer terror induced at Salem. Similarly, it was probably with Kittredge in mind that Perry Miller commented impatiently, "Sober historians, trying to restore the true setting, slide into the accents of apology and gloss over a crime." In this way, absolutist religious ideology and communal viciousness reentered the post–World War II understanding of the witch hunt, an interpretative shift that the New Left scholars have sought to reverse through their own romantic appeals to the everyday virtues of New England's common people.[5] Karlsen's study almost offered an exception to this generalization, since her work did focus on the victims of seventeenth-century witchcraft accusations and included a substantial, critical discussion of Puritanism's role in these persecutions. Moreover, Karlsen helpfully included the little-studied Hartford, Connecticut, witchcraft panic of 1662, which likely claimed four lives amid fourteen indictments, along with Salem in her examination of the general seventeenth-century phenomenon, allowing readers to recognize that the potential for a full-fledged panic to erupt always lurked within Puritan New England. The Salem witch hunt, in other words, was not nearly as peculiar as many historians wished to regard it. Yet in the end, *The Devil in the Shape of a Woman* only interested itself in the victims of witchcraft accusation insofar as they were women, not because they were victims of an irrational burst of scapegoating. Similarly, the book implicated Puritanism not for the particular ways that its impossibly high expectations of piety contributed to scapegoating (by generating an often intolerable level of self-doubt) but only for representing an expression of a larger faith, Christianity, whose central creation myth blamed women for the misfortunes of humanity. In these ways Karlsen, too, returned to the romantic interpretation that saw witch hunting as "ordinary"—the ordinary oppression of women by men—and in which heroes could be found not among the suspects who refused to confess to crimes they had never committed but rather among the most extravagant female accusers, whose other-worldly rebellion against patriarchal control took the form of naming innocent victims.[6]

Is it necessary to arrive at a middle ground between these two overarching views of colonial American witch hunting, the post–World War II liberal consensus and the New Left revision? My study has aimed at answering no to this question, for if ever there were an instance of "throwing the baby out with the bathwater," the post-1960s historians of witchcraft have produced one. Let us return to their works one last time and ask, what has been gained and what has been lost in the scholarly products of the last forty-five years?

There are some definite gains. We now know that Samuel Parris's slave, Tituba, did not place herself at the head of any occult circle in Salem village. Whatever fortune-telling or other small-scale, illicit activities may have touched off the girls' psychosomatic responses, Tituba probably had nothing special to do with them. We now know quite a bit more about the social relationships, especially concerning the Putnam clan, that comprised what Starkey memorably called Salem's "web of spite" that underlay many of the witchcraft accusations. Even more important may be the genealogical investigations—really, just begun—that have uncovered links among a great many of the suspects all across Essex County, for witchcraft was believed to run through family ties. We now have a more vivid understanding of how the posttraumatic scars left by Indian attacks on settler families of the Maine frontier may have fed into the Salem panic through a terrible leap of imagination on the part of several refugee accusers. And most significant of all the new contributions of the past four and a half decades, a substratum of misogyny (or perhaps patriarchalism is the more precise term), shared by women and men, beneath the general charge of witchcraft has now been so clearly identified that it is hard to foresee any future account of Salem failing to take note of it.

But more has been lost than gained. The emotional intensity of an entire community thrown into a fearful frenzy by the threat of hidden danger, captured so brilliantly in Starkey's history, is absent from all of the leading post-1960s accounts except Norton's, in which it is greatly downplayed. Some of the New Left studies—Norton's especially—sharply criticize the colony's magistrates and judges for the miscarriage of justice at Salem, just as the accounts after World War II did. These officials deserve criticism for departing significantly from most of their own era's standards of legal restraint. But the judicial examinations of witchcraft suspects acquired their inexorable logic, in which no responses were acceptable except those that confirmed the findings of guilt, chiefly from the presence of an aroused community of spectators, sometimes three hundred strong, who watched these cross-questionings and participated right along with the afflicted accusers. The eclipse of the term "witch hunt," which had appeared frequently in Starkey's account, in favor of the more neutral and static "witchcraft" or "witch trials" in the post-1960s histories registered this loss of interest in the social psychology of the Salem events. And with this loss went the earlier generation's instinct that figuring out the precise trigger of a social panic held less importance than laying bare the dynamics of the process once it had taken hold. For Salem, did that trigger lie in the local challenge to Reverend Parris's authority, or the resumption of Indian warfare, or the political fluctuations following the colonial charter's revocation, or the continuing scourge of smallpox, or the presence of neighboring Quakers, or some combination of these? Or, as seems more likely, was it simply the shock to a profoundly religious community of witnessing the horrifying physical symptoms of apparent diabolism in vulnerable young people?[7]

Scapegoating arises when an adequate explanation for extreme misfortune cannot be found and especially when individuals fear that they may harbor some portion of a stigmatized characteristic that might be blamed for the misfortune.[8] Under these circumstances the impulse to draw a sharp line between self and other and to externalize the blame often becomes irresistible. We know little more today about how this human propensity worked at Salem than we did after reading Starkey's 1949 account, because the New Left historians were not interested in the problem of scapegoating, at least not when the victims were white, Anglo-American women and men of mostly middling and sometimes upper ranks. Thus, readers of the recent histories of colonial witch hunting come away knowing far less about Salem's victims than the previous generation's readers did. They may not even know their names. There is something sad about this, considering that the first memorial to Rebecca Nurse was constructed by some of her descendants in 1885. In fact, whatever new details have emerged about the lives of the innocent victims of the Salem witch hunt mostly paint unflattering portraits of them. Even leaving aside Norton's excessively negative evaluations of the actions of George Burroughs, John Flood, and John Alden, the main new pieces of information about the Salem victims have centered on the abrasive personalities of some of the women (Sarah Good, Bridget Bishop, Martha Cory, and Wilmot Redd) and the possibility that several of the men (John Procter, John Willard, George Jacobs Sr., and Burroughs) had been either verbally or physically abusive toward their wives or female servants. Now missing are the longer descriptions, found in Starkey's account, of the ways these same individuals—thoroughly average in their everyday weaknesses and strengths—somehow found the courage at the height of the witch hunt to defy both the crowd and colonial officials and to do so with dignity, eloquence, and tenacity to the end. By denouncing the judicial flaws of the proceedings against them and by proclaiming their innocence, the Salem victims, it may not be too much to suspect, contributed in some important way to the evolution of modern legal defenses for anyone accused of a crime.[9]

Puritanism, without a doubt, had much to do with the remarkable courage shown by these women and men, just as it had so much to do with generating the witch hunt in the first place. Puritanism's contribution is the other aspect of the story (after the social psychology of the panic) to receive weaker treatment in the New Left scholarship than in the works that preceded it. Perhaps it should not be surprising that the social historians—as distinct from religious historians—who grabbed the field of witchcraft studies in the years following the 1960s should have underplayed the role of religion in the Salem witch hunt, notwithstanding an attempt to analyze Samuel Parris's sermons in Boyer and Nissenbaum's book and valuable explications of Puritan ideas about witchcraft in Norton's and Karlsen's. Each of the four leading New Left works about colonial witchcraft, a subject that would seem to belong to the realm of religion, may be seen as subtly reductionist in its own way, explaining witch hunting in terms of economics, social solidarity (or ambivalence toward mothers), gender oppression, and racial politics, respectively. But the scholars of Puritanism itself, who have produced some of the finest historical works of the past generation, deserve some of the blame for this shortcoming by abandoning what should have been their own field of study. One senses they did so because witch hunting would have marred the picture of a seventeenth-century Calvinism that had amazingly—but deservedly—come back into academic favor after two centuries of disrepute, owing first to the rise of Protestant Neo-Orthodoxy during the 1930s and 1940s and then to the evangelical resurgence of the 1960s through 1980s.

Two historians of Puritanism, Stephen Foster and David D. Hall, did address the subject but still found ways to avoid criticizing the Reformed Protestant tradition head on. Foster leaned toward the conservative or sectarian side of the Reformed spectrum (he calls these sorts of Puritans variously the "insurgents," "resisters," "stalwarts," and "anticlericals") whose "purism" (Hall's term) kept these members of congregations like Boston's First Church at arm's length from the political thrust of ministers like the Mathers, who believed that God enjoined them to dirty their hands in the secular world, whether by supporting the magistrates in upholding the colony's moral standards or by negotiating with the king's ministers to preserve as much independence as possible for Massachusetts. The abominations of the witchcraft court, whose members had been selected by Increase Mather's handpicked governor, could therefore be laid, in Foster's view, at the doorstep of an overly politicized clergy that had momentarily forsaken its true Puritan calling. Hall was more even-handed and more persuasive in recognizing the ways in which the prosecution of "witches" at Salem brought unity and even, briefly, millennial hopes to all shades of Puritan opinion. Like Foster, Hall had no trouble labeling the court's persecution of its innocent victims as a "witch hunt," but his appreciation for the determined piety of New England's lay Puritans—their strenuous efforts to live according to the precepts of love and to guard themselves against the incursions of sin—left him assimilating all witch hunting, Salem's included, into a ritualized cycle of repentance and renewal that made the sacrifice of these innocents not so very different from Puritan fast days, public confessions, or even simple prayer.[10]

Dominant as the New Left interpretations of the Salem witch hunt have been over the past forty-five years, there are signs that a new era of scholarship on the subject has already dawned, one that is likely to return to many of the preoccupations of the post–World War II intellectuals and build on the moral foundation constructed by them. In the 2008 special issue of the *William and Mary Quarterly* devoted to a retrospective assessment of *Salem Possessed* (noted in my introduction), two articles and one shorter commentary by new historians rejected Boyer and Nissenbaum's economic argument in favor of approaches that placed the religious inclinations of the Salem villagers at the center of their explanations for the witch hunt. Two of the most recent books on the panic, Benjamin C. Ray's *Satan and Salem: The Witch-Hunt Crisis of 1692* and Stacy Schiff's *The Witches: Salem 1692*, both published in 2015, have likewise retold the Salem story as a tragedy for which Puritanism in one way or another could be held chiefly responsible. Ray's book, restating the author's argument from one of the articles in the 2008 *William and Mary Quarterly* roundtable, emphasizes the zealousness of Salem village minister Samuel Parris and the leading members of his congregation as the prime factor in the witch hunt, even if it falls short of offering a broad examination of Puritanism and its propensity for intolerance. By contrast, *The Witches*, with its narrative format and journalistic penchant for describing the more sensational aspects of witch belief, may be regarded as an updated version of Starkey's *Devil in Massachusetts*, which in similar fashion brought Puritanism, adolescent psychology, local grudges, and political vulnerability—roughly in that order—together to produce Salem's deadly amalgam. Their weaknesses aside, both accounts succeed in bringing religion back to the analytical center of their explanations for the witch hunt.[11]

Even as early as the 1990s, changes pointing in a new ethical direction could be spotted in the large number of books on Salem that greeted the three-hundredth anniversary of the witch hunt. Most of these books aimed at a popular audience, drawing synthetically on the published work of previous scholars, along with some of the primary sources. While all accepted to varying degrees the village factional argument set forth in *Salem Possessed*, all also adopted the narrative approach first utilized so effectively by Starkey to convey the mounting sense of fear that drove the witch hunt forward. Starkey's own formulations featured prominently again among the references in some of these narratives, after they had virtually disappeared from citations in the first three New Left accounts. The victims of the witch hunt also began to come back into sympathetic focus at this time. Larry Gragg's *Salem Witch Crisis* (1992) included a chapter that described the horrifying conditions of Essex County's jails, where over 150 suspects were kept, often in chains, for periods of many months. Bernard Rosenthal's *Salem Story* (1993), the most original and provocative of these books, both because it tacked back and forth between the Salem events and their later literary representations and because it resurrected—unconvincingly, in my view—the eighteenth-century argument that fraud mostly motivated the afflicted girls and women, structured four of its ten chapters directly around the execution dates of the Salem victims, entitling them, "June 10, 1692," "July 19, 1692," "August 19, 1692," and "September 22, 1692." Peter Charles Hoffer's companion volumes, *The Devil's Disciples* (1996) and *The Salem Witch Trials* (1997), devoted their most valuable pages to discussions of the legal aspects of the defendants' treatment, and Hoffer dedicated the second of his books to little Dorothy Good, Sarah Good's four-year old daughter, who was locked up for months along with her mother and the rest of the witchcraft suspects.[12]

The renewed emphasis on the victims of the Salem panic—together with the return of the term "witch hunt" to describe what had happened in 1692—continued into the new century, fed not only by the tercentenary's popular focus on Salem's victims but also by the spate of attention given to a series of child-abuse scares at daycare centers and schools in the 1980s and 1990s. As these cases moved into the legal arena, the testimony of young children figured prominently in the prosecution of adult defendants, and an element of social panic, sometimes connected to the belief that the suspects were followers of a Satanic religion, swirled around the charges. Parallels to the events of 1692 were noted in the press, as the popular understanding of the Salem witch hunt, based on the post–World War II era's consensus, reasserted itself, and this interpretation in turn influenced many of the more recent scholars of seventeenth-century witch hunting. At least six historians, whose works came out between 1993 and 2008, mentioned the child abuse scares or similar events in their writings. Where Salem's New Left historians had been attracted to the afflicted accusers precisely because of their marginal social or psychological characteristics—regarding them sympathetically as rebels— historians of witch hunting who read about young children testifying in the abuse cases and saw the potential for their words to be manipulated vindictively by adults were now prepared in their scholarly work to empathize instead with the suspects named in the fantasies of the witchcraft accusers. And yet, the return of the Salem victims in all these accounts could serve little more than a sentimental purpose, so long as the causal relationships presented to explain the witch hunt remained tied to the prevailing theories of economic factionalism, simple gender conflict, or frontier warfare. Logically, these explanations set their readers up for sympathizing with the perpetrators of the witch hunt (anti-capitalist farmers, female servants, and Indian war refugees), not its victims. By downplaying the more important contributions of Puritanism and communal scapegoating to witch hunting, most of these recent accounts continued to miss the opportunity to link the Salem panic's deepest underlying causes to its terrifying results.[13]

One of the historians influenced by the child-abuse allegations was John Demos, who revisited the subject of seventeenth-century witchcraft in his book *The Enemy Within: 2,000 Years of Witch Hunting in the Western World* (2008). As the subtitle of his book, featuring the term, "Witch Hunting," suggests, Demos's overt sympathies had evolved since the publication of his 1982 study, *Entertaining Satan*, whose subtitle, "Witchcraft and the Culture of Early New England," gave no hint of either the victimization involved in witchcraft accusations or the social panics so often connected to them. In his new book, however, no reader could miss the author's strong condemnation of the "injustice" of such "scapegoating" against "innocent targets." Significantly, Demos this time devoted almost one-third of the book to Salem, the very subject he had omitted from his 1982 account. He began with a highly sympathetic portrait of Rebecca Nurse, describing her helplessness at her examination, as she was "cornered" and "persecuted" by Magistrate Hathorne's questioning. After presenting a substantial summary of the Salem events, along with a peculiarly ironic run-through of every conceivable argument that had been offered to explain them—out of them all, Demos endorsed Boyer and Nissenbaum's and Norton's—he concluded with a nuanced portrait of Cotton Mather's role in the panic, adding, "history will not easily forgive him." What a far cry from this same historian's dismissal in 1970 of the "unending effort to judge the participants—and above all, to affix blame" in the historiography of the witch hunt.[14]

In truth, it was always impossible *not* to affix blame.[15] The New Left historians did so in their own way: Boyer and Nissenbaum by imagining the deviously successful "Porters" as agents of a creeping mercantile capitalism that upended the hardworking Putnams and their neighbors, Norton by positing Massachusetts officials looking for a way to divert attention from early setbacks in the colony's war with the Wabanakis, and Demos (in 1982) and Karlsen by shifting the focus away from Salem toward witchcraft accusations in general, where responsibility could be lodged either with an interplay of the local community and the deviant personalities of the accused, or simply with men. There is nothing wrong with the fact that these histories contained implicit and sometimes explicit moral judgments. Historical writing in the last analysis is a form of moral discourse, enabling us to use our best understanding of the human past to adjust our moral compasses in the present. It fails not when it takes a stand but when it overtly allows its ethical positions to override long-established canons of objectivity (temporarily suspending judgment, acknowledging conflicting evidence, and entertaining multiple points of view, to name a few) by which we all inch forward toward a greater grasp of the truth. None of the works examined here fails that test; indeed, all represent superior products of scholarly effort. But often it is precisely the limited or distasteful moral implications of historical arguments that direct attention back to the explanations themselves and invite closer scrutiny of their hidden biases. That is what this study has aimed to accomplish for the New Left era in Salem scholarship. One hopes this era will now be superseded by a period in which new works will rise to dominance, influenced again by the liberal, universalistic values that fell out of favor during the time of 1960s-inspired radicalism.[16]

Appendix 1
DATA POINTS ON BOYER AND NISSENBAUM'S
"GEOGRAPHY OF WITCHCRAFT" MAP

Inferred correspondences between data points on Boyer and
Nissenbaum's "Geography of Witchcraft" map and names shown on
Boyer and Nissenbaum's lists of accusers, accused witches, and
defenders, based on residences displayed on
Charles W. Upham's 1867 map

Numbers are the ones shown on Upham's map, with three letters (*c*, *p*, *i*) used by Boyer
and Nissenbaum to replace three symbols on Upham's map. The list proceeds in imaginary rows superimposed on Boyer and Nissenbaum's map, moving from north to south,
and within each row moving from west to east. The reader can lay a ruler horizontally
across the page of the map and move downward to recreate the order shown here.

Accusers on western side
18. Lydia Nichols (at residence of John Nichols Jr.)
16. Phillip and Margaret Knight
10. Thomas and Elizabeth Bailey
8. Benjamin, Bray, and Henry Wilkins Sr. (at single residence shown for Bray Wilkins)
25. Peter Prescott
8. John, Rebecca, and Samuel Wilkins (at single residence shown for Bray Wilkins)
23. Edward Putnam
28. Henry Kenny
26. Ezekiel Cheever
24. Thomas Jr. and Ann Putnam Sr.
37. John Putnam Jr.
44. Hannah Small
58. William Allen
57. John Buxton
59. Samuel Braybrook
c. Johnathan Walcott
p. Samuel Parris (at parsonage)
   [unidentified "A" symbol]
i. Nathaniel Ingersoll
76. Joseph Holton Sr.
90. Benjamin Hutchinson
   [unidentified "A" symbol]

115. John Walcott
114. Samuel Abbey
119. Thomas Flint
120. Joseph Flint

Accusers on eastern side

70. Thomas Raiment
51. Joseph Whipple

Accused witches on western side

1.   John Willard
72. Sarah Buckley and Mary Withridge
128. Giles and Martha Cory

Accused witches on eastern side

35. Daniel Andrew
42. George Jr. and Rebecca Jacobs
43. Sarah Cloyce
40. Sarah Osborne
69. Edward and Sarah Bishop
68. Bridget Bishop
p.   Tituba and John Indian (at Parris parsonage)
79. Mary Black (at Nathaniel Putnam residence)
95. Rebecca Nurse
139. John, Elizabeth, Benjamin, Sarah, and William Proctor

Defenders (of accused witches) on western side

8.   Thomas Wilkins (at single residence shown for Bray Wilkins)
57. Elizabeth Buxton
73. Joseph Holton Jr.
91. Job Jr. and Esther Swinnerton
138. Robert Moulton

Defenders (of accused witches) on eastern side

34. Benjamin and Sarah Putnam
35. Sarah Andrew
32. Joseph Putnam
36. Sarah Leach (closest listed defender to "D" symbol)
41. Jonathan Putnam
43. Peter Cloyce
46. John Sr. and Rebecca Putnam
48. Daniel and Hepzibah Rea
66. Joshua and Sarah Rea
77. Joseph Sr. and Lydia Hutchinson

80. Israel and Elizabeth Porter
75. John Holton
76. Sarah Holton (at residence of Joseph Holton Sr.)
98. Rebecca Preston
97. John and Mary Tarbell
93. Samuel Nurse and Sarah Nurse (residence of latter unclear)
123. Walter and Margaret Phillips
132. Nathaniel Felton Sr.

Sources: Boyer and Nissenbaum's map, *Salem Possessed*, 34; "List of Accused Witches Who Lived in or around Salem Village," S-VW, 375; "List of All Persons Accused of Witchcraft in 1692," S-VW, 376–378; "Selected List of Accusers and Persons against Whom They Testified," S-VW, 379–380; "List of Defenders Connected with Salem Village," S-VW, 381–382; "Map of Salem Village, 1692," Charles W. Upham, *Salem Witchcraft*, 1: insert in frontispiece, with numbered index to map, xix–xxi. Boyer and Nissenbaum reproduced Upham's map and index in S-VW (394–397), but I found it easier to use a photocopy of the original. Where discrepancies exist in spellings of names, I have used those appearing in Boyer and Nissenbaum's lists of accusers, accused witches, and defenders, rather than those found in Upham's index (or in the later *Records*).

Appendix 2
Chronological List of Accused Suspects
in Salem Witch Hunt

Used to construct figure 7: accused suspects in Salem witch hunt,
arranged chronologically by date (shown in fourth column) of
first formal legal action, showing suspect's town of origin
and type of initial surviving legal document

Abbreviations: W=arrest warrant, C=complaint, D=deposition, T=testimony,
E=examination, S=statement, O=other legal document.

Good	Sarah	Salem Village	2/29/1692	W
Osburn	Sarah	Salem Village	2/29/1692	W
Tituba		Salem Village	2/29/1692	W
Cory	Martha	Salem Village	3/19/1692	W
Good	Dorothy	Salem Village	3/23/1692	W
Nurse	Rebecca	Salem Village	3/23/1692	W
Clinton	Rachel	Ipswich	3/29/1692	W
Cloyse	Sarah	Salem Village	4/04/1692	C
Procter	Elizabeth	Salem Farms	4/04/1692	C
Procter	John	Salem Farms	4/11/1692	D
Bishop	Bridget	Salem Town	4/18/1692	W
Cory	Giles	Salem Farms	4/18/1692	W
Hobbs	Abigail	Topsfield	4/18/1692	W
Warren	Mary	Salem Farms	4/18/1692	W
Abbott	Nehemiah Jr.	Topsfield	4/21/1692	W
Bishop	Edward Jr.	Salem Village	4/21/1692	W
Bishop	Sarah	Salem Village	4/21/1692	W
Black	Mary	Salem Village	4/21/1692	W
English	Mary	Salem Town	4/21/1692	W
Esty	Mary	Topsfield	4/21/1692	W
Hobbs	Deliverance	Topsfield	4/21/1692	W
Hobbs	William	Topsfield	4/21/1692	W
Wilds	Sarah	Topsfield	4/21/1692	W
Burroughs	George	Wells, Maine	4/30/1692	C
Dustin	Lydia	Reading	4/30/1692	C
English	Phillip	Salem Town	4/30/1692	C

Hoar	Dorcas	Beverly	4/30/1692	C
Martin	Susannah	Amesbury	4/30/1692	C
Morey	Sarah	Beverly	4/30/1692	C
Carter	Bethia Jr.	Woburn	5/08/1692	W
Carter	Bethia Sr.	Woburn	5/08/1692	W
Dustin	Sarah	Reading	5/08/1692	W
Sears	Ann	Woburn	5/08/1692	W
Churchill	Sarah	Salem Village	5/10/1692	T
Jacobs	George Sr.	Salem Town	5/10/1692	W
Jacobs	Margaret	Salem Town	5/10/1692	W
Jacobs	George Jr.	Salem Village	5/10/1692	T
Jacobs	Rebecca	Salem Village	5/10/1692	T
Willard	John	Salem Village	5/10/1692	W
Parker	Alice	Salem Town	5/12/1692	W
Pudeator	Ann	Salem Town	5/12/1692	W
Soames	Abigail	Salem Town	5/13/1692	W
Andrew	Daniel	Salem Village	5/14/1692	W
Buckley	Sarah	Salem Village	5/14/1692	W
Colson	Elizabeth	Reading	5/14/1692	W
Farrar	Thomas Sr.	Lynn	5/14/1692	W
Hart	Elizabeth	Lynn	5/14/1692	W
Whittredge	Mary	Salem Village	5/14/1692	W
Toothaker	Roger	Billerica or Salem Town	5/18/1692	W
Bassett	Sarah	Lynn	5/21/1692	C
Procter	Sarah	Salem Farms	5/21/1692	C
Roots	Susannah	Beverly	5/21/1692	C
Cary	Elizabeth	Charlestown	5/23/1692	O
De Rich	Mary	Salem Village	5/23/1692	C
Pease	Sarah	Salem Town	5/23/1692	C
Procter	Benjamin	Salem Farms	5/23/1692	W
Bradbury	Mary	Salisbury	5/26/1692	S
Fosdick	Elizabeth	Malden or Charlestown	5/26/1692	S
Redd	Wilmot	Marblehead	5/26/1692	S
Rice	Sarah	Reading	5/26/1692	S
Abbott	Arthur	Topsfield	5/28/1692	C
Alden	John	Boston	5/28/1692	C
Carrier	Martha	Andover	5/28/1692	C
Flood	John	Rumney Marsh	5/28/1692	C
How	Elizabeth	Ipswich	5/28/1692	C
Procter	William	Salem Farms	5/28/1692	C
Toothaker	Mary	Billerica	5/28/1692	C
Toothaker	Margaret	Billerica	5/28/1692	C
Paine	Elizabeth	Malden	5/30/1692	C

Ireson	Mary	Lynn	6/04/1692	C
Tookey	Job	Beverly	6/04/1692	T
Dolliver	Ann	Salem Town	6/06/1692	W
Candy		Salem Town	7/01/1692	C
Hawkes	Margaret	Salem Town	7/01/1692	C
Foster	Ann	Andover	7/15/1692	E
Lacey	Mary Sr.	Andover	7/19/1692	C
Lacey	Mary Jr.	Andover	7/19/1692	C
Carrier	Andrew	Andover	7/21/1692	W
Carrier	Richard	Andover	7/21/1692	W
Emerson	Martha	Haverhill	7/22/1692	W
Bridges	Mary Sr.	Andover	7/28/1692	W
Bromage	Hannah	Haverhill	7/28/1692	W
Green	Mary	Haverhill	7/28/1692	W
Post	Mary	Rowley	8/02/1692	W
Clark	Mary	Haverhill	8/03/1692	C
Scott	Margaret	Rowley	8/04/1692	D
Carrier	Thomas Jr.	Andover	8/10/1692	E
Carrier	Sarah	Andover	8/10/1692	E
Johnson	Elizabeth Jr.	Andover	8/10/1692	E
Faulkner	Abigail Sr.	Andover	8/11/1692	E
Eames	Daniel	Boxford	8/13/1692	E
Hutchins	Frances	Haverhill	8/18/1692	W
Wilford	Ruth	Haverhill	8/18/1692	W
Eames	Rebecca	Boxford	8/19/1692	E
Barker	Mary	Andover	8/25/1692	W
Barker	William Sr.	Andover	8/25/1692	W
Bridges	Mary Jr.	Andover	8/25/1692	E
Bridges	Sarah	Andover	8/25/1692	E
Howard	John	Rowley	8/25/1692	C
Jackson	John Sr.	Rowley	8/25/1692	C
Jackson	John Jr.	Rowley	8/25/1692	C
Marston	Mary	Andover	8/25/1692	W
Post	Hannah	Boxford	8/25/1692	E
Post	Susannah	Andover	8/25/1692	E
Johnson	Abigail	Andover	8/29/1692	W
Johnson	Elizabeth Sr.	Andover	8/29/1692	W
Barker	William Jr.	Andover	9/01/1692	E
Hawkes	Sarah	Andover	9/01/1692	E
Johnson	Stephen	Andover	9/01/1692	E
Wardwell	Samuel	Andover	9/01/1692	E
Wardwell	Sarah	Andover	9/01/1692	E
Wardwell	Mercy	Andover	9/01/1692	E

Parker	Mary	Andover	9/02/1692	E
Dicer	Elizabeth	Boston or Gloucester	9/03/1692	W
Prince	Margaret	Gloucester	9/03/1692	W
Colson	Mary	Reading	9/05/1692	E
Emons	Joseph	Manchester	9/05/1692	C
Frost	Nicholas	Piscataqua, New Hampshire	9/05/1692	C
Lilly	Jane	Reading	9/05/1692	E
Taylor	Mary	Reading	9/05/1692	E
Johnson	Rebecca Sr.	Andover	9/07/1692	E
Salter	Henry	Andover	9/07/1692	E
Barker	Abigail	Andover	9/08/1692	O
Dane	Deliverance	Andover	9/08/1692	E
Osgood	Mary	Andover	9/08/1692	E
Carroll	Hannah	Salem Town	9/10/1692	W
Cole	Sarah (Davis)	Salem Town	9/10/1692	W
Penny	Joan	Gloucester	9/13/1692	C
Draper	Joseph	Andover	9/16/1692	E
Faulkner	Dorothy	Andover	9/16/1692	E
Faulkner	Abigail Jr.	Andover	9/16/1692	E
Tyler	Johannah	Andover	9/16/1692	E
Tyler	Martha	Andover	9/16/1692	E
Wilson	Sarah Jr.	Andover	9/16/1692	E
Cole	Sarah (Aslebee)	Lynn	10/01/1692	C
Dike	Rebecca	Gloucester	11/05/1692	W
Elwell	Esther	Gloucester	11/05/1692	W
Row	Abigail	Gloucester	11/05/1692	W

Source: "Records of the Salem Witch-Hunt" (chronological list of titles of the 977 documents in the collection), in *Records*, pp. 101–124. (*Records* uses "Salem Farms" to denote a subdivision of Salem town, located just south of the Salem village line.) My procedure was to search for the first appearance of any suspect's name in the document titles and then to read the corresponding document. This procedure resulted in identifying the 138 suspects included here and in figure 7. In his "General Introduction," Rosenthal speaks of "about 150" as the number most scholars settle on for the number of accused (p. 23). I omitted the names "Mrs. White," "Faith Black," and "Goodwife (Elizabeth?) Jackson," due to insufficient identification or uncertainty as to legal action.

A longer list of 156 names has been compiled by Margo Burns, based on a more thorough knowledge of the documents in the *Records* collection, including internal references to names not appearing in document titles. This list has been reprinted as appendix 1 in Baker, *Storm of Witchcraft*, 287–292. Of the eighteen names in the Burns group not included in my list, one (Martha Sparks) predates the Salem witch hunt, and three (John Busse, Thomas Hardy, and Elizabeth Jackson) show no evidence of a formal complaint or arrest. The other fourteen suspects (Rebecca Johnson Jr., Rachel Slue, Joseph Procter, Phoebe Day, Mehitable Downing, Edward Farrington, Eunice Frye, Sara Parker, Mary Rowe, John Sawdy, Hannah

Tyler, Mary Tyler, Rachel [or perhaps Sarah] Vincent, and Sara Wilson Sr.) do show evidence of having been formally accused and usually jailed in the witch hunt, but no firm date can be established for these actions, so it would be impossible to add them to my weekly graph. A majority, however, came from Andover and appear to have been named during the month of September.

Notes

Abbreviations

Burr   George Lincoln Burr, ed. *Narratives of the Witchcraft Cases, 1648–1706.* New York: Charles Scribner's Sons, 1914.

Records   Bernard Rosenthal et al., eds. *Records of the Salem Witch-Hunt.* New York: Cambridge University Press, 2009.

RFQCE   George Francis Dow, ed. *Records and Files of the Quarterly Courts of Essex County, Massachusetts.* 9 vols. Salem, MA: Essex Institute, 1911–1975. http://salem.lib.virginia.edu/Essex/index.html.

S-VW   Paul Boyer and Stephen Nissenbaum, eds. *Salem-Village Witchcraft: A Documentary Record of Local Conflict in Colonial New England.* Belmont, CA: Wadsworth, 1972.

SWP   Paul Boyer and Stephen Nissenbaum, eds., *The Salem Witchcraft Papers: Verbatim Transcripts of the Legal Documents of the Salem Witchcraft Outbreak of 1692.* 3 vols. New York: Da Capo, 1977.

Introduction

1. For the numbers jailed and dying in prison, see Richard B. Trask, *"The Devil Hath Been Raised": A Documentary History of the Salem Village Witchcraft Outbreak of March 1692* (1997), ix; for the number of confessors naming other suspects, see Mary Beth Norton, *In the Devil's Snare: The Salem Witchcraft Crisis of 1692* (2002), 323–324. Margo Burns counts fifty-five confessors, though not all may have named additional suspects ("'Other Ways of Undue Force and Fright': The Coercion of False Confessions by the Salem Magistrates" [2012], 24). On problems in defining and counting the number of accused suspects, see Burns and Bernard Rosenthal, "Examination of the Records of the Salem Witch Trials" (2008), 408–409. A useful summary of the numbers involved also appears in Rosenthal, "General Introduction," in *Records*, p. 23. A chronological list of the accused may be found in appendix 2 of the present study.

Technically, the witchcraft trials did not end with the last sitting in September of the special court of oyer and terminer (literally, "to hear and to determine"; often referred to as the witchcraft court in histories of the witch hunt). The newly appointed superior court of judicature, the highest court in the colony, took over in January 1693 and, using much stricter rules, dispensed with the remaining cases over the next five months. All but three suspects were either acquitted or released without indictment, and the three who were convicted quickly received pardons from the governor (*In the Devil's Snare*, 290–293).

2. Shapiro, "The Lesson of Salem" (1992), 64–67. The tercentenary committee chose Arthur Miller to unveil the monument in 1991 and Holocaust survivor Elie Wiesel to dedicate it in 1992 (Rosenthal, *Salem Story: Reading the Witch Trials* [1993], 208). Miller acknowledged his debt to Starkey for *The Crucible* in his autobiography, *Timebends: A Life* (1987), 330. I discuss the relationship between Miller's play and Starkey's study more fully in chapter 1.

3. One review essay noted that twenty important books on the subject, not counting documentary collections, had come out from 1969 to 2003 (John M. Murrin, "The Infernal Conspiracy of Indians and Grandmothers" [2003], 485–494). Many valuable scholarly articles also appeared during the same period, and new books and articles have continued to be written in the years since 2003.

4. The textbooks consulted were Robert A. Divine, T. H. Breen, George M. Fredrickson, R. Hal Williams, and Randy Roberts, *America, Past and Present*, brief 3rd ed., vol. 1 (New York: HarperCollins, 1994); John M. Murrin et al., *Liberty, Equality, Power: A History of the American People*, vol. 1 (Fort Worth, TX: Harcourt Brace, 1996); Mary Beth Norton et al., *A People and a Nation*, 6th ed., vol. 1 (Boston: Houghton Mifflin, 2001); George B. Tindall and David E. Shi, *America: A Narrative History*, 6th ed., vol. 1 (New York: W. W. Norton, 2004); James Henretta, David Brody, and Lynn Dumenil, *America: A Concise History*, 3rd ed., vol. 1 (Boston: Bedford/St. Martin's, 2006); Mark C. Carnes and John A. Garraty, *The American Nation: A History of the United States*, 12th ed., primary source ed. (New York: Pearson Longman, 2006); Robert A. Divine et al., *The American Story*, 3rd ed. (New York: Pearson Longman, 2007); Alan Brinkley, *The Unfinished Nation: A Concise History of the American People*, 6th ed. (New York: McGraw-Hill, 2010); Eric Foner, *Give Me Liberty! An American History*, 3 ed., vol. 1 (New York: Norton, 2011); John M. Murrin et al., *Liberty, Equality, Power*, 6th ed. (Boston: Wadsworth, 2012); Carol Berkin, Christopher Miller, Robert Cherny, and James Gormly, *Making America: A History of the United States*, 6th ed. (Boston: Wadsworth, 2012); Michael Schaller et al., *American Horizons: U.S. History in a Global Context* (New York: Oxford University Press, 2013); and James Oakes et al., *Of the People: A History of the United States*, 3rd ed., vol. 1 (New York: Oxford University Press, 2017). In a class by itself is Howard Zinn's *A People's History of the United States, 1492–Present*, rev. and updated ed. (New York: Harper Perennial, 1995), which ignores the Salem witch hunt entirely.

In a separate examination of thirteen major United States history textbooks published between 2004 and 2007, Benjamin C. Ray found that Boyer and Nissenbaum's *Salem Possessed* particularly dominated explanations for the unprecedented sweep of the witch hunt ("'The Salem Witch Mania': Recent Scholarship and American History Textbooks" [2010], 53–55). In the years following 2007, however, it appears to me that Norton's *In the Devil's Snare* has replaced *Salem Possessed* in this capacity. Of the five textbooks on my list dated 2011 or later, four (all but Oakes) give prominence of place to Norton's perspective. Most nontextbook secondary works on Salem and related subjects that have appeared since 2002 have also allowed Norton's arguments to dominate their explanations for the magnitude of the witch hunt, as I describe in chapter 5, note 14.

The textbooks' treatments of the Salem witch hunt stand somewhere between the dominant scholarly approaches that I focus on in this book and the event's popular understanding, which has also endured up through the present. The textbooks loosely adopt many of the arguments of the post-1960s era of scholarship for their explanations of the witch hunt, yet these same textbooks still wish to appear sympathetic to the victims of the panic, particularly its female victims. As I point out in my conclusion, this is an intellectually unstable combination, since the explanations themselves engender sympathy for the witch hunt's perpetrators. More fully in line with the leading Salem monographs of the past four and a half decades, however, the modern textbook treatments have dropped the post–World War II generation's focus on the heroic actions of the accused.

5. "Forum: Salem Repossessed." The journal's fifth respondent, Sarah Rivett, is not principally a witchcraft scholar. I take note of her commentary on *Salem Possessed* and her later book on the epistemology of Puritan religious beliefs, which contains a chapter on the treatment of spectral evidence in witchcraft cases, in the conclusion, note 11. I discuss in chapter 2 the two substantive critiques of *Salem Possessed* that appeared in the 2008 forum. The third article in the forum was more narrowly technical in focus. Watson, "Salem's Dark Hour" (1992), 117–131; Shapiro, "Lessons of Salem." Reviews of Norton's book appeared in the *Boston Globe, Los Angeles Times, Christian Science Monitor, Newsweek, Christian Century,* and *Atlantic Monthly.*

6. In focusing on the four leading books of the post-1960s generation, I have no intention of slighting the contributions made by many other fine historians of Salem and colonial witchcraft, whose works have also added to the knowledge of this field over the past five decades. A list of these historians includes in rough chronological order: David Levin, Kai T. Erikson, Sanford J. Fox, Larzer Ziff, Robert Middlekauff, Chadwick Hansen, Roger Thompson, David Thomas Konig, David L. Greene, Ann Kibbey, Richard Slotkin, Richard Weisman, Stephen Foster, David D. Hall, James E. Kences, Richard P. Gildrie, Christine L. Heyrman, David C. Brown, Jon Butler, Larry Gragg, Lyle Koehler, Daniel G. Payne, Wendel D. Craker, Jane Kamensky, Enders A. Robinson, Richard Godbeer, Richard B. Trask, Bernard Rosenthal, James F. Cooper Jr., Kenneth P. Minkema, David Harley, Cedric B. Cowing, Peter Charles Hoffer, Amanda Porterfield, Louis J. Kern, Frances Hill, John McWilliams, Bryan F. Le Beau, Elaine G. Breslaw, Elizabeth Reis, Emerson W. Baker, John G. Reid, John M. Murrin, Richard Francis, Marilynne K. Roach, Margo Burns, Richard Latner, Benjamin C. Ray, Gretchen Adams, Sarah Rivett, Alison Games, and Stacy Schiff.

I refer to the works of all these historians at various points in this book, mostly within the notes but sometimes within the text, when their works have played a part in influencing the main lines of argument in Salem scholarship. My first aim, however, has been to explain the powerful influence of the four leading, post-1960s Salem books in terms of their preeminent ability to articulate ideas common to their academic peers and readers—in essence, to express the academic *zeitgeist*, or "spirit of the age," in relation to their subject. Nevertheless, as I take note in my conclusion, the insights and sympathies of some of the lesser known Salem scholars, especially those who have brought renewed attention to the religious aspects of the story, point toward the welcome possibility of a new interpretative era that may supersede the current one.

7. I am grateful to my colleague Richard S. Taylor for suggesting the image at the close of the paragraph.

CHAPTER 1: Starkey's *Devil in Massachusetts* and the
Post–World War II Consensus

1. Starkey, *Devil in Massachusetts*, 14–15.

2. Ibid., 46, 216, 269. Starkey drew out the contemporary lessons of Salem again at the conclusion of her book, writing in the final paragraph:

> Late in the nineteenth century, when it was much the fashion to memorialize the witchcraft delusion, honest men discussed it with wondering pity as something wholly gone from the world and no longer quite comprehensible. But such condescension is not for the twentieth century. Heaven forgive us, "demoniac possession" is with us still, even if the label is different, and mass mania, and bloodshed on a scale that the judges of old Salem would find incredible. Our age too is beset by ideological "heresies" in almost the medieval sense, and our scientists have taken over the office of Michael Wigglesworth [author of the apocalyptic Puritan text, *Day of Doom*] in forcing on us the contemplation of Doomsday. (269–270)

For Starkey's birth date, see *Boston Globe*, February 19, 1993, 68.

3. Starkey, *Devil in Massachusetts*, 64–68, 72–75. The names of individuals involved in the Salem witch hunt went by various spellings in the original documents, resulting in variations to be found in the works of later historians. In constructing my account, I relied on the versions found in the widely employed anthology *SWP* (1977). However, I have checked these usages against the still more authoritative *Records* (2009) and adopted spellings from the latter source in cases of discrepancy.

4. The delay in holding the first trial may have reflected the reluctance of acting governor Simon Bradstreet to go along with the witch hunt. Massachusetts had been operating under a provisional government since the overthrow of Gov. Edmund Andros in April 1689, an outgrowth of the Glorious Revolution in England. When the newly appointed governor, William Phips, arrived in mid-May 1692, he quickly appointed the special court of oyer and terminer to begin the trials of the jailed suspects. Bernard Rosenthal credits Charles W. Upham, the leading nineteenth-century historian of the Salem witch hunt, for this observation (*Salem Story*, 30, 225n44). Late in the witch hunt (in mid-September), largely in response to criticisms from suspects who had refused to confess and from some outside observers, confessors did begin to be tried. Before the special witchcraft court was disbanded, it appears that six confessed "witches" were tried and convicted or convicted based on their guilty pleas: Abigail Hobbs, Ann Foster, Mary Lacey Sr., Rebecca Eames, Abigail Faulkner Sr., and Samuel Wardwell. Wardwell recanted his confession before his trial, but the decision had already been made to try him based on his confession. Wardwell alone of this group was executed. For slightly differing accounts of these actions, see Norton, *In the Devil's Snare*, 274–276, and Baker, *Storm of Witchcraft*, 37, 190–191. For more on ways that the legal proceedings at Salem departed from previous norms in witchcraft prosecutions, see chapter 2, note 6.

5. Starkey, *Devil in Massachusetts*, chap. 6 (Rebecca Nurse); chap. 7 and 190–194 (John Procter); chap. 9 and 193–198 (George Burroughs); 111–114, 203–204 (Mary Esty); and 84, 189 (on the "true Puritan spirit"). The role of Cotton Mather at George Burroughs's hanging has been questioned by some later historians. For more on this issue, see chapter 2, note 5.

6. Starkey sets forth her psychological approach in *Devil in Massachusetts*, 17, 23–26, 32, 34, esp. 45–47. Her annotated bibliography characterizes Freud's *Selected Papers on Hysteria and Other Psychoneuroses* as "my authority in describing the probable origin of hysteria among the afflicted girls" (301). The long history of the medical diagnosis "hysteria," named by the ancient Greeks to indicate disorders caused by the faulty position of the uterus (*hystera*), is traced in Mark S. Micale, *Hysterical Men: The Hidden History of Male Nervous Illness* (2008). Micale explains that while Freud and other turn-of-the-century psychologists did not regard hysteria as limited to females, the continued use of the diagnostic term, its presumed etiology in sexual development, and patriarchal cultural norms all conspired to maintain its association with women. Carroll Smith-Rosenberg also emphasizes the association of the diagnostic term with women along with its pejorative implications in "The Hysterical Woman: Sex Roles and Role Conflict in 19th-Century America" (1972), 652–678, esp. 652, 677–678. For Starkey's slurs, see *The Devil in Massachusetts*, 141, 13, 14, 167, 94. Chadwick Hansen is one later historian who thought Starkey emphasized fraud over hysteria, but the confusion did not stem, as Hansen suggests, from Starkey's insufficiently clinical definition of hysteria but rather from her anger at the accusers spilling over into misogynist epithets long associated with the diagnosis itself. Hansen provides a more clinical discussion of hysteria in the behavior of the accusers than Starkey does, but their explanations remain essentially the same. See Hansen, *Witchcraft at Salem*, ix, xiv, chaps. 2–4. Ann Kibbey also mistakenly characterized Starkey's assessment of the afflicted females as frauds ("Mutations of the Supernatural: Witchcraft, Remarkable Providences, and the Power of Puritan Men" [1982], 126n2).

Starkey's poorly disguised anger toward the afflicted girls (with the resulting confusion over whether she regarded their behavior as fraudulent) may have been influenced by Lillian Hellman's powerful 1934 play, *The Children's Hour*, depicting the lethal results of a false rumor purposely spread by a child about her teachers at a private girls' school. There is a possible allusion to that play in Starkey's account of Mercy Lewis, one of the afflicted adolescents at Salem, whom Starkey described as "a sly piece, the kind of child who listens at door jambs" (*Devil in Massachusetts*, 127), an image that fits with one of the early scenes that unfolds in Hellman's play. *The Crucible*, too, would later be compared with *The Children's Hour* (Bigsby, *Arthur Miller*, 450–451). In this era, attitudes toward children were considerably less sentimental than those that developed in the later twentieth century. For an overview of these contrasting attitudes, see Mintz, *Huck's Raft*, chaps. 14, 16.

7. The quotation is from H. Erik Midelfort, *History of Madness*, 31. I am indebted to Margaret Chowning's discussion of an epidemic, likely of psychosomatic origins, that broke out in an eighteenth-century Mexican nunnery for pointing me toward Midelfort's observation (Chowning, *Rebellious Nuns*, 105–118.) The leading Enlightenment historian of Salem was Thomas Hutchinson, the colonial governor of Massachusetts in the years leading up to the American Revolution. Hutchinson, a great-grandson of the banished Puritan heretic Anne Hutchinson, seems to have misunderstood the authenticity of the afflictions of the Salem accusers in much the same way that he underestimated the depth of the grievances held by the Revolutionary-era Bostonians who mercilessly harassed him, even if he was correct about identifying the mob psychology operative in both social settings. Thomas Hutchinson's interpretation of the witch hunt

appeared in his *History of the Colony and Province of Massachusetts-Bay*, 2:9–47. On Hutchinson's role in the years before the American Revolution, see Bailyn, *Ordeal of Thomas Hutchinson*. Within the post-1960s scholarship on Salem, Bernard Rosenthal's *Salem Story* (1993) carries forward Hutchinson's argument that the accusers' afflictions were chiefly fraudulent. Rosenthal has continued to argue along the same lines in his "General Introduction," to *Records*, pp. 26–32 (esp. through his expressed skepticism toward any psychological explanation for the accusers' afflictions) and pp. 34–37 (in his emphasis on how Massachusetts officials specifically ignored prior English concerns about "counterfeit" charges in witchcraft proceedings).

8. I discuss the persuasive documentary evidence for fortune-telling as the likely initial cause of the girls' afflictions in chapter 5. Starkey's description of the details connected to the fortune-telling activity, however, has turned out to be inaccurate. Here she drew on the influential work of Charles W. Upham, imagining Samuel Parris's slave, Tituba, to have led a "young people's circle" (the title of her second chapter) in occult practices out of the living quarters of the Parris home. Chadwick Hansen first questioned the evidentiary basis for this assertion ("Metamorphosis of Tituba," 3–12), and Bernard Rosenthal has since made clear that no evidence in the primary sources exists for any such organized activity or for Tituba's role in the fortune-telling that went on in the community ("Tituba's Story," 190–203). Starkey herself attributed this portion of her account to "tradition" (*Devil in Massachusetts*, 272), unlike the rest of her study, which was well rooted in the surviving documents of the period. I describe Tituba's place in the recent historiography of the Salem witch hunt in chapter 5.

The idea that guilt and fear within a highly religious environment could produce physical symptoms attributable to witchcraft comes up in a number of secondary sources. In addition to Starkey's and Hansen's treatments, referenced in note 6 above, see Ogden, "Binding Spells: Curse Tablets and Voodoo Dolls in the Greek and Roman Worlds" (1999), 82–85. For a longer discussion of the phenomenon, see Levack, *The Devil Within: Possession and Exorcism in the Christian West* (2013), esp. vii–x, 133–138, 206–214. Starkey's phrase "web of spite" appears in *Devil in Massachusetts*, 152.

9. In addition to the false attribution of Tituba as the head of a fortune-telling circle, Starkey carried forward a few other mistakes from earlier sources. She misidentified Bridget Bishop, the first accused suspect to be brought to trial and the first to be hanged, as a bawdy tavern keeper who lived just outside Salem village. In reality, Bishop was a resident of Salem town and not a tavern keeper at all, although she had run afoul of the town authorities on various charges of domestic fighting, witchcraft, and theft from as early as 1670. In this case the error stemmed from confusion by some of the original Salem participants concerning two different women, Sarah Bishop and Bridget Bishop, both married to men named Edward Bishop and both accused in the witch hunt. Rosenthal credits David L. Greene with unearthing this error in 1981 and adds more about the real and the presumed Bridget Bishop in *Salem Story*, 71–85.

Starkey also misdated the vision that seventeen-year-old Wenham resident Mary Herrick had of the ghost of executed "witch" Mary Esty, shifting it forward a month from November to October, a mistake that again stemmed from an ambiguity in one of the primary sources. The vision was significant, Starkey asserts, not only because it proclaimed Mary Esty's innocence in a convincing way to a population by then increasingly skeptical of the witchcraft trials but also because it proved influential in changing the mind of Rev. John Hale, a supporter of the trials up until that point, by outlandishly identifying his wife as a spectral associate of Esty. Starkey portrays this event as one of several that led leaders in the colony to halt the trial proceedings. Even if proper dating of Mary Herrick's vision removes this incident from one of the many factors causing the shutting down of the special witch-hunting court, which occurred on October 29, I am unpersuaded by an argument advanced by Bernard Rosenthal that this mistake helps undermine the general notion, subscribed to by Starkey and most others, that the naming of prominent people as witches (perhaps ending with Mrs. Hale) contributed ultimately toward the colony's frightened elite taking action against the witch hunt. While it is true, as Rosenthal maintains, that prominent people had on occasion already been named (with some arrested and others ignored) without slowing the witch hunt, the cumulative effect of such accusations seems to have added to the growing doubts among the colony's leaders about the prosecutions. Boston minister Increase Mather conceded as much when he wrote in early October, "And the Devils have of late accused some eminent persons. It is an awful thing which the Lord has done to convince some among us of their error" (*Cases of Conscience*, 121). On this issue, see *Salem Story*, 178–179. Chadwick Hansen also clarifies the more limited effect that Mary Herrick's vision was likely to have had on Reverend Hale and the ending of the witch hunt in his introduction to Calef, *More Wonders of the Invisible World* [1700], facsimile reproduction (1972), x.

10. Morgan, review of *Devil in Massachusetts*, 616–617. Morgan exaggerated the legal irregularities in the Salem trials, given their era. The witchcraft trials were not cynically staged, as were the Communist show trials. Still, the general analogy was apt. See chapter 2, note 6, for more on the legal departures at Salem.

In *The Specter of Salem: Remembering the Witch Trials in Nineteenth-Century America* (2008), Gretchen A. Adams inexplicably refers to Starkey's book as a work of "historical fiction" (153). It is not that at all but a serious historical monograph based on careful research in the primary and secondary sources available at the time of her writing. Starkey does on rare occasion embellish her account with imaginative descriptions of the village or the personal characteristics of some of its residents, but she tells the reader when she is doing this (see *Devil in Massachusetts*, 18, and the notes on 271–291).

11. Huxley, *Devils of Loudun*; the quotation appears on 122–123. Unlike most intellectuals of the postwar period, Huxley was not a committed rationalist. As his epilogue also reveals, he held out hope for mystical experiences that would be based on human innocence and love, what he termed "upward self-transcendence." See Marion L. Starkey, *The Devil in Massachusetts: A Modern Inquiry into the Salem Witch Trials*, with an introduction by Aldous Huxley (Alexandria, VA: Time-Life Books, 1963); the quotation appears on xxi. (This is the sole reference to the 1963 Time-Life edition of Starkey's book in my study. This edition also changed "Enquiry" from the book's original title to "Inquiry.")

12. On these aspects of the political environment in postwar America, see Patterson, *Grand Expectations*, esp. chaps. 4, 5, 7; Kloppenberg, *Virtues of Liberalism*, chap. 8. In another connection between Starkey and postwar liberal thinkers, historian and ex–New Dealer Arthur Schlesinger Jr., author of the influential liberal manifesto, *The Vital Center* (1949), offered advice to Starkey at the final manuscript stage of her work (*Devil in Massachusetts*, 10).

13. Arthur Miller, "Journey to 'The Crucible,'" X3. Miller left his home in Connecticut for Salem on April 2, 1952, and returned on April 10 (Bigsby, *Arthur Miller*, 415, 423, 426). In his autobiography, Miller wrote that while he had first learned about Salem in his college American history class, it was only when a copy of Marion Starkey's book, "as though it had been ordained . . . fell into my hands, [that] the bizarre story came back as I had recalled it, but this time in remarkably well-organized detail" (*Timebends*, 330). He added, "In fact, there was little new I could learn from the court record, but I wanted to study the actual words of the interrogations, a gnarled way of speaking, to my ear" (336). Bigsby notes that Miller had begun work on his play before going to Salem, and he quotes a 2002 interview with the playwright in which Miller acknowledged that he went to Salem "so that I could especially study the language" (*Arthur Miller*, 423).

14. Arthur Miller, *Crucible*, 1–154; Miller, "Introduction to *Collected Plays*" [1957], in *Crucible*, 165; Miller, "Brewed in *The Crucible*" [1958], in *Crucible*, 171–172. In *Timebends*, Miller said of Procter, "I suppose I had been searching a long time for a tragic hero, and now I had him; the Salem story was not going to be abandoned. The longer I worked the more certain I felt that as improbable as it might seem, there were moments when an individual conscience was all that could keep a world from falling" (342).

15. Miller claimed to have hit upon the sexual triangle for the centerpiece of his play from his research in the primary sources, but the specifics of his claim changed over time. In 1957 he wrote, "I doubt I should ever have tempted agony by actually writing a play on the subject [of the witch hunt] had I not come upon a single fact. It was that Abigail Williams, the prime mover of the Salem hysteria, so far as the hysterical children were concerned, had a short time earlier been the house servant of the Procters and now was crying out Elizabeth Procter as a witch; but more—it was clear from the record that with entirely uncharacteristic fastidiousness she was refusing to include John Procter, Elizabeth's husband, in her accusations despite the urgings of the prosecutors. Why? I searched the records of the trials in the courthouse at Salem but in no other instance could I find such a . . . clear attempt to differentiate between a wife's culpability and a husband's" (*Crucible*, 164). Yet, as Gerald Weales points out in a note to this text (ibid., 164n2), the examination records clearly showed Abigail Williams (and she was not the only one) accusing John Procter right along with his wife (see also *SWP*, 2:677–678). Nor is there any evidence in the examination records or indictments that Abigail Williams had ever been a house servant for the Procters.

In his 1987 autobiography Miller remembered his "discovery" differently: "Like every criminal trial record, this one was filled with enticing but incomplete suggestions of relationships, so to speak, offstage. Next day in the dead silence of the little Historical Society building . . . I found Charles W. Upham's quiet nineteenth-century masterpiece *Salem Witchcraft*, and in it, on my second afternoon, the hard evidence of what had become my play's center: the breakdown of the Procter marriage and Abigail Williams's determination to get Elizabeth murdered so that she could have John, whom I deduced she had slept with while she was their house servant, before Elizabeth fired her" (*Timebends*, 337). But I have been unable to find any such evidence in Upham's two-volume work, nor have I ever seen any reference to Upham's work in a secondary source that would support Miller's claim. Moreover, Abigail Williams, who was really only eleven in 1692, appears to have been taken into her uncle Samuel Parris's family when the Parrises were still living in Boston prior to their arrival in Salem "before June 1688" or else just when they moved to Salem (Roach, "That Child, Betty Parris," 4; Roach, *Salem Witch Trials*, xxxiv; Gragg, *Quest for Security: The Life of Samuel Parris, 1653–1720* [1990], 35). It therefore seems unlikely that Williams could have been a servant in the Procter home seven months before the outbreak of the witch hunt, as the play contends.

Why Miller went to such lengths to make it seem that his fictional plot line stemmed from some factual basis to be found in the Salem documents remains a mystery. A more likely source for the playwright's idea of a triangular relationship based on sexual attraction and jealousy would again seem to lie in his reading of Starkey, which offers a hint of just such a relationship involving the Procters' actual servant, twenty-year-old Mary Warren (Starkey, *Devil in Massachusetts*, 95–96). This hypothesis also fits with another passage in *Timebends*, in which Miller admits that "even in the first weeks of thinking about the Salem story [i.e., before he took his research trip to Salem], the central image, the one that persistently recurred as an exuberant source of energy, was that of a guilt-ridden man, John Procter, who, having slept with his teen-age servant girl, watches with horror as she becomes the leader of the witch-hunting pack and points her accusing finger at the wife he has himself betrayed" (*Timebends*, 332). If true, these observations explain further why Starkey's book supplied *The Crucible* with far too much material for Miller to have been able to acknowledge its contribution until late in his life, and even then incompletely. Asserting that he had found the germ of the play's sexual relationship in the Salem records may additionally have helped Miller obscure any connection that audiences might draw between his play and his life. Miller divorced his first wife, Mary Slattery, in 1956 and in the same year married Marilyn Monroe, with whom he had had an intimate relationship dating back to 1951. According to Miller's biographer, Christopher Bigsby, "Mary could see herself in the unyielding figure of Elizabeth Procter, and something of her husband in John Procter, disabled by his affair with a woman out to displace his wife" (Bigsby, *Arthur Miller*, 398).

16. Miller spoke on several occasions about the larger role played by guilt in his play. "The central impulse for writing [the play] at all," he wrote in 1957, "was not the social but the interior psychological question, which was the question of that guilt residing in Salem which the hysteria merely unleashed but did not create. Consequently, the structure reflects that understanding, and it centers in John, Elizabeth, and Abigail" (*Crucible*, 165). See also *Timebends*, 341; and Miller, "Again They Drink," H36.

17. For the development of Miller's political and ethnic identity and its relationship to *The Crucible*, see Bigsby, *Arthur Miller*, 55–60, 77, 114–134, 158–163, 409–410, chap. 8. Similar themes are addressed in *Timebends*, 36–43, 330–352, 449–456. The passage critical of communism from Act 1 may be found in *Crucible*, 34. Miller wrote about the reception of the play in China in *Timebends*, 348, and in "Again They Drink," H36. In the former instance, he observed, "The writer Nien Cheng, who spent six and a half years in solitary confinement and whose daughter was murdered by the Red Guards, told me that after her release she saw the Shanghai production and could not believe that a non-Chinese had written the play. 'Some of the interrogations,' she said, 'were precisely the same ones used on us in the Cultural Revolution.'" Yet at the time *The Crucible* was released, Miller was criticized by reviewers Robert Warshow and Eric Bentley for his naiveté and evasiveness about communism and for structuring the play

in such a fashion that his leftist audiences would comfortably look only to the Red hunt-ers as analogues to his Puritan magistrates and not see the latter's closer resemblance to the Communist prosecutors in Prague. Moreover, these critics insisted, communists really existed as a danger, while witches did not, so the parallel between the Salem witch hunt and modern anti-communism was not a fair one. (See Warshow's and Bentley's reviews in *Crucible*, 210–226, 204–209.) While there was merit in the first of these criticisms, if not the second (since nearly everyone in late-seventeenth-century New England believed in the existence of witches), the fact that *The Crucible* proved so successful over the next fifty years, speaking to audiences the world over who knew little or nothing about American McCarthyism, suggests that Miller was also correct in his general defense of the play as one dealing with a universal human propensity.

Miller's worries about the dangers inherent in emotion-driven crowd behavior can be traced as well to a more longstanding fear among Jews, given their historic experi-ence with persecutions and pogroms (see Heinze, *Jews and the American Soul*, 184–191). For understanding Miller's place in the postwar world, I also found helpful Adam Kirsch's review of Bigsby's biography, "Great Disconcerting Wipeout," 43–48.

18. The parts of Perry Miller's writings most relevant to the Salem witch hunt ap-pear in *New England Mind: From Colony to Province*, 179–190, chap. 13. (The first volume of this work, *The New England Mind: The Seventeenth Century*, had appeared in 1939.) The two sentences that have often been misinterpreted read, "The most curious of all the facts in that welter we call Salem witchcraft is this: . . . the intellectual history of New England up to 1720 can be written as though no such thing ever happened. It had no effect on the ecclesiastical or political situation, it does not figure in the institutional or ideological development [of the region]" (191). For examples of later works that have cited this passage as a way of diminishing the significance of the 1692 witch hunt, see Fred-erick C. Drake, "Witchcraft in the American Colonies" (1968), 697n12; Demos, "Under-lying Themes" (1970), 1311; Karlsen, "On Witchcraft and Witch-Hunting" (1983), 612; Demos, *Entertaining Satan* (1983), 4n2; and, for the purpose of diminishing the respon-sibility of Puritanism in witch hunting, Hall, "Witchcraft and the Limits of Interpreta-tion" (1985), 262; and Rosenthal, *Salem Story* (1993), 212. The same misunderstanding of Perry Miller's position persists, though not for the purpose of discounting the impor-tance of the Salem witch hunt or Puritanism's role in it, in Latner, "Salem Witchcraft, Factionalism, and Social Change Reconsidered" (2008), 424; and Baker, *Storm of Witchcraft* (2015), 6.

19. Quotations (in order) are from Perry Miller, *New England Mind*, 195, 200, 202, 195, 194, 199.

20. The Puritans had terms to indicate this distinction (although even they did not always employ them strictly). If an individual were tormented by the specter of a person who had entered into a pact with the Devil, the sufferer was said to be "bewitched." If, on the other hand, an individual showed the same outward signs of spectral torment but it was believed that the person corresponding to the specter was an upstanding fol-lower of Christ, then the afflicted individual was said to be "possessed," having been misled by the Devil to believe that a witch was involved. The implications of the dis-tinction were significant, since in the former case a crime had been committed and the legal authorities of the community were called upon to find and prosecute the witch, while in the latter case the suffering pointed to a spiritual crisis for the individual (and

family) in distress, even the likelihood that the Devil was at that very moment attempting to win over the sufferer's soul. (There was still another form of diabolical torment, known to the Puritans as "obsession," in which the Devil, often with the help of a witch, vied for the sufferer's body but had not yet entered into battle for her or his soul, but this status did not figure importantly in the controversies at Salem.) For more on this issue, see David Harley, "Explaining Salem: Calvinist Psychology and the Diagnosis of Possession" (1996), 307–330. Harley argues that a gradual shift in the Puritan elite's diagnosis of the afflicted young women's conditions from "witchcraft" (or "obsession") to "possession" helped bring about the end of the witch hunt, which seems true enough. But he fails to explain the ease with which the afflictions at Salem were so quickly attributed to witchcraft as opposed to possession in the first place. (Brian Levack observes that the symptoms of affliction at Salem correspond only to the definition of obsession, not possession, as those terms were used by early modern demonologists. This may be so, but, as Harley's discussion shows, New England's Puritans, including no less an authority than Increase Mather, blurred the boundaries between these two terms. See Levack, *The Devil Within*, 17–18, 270n95.)

21. For the quotation, see Miller, *New England Mind*, 194. In 1684 Increase Mather had published his *Essay for the Recording of Illustrious Providences* (often referred to as *Remarkable Providences*, from its subtitle), and in 1689 Cotton Mather came out with *Memorable Providences, Relating to Witchcraft and Possessions*. Both works documented presumed cases of witchcraft, using the latest scientific terminology, and both pursued the secondary purpose of joining in the efforts of English divines to defend the claims of revealed religion against the emergence of materialistic thinking in the English-speaking world. Cotton Mather's volume included a lengthy description of the 1688 Boston instance of the apparent bewitching of the Goodwin children by Goodwife Glover, the mother of a neighboring Irish washerwoman with whom one of the children had quarreled. Samuel Willard and three other leading ministers signed a prefatory endorsement of the book. Miller discusses these works on 180–183.

Aside from the publicity given to purported acts of witchcraft in the works of the two Mathers, knowledge of similar episodes elsewhere in the Western world would likely have played a role in the thinking of New England's Puritans. In his *Wonders of the Invisible World*, which appeared just after the Salem court had been disbanded, Cotton Mather noted that a 1662 witchcraft trial at Bury St. Edmunds, England, resulting in the execution of two women for bewitching seven children and teenagers, had been "much considered" by the court. In the same work Mather spoke of the mass execution of presumed witches in Sweden during the 1660s and 1670s, again for the bewitchment of children, as providing another precedent for what had happened in New England. I have not seen evidence that the Swedish cases were known to or considered by the Salem judges, but it is hard to believe that the Massachusetts magistrates would not at least have heard of them, contributing to the general plausibility of the accusations that issued from Salem village's afflicted young people. On these precedents, see Norton, *In the Devil's Snare*, 36–38, 285; Mather, *Wonders of the Invisible World* [1693] in *Witchcraft Delusion*, 1:140–151, for the English case; 141, for "much considered"; and 211–217, for the Swedish examples.

22. The quotations may be found in Miller, *New England Mind*, 202, 207. For Starkey's treatment of Cotton Mather, see Starkey, *Devil in Massachusetts*, chap. 20. In

fairness to Willard, it is likely that the minister issued his critical dialogue between "S" and "B" (its formal title was *Some Miscellany Observations on Our Present Debates Respecting Witchcrafts*) under the alias "J. A. and P. E." (initials selected to point to the plight of John Alden and Philip English, two high-status, fugitive suspects of the witch hunt) as a means of evading an order by Governor Phips, announced shortly before October 12, banning published discussions of the trials. Thomas Brattle's critical letter, dated October 8, for example, was also never published, while Increase Mather's *Cases of Conscience* and Cotton Mather's *Wonders of the Invisible World* were exceptions allowed by the governor. Willard had also made his growing unease with the witchcraft trials known as early as June 19, when he preached a sermon questioning the reliability of spectral evidence, although the minister seems to have drawn back from his open criticism following his own naming as a suspect by one of the afflicted sometime before July 11. Nothing came of this stray accusation, but Willard joined in another statement, issued by the Boston-area ministerial Cambridge Association on August 1, minimizing the likelihood that Satan would be permitted to impersonate innocent people in the form of their specters. By late September, however, Willard had recovered his courage to oppose the trials, and contemporaries apparently knew him to be the true author of the dialogue between "S" and "B." Still, he refrained from attacking the work of the judges themselves. On these points, see Norton, *Devil's Snare*, 201–203, 215–216, 224–225, 280–282, 386n42, 403n33, 403n34.

In keeping with Perry Miller's emphasis on the transformative effects of the witch hunt on New England Puritanism, Elizabeth Reis argues persuasively that the excesses of the Salem trials led to an attenuation of Satan's role in the religious life of Puritans and their descendants. Satan was no longer thought of as a physical entity who could suddenly appear in the midst of a human situation; he receded to become simply the guardian of hell, although he could still function from a distance as a tempter of human souls. See her *Damned Women: Sinners and Witches in Puritan New England* (1997), chap. 5. John Murrin makes the same point, noting that in the years following the witch hunt, references to Satan, which carried the risk of an association with witchcraft, began to disappear from the sermons of Congregationalist ministers. A little later on, evangelical preaching brought forward the image of hell fire, still frightening but without the connotation of outside human agents working along with the Devil. See his "Coming to Terms with the Salem Witch Trials" (2000), 346.

Perry Miller's harsh judgment concerning the role of Puritanism in the witch hunt influenced a number of subsequent scholars, though all softened Miller's blows. In his brief treatment of the Mathers' role in the witch hunt, Robert Middlekauff, for example, drew much from Miller's and Starkey's accounts, but he emphasized Increase Mather's skepticism toward the witchcraft court's sense of certainty in fathoming God's ways (Middlekauff, *The Mathers* [1971], 143–161). In their essays on Arthur Miller's *The Crucible*, David Levin and Edmund Morgan recognized the power and virtues of the play, but both felt the playwright could have intensified the tragic dimensions of his drama by showing a wider spectrum of Puritan responses to the witch hunt instead of making its representatives appear either blindly moralistic (in the characters of Reverend Parris and Judge Danforth, a stand-in for Stoughton) or comically ineffectual (in the character of Reverend Hale). As criticisms of the play, these points are well taken, but as commentaries on the actual history of the witch hunt, they go too far in exculpating the Puritan faith from its absolutist tendencies. See Levin, *In Defense of Historical Literature* [1967], chap. 4, and Morgan, "Arthur Miller's *The Crucible* and the Salem Witch Trials" [1985], 171–186. The two leading modern biographies of Cotton Mather retained more of Perry Miller's hard-hitting criticism of the minister's role in the Salem witch hunt while at the same time presenting humane portraits of the man. Both biographies show Cotton Mather's actions to have been shaped not only by the Puritans' general providential doctrines (along with social and political pressures) but also by his strong beliefs in the nearness of the Day of Judgment and in a vivid spirit world of angels and demons, whose interventions, he would have been the first to acknowledge, were extremely difficult to interpret. See Levin, *Cotton Mather* (1978), chaps. 5–7, esp. 157, 200; and Kenneth Silverman, *Life and Times of Cotton Mather* (1985), chap. 4.

Starkey's and Perry Miller's understanding of Puritanism's responsibility for generating the Salem witch hunt also directly influenced Kai T. Erikson's sociological treatment of the 1692 events in his *Wayward Puritans: A Study in the Sociology of Deviance* (1966). While emphasizing—in line with the principles of functionalist sociology—the need for all societies to have "wayward" members (or "criminals") who, by their transgressions, reinforce social boundaries, Erikson's study blamed the Puritans' "religious absolutism" (187) for bequeathing to America a particularly intolerant way of handling its law-breakers, one lacking in compassion and in the belief that rehabilitation was possible. For Erickson, it was less important whether society invented its criminals (as he believed the Puritans had done with their "witches") or whether it simply exaggerated their threat (as the Puritans had done earlier with their "antinomian" and Quaker adversaries). What counted was how a conformist majority treated its dissidents.

CHAPTER 2: **Boyer and Nissenbaum's *Salem Possessed***
and the Anti-capitalist Critique

1. Demos, "Underlying Themes," 1311 (italics in the original). I take up the substance of Demos's inquiry when I consider his later book, *Entertaining Satan*, in chapter 3.

2. In *Witchcraft at Salem*, Hansen named only five of the twenty executed individuals as probable, likely, or possible witches (Bridget Bishop, Wilmot "Mammy" Redd, George Burroughs, Sarah Good, and Samuel Wardwell [see *Witchcraft at Salem*, chap. 5, for his evidence]), yet he also wrote, "Twenty people died. . . . But at least a dozen now seem to be clearly innocent" (88). In a later article Hansen named two more of the executed suspects in 1692 as likely practitioners of witchcraft: Martha Carrier and Mary Parker ("Andover Witchcraft and the Causes of the Salem Witchcraft Trials" [1983], 38–57). Hansen summarizes his argument in the preface and on pp. 225–227 of *Witchcraft at Salem*.

I use the term "witch hunt" throughout my study, in keeping with its common usage by Starkey and others in the post–World War II period. (Although Starkey used "Salem Witch Trials" in the subtitle to her 1949 book, the term "witch hunt" appeared frequently throughout her text to refer to the entire, year-long social process she was describing.) As I show in the chapters that follow, "witch hunt" fell out of favor with the leading historians of Salem during the post-1969 era. In the conclusion I explain how the designation has returned to scholarly use, beginning in the mid-1990s. As for the term's origins, I have not run across a detailed explication. Historian of Scottish witch hunting Christina Larner asserted that the term was coined in the United States in the twentieth century, although not in the first instance to describe the historical persecution of people believed to practice witchcraft. However, she provided no further guidance in a work cut short by her untimely death (*Witchcraft and Religion* [1984], 88, 90). The earliest use of the term I have seen appears in an editorial footnote by the American historian of witchcraft George Lincoln Burr in his widely used anthology of primary sources from the New England experience, *Narratives of the Witchcraft Cases* (1914), 424n1. As Larner pointed out, the term's value lies in shifting the emphasis from the alleged behavior of suspects ("witchcraft") to the actions of those who would pursue certain persons on the belief they had committed a crime (*Enemies of God: The Witch-hunt in Scotland* [1981], 1).

3. Hansen, *Witchcraft at Salem*, 64–70. For the testimony about the puppets by John Bly Sr. and William Bly and the story of the conflict over the sow, see SWP, 1:101, 103. Effigies planted under floors or within walls were known in the Greco-Roman world to be used against feared enemies (Ogden, "Binding Spells," 25). One example from the Salem records that also points in the direction of countermagic to explain this piece of evidence comes from a passage in the later examination of suspect Ann Dolliver. When asked if she had made any puppets, Dolliver replied, "yes one: afterward she ownd two popits & it was becau(s) she thought she was bewitched & she had read in a book: that told her: that that: was the way to afflict: them that had afflicted her" (*Records*, #309). Hansen's acceptance of the Blys' testimony as credible evidence against Bishop is also rejected by Lyle Koehler (*A Search for Power: The "Weaker Sex" in Seventeenth-Century New England* [1980], 415n94), and Hansen's overall case against Bishop is criticized by Rosenthal in *Salem Story*, 75–76, 78–81. Marilynne K. Roach offers yet another possible explanation for the puppets, assuming the Blys were telling the truth. Since the effigies were found in the old structure that had belonged to Bishop's second husband, Thomas Oliver, they had likely been inserted into the wall when the house had been built, which predated Bishop's arrival in New England and her marriage to Oliver. If so, they had nothing to do with Bridget Bishop at all (*Six Women of Salem*, 23).

While Rosenthal raises an important caveat about the need to regard all depositional testimonies cautiously, especially those that contained stories of events said to have occurred years earlier, he takes the added—and what seems unwarranted—step of suggesting that the court discounted most of the accusations and corroborating evidence contained in these testimonies, since these charges did not appear in the formal indictments of the suspects, which only cited spectral torments occurring during the examination process or at times closely related to it (*Salem Story*, 75–76, 78–81). But indictments took that form in order to align with the language of current English law, necessary now that a new colonial charter had arrived with Governor Phips, and indictments did sometimes add the phrase "and Sundrey other Acts of witchcraft" to cover nonspectral forms of witchcraft (Norton, *In the Devil's Snare*, 205, 226). Moreover, Increase and Cotton Mather both asserted that the justices never convicted any suspect based on spectral evidence alone but relied on what they took to be other forms of corroborating evidence (or "presumptions") from the depositions. See Increase Mather, "Postscript" to *Cases of Conscience*, 126; Cotton Mather to John Foster, August 17, 1692, in S-VW, 118–119; and Cotton Mather, *Wonders of the Invisible World*, in Burr, 215–216, 223, 229, 237, 241–244.

Wendel D. Craker's study of the grounds for selecting which of the 150 or more accused suspects would be brought to trial offers considerable support for the Mathers' assessments. Craker argues that the court's prosecuting attorneys selected for trial only the cases (22 in all) where spectral evidence was supplemented by accusations of non-spectral forms of witchcraft (the types of evidence I outlined in chapter 1), adding toward the end of the court's existence cases where spectral evidence was supplemented by confessions (6 in all). See his "Spectral Evidence, Non-spectral Acts of Witchcraft, and Confession at Salem in 1692" (1997), 331–358. In concluding that spectral evidence did not play such a decisive role in the witchcraft prosecutions, however, Craker goes too far in the opposite direction from Rosenthal's. In some of the trials—for example, those of John Procter and George Jacobs Sr.—no pieces of nonspectral evidence were brought out against these individuals, at least so far as surviving data indicate. Two other suspects against whom no nonspectral testimony has survived, Sarah Buckley and her daughter Mary Whittredge, were also selected for trial and served with indictments by the grand jury, although their trials were delayed beyond the existence of the court. For still other victims—e.g., Rebecca Nurse and Elizabeth Procter—spectral testimony clearly dwarfed the scant presentation of nonspectral evidence. (For these examples, see the entries gathered under the names of the six individuals, arranged alphabetically, in SWP.) Moreover, spectral evidence, resulting from highly visible, physical symptoms in the afflicted accusers, was typically attested to by at least two witnesses, a judicial safeguard that Craker implies only pertained to nonspectral evidence (Craker, "Spectral Evidence," 336). Spectral assault was thus considered just as empirically valid to most participants as reports of a suspect's "superhuman" feats of strength, malign curses, or suspicious skin growths. In the absence of confession (always considered the best proof of all), the judges do seem to have looked for a wide range of corroborating evidence in determining a suspect's guilt, but spectral evidence, while not new in the Salem witch hunt, deserves a special place in its story. Spectral evidence most dramatically got the entire frenzy going, while doubts about its misuse ultimately brought the panic to a close. For balanced treatments of the subject, see Daniel G. Payne, "Defending against the Indefensible: Spectral Evidence at the Salem Witchcraft Trials" (1993), 62–83, and Norton, *In the Devil's Snare*, 30–42, 199–204, 213–216.

4. Hansen, *Witchcraft at Salem*, 71–72 (Redd), and 126–127, 172–173 (Good). Hansen provides little better evidence of actual witchcraft in his later article focusing on several Andover suspects. The article's sole piece of evidence that suggests even the possibility of an occult practice with harmful intent comes from testimony prepared for the August 1692 witchcraft trial of Martha Carrier by a former neighbor, John Rogers of Billerica. Rogers reported that seven years earlier he had found one of his sows dead with its ears cut off following an argument with Carrier. Since this same witness also held Carrier responsible for another sow wandering off and a cow abruptly stopping to give milk, all during the same summer in which "some difference betwixt us" caused Carrier to "[give] forth several threatening words as she often used to doe," it seems equally likely that Rogers later embellished the part about the dead sow's ears to strengthen his complaint against Carrier in the context of the ongoing witch hunt. Still

another possibility is that Carrier resorted to an act of symbolic aggression as a way to use her reputation for witchcraft as a form of intimidation, a different sort of criminality than witchcraft itself. No record of any reply Carrier might have made to the charge has survived. The rest of Hansen's evidence in the article consists of two other reported curses, one case of countermagic (used to ward off presumed witchcraft), and a number of hallucinations imagining torments at the hands of specters of presumed witches—all signs of the fear of witchcraft but not the practice of it. See "Andover Witchcraft," esp. 42–43, 48. Yet the author still concludes, "From the evidence of the surviving documents it also seems clear that white witchcraft [occult techniques not meant to do harm] was commonly practiced and that black witchcraft was not uncommon. . . . Without the near-universal belief in witchcraft and the regular practice of it, it is hard to see how witchcraft could have remained a capital crime, as it did in both England and English America until a generation after the Salem trials" (54). I address the subject of how there could be fear of witchcraft without the presence of any practicing witches in the Aside that follows chapter 2.

   5. Hansen, *Witchcraft at Salem*, 150–151 (for the quotation about Wilmot Redd); 32–35 (on Sarah Good); 74–77 (on George Burroughs); 58–59, 127–131, 151–153 (on Rebecca Nurse, Mary Esty, and Elizabeth Procter); and 192–193 (for the remarks on Calef's "insolence"). In another example of the disdain he showed toward Sarah Good, Hansen judged her "so liberal with her curses" (218), even though she had directed her two documented outbursts at individuals (Rev. Nicholas Noyes and Mercy Short) who had shown abuse toward her during the witch hunt itself. Hansen called the behavior of Cotton Mather "sane and temperate" up until the point in late September when the minister drafted his defense of the trials in *Wonders of the Invisible World* (168), but this judgment overlooks the public support (despite his private misgivings) Mather gave throughout the summer to the trials and in particular to the five hangings that he personally witnessed on August 19.

   Exactly what role Mather played at the time of George Burroughs's hanging (one of those executed on August 19) remains a matter of dispute. Starkey followed Calef's account, written four years after the fact (and published four years later still, in 1700), which asserted that Mather, mounted on a horse in front of the gallows, quieted the restive crowd and allowed the hanging to proceed, after Burroughs had offered with great decorum his last words, proclaiming his innocence and reciting the Lord's Prayer (Starkey, *Devil in Massachusetts*, 197–198). Although Hansen is elsewhere extremely critical of Calef's treatment of Mather, he, too, seems to have accepted Calef's version of Mather's role at Burroughs's hanging (Hansen, *Witchcraft at Salem*, 146–149). Mather's recent biographers have been more cautious about the evidence for the minister's intervention at the event (though not about the disquieting effect that Burroughs's behavior at the gallows had on the crowd, which was corroborated by other eyewitnesses). David Levin believes that Calef probably exaggerated Mather's response, while Kenneth Silverman accepts the merchant's account with only minor qualification. See Levin, *Cotton Mather*, 212–215; and Silverman, *Life and Times of Cotton Mather*, 109–111.

   6. One study that followed quite closely in the footsteps of Hansen's book was David Thomas Konig's *Law and Society in Puritan Massachusetts: Essex County, 1629–1692* (1979). Konig's sympathies lay with New England's legal system, which had been developed over the course of the seventeenth century, gradually weaning Puritans away from

religiously based forms of social control, such as personal arbitration and neighborly watchfulness, toward more formal court procedures. Legal formality, in Konig's view, socialized the colonists to live according to preestablished rules, respect personal boundaries, and accept outsiders. According to Konig, the witchcraft trials of 1692—like Hansen, Konig rarely spoke of a "witch hunt"—resulted from the response of this newly empowered legal system to the threat posed by people adopting backward-looking, "extralegal" means of achieving their ends: people who used violence against their neighbors' property or animals, people who spoke in an antinomian fashion against the authority of law in general, and people who practiced witchcraft. Much as did Hansen (whom he cited approvingly), Konig assumed that some of those accused of witchcraft during the Salem witch hunt, including Martha and Giles Cory, were actual practitioners of malicious magic, although he presented no evidence apart from the charges of accusers. More generally, he simply accepted at face value that most accusations (until the very end of the witch hunt) corresponded truthfully to unlawful and defiant social behavior by the accused, who may or may not have resorted to the help of the Devil. Even Rebecca Nurse, according to Konig, fell into this "extralegal" category (because of an argument she had with a neighbor over the latter's pigs crossing into her property), despite the fact that her husband, Francis, as Konig acknowledged, participated in the county legal system quite successfully.

In defending the legality of the special court of oyer and terminer that prosecuted the accused witches, Konig oddly overlooked the wider environment of what could properly be called an extralegal panic that gave rise to the witch-hunting court in the first place. This same atmosphere of panic equally accounted for most of the special court's many unusual legal decisions. These included adopting the mostly discredited "touch test," which produced incriminating evidence against a suspect if her or his touch brought relief from torment to the afflicted (on the belief that demonic "effluvium" flowed back to the "witch" through physical contact); failing to examine accusers and suspects insulated from the reactions of other accusers and the large crowd; permitting on occasion accused suspects to be subject to torture, a practice generally discouraged under English law but allowed for those already convicted of a felony in order to force disclosure of accomplices; delaying the trials of confessors; and refraining from requiring complainants to post the customary monetary bond along with their formal accusations. (This last anomaly, as Bernard Rosenthal points out, made it easier than usual in such felony cases to advance accusations, since by guaranteeing that accusers would follow through with legal proceedings, bonds typically functioned as a brake on frivolous complaints ["General Introduction" to *Records*, pp. 18, 31].) By neglecting to discuss these departures from prudent legal practices of their day, Konig's study, like Hansen's, shifted sympathies away from the victims of the Salem witch hunt, yet it, too, failed to strike a responsive chord in the increasingly radicalized university culture of the late twentieth century, probably because it championed the established legal system rather than a subordinate group in society. (See *Law and Society*, esp. chaps. 6–7.)

An earlier study of the legal aspects of the witchcraft trials, Sanford J. Fox's *Science and Justice: The Massachusetts Witchcraft Trials* (1968), while much less extensive than Konig's, had also found the Puritans' legal procedures sound for their era. Fox, however, took nearly all of his examples from seventeenth-century legal actions brought against individuals accused of witchcraft under nonpanic circumstances, while he mostly ignored the Salem cases, where departures from cautious legal norms were far more common. Fox's is a curious study, since it aimed to illustrate the general proposition that justice suffers when legal proceedings fail to utilize relevant scientific (or social scientific) knowledge. Yet, as Fox was forced to concede repeatedly, the relevant medical knowledge in the late seventeenth century (concerning, for example, the understanding of the causes of death and illness, or of the mental states of people thought to be afflicted by witchcraft) was still insufficiently separated from the religious assumptions of its day to offer much help to the accused, even had the legal system been better prepared to make use of such knowledge. Fox may have initiated his study out of sympathy for the Salem victims, but it quickly left those victims far behind.

In reviewing these studies of the Salem witch hunt and the law, my point is not to charge the witchcraft court with running roughshod over all legal procedures. In most respects, including in its handling of the all-important matter of spectral evidence, the court adhered to common practices in witchcraft prosecutions. (In support of this general observation, in which most historians concur, see also David C. Brown, "The Forfeitures at Salem" [1993], 85–111.) Nevertheless, the violations of prudent legal standards noted above, not to mention the magistrates' evident leanings in favor of the accusers—against which such institutional protections as defense counsel and the principle of judicial neutrality had not yet been developed for criminal cases—injected substantial, probably decisive, bias against the accused into the examinations and trials. For the legal context, see, in addition to Konig's book, John M. Murrin, "Magistrates, Sinners, and a Precarious Liberty: Trial by Jury in Seventeenth-Century New England" (1984)," 152–206. Also helpful on legal aspects of the Salem witch hunt is Peter Charles Hoffer, *Devil's Disciples: Makers of the Salem Witchcraft Trials* (1998), chaps. 6–7.

7. Boyer and Nissenbaum, *Salem Possessed*, 22 ("dramatic set piece"). In 2008, Jane Kamensky reported that as of that year, the book was in its twenty-sixth printing, had sold over 180,000 copies, and was "still going strong" ("Salem Obsessed," 392).

8. See Boyer and Nissenbaum, *Salem Possessed*, chaps. 2–6, for the heart of the factional argument; the map of accusers, accused, and defenders appears on 34. I have reproduced this map as my figure 4, which I present later in the chapter as part of my critique of Boyer and Nissenbaum's argument, but readers may wish to glance ahead at it at this point.

9. The quotations in order may be found in ibid., 115, 117, 88–89, 178, 209. The authors discuss Samuel Parris in chap. 7. They describe Israel Porter elsewhere as "cool as always" and "a master of the passive voice" (141), as "cool and ambitious" (179), and as "always hovering in the background, whispering advice, devising strategy, but never giving vent to passion, never backed into any corners" (115). The authors characterize him as a veritable Svengali when discussing his role in writing the will of Mary Veren Putnam, Thomas Putnam Jr.'s stepmother (139–142). Other easterners are similarly described in negative terms related to monetary aspirations, including the executed John Procter, said to have had a "successful career shrewdly built upon the varied economic opportunities available in the fluid Essex County situation" (200), and jailed suspect Sarah Osburn's husband, Alexander, called a "shrewd operator" because he and Sarah contested the will of Sarah's first husband, a man allied to the Putnam clan (194).

Salem Possessed also contained a secondary, psychological argument based on the assumption that the village's western farmers could not face their own desires for commercial gain. Thus their resentments toward their more successful neighbors to the east were fueled by feelings of envy and then guilt for harboring such unacceptable desires in the first place. These themes are drawn upon in chaps. 6–7 and brought back in the final pages of the book's last substantive chapter (209–216). In that chapter's last paragraph, I found the only tribute in *Salem Possessed* to the heroism of the executed victims, who, the authors rightly say, died because they "insisted on remaining faithful to the essential requirement for stable social relationships: simple honesty" (216). Even here, however, no names are mentioned and no details presented about the actions of these people. In general, the psychological argument, which might have granted to scapegoating the central role it deserved in the witch hunt, remains attenuated throughout the book. Far more prominent is the argument that emergent capitalism produced conflict between two distinct social groups, "capitalists" and "Puritans." Boyer and Nissenbaum credited Michael Walzer's article, "Puritanism as a Revolutionary Ideology" (1963), 59–90, for the germ of their psychological argument (*Salem Possessed*, xiii), and indeed it can be found on pp. 78 and 81 of that article. Yet it is significant that the authors did not pick up the larger, critical thrust in Walzer's treatment of the Puritans, which was to liken them to the Jacobins and Bolsheviks in their capacity for single-minded repressiveness and even "terror." Boyer and Nissenbaum's Puritans come across as much too innocent to allow for such associations.

10. Boyer and Nissenbaum, *Salem Possessed*, 105, 109 ("private will" vs. "public good"), xiii ("Watts and Vietnam"), and 180 ("Oddly enough"). It is possible that in their reference to the Watts riot of 1965 and the Vietnam War, Boyer and Nissenbaum may have meant their analogy to point to the "violent roles" played by members of the Los Angeles police force and by American soldiers, but the context (having just mentioned "revolutionary" Puritans) suggests that they were likening the witch hunters to radicals who adopt violent means to pursue otherwise laudable ends—people, in other words, who "go a little too far." This interpretation is supported by the authors' later remembrance of writing that same passage: "As we note in the preface of *Salem Possessed*, the book was also the product of a tumultuous era in the nation's history, with society torn by clamorous disagreements over what many saw as a disastrous and ill-considered war waged by an arrogant and blundering administration" ("*Salem Possessed* in Retrospect" [2008], 531).

In light of the qualified sympathy expressed in *Salem Possessed* for the Watts rioters, it is noteworthy that the first annual Salem Award, an honor created in 1992 to go along with the tercentenary of the witch hunt, was presented to Gregory Allen Williams, an African American man from Inglewood, California, who risked his life in the midst of later Los Angeles riots (following the verdict in the Rodney King trial) to save an Asian American under attack by a mob (Shapiro, "The Lessons of Salem," 64). Almost thirty years separated the Watts and Rodney King riots (1965 and 1992), and Paul Boyer and Stephen Nissenbaum might well have personally applauded the choice of Williams to receive the Salem Award in 1992. Yet the two different vantage points represented, respectively, by the authors' stance in *Salem Possessed*, still assigned today in university classrooms, and the selection of Williams by the Salem Award committee provide a striking illustration of how prevailing academic views of the Salem witch hunt diverge from popular understanding of the event.

The authors' sympathy for the witch hunters—although not the ethical peculiarity of this position—was also noted by Cedric Cowing in his review of *Salem Possessed* (1975), 1381–1382, and by Ann Kibbey, "Mutations of the Supernatural" (1982), 126n2.

11. The key works about crowd behavior were George Rudé, *The Crowd in History: A Study of Popular Disturbances in France and England, 1730–1848* (1964), and E. P. Thompson, "The Moral Economy of the English Crowd in the Eighteenth Century" (1971). Pauline Maier applied the same ideas to American colonial history in an influential article, "Popular Uprisings and Civil Authority in Eighteenth-Century America" (1970), in which she explained the chief characteristics of crowd actions: crowds used extralegal means often to implement laws not otherwise enforceable, they did not rely exclusively on lower-class people and often had the support of local officials, they were discriminating in selecting the targets of their anger, they showed restraint in the use of violence, and they were an ambiguously accepted part of the constitutional framework of government.

12. For the two earliest responses to *Salem Possessed*, see Cowing's four-paragraph review in the *American Historical Review* cited in note 10, and Keith Thomas, "Satan in Salem" (1974), 22–23 (Thomas's use of "ragged" appears on p. 23). A typical later response that accepted Boyer and Nissenbaum's factional argument while noting that it might only account for nineteen of the witch hunt's sixty-nine accusations up through May 31, 1692, may be found in Richard Weisman, *Witchcraft, Magic, and Religion in 17th-Century Massachusetts* (1984), 128–129, 133–134, 141–142, 172–174, 244–245n136. More substantively, David D. Hall questioned Boyer and Nissenbaum's general proposition that capitalism and Puritanism stood at odds with one another, as well as their underlying assumption (to help explain the motivations of the witch hunters) that rural communities in late-seventeenth-century New England faced a social crisis due to shrinking landholdings. Hall, however, did not develop these comments into a critique of the factional argument in *Salem Possessed*. For Hall's observations, see "Witchcraft and the Limits of Interpretation" (1985), 263–265, 272, and his "Religion and Society" (1984), 335–336. I note other criticisms made by scholars about particular points in the argument of *Salem Possessed* as my discussion proceeds in this chapter.

13. In *Salem Possessed*, Boyer and Nissenbaum present only two names from the dispute over the village's first minister: Nathaniel Putnam and Bray Wilkins, both opponents of Reverend Bayley (for the full discussion of the dispute, see 45–53). But in their highly valuable, edited collection of documents about the witch hunt produced two years earlier, *Salem-Village Witchcraft: A Documentary Record of Local Conflict in Colonial New England*, the authors provide many more details and names. The two most usable petitions against and for Bayley appear, respectively, on 242–243 (14 names) and 250–251 (24 names); these are the same two petitions that Boyer and Nissenbaum highlight in their discussion in *Salem Possessed* without giving any further details. Later supporters of the witch hunt include, from the anti-Bayley petition, Benjamin Wilkins, Henry Wilkins, Bray Wilkins, John Putnam ["Jr."], and Nathaniel Putnam and, from the pro-Bayley petition, Capt. John Putnam, Thomas Putnam Jr., Jonathan Walcott, Nathaniel Ingersoll, and John Buxton. Later opponents of the witch hunt include, from the anti-Bayley petition, Thomas Wilkins, and, from the pro-Bayley petition, Peter Cloyse and Daniel Andrew. (I added "Jr." in quotation marks and brackets to the first John Putnam's name because this man was actually the son of Nathaniel Putnam, even though he was known as John Jr. He should not be confused with yet another John Putnam, the son of Nathaniel's brother, Capt. John Putnam. This John, sometimes designated "John, III," does not figure prominently in the historical records of the witch

hunt. The "Jr." is missing on the anti-Bayley petition noted above, but it is clear from a related anti-Bayley petition shown on p. 244 that John Jr. was meant.)

In *Devil's Disciples*, Peter Charles Hoffer also notes that the Putnam clan was divided in the dispute over Reverend Bayley, but in the rest of his treatment of social relationships in Salem village leading up to the witch hunt, Hoffer relies on the factional argument of *Salem Possessed* with only minor modifications (see pp. 46–47 for the Bayley dispute, and chap. 2 for the village factionalism generally).

14. On George Burroughs's Salem ministry (which may actually have started in late November, 1680), see *Salem Possessed*, 54–56, quotation on 56. In their presentation of the conflict over Burroughs, Boyer and Nissenbaum state that the six men who posted bail for him "had been almost unanimously pro-Bayley, or closely identified with pro-Bayley families" (56), and the authors simply list their names in a footnote. But a check of these six names against the pro-Bayley petition noted earlier shows that only four had signed it (Nathaniel Ingersoll, John Buxton, Thomas Haynes, and William Sibley), while two had not (Samuel Sibley and William Ireland Jr.). If "William Ireland, Jr." is the same man as "William Iorland," then Ireland, in fact, had signed a secondary anti-Bayley petition in October 1679 (S-VW, 252). For the names of the five committee members, see S-VW, 173–174. The Salem Village Committee, elected annually by the male householders in the village, was the sole governing body of the "parish," legally a subsection of Salem Town. A brief treatment of this dispute that places Burroughs in a more favorable light than does *Salem Possessed* appears in Konig, *Law and Society*, 105.

15. The Lawson ministry is discussed in *Salem Possessed*, 56–59. In this discussion the authors only give the names of two Lawson supporters, Capt. John Putnam and his nephew, Thomas Putnam Jr. But later in the book (p. 93), Boyer and Nissenbaum mention that the five members of the Salem Village Committee in 1686 (which included the two Putnams) all supported Lawson as well. The names of these five are given in the Salem-Village Book of Record, reprinted in S-VW, 337, from which I drew the names presented in the text. Actually, the village records do not reveal who took the lead in pushing for Reverend Lawson's ordination, but it is reasonable to assume that the elected officials of the village for that year did so. The first mention of arranging for Lawson's "full settlement with us" occurs in the entry for December 10, 1686, "by order of the Committee." Two others who also appear to have been involved in the ordination drive were Jonathan Walcott, a strong supporter of the later witch hunt, and Joseph Herrick, a moderate supporter of the witch hunt who nevertheless came to the defense of Rebecca Nurse (S-VW, 337–342).

16. *Salem Possessed*, 56–59; S-VW, 243, 245, 248 (for names on Bayley petitions), 324 (for committees to invite Lawson), 344–345 (for the February 1687 Salem town statement, including both quotations), 183 (for committees to invite Parris; these included Francis Nurse and John Tarbell, both later opponents of the witch hunt), and 348, 349, 351, 352, 355 (for other examples of the villagers working together). It is also noteworthy that the names of Joseph Hutchinson, Daniel Andrew, and Joseph Porter, three of the four prominent Lawson opponents, did not appear on a list of thirty-eight villagers delinquent in their payments to support the ministry, recorded on December 17, 1689, covering the period marking the transition from Lawson's tenure to Parris's. The fourth, Job Swinnerton, whose name did appear on the same list, died in April of that year, which probably explains why his household was delinquent (ibid., 350). (I assume

that the "Job Swinnerton" mentioned in these citations was Job Swinnerton Sr. Job Swinnerton Jr., a man in his fifties during the 1680s, also lived in the village at this time and was certainly capable of playing a public role. However, since the village record book never adds "Sr." or "Jr." when the name appears, beginning with the Bayley petitions of 1679, it seems likely that the elder Swinnerton is meant. Upham also speaks of Job Swinnerton in this role without indicating a change from an earlier reference that clearly refers to the older man [Upham, *Salem Witchcraft*, 1:140, 270].) In *Salem Possessed*, Boyer and Nissenbaum call attention to a phrase, "the effects of settled prejudice and resolved animosity," used by the Salem town officials when describing the villagers' conflict over the prospect of Lawson's ordination, to support the authors' interpretation of longstanding factionalism in the village. But the town's magistrates and ministers may have meant by this usage to characterize the intensity of the conflict rather than its duration (58).

Stephen Foster offers a very different interpretation of the disputes over the Salem village ministry. Based on persuasive inferences, Foster suggests that the four ministers who occupied this post held a succession of differing views about the Halfway Covenant, a controversial policy adopted at a colony-wide synod in 1662 aimed at broadening participation in the Puritan churches. The new policy, which was not binding on individual congregations, made the sacrament of baptism open to children of parents who, while morally upright, had not testified to having had a saving experience of grace. Such parents, not considered full members of a Puritan church, would formerly have been disallowed from presenting their children for baptism; now, as "halfway" members of their congregations, they could do so. Foster believes that Bayley and Lawson favored the Halfway Covenant, while Burroughs and Parris opposed it (*The Long Argument: English Puritanism and the Shaping of New England Culture, 1570–1700* [1991], 212, 358n99). Although there is not enough detail in the surviving records from the Salem village church to indicate why certain villagers lined up behind one or another of the ministers, this religious dimension to the ministers' differences might offer just one reason among many to explain why Boyer and Nissenbaum's argument based on economic factions is far less conclusive than the authors claim. Doctrinal differences, however, cannot offer a master key to the controversies over the four ministers, much less to the witch hunt, because, if Foster is correct, a core of the liberal Bayley supporters (including Capt. John Putnam, Thomas Putnam Jr., Nathaniel Ingersoll, and John Buxton) would have had to shift their doctrinal beliefs all at roughly the same time in order to become supporters of the conservative Parris and the witch hunt, which seems far-fetched. More likely is that factors other than support for or opposition to the Halfway Covenant played equally decisive roles in determining the villagers' leanings towards their ministers. To add to these complications, the supposedly liberal Bayley (if Foster is correct) preached a resolute sermon at Samuel Willard's pro–Halfway Covenant Third Church in Boston, backing the witch hunt just after Bridget Bishop's hanging (Francis, *Judge Sewall's Apology*, 123), and doctrinal compatibilities did nothing to prevent Samuel Parris from seeking a death sentence for the accused witch George Burroughs. Other historians align Deodat Lawson with the conservatives: Marilynne Roach says he took a position at Boston's anti–Halfway Covenant First Church after leaving Salem village around 1688 or 1689 (*Salem Witch Trials*, xxxiii). Moreover, positions held by individuals concerning the Halfway Covenant could change over these years. I return to this subject at the end of this chapter.

17. The history of Salem, omitting the events of 1692, is presented in *Salem Possessed*, chaps. 2–3. The two petitions from 1695 are introduced on p. 80 and used to analyze the two factions in chap. 4. Examples of the authors utilizing post-1692 events to help explain the causes of the 1692 witch hunt include: Reverend Parris's sermons (chap. 7); the conflict over Mary Veren Putnam's will (139–143); and the construction of the "Anti-Parris Network" that links many of the victims of the witch hunt to Israel Porter (184), in which no fewer than six linkages are based on events occurring during or after the witch hunt. (I discuss Boyer and Nissenbaum's chart displaying this network later in this chapter.) Perhaps sensing the problem of having relied on 1695 petitions to constitute the names of the two factions said to have caused the earlier witch hunt, the authors make one attempt in their final chapter (185) to link their two 1695 lists to the names of Salem villagers whose position during the witch hunt is known, and they find a high correlation. But here again, they have only linked pro- and anti-Parris petitioners to the events of 1692, not to any point in time before 1692. If, as I am suggesting, the witch hunt itself crystalized the factions that would, from late 1692 through 1697, express themselves in conflict over the question of whether to keep or remove Reverend Parris as the village minister, then linking 1695 data back to 1692 does not shed light on the factors producing the witch hunt.

In fairness to Boyer and Nissenbaum's interpretation of the motivation behind Ann Carr Putnam's charge of witchcraft against Rebecca Nurse, the authors do provide evidence of resentment held by Thomas Putnam Jr. toward Thomas's stepmother, Mary Veren, that dated back to a time prior to the witch hunt. When Thomas's father, Thomas Putnam Sr., died in 1686, Thomas joined with his brother, Edward, and two brothers-in-law from his father's first marriage in a failed legal action to contest the terms of their father's will, which the siblings blamed on the influence of his second wife (*Salem Possessed*, 136–137). One may well hypothesize, as Boyer and Nissenbaum do, that displaced personal resentments like this one fueled many of the witchcraft accusations lodged from the household of Thomas Putnam Jr., as well as those from other households. Still, to present data that postdates the witch hunt (*Salem Possessed* devotes four pages to the episode surrounding Mary Veren's will) to add strength to an argument for the causes of the witch hunt contributes to obscuring more likely explanations for the tragedy.

Boyer and Nissenbaum also note that Ann Carr Putnam had been involved in a still earlier protest, together with her husband and other members of the Carr family, against the terms of her own father's will when he died in 1682 (*Salem Possessed*, 135). The authors say the protest had little effect, with Ann and the others receiving "modest cash bequests" compared to the 60% of the estate going to two of the sons. Yet not only were such unequal distributions common in seventeenth-century Massachusetts, but a slightly later settlement of the will (in 1683), overlooked by Boyer and Nissenbaum, raised Ann's portion to 10% of the estate's value, a reasonable sum, considering the presence of nine children in the family. (On the 1683 settlement, see Baker, *Storm of Witchcraft*, 122, 330n63.)

18. *Salem Possessed*, 69–78. The actions of the four leaders (and their supporters) in the drive to remove Samuel Parris (1693–1697) may be traced in the village church records, where they are variously called "the dissenting brethren" or "the displeased brethren" or else are mentioned by name (S-VW, 281–312, esp. 296–297 for a summary of

their grievances in November 1694). See also p. 266 for a summary of their position in 1697. The church activities of these same four men during the 1689–1691 period may be traced in *S-VW*, 268–277.

The precise relationship between Thomas Wilkins and the executed John Willard, not known to Boyer and Nissenbaum when they wrote *Salem Possessed*, was established by David L. Greene in his article, "Bray Wilkins of Salem Village MA and His Children" (1984), 1–18, 101–113. Boyer and Nissenbaum believed, erroneously, that Thomas Wilkins had married a niece of Rebecca Nurse (actually it was Thomas Wilkins's son, also named Thomas, who married Rebecca's niece, Elizabeth Towne, although only after the witch hunt in 1694), yet they still failed to note this personal relationship to a victim of the witch hunt in their treatment of the actions of the four anti-Parris "faction" leaders. The relationship is noted only in a different context near the end of the book (197).

19. This document is discussed in *Salem Possessed*, 67–68, and presented in full in *S-VW*, 255–256.

20. See *Salem Possessed*, 65–68 ("coup" appears on 66), and 109 for "archaic strategy." The full sentence containing the latter phrase reads, "Unable to relieve their frustrations politically, the members of the pro-Parris faction unconsciously fell back on a different and more archaic strategy: they treated those who threatened them not as a political opposition but as an aggregate of morally defective individuals"—i.e., as witches (109). In his works, *Primitive Rebels: Studies in Archaic Forms of Social Movement in the 19th and 20th Centuries* (1959) and *Bandits* (1969), Eric Hobsbawm employed the terms "primitive" and "archaic" as a way of criticizing such groups as the Mafia, millenarian anarchists, certain secret societies, and bands of outlaws for being naively and ineffectively "pre-political," while still holding them up as heroes who championed the interests of peasants and other common people of Europe and America against the incursions of market forces.

21. Technically, the village committee raised the question of whether Reverend Parris's maintenance ought to be shifted to voluntary contribution, an older method of ministerial support that had sometimes been employed in colonial Massachusetts (*S-VM*, 356). The salary for Salem town's minister, John Higginson, for example, who assumed his post in 1660, had at first been paid by voluntary subscription, but this method yielded to a compulsory assessment by 1667 (Perley, *The History of Salem*, 2:289).

In *Salem Possessed*, Boyer and Nissenbaum only briefly note the 1689 transfer of title to the village parsonage in their treatment of the "factional" divide over the four ministers (61–62) and then return to the subject of Parris's terms of maintenance in their biographical chapter on the minister (156–160). By relegating their longer discussion of these terms to the later chapter, the authors suggest—mistakenly, I believe—that these developments hold greater meaning for understanding Parris's ambivalence toward the world of commercial negotiation (thus turning Parris, like the economically "bumbling" Putnams, into another symbolic victim of emerging market forces) than these events do for recognizing the actual, more limited issues in contention between the minister and a number of the villagers.

A more persuasive treatment of the dispute over Reverend Parris's maintenance, centering on the discovery of the transferred title to the parsonage, may be found in Upham, *Salem Witchcraft*, 1:286–298. Upham notes that the record of the October 10, 1689, meeting that voted to grant the parsonage with its surrounding land to Parris and to rescind the 1681 prohibition on doing so was "not signed by the clerk, and there is no evidence that the meeting was legally warned [announced]," suggesting that it was carried out secretively by a subgroup of the villagers (297). The text of the minutes of the meeting in the village's book of records, however, does not appear unusual, since not all minutes show signatures at their end nor announcements in advance (S-VW, 349). Thus it is possible that the meeting, whose minutes begin with the common phrase, "At a general meeting of the inhabitants of Salem Village," was simply unattended by those villagers who would have strenuously disagreed with what transpired. Meanwhile, the men who would shortly emerge as Parris's opponents apparently believed that the terms of the minister's maintenance had already been set at the village meeting of June 18, 1689, whose minutes stated clearly that Parris and his family would enjoy only the "use," not the ownership, of the ministry lands so long as he held the position (348).

The timing of when these opponents learned of the property conveyance is also not clear from the village records. The only indication that an angry meeting occurred when the disputants recognized the significance of what had happened comes from two later depositions submitted to the county court in 1697 by Samuel Parris and by Joseph Porter, Daniel Andrew, and Joseph Putnam, respectively. The first (by Parris) speaks of the heated exchange not occurring "till after my Ordination a good while" (quoted in Fowler, "Account, of the Life and Character of Samuel Parris," in *Witchcraft Delusion* [1866; 1970], 3:201), and the second (by Porter, Andrew, and Putnam) speaks similarly of the recognition and heated confrontation occurring at a meeting held "a considerable time after Mr. Parris his ordination" (Upham, *Salem Witchcraft*, 1:295– 296). Larry Gragg suggests that this meeting would likely have been held in October 1690, which makes sense within the sequence of events (*Quest for Security*, 93–94). Gragg, however, follows the interpretation of another nineteenth-century Salem historian, Samuel P. Fowler, in believing that the crux of the dispute over Samuel Parris's maintenance revolved around the question of how the minister would be supplied with firewood (*Quest for Security*, 46–49, 87–88, 93–98, 155; Fowler, "Account of the Life," 198–203, 220). I find Upham's emphasis on the transfer of property to be more convincing.

(In his discussion, however, Upham does seem to mix up what transpired at two different meetings. At the May 17, 1689, village meeting, which occurred *before* Parris's ordination, there were initial disagreements over how the minister would be provisioned with firewood and whether outsiders attending the village church would contribute to the minister's salary, both of which issues were resolved at the time. Upham seems to confuse this meeting with the still more contentious one held *after* the minister's ordination, probably during October 1690. This meeting, over the title to the minister's house and land, according to the Porter-Andrew-Putnam deposition, ended in a bitter face-off. Seemingly misled by Parris's use of the phrase "much agitation" to describe the earlier disagreement about the outsiders' contributions, Upham erroneously applied the phrase to a characterization of the entire meeting, thereby surmising that the altercation over the transfer of property must have come up at that time. On the subject matter of the May 17, 1689, meeting, Fowler's account appears more reliable than Upham's. It also conforms more closely than Upham's to a handwritten "declaration" that Parris drafted for use in the 1697 court proceeding ["A general account of the transactions between the inhabitants of Salem village and my self Samuel Parris"]. On these points, see Fowler, "Account of the Life," 199–201 [201 for "much agitation"]; Upham, 1:293–294 [293 for "much agitation"].)

22. S-VW, 357–358 (for the three meetings in early 1692), 277–278 (for Thomas Wilkins), and 268–278 (for the church records generally from Parris's ordination until the witch hunt). Boyer and Nissenbaum also attempt to link the themes found in Parris's sermons to the specific conflicts he was having with his opponents over the issues concerning his maintenance (*Salem Possessed*, 168–172, and chap. 7), but this line of reasoning is unpersuasive. The themes of his sermons do paint a picture of the godly under constant threat of attack by the forces of Satan, but the minister's sermonic references are entirely biblical, and in nearly every case can best be explained simply by his conservative Calvinist outlook. (Parris's sermons, excerpted in *Salem Possessed*, may be read in their entirety in Cooper and Minkema, eds., *Sermon Notebook of Samuel Parris, 1689–1694* [1993].) Parris's sole direct reference to "this poor little village" prior to the witch hunt (*Salem Possessed*, 169), for example, comes when the minister warns his parishioners not to resort to false words, as even the apostle Peter did in denying the divinity of Christ (Cooper and Minkema, *Sermon Notebook*, 83–84). There is nothing more specific than this. In one sermon, two phrases Parris selected to characterize Christ's ministry ("holy sermons" and "maintenance of pure religion") may have carried oblique references to the Salem minister's own embattled situation (*Salem Possessed*, 169). But even if he intended to make such connections to local developments, Parris was only doing what would have been expected of any minister: he was offering a providential interpretation of daily events.

No doubt Reverend Parris's conservative religious outlook played a critical role in setting the stage for the witch hunt, as I point out at the end of this chapter, but there is no reason to think Parris's sermon topics heralded a more pointed strategy of counterattack against his village opponents by means of witchcraft accusations. In fact, by late 1691 Parris was just as disappointed with the lack of support shown by most of his own church members as he was worried about what the village committee had done (see the minister's entries in the church record book for November 10 and November 18, 1691, in S-VW, 277). Parris had already adopted his strategy to counter the actions of the village committee. It was to go to court to force the committee to collect the minister's tax.

Larry Gragg follows Boyer and Nissenbaum's line of argument concerning the factionalism in Salem Village surrounding Reverend Parris, but his presentation of the evidence falls short (as does theirs) in justifying his assertion that a group of village members prior to the witch hunt "wished to remove [Parris]" and were simply using "the questionable circumstances surrounding his contract to accomplish their task" (*Quest for Security*, chap. 7, quotations on p. 93). In work published before *Salem Possessed* appeared, David D. Hall showed that many New England ministers in the second half of the seventeenth century faced problems similar to Samuel Parris's in meeting their needs for maintenance and securing land for their families from among their congregations and townsmen (*The Faithful Shepherd: A History of the New England Ministry in the Seventeenth Century*, 185–194). David Thomas Konig echoes this observation in his legal study of seventeenth-century Essex County. Applying his findings to the case of Salem village, Konig writes, "Resistance to paying the ministers' rate, like tax evasion in any society, was not uncommon in Essex, but it took on a more serious, collective form when town meetings attempted to escape the financial responsibilities of maintaining a minister. The disputes at Salem Village have dominated historical attention and have been portrayed as a unique backdrop—and hence plausible cause—of the later witchcraft accusations, but they were not at all unique" (*Law and Society*, 98–104, quotation on 101).

23. See *Salem Possessed*, 184 (for the "Anti-Parris Network" built around Israel Porter) and 181 (on Andrew's election as a town selectman). See Norton, *In the Devil's Snare*, 30 (for the date of Elizabeth Procter's first naming); Karlsen, *Devil in the Shape*, 142–143; and Demos, *Entertaining Satan*, 83–84 (for background on Procter's grandmother). Sources for the order of accusations against the Jacobs group are listed in the notes to my figure 3. On Jacobs-Andrew family ties, see Enders A. Robinson, *The Devil Discovered*, 335–343. Rebecca Andrew Jacobs, by all accounts, was mentally disturbed at the time of her arrest, and it is likely that her mental condition contributed to the accusation of witchcraft against her. Her daughter, Mary, at just under the age of two, had fallen into a well and drowned, and, as Rebecca's mother, Rebecca (Andrew) Fox, pointed out in a petition to secure release of her daughter from jail, the younger Rebecca "at some times has uttered hard words of her self as tho she had killed her Child, which words are much accounted of as is famed [i.e., as is reputed]" (*SWP*, 2:497). If Rebecca held herself responsible for the death of her daughter, others in Salem village may have done so as well, offering another potent line of seeming transmission between the witchcraft imputed to George Jacobs Sr. and that charged against Rebecca's brother, Daniel Andrew.

It is even possible that there was yet another connection between the Jacobs and Andrew families. George Jacobs Jr.'s sister, Ann (or Anna), was married to a man named John Andrews, whose Ipswich family of origin may have been related to Daniel Andrew's Watertown or Cambridge family of origin ("Andrew" was sometimes spelled "Andrews"). On both of these latter points, see David L. Greene's helpful article, "Salem Witches II: George Jacobs," 65, 72–74. Charles Upham thought John Andrews may have been Daniel's brother (Upham, *Salem Witchcraft*, 2:170, 319), but Upham appears to have been misled in this supposition by his apparent failure to recognize that Daniel Andrew was Rebecca Andrew Jacobs's brother; hence, Upham explained the use of the term "uncle" by the junior Jacobs daughter, Margaret, also accused of witchcraft in 1692, to describe "D. A." as a contemporary extension of the term to cover Margaret's Uncle John's brother. As Daniel Andrew was Margaret's mother's brother, there was no need to posit the more circuitous relationship via John.

Jane Kamensky unwittingly compounds Boyer and Nissenbaum's Porter problem when she suggests that "the surviving descendants of John Porter Sr. figured prominently among the accused during the Salem witch trials" because of the community's likely memory of the severe personal transgressions of John Porter Jr., Israel and Joseph Porter's older brother. John Porter Jr., had once been forced by the Massachusetts Court of Assistants to endure a symbolic hanging for contempt of authority, and he died in isolation and poverty in 1684. However, no Porters actually figured among the accused at Salem in 1692, and there are no references in the surviving Salem witch-hunt literature to the memory of John Porter Jr.'s misdeeds. For the story of John Porter Jr., see Kamensky, *Governing the Tongue*, 103–117, 111, and 243n55 (for the purported connection to the Salem witch hunt).

24. The best summary of the Topsfield land dispute and its relationship to the families of some of the witch hunt's victims may be found in Upham, *Salem Witchcraft*,

1:238–242; 2:128, 135–136, 137–139. Some historians refer also to land disputes between the Putnams and the Nurses, but for the most part these two families seem to have been on the same side of a broader conflict over lands originally claimed by the Endicotts, especially by the family's descendant, Zerubabel Endicott (on this complicated issue, see ibid., 1:69–96). Boyer and Nissenbaum mention a Nurse-Putnam land dispute from the 1670s in one sentence (*Salem Possessed*, 149).

On Joanna Towne, see Norton, *In the Devil's Snare*, 77, and *SWP*, 2:601; on Elizabeth How, see *SWP*, 2:437–439, 443–455; and on Sarah Wilds, see *SWP*, 3:808–810, 812–818. More work needs to be done in systematically tracing the family ties of all the accused in the Salem witch hunt, including those named during the panic's second phase, centered in the town of Andover. A number of historians have noted the large number of relatives of Andover's minister, Francis Dane, who found themselves accused—though Dane himself was not—during the witch hunt's later months (see, e.g., Baker, *Storm of Witchcraft*, 137). Richard Latner also offers valuable observations along these lines in "The Long and the Short of Salem Witchcraft," 137–156. Adding maiden names alone to the list of the accused that appears in my appendix 2 would reveal a surprising number of connections. The most extensive start in cataloging these genealogical ties appears in two books by Enders A. Robinson: *Devil Discovered*, on the Salem phase, and *Salem Witchcraft and Hawthorne's House of the Seven Gables*, on the Andover phase. The works of Marilynne K. Roach (*Salem Witch Trials* and *Six Women of Salem*) also contain a wealth of genealogical data.

25. Richard Latner, "Salem Witchcraft, Factionalism, and Social Change Reconsidered," 423–448, quotation on 446–447. In a reply to Latner, Boyer and Nissenbaum attempt unsuccessfully to discredit his findings by arguing that means provide a better measure of comparison than medians in this case, because they take into account extremes of wealth (or poverty), which would be likely to influence perceptions. But Latner uses means and medians throughout his analysis, noting that each offers different strengths, although he settles on medians as the more valuable. The trends are exactly the same using either measure. Concerning the all-important decade that preceded the witch hunt (1681–1690), Latner offers two comparisons between the pro-Parris and anti-Parris groups, one using only 1695 petition signers present both in 1681 and 1690, and a second using 1695 petition signers present in either 1681 or 1690. Using means as the measure in the first comparison, the pro-Parris group improved from 90 to 100% of the anti-Parris group's level of wealth; in the second comparison the pro-Parris group improved from 88 to 93% of their opponents' level of wealth. Using medians as the measure in the first comparison, the pro-Parris group improved from 83 to 130% of the anti-Parris group's level of wealth; in the second comparison the pro-Parris group improved from 80 to 100% of their opponents' level of wealth (435–438). Thus, while Latner highlights the last of these measures of change in economic position between the two groups (see his final chart on p. 447), all of his comparisons point in the same direction. Indeed, he even offers initially yet another measure of this same change, one that compares the movement in percentile ranking of each group's members in relationship to the village's entire list of taxable householders. Using this measure Latner finds that, over the 1681–1690 period, about 43% of the pro-Parris group improved their ranking and 19% experienced a drop in their ranking, while for the anti-Parris group only about 30% improved their ranking and 30% showed a decline (432–434). Here

again, the people who would later support the village minister in 1695 are shown to have been advancing, not declining, during the 1680s, relative to the people who would later oppose the minister. Boyer and Nissenbaum also criticize Latner for not addressing wider aspects of their argument in *Salem Possessed*, but that is hardly a fair complaint. Carefully scrutinizing one important building block in a major argument is a worthy contribution. For Boyer and Nissenbaum's response to Latner, see "*Salem Possessed* in Retrospect," 518–522.

26. To be more precise, Boyer and Nissenbaum did make use of exactly the same data set (the names of the roughly 200 petition signers from 1695) to construct one of their maps (Map 3, "The Geography of Factionalism: Residential Pattern of the Signers of the Pro-Parris and Anti-Parris Petitions of 1695," *Salem Possessed*, 84), showing a strong preponderance of anti-Parris inhabitants living on the eastern, town side of the village and an equal preponderance of pro-Parris inhabitants on the western, interior side. But their study's most famous map, one frequently reproduced by other authors in later articles and textbooks, was the one displaying a selection of thirty-five "accusers," twenty-two "accused witches," and thirty-three "defenders" who were living in Salem village or its immediate vicinity during the 1692 witch hunt (Map 1, "The Geography of Witchcraft: Salem Village, 1692," 34). My discussion centers on the latter map. In *Salem Possessed*, Boyer and Nissenbaum remarkably never identified the names corresponding to the ninety data points placed on their map 1, but all but two of these names can be inferred from the lists of accusers, defenders, and accused witches, along with the copy of Charles W. Upham's residential map of Salem village, provided in S-VW, 375–382, 394–399. For my list of best guesses for these correspondences, see appendix 1.

27. Ray, "The Geography of Witchcraft Accusations in 1692 Salem Village," 449–478, quotation on 468. Ray returned briefly to his critique of Boyer and Nissenbaum's map in his later book, *Satan and Salem: The Witch-Hunt Crisis of 1692* (2015), 187–191, where he chose to highlight the geographic division within the formal boundaries of the village alone: 57% of accusers (33 out of 58) lived on the western side, while 86% of the accused witches (12 out of 14) lived in the east. Here he drew a slightly more qualified conclusion: "The vast majority of the accused in Salem Village lived on the eastern side of the Village, but so did half of their accusers. There was therefore no real east-west division between accusers and accused" (*Satan and Salem*, 188). The map that displays his data (which covers both the village and its immediate environs), however, is virtually identical to the one (reproduced as my figure 5) that appeared in Ray's earlier article (as his figure X), the only difference being the addition of two accused witches (Sarah and Dorothy Good) to the eastern half of the village. The Goods' residence in 1692 has always been unknown, but Ray reasonably assigned them to a place where they were known to have lived previously. (The text on p. 188 of *Satan and Salem* gives three erroneous numbers compared to the data shown on the accompanying map: it speaks of fifteen, rather than fourteen, accused witches in the village; fifty-seven, rather than fifty-eight, village accusers; and thirty-two, rather than thirty-three, accusers living on the village's western side.) The account in the book is far more cursory than the one appearing in Ray's earlier article, and the book cites the article instead of providing documentation of its own for the asserted distribution. Accordingly, my analysis of Ray's methods proceeds on the basis of his article.

Ray discusses his corrections to Boyer and Nissenbaum's map on pp. 458–469 of "The Geography of Witchcraft Accusations." As for the accusers, Ray places on the map nine young, female, afflicted accusers—nearly all extremely active in the witch hunt and all of whom Boyer and Nissenbaum had omitted—but I am unpersuaded by his thinking in doing so for all in this category. Most (Ann Putnam Jr., Mercy Lewis, Mary Walcott, Betty Parris, Abigail Williams, Elizabeth Hubbard, and Susannah Sheldon) deserve to be included, because their accusations seemed to emerge out of the sentiments and gossip absorbed from the adults in their households; thus their presence on the map helps define the residential patterning of the witch hunt. But others (Mary Warren, Sarah Churchill—whom Ray omits for a different reason, as explained below— and Jemima Rea) became accusers against the wishes of the adults in their household; thus, they do not seem to indicate anything about the geography of accusation but only its sociology.

Ray adds another five new accusers (Joseph Herrick Sr., James Holton, James Kettle, Nathaniel Putnam, and Samuel Sibley) whom Boyer and Nissenbaum had probably omitted from their map because these Salemites had functioned both as accusers and occasional defenders of one or another suspect. (It was the authors' stated policy to omit from their map any individuals who functioned ambiguously in this way, although they violated this rule in the cases of Joseph Holton Sr., his wife Sarah Holton, Joseph Hutchinson Sr., John Putnam Sr., and Jonathan Putnam, all of whom also appear on Boyer and Nissenbaum's lists of both accusers and defenders yet were placed on the authors' map: Holton Sr. as an accuser and the other four as defenders.) Ray's reasoning is persuasive that the five listed above functioned chiefly as accusers, although his documentation is maddeningly thin.

Ray is again mostly persuasive in shifting six additional names (Jonathan Putnam, Joseph Hutchinson Sr. and his wife Lydia, John Putnam Sr. and his wife Rebecca, and Joseph Holton Sr.) from the ranks of Boyer and Nissenbaum's "defenders" to his own corrected group of "accusers," although it seems to me that Boyer and Nissenbaum must have already assigned one of their As to Joseph Holton Sr., a man whom the authors list as having brought formal witchcraft complaints against at least ten people. In any case, like the previous group of five, these six typically accused several individuals while defending a single suspect (almost always Rebecca Nurse), although a case could be made for the removal of the Hutchinsons from among the accusers, since Joseph accused no one after he joined the initial complaint against the first three suspects, and there is no record of Lydia accusing anyone. Here, too, Ray fails to provide adequate documentation, but his assessments fit with known data from other sources.

Ray adds a final group of thirteen accusers whom he believes Boyer and Nissenbaum overlooked. Of these, Indian John makes good sense, while Tituba does not, since she is already included as an accused witch. (Even though the net geographic effect of counting an individual in both categories of accuser and accused would be nil, it would seem best to adhere with consistency to the principle of deciding how an individual chiefly functioned during the witch hunt in placing them on the map). Similarly, I do not agree with Ray's decision to count Abigail and Deliverance Hobbs as accusers, since he has also decided to add them as accused "witches," which was their primary role in the witch hunt. Ray's remaining nine accusers (Samuel Parris, Lydia Nichols Jr., her sister Elizabeth and her brother Thomas, Sarah Holton, Bathshua Pope and her husband Joseph, Joseph Herrick Sr. and his wife Mary) seem sound, except that he has already counted Herrick in an earlier category of additional accusers, and Parris appears to have already been included in Boyer and Nissenbaum's original map.

Ray has also chosen to omit Sarah Churchill and Elizabeth Booth, both accusers, from his map, together with George Jacobs Sr., whom Churchill and others accused of witchcraft, because their residences lay just beyond the bounds of Boyer and Nissenbaum's original map. But all three of these important figures in the witch hunt lived as close to Salem village to the south as Ray's Topsfield additions, noted in the next paragraph, did to the north.

As for the accused "witches," I agree with Ray that Bridget Bishop (her residence had been incorrectly identified as close to the village) and Indian John (he was never accused and is now correctly identified as an accuser) should be removed as "witches" from the map and that four Topsfield residents (Abigail, Deliverance, and William Hobbs, and Mary Towne Esty) should be added, since Boyer and Nissenbaum had placed three nearby Topsfield accusers on their own map. (For that matter, I see no reason not to include Elizabeth How and Sarah Wilds, the other two Topsfield residents whose naming as witches was quite integral to the early development of the Salem witch hunt, but Ray has chosen not to do so.) I do not agree that Mary Warren should be added to the number of accused witches, since she functioned in the witch hunt chiefly as an accuser.

Ray also decided to ignore the remainder of Boyer and Nissenbaum's "defenders" without comment, removing that category entirely from his corrected map. The full list of defenders, from which Boyer and Nissenbaum selected about half to place on their map, appears in S-VW, 381–382. Logically, some of these people—for example, Rebecca Nurse's relatives Sarah Nurse, Samuel Nurse, Rebecca Preston, and John and Mary Tarbell—should probably be included on any map illustrating the geography of the witch hunt, since these people likely became known opponents of the witch hunt early on. Most of the remaining "defenders," however, were similar to the members of Ray's groups of five and six additional accusers described in the previous paragraphs—that is, they probably approved of the witch hunt (and may even have testified against several suspects) but acted to defend one or another of its victims, usually Rebecca Nurse. All in all, my own questioning of Ray's decisions would probably work to shift Ray's modifications back somewhat in the direction of Boyer and Nissenbaum's geographic disproportions but certainly not all the way. Thus, I find Ray's modifications to the geographic distribution shown on Boyer and Nissenbaum's original map to be mostly valid. Still, they do not eliminate the disproportions entirely, as I point out in the text.

In a reply to Ray's argument, Boyer and Nissenbaum conceded that in *Salem Possessed* they mistakenly placed Ray's group of six new accusers (Jonathan Putnam, Joseph and Lydia Hutchinson, John Putnam Sr. and his wife Rebecca, and Joseph Holton Sr.) as defenders when each of these individuals had also accused a number of suspects; hence they should have been eliminated from the map, according to the authors' own rules. (Actually, however, Lydia Hutchinson never accused anyone, and Ray has transferred these six to the category of accusers. It still seems likely to me that in preparing their map for *Salem Possessed* in 1974, Boyer and Nissenbaum assigned Joseph Holton Sr. one of their *A* symbols, even as they might have also placed him on the map as a defender. Double counting in this instance might have occurred as a mistake. Even in 2008, the authors still never provided a list of correspondences for the symbols shown on their map, so it is impossible to know for sure where Joseph Holton Sr. was placed.) Boyer and Nissenbaum equally acknowledged that they might have overlooked some additional accusers from Ray's final group of thirteen (they inexplicably number this group at fourteen), without going into further details. However, they strongly defended their original decision to omit the afflicted accusers from their map, since, as the authors put it, "their specific accusations were so tainted by adult intervention or, as Ray suggests, by 'village gossip' that their residences were not germane to the geographic pattern we were documenting." Ray's judgment to include the afflicted accusers on the map seems stronger, however, since for most of the afflicted, it was not adults in general or village gossip as a whole that influenced their accusations but the specific stories, beliefs, and prejudices they would have heard from their immediate household surroundings, at least in the many instances in which the afflicted were regarded sympathetically by their household members. Boyer and Nissenbaum concluded their response to Ray's article by dismissing its significance for altering the geographic pattern of the witch hunt that *Salem Possessed* first set forth. Boyer and Nissenbaum are only partly correct on this point, since the east-west disproportions have been substantially mitigated by Ray's modifications, though not eliminated, as the percentages reported in my text demonstrate. For Boyer and Nissenbaum's response to Ray's article, see their "*Salem Possessed* in Retrospect," 522–530, quotation on 525.

28. The personal details of these accusations are available in many accounts of the witch hunt. Documentation may be found, for example, in Norton, *In the Devil's Snare*, 77, 196 (for Rebecca Nurse); *Salem Possessed*, 193–194 (for Sarah Osburn); and *Salem Possessed*, 195–198 and *In the Devil's Snare*, 157–158 (for John Willard). The particular accusations noted in the text did not preclude additional reasons for suspicion directed against the same individuals by these or other members of the community or colony. A number of the accused (including Rebecca Nurse, George Burroughs, Elizabeth Procter, and Andover resident Samuel Wardwell, all of whom were convicted and all but Procter executed), for example, were perhaps tainted by real or reputed associations with Quakers or Baptists, both still regarded as heretical sects by some Puritans in 1692. On the latter point, see Christine Leigh Heyrman, "Specters of Subversion, Societies of Friends: Dissent and the Devil in Provincial Essex County, Massachusetts" (1984), 45–61. In an implicit criticism of Boyer and Nissenbaum's thesis, Heyrman adds that the concentration of Quaker families on the eastern side of Salem village might explain the geographic distribution of accusers and accused in the village better than the proximity of the easterners to Salem town (53). Yet the number of Quaker families in Salem village was small, and Heyrman acknowledges that practicing Quakers themselves were not especially targeted in the countywide witch hunt (51). More questionable still is her claim that Rebecca Nurse was disliked because in 1677 she and her husband had taken in the orphaned son of Salem Quaker John Southwick as a ward (52). John Southwick, like most of Salem's Quakers, had become very well accepted in the town before his death in 1672 (Jonathan M. Chu, *Neighbors, Friends or Madmen: The Puritan Adjustment to Quakerism in Seventeenth-Century Massachusetts Bay* [1985], 129, 132, 139, and chap. 7.) Carla Gardina Pestana presents a similar picture of Quaker assimilation in Salem, certainly from 1680 onward. She also notes that several Lynn residents, including Sarah Hood Bassett, Elizabeth Procter's sister-in-law, joined the Quakers in

reaction to having been jailed as a suspect in the Salem witch hunt. "Rather than Quakerism sparking accusations of witchcraft, as one scholar [Christine Heyrman] has recently suggested," Pestana writes, "the witch controversy led to the growth of Quakerism" (*Quakers and Baptists in Colonial Massachusetts* [1991], 94, 162, and, on the Lynn Quakers, 123–124). Some Quakers, including Samuel Shattuck and probably Naomi Maule, also provided testimony against Bridget Bishop at her trial (Roach, *Salem Witch Trials*, 159), even as Naomi's husband, Thomas Maule, would later produce a biting critique of the witch hunt that was published in 1695. (A nearly identical version of Heyrman's article appears as chap. 3 in her book, *Commerce and Culture: The Maritime Communities of Colonial Massachusetts, 1690–1750* [1984].)

For the family groupings shown in figure 6, most can be identified simply by surname in the list of correspondences to the data points on Boyer and Nissenbaum's map supplied in my appendix 1. Thus, for example, the four Putnam (PT) symbols correspond to Edward Putnam, Thomas Putnam Jr., Ann Putnam Sr., and John Putnam Jr. For the Wilkins extended family (WK), however, the six accusers with the Wilkins surname are joined by Thomas and Elizabeth Bailey (Elizabeth was Bray Wilkins's granddaughter), Phillip and Margaret Knight (Margaret was Bray Wilkins's daughter), and Lydia Nichols (Lydia was another of Bray's daughters). On these relationships, see Greene, "Bray Wilkins of Salem Village," 11, 7. The Jacobs extended family (JA) includes George Jacobs Sr. and his granddaughter Margaret, with whom he lived to the southeast of the village boundary (not shown on Boyer and Nissenbaum's original map); George Jr. and Rebecca Andrew Jacobs, as shown among the accused witches listed in appendix 1; Daniel Andrew (the brother of Rebecca Andrew Jacobs); and Sarah Porter Andrew (Daniel Andrew's wife, included on Boyer and Nissenbaum's map as a defender). For documentation of these relationships, see Greene, "Salem Witches II: George Jacobs," esp. 72, and *Records*, pp. 928 and 947. For the Nurse/Towne family (NT), members include Mary Towne Esty (just north of the village boundary, not included on Boyer and Nissenbaum's original map), Sarah Towne Cloyce and her husband Peter Cloyce (the latter shown as a defender on the original map), the accused witch Rebecca Nurse, and five of Boyer and Nissenbaum's defenders (Rebecca Preston, Rebecca Nurse's daughter; Mary and John Tarbell, Rebecca Nurse's daughter and son-in-law; Samuel Nurse Sr., Rebecca Nurse's son; and Sarah Nurse, Rebecca Nurse's daughter-in-law). The Wilds family (WL) includes Sarah Wilds Bishop, her husband Edward, both of Salem village, and her mother, Sarah Wilds, of Topsfield, living just to the north of Salem Village. (Sarah Wilds did not appear on Boyer and Nissenbaum's original map.)

Despite his endorsement of Boyer and Nissenbaum's factional argument, Peter Charles Hoffer seems exactly right when he observes that the geographic pattern of accusers and accused in Salem village is better explained by the location of the land holdings of a few critical families than by any larger economic axis (*Devil's Disciples*, 242n91).

29. Robert G. Pope, *The Half-Way Covenant: Church Membership in Puritan New England* (1969), contains much valuable information on the role of Rev. John Higginson and the Salem town church in the evolution of the Halfway Covenant. See, esp., 142–147, 150, 247–248. The estimate of 80% may be found on p. 185. It is necessary to add, however, that the movement toward liberalization in the rules of participation in

the Puritan churches in the mid-seventeenth century—in effect, a step back in the direction of Anglican practice—at first often went with heightened intolerance toward the dissenting sects on the Puritans' opposite flank, the Quakers and the Baptists (Foster, *Long Argument*, 189–203, esp. 198, 355n64). Higginson himself was anti-Quaker when he was ordained in the Salem church in 1660, but the conciliatory policies he soon pursued toward the Society of Friends, even while aimed at winning its converts back to his own church, put an end to the violent clashes that had occurred between Salem's Puritans and Quakers during the previous few years and produced, in the words of Richard P. Gildrie, "a permanent détente . . . by the mid-1660s" (*Salem, Massachusetts, 1626–1683: A Covenant Community*, 130–137). By all accounts Higginson, whose own mentally ill daughter was among those accused and jailed in 1692 (Heyrman, "Specters of Subversion," 46n11), was not an avid supporter of the witch hunt, and he wrote a thoughtful, approving preface to Rev. John Hale's reevaluation of the tragedy, *Modest Enquiry*, when it was first completed in 1698. Yet it is a mark of just how powerful the witchcraft panic was in 1692 that Higginson did not, so far as is known, speak out against the tide during that year (he was admittedly seventy-six years old and in ill health), and the younger minister at his church, Rev. Nicholas Noyes, was an avid proponent of the witch hunt.

Pope made the important point throughout his study that over the course of the seventeenth century it was generally the laity, not the clergy, in New England who stood for conservatism in Puritan practice; conservatism here means the (once radical) tendency to maintain a sharp distinction between the visible saints and everyone else. This observation may be broadened to say that, given how thoroughly most New Englanders had internalized Calvinist principles, liberalization came first to the more educated members of the ministry and the more cosmopolitan sections of the population (although to some degree liberal versus conservative interpretations of Calvinist principles remained a matter of personal temperament). These social generalizations aptly describe the contrasting pace of religious change in Salem town and village. On the conservatism of the Salem village church under Samuel Parris, see Gragg, *Quest for Security*, 73–75. Although Parris had attended Harvard College, he had never graduated, and he pursued a merchant career in Barbados and Boston before turning to the ministry in the mid-1680s. Parris's religious ties were to Boston's conservative First Church, where his uncle John Oxenbridge had previously ministered. First Church resisted the Halfway Covenant until 1730. On these points, see Gragg, *Quest for Security*, 10–11, 31–33; Pope, *Half-Way Covenant*, chap. 6, and p. 200; and Cooper, *Tenacious of Their Liberties: The Congregationalists of Colonial Massachusetts*, 242n47. Gragg strenuously rejects Boyer and Nissenbaum's portrait of Parris's religious views as driven by failure in business or resentment over the terms of his father's will. In fact, he shows Parris to have been moderately successful economically while maintaining a restless drive for status and the security of his family (*Quest for Security*, xi, xviii, 13, 47–48, 51, 61, 195–199). Gragg asserts persuasively that Parris's religious beliefs and those of the Salem villagers cannot be reduced to their economic positions (xviii, 149n8), while at the same time he accepts Boyer and Nissenbaum's factional argument to explain the conflicts during Samuel Parris's ministry, an unresolved tension in his argument that persists in Gragg's later narrative account, *The Salem Witch Crisis* (1992).

In valuable recent works, Richard Latner and Benjamin C. Ray have also called attention to the centrality of religious factors in unleashing the Salem witch hunt. Latner argues for the importance of Salem village's opposition to the Halfway Covenant as an index of conservative Puritan practice, which is indisputable for the ministry of Samuel Parris but seems questionable when he asserts the same for Parris's predecessor, Deodat Lawson. (The scant evidence presented is not convincing, and see note 16 above for Stephen Foster's contrasting view.) Latner also offers a suggestive religious interpretation of how the witch hunt spread to Andover in July 1692, based on conflict between the community's older, more liberal minister, Francis Dane, many of whose family members were accused of witchcraft, and Andover's younger, more conservative minister, Thomas Bernard, who initially supported the witch hunt until reversing course in October 1692. See Latner, "'Here Are No Newters': Witchcraft and Religious Discord in Salem Village and Andover" (2006), 92–122. Latner might have added that Bernard had been raised in Hadley, Massachusetts, a conservative Puritan community formed out of a schism in the Wethersfield, Connecticut, congregation. On this subject, see Demos, *Entertaining Satan*, 351.

Ray argues that the witch hunt grew out of Samuel Parris's and his congregation's conservative sense of embattlement against a profane, Satanically inspired world and more particularly against local opponents within Salem village. When he sticks to the general religious outlook of conservative Puritanism, Ray is persuasive. Unfortunately, the weight of his interpretation falls on the actions Parris and the members of his congregation are said to have taken to strike back at particular religious foes, especially the unchurched members of the community and the village committee of 1691. Adopting Boyer and Nissenbaum's language to describe the village at war with itself over its minister, Ray writes, "As early as December 1689, only a month after Parris had been ordained, his opponents took decisive action. Thirty-eight Village men, none of them church members, withheld their tax payments for the minister's salary" (*Satan and Salem*, 22). In October 1691, the (non-church member-dominated) village committee "staged a political coup," leading to "'total institutional polarization'" by the end of the year (24; the internal quotation comes from *Salem Possessed*). "The battle lines were drawn, and Parris fought back" (25). I have shown earlier in this chapter how this characterization of the first several years of Parris's ministry misconstrues the extent and sources of conflict in the village. The early delinquency of thirty-eight households to pay their portions of the minister's salary was run-of-the-mill for the village (as for other Massachusetts towns). The total deficit amounted to less than one-quarter of the minister's annual salary, and, significantly, the households involved included several relatives of church members or future church members and none of the five men who in the next year or two would challenge Parris over the discovered transfer of title to the parsonage (the list of delinquent householders appears in S-VW, 350).

Moreover, in his earlier article, "Satan's War against the Covenant in Salem Village" (69–95), and later book, *Satan and Salem*, Ray blurs the boundaries between non-church members and community members who simply belonged to other churches outside Salem village. A number of local victims of the Salem witch hunt were members of the church in Salem town (Rebecca Nurse, Sarah Buckley, Giles Cory, and probably Elizabeth and John Procter). Daniel Andrew is also listed in the records of the Salem town church as having several children baptized there, where his wife was a member (Pierce, *Records of the First Church in Salem*, 37, 38, 40). Mary Esty belonged to the church in neighboring Topsfield ("Records of the Topsfield Church," 6). The Salem village church itself counted among its members three witchcraft suspects: Martha Cory, Sarah Cloyce, and Sarah Bishop. As the witch hunt moved into other communities, local church members again were often targeted. While it is true, as Ray points out, that stalwart members of Reverend Parris's village congregation, with the family of Thomas Putnam Jr. in the lead, did most of the accusing, the accusations themselves did not in the first instance spring from differing religious positions (churched vs. unchurched, for or against the Halfway Covenant) but rather from longstanding personal prejudices, based on community gossip, about individuals thought likely to be Satan's agents. These individuals might or might not be church members. Ray is even forced to acknowledge that Parris's immediate local opponents were mostly ignored in the accusations (*Satan and Salem*, 190). Conservative Puritan beliefs were indeed critical for activating the Salem witch hunt, but these beliefs should not be emphasized to the exclusion of recognizing the equally important role played by personal fears and enmities that typically proceeded along family lines.

In a still earlier argument for the importance of religious conflict in generating the witch hunt, Cedric B. Cowing attempted to use the English regional origins of Salem settlers as an index of religious stance, in which settlers from the southeast of England were said to represent a comparatively rational, orderly form of Puritanism, while settlers from the northwest of England were said to represent a comparatively raw, emotional form of the faith. In Cowing's view, the witch hunters stemmed disproportionately from southeastern families, while the accused hailed disproportionately from northwestern families, whose "growing sectarianism . . . posed a serious threat to Puritan order. . . . Orthodox Southeasterners feared 'enthusiasm' and believed that these people were reviving the religious chaos of the [English] Interregnum." But there appears to be little evidence of any such growth in "sectarianism" or "enthusiasm" in the years prior to 1692. Quakers and Baptists had become increasingly institutionalized and accepted by their Puritan neighbors. Secular ways seemed to pose a far greater threat, from the standpoint of the ministry. Cowing also provides no evidence for his most striking assertion ("more than five out of six among the accused witches had origins in the Northwest") and only shaky evidence for his more limited claim that two-thirds of accused males possessed surnames linking them with the Northwest. The data he presents for the latter claim show 58% of thirty-eight names roughly associated with the Northwest, but the original list of names lacks precision as a complete set of the men and boys who were accused. The list also features a number of family subgroups (for example, three Procters), which raises the question of whether the individuals were associated because of their regional roots or because of their family ties. Above all, regional surnames simply offer too blunt an instrument with which to uncover religious proclivities. The Procter surname may indeed be associated with the north of England, but knowing that John and Elizabeth Procter were members of the Salem town church (if indeed they were) seems much more important for inferring their religious leanings than identifying the likely geographical origin of John's forbears. (I have not found the Procters' names in the church's published records, edited by Richard D. Pierce, but local historian Sidney Perley, writing in the 1920s, stated that they were assigned seats in the church's new building in 1677 [*History of Salem*, 2:433].) Ancestral regional distinctions, however, might have come into play in generating or maintaining personal prejudices within New England's towns. See Cowing, *The Saving Remnant: Religion and the Settling of New England* (1995), 1–41, 68–108, quotations on 96 and 80.

30. The connection between the merchant class and liberalization of Puritan values was persuasively argued in Bernard Bailyn, *The New England Merchants in the Seventeenth Century* (1964), esp. 44, 106–111, 139. On John Hathorne's conservatism, see Gildrie, *Salem, Massachusetts*, 138, 161. Boyer and Nissenbaum imply, citing Gildrie, that Hathorne was not part of the merchant class (introduction to SWP, 1:30n11). But he had inherited ownership of his father's substantial merchant shipping business, and the longer quotation of Gildrie's, from which Boyer and Nissenbaum excerpt only the phrase, "a leader of the orthodox, anticommercial party in colonial politics," makes this clear: "His [Eleazer Hathorne's] younger brother John, also a merchant, aspired to the role played by his father [i.e., participation in public service] and largely succeeded, becoming a leader of the orthodox, anticommercial party in colonial politics. His dedication to the old values was intense enough to make him one of the two merchant sons of leading families to serve [the customary apprenticeship] in lesser posts. Hence he was an obvious exception" to the new rule that merchants either moved directly into high official positions or else avoided public service altogether (Gildrie, *Salem, Massachusetts*, 138). In *Salem Possessed* the authors do identify Hathorne on one occasion as a "wealthy merchant" (58), but overall he barely appears in the book—not surprising, because his alliance with the supposedly anti–Salem town "Parris faction" made him an anomaly in terms of Boyer and Nissenbaum's economic explanation for the witch hunt. Hathorne's religious conservatism can also be seen in his opposition to the longtime Salem minister, John Higginson, which manifested itself in the leadership Hathorne provided for a failed attempt in 1680 to form a second church in the town. Hathorne appears to have followed his father, William, in interpreting Higginson's religious innovations as allying the church too closely with the secular world. It would be a mistake, however, to regard either the Hathornes' or Higginson's religious stances as "anticommercial" in any meaningful sense, although each position has on occasion been labeled as such by historians. Both sides in their religious conflicts attempted in their respective ways to bring the discipline of Puritan godliness to business pursuits, and both spoke for urban constituencies dominated by people with commercial callings. On these points, see Christine Alice Young, *From "Good Order" to Glorious Revolution: Salem, Massachusetts, 1628–1689* (1980), 126–138; and Foster, *Long Argument*, 195–196, 202, 208–211, 356n76.

On the orthodox views of Richards and Stoughton, see Pope, *Half-Way Covenant*, 195–196 (Richards), 167 (Stoughton). On Stoughton's Manichean cast of mind as early as 1668, see Foster, *Long Argument*, 216. For Sewall's conservatism, see Bailyn, *New England Merchants*, 134–135, 193–194; David D. Hall, *Worlds of Wonder, Days of Judgment: Popular Religious Belief in Early New England* (1990), 216–217, 220, 226–228; and Francis, *Judge Sewall's Apology*, part 1. One may also characterize Wait Winthrop, another of the trial judges, as perhaps a temperamental conservative at the time of the witch hunt. Although in his youth an Anglophile who resisted covenanting with any church, Winthrop's growing opposition to the authoritarian regime of Edmund Andros moved him in the direction of New England orthodoxy. After participating in the rebellion that overthrew Andros in April 1689, Winthrop joined Boston's Third Church and began to identify fully with the New England of his illustrious forbears. His leading biographer writes of this turning point in Winthrop's life, "The Glorious Revolution started Wait Winthrop off in an entirely new direction. Not only was he henceforth an active public figure, regularly elected to the Massachusetts council from 1689 till his death in 1717, but he became increasingly a champion of Massachusetts' 'antient liberty,' the religious orthodoxy and chartered privileges established by his grandfather. Having at last joined the church, Wait became the protégé of Cotton Mather, a zealous judge in witchcraft trials, a pious critic of his colleagues' self-seeking greed in office, and a stern defender of the old-time New England virtues" (Richard S. Dunn, *Puritans and Yankees: The Winthrop Dynasty of New England, 1630–1717*, chaps. 9–12, quotation on p. 258).

The persistent appeal of Boyer and Nissenbaum's factional argument can be seen in the way a number of the more recent historians, despite their welcome insistence on the importance of religious ideas in generating the witch hunt, cannot shake their reliance on the categories of social conflict set forth in *Salem Possessed*. In addition to Gragg (as described in the previous note), see, e.g., Richard Gildrie, "Visions of Evil: Popular Culture, Puritanism, and the Massachusetts Witchcraft Crisis of 1692" (1985), 17–35, and *The Profane, the Civil, and the Godly: The Reformation of Manners in Orthodox New England, 1679–1749* (1994), 157–181. In both works Gildrie accepts the alleged "entrenched factionalism" of Salem village (citing *Salem Possessed*) as one of the causes of the witch hunt ("Visions of Evil," 22; *The Profane, the Civil, and the Godly*, 167), while at the same time writing convincingly of the guilt-ridden, conservative Calvinist perspective that could lead so many common people to confess to the crime of witchcraft: "The Salem witchcraft investigations were ceremonies about evil and the greatest of the evils was the inability of people who so badly wished to embrace Puritan experience to do so" ("Visions of Evil," 30). Similarly, in the introduction to their edited volume, *The Sermon Notebook of Samuel Parris, 1689–1694* (1993), James F. Cooper Jr. and Kenneth P. Minkema explain many of the collection's passages from Parris's sermons as thinly disguised references to the factional dispute in the village, before concluding—jarringly—that it was neither "capitalist contention" nor "family rivalries" that lay at the center of the tensions that produced the witch hunt but rather Parris's own inclination to draw a sharp line in his sermons between those good Christians who lived within the covenant and those who remained outside it (1–36, esp. 4, 11, 13–17, with their conclusion on 34). Both Latner ("Here Are No Newters," 101–104) and Ray (documented in the previous note) equally assume the existence of an "anti-Parris" faction, as described in *Salem Possessed*, whose actions are taken to be the cause of Parris's extreme response in preaching about the encirclement of the congregation by Satan's forces. Ray's attempts to tie some of the themes and quotations from Parris's sermons to the conflict in the village over the minister's maintenance are as unconvincing as those of previous historians, Boyer and Nissenbaum included ("Satan's War," 79–81; *Satan and Salem*, 22–23). In *Storm of Witchcraft* (2015), Emerson Baker defers to Boyer and Nissenbaum's factional argument (77–90, 94–96, 119–123, 230, 273), even as he undercuts it with a limiting footnote (322n49) and emphasizes instead the causal significance of the northern Indian war and Reverend Parris's polarizing religious views. *Salem Pos-*

sessed has indeed cast an exceedingly long shadow over the subsequent scholarship on the Salem witch hunt.

CHAPTER 2: An Aside

1. For some of the European influences on witchcraft studies at this time, see H. C. Erik Midelfort, "Were There Really Witches?" (1974), 189–205. While skeptical of previous claims for witches in early modern Europe, Midelfort nevertheless left the door open to their presence, especially owing to the recent scholarship of Keith Thomas (on England) and Carlo Ginzburg (on Italy). Jon Butler also highlighted European scholarly trends in his review essay, "Witchcraft, Healing, and Historians' Crazes" (1984), 111–118.

2. On "cursing tablets," see Thomas, *Religion and the Decline*, 508–509; and Kittredge, *Witchcraft in Old and New England*, 132–133. After Thomas's study appeared, an important archeological discovery of as many as 700 cursing tablets from Roman Britain was made at Bath, England. Inscribed on rolled metal plates, dedicated nearly exclusively to the local goddess Sulis (identified with Minerva, the Roman goddess of wisdom and magic), and deposited in a sacred spring associated with her, these tablets fall into the category of "prayers for justice." Nearly all sought the help of the goddess to recover items stolen from individuals at the public baths near the site of the temple of Sulis. Yet while the inscriptions aim to have the goddess punish the thief and recover the stolen goods, they bear little resemblance to purported witchcraft of either the ancient or early modern type. Most seem to have been written not by a "sorcerer" or "witch" but rather by or for the wronged individuals themselves, using texts based on formulations transmitted orally or through consulting a handbook. Moreover, the tablets address a respectable deity, whose powers were referred to with humility and deference, suggesting, according to Daniel Ogden, that the Sulian tablets had "more in common with ordinary pious religious practice than 'magic'" (Ogden, "Binding Spells," 4–5, 11, 13, 15, 23, 28, 37–43, 46, 55–59, 68). Two other Roman-era curse tablets uncovered in 2005 at Leicester similarly appealed to deities to punish thieves and recover stolen belongings (a slave's cloak and a man's silver coins). See Tomlin, "Paedagogium and Septizonium," 207–218.

3. On the use of effigies, see Thomas, *Religion and the Decline*, 513–514; and Kittredge, *Witchcraft in Old and New England*, 73–90.

4. Thomas, *Religion and the Decline*, quotation on 526. I discuss Thomas's explanation for the rise in witchcraft prosecutions during these two centuries in chapter 3.

5. Jon Butler, "Magic, Astrology, and the Early American Religious Heritage," 331–333, 335–338, 343, and quotation on 332n31; Butler, *Awash in a Sea of Faith*, chap. 3, quotation on 311n10.

6. Weisman, *Witchcraft, Magic, and Religion in 17th-Century Massachusetts*, 85–86, 139–140 (for examples of confusing reputation with practice), 39–42 (for examples of supposed witchcraft), and 76, 89, 95, 123–126, 184–189 (for the de facto substance of his argument). Weisman's interpretation thus continued in the sociological tradition of Kai T. Erikson's 1966 study, *Wayward Puritans*, which he acknowledged (xiv). For a summary of Erikson's position, see chap. 1, note 22.

7. David D. Hall, "Witchcraft and the Limits of Interpretation," 265 (for his early openness to Hansen's hypothesis); Hall, *Worlds of Wonder*, 7 (and throughout for the

omission of witchcraft from occult practices); Hall, introduction to *Witch-Hunting in Seventeenth-Century New England: A Documentary History, 1638–1692* (1991), 15n4, 4–5 (for his direct disagreement with Hansen); and Hall, *Worlds of Wonder*, esp. 74, 82–89, 94, 98–102, 106–109, 140, 144–147, 150, 168–169, 189–196 (for the rest of the material in this and the next paragraph).

8. Hall, "Witchcraft and the Limits of Interpretation," 274 (for "perhaps not unwilling"); Hall, *Worlds of Wonder*, 284n103 (for the story of Mary Parsons, whom Hall mistakenly calls Mary Johnson); Hall, "Middle Ground on the Witch-Hunt Debate" (1998), 346 (for the final quotation). For Hall's own explanation of the Salem witch hunt, see my discussions in chapter 2, note 12; chapter 3, note 12; and the conclusion.

9. Godbeer, *Devil's Dominion*, 39n70 (for its endorsement of Hansen's work), 7, 38–39, 41, 213–214 (for the presence of witches in New England and during the Salem witch hunt), and 213–214 (on Mary Lacey). For the rest of Lacey's confession, see SWP, 2:514.

10. Godbeer, *Escaping Salem*, 147 (for the ambiguous paragraph); Godbeer, ed., *The Salem Witch Hunt*, 9, 107, 109–110, 113, 151. In a still later article, Godbeer expresses greater equivocation about the actual practice of image magic at Salem, but he nevertheless implies that given the large number of such accusations, "this magical technique" must have sometimes been employed ("Folk Magic in British North America" [2015], 263–264).

The assertion that witches really existed appears as well in Alison Games, ed., *Witchcraft in Early North America* (2010), 4, but the long introductory essay that precedes the book's collection of documents provides no evidence of any such practice among colonial British Americans. Writing in 2015, Emerson Baker also follows Godbeer and Hansen, both of whose works he cites, in accepting the limited presence of actual witches at Salem: "Clearly there were some who not only believed in the power of poppets and black magic but also were willing to use it. . . . At best there were only a handful of people practicing magic—especially black magic—in Essex County in 1692" (*Storm of Witchcraft*, 131–133).

11. The contradictions present in this line of scholarship and their potential for adding confusion to the understanding of the Salem witch hunt are best on display in Godbeer's *Devil's Dominion*. Godbeer devotes the last chapter to the events of 1692, arguing that Puritanism's strict doctrines of sin and predestination encouraged (as a means of seeking relief from such intense personal responsibility for salvation) the scapegoating that went on, especially when triggered by the perception of a host of external threats to the colony. This argument is a useful summary of the leading religious component in the witch hunt, but its insight is hard to reconcile with the rest of Godbeer's book, which adopts a sympathetic stance toward the beliefs and practices of New England's common people. Their religious life is depicted as laced with occult traditions (protective magic, divination, astrology, healing, and witchcraft) that are said to have supported the average person's self-worth against the deadening weight of Puritanism. ("Religion thus empowers the supernatural," Godbeer observes in his introduction, "whereas magic empowers human beings through their command of the supernatural" [9].) In an early chapter devoted to the pre-Salem cases of witchcraft accusation, the reader is encouraged to side with "the people," whose attempts to see the occasional community witch successfully prosecuted are often thwarted by the scrupulosity of

Puritan magistrates and ministers. Had the people prevailed in more of these cases, Godbeer implies, the backlog of popular resentment that fed into the Salem witch hunt would have been dissipated and the panic possibly avoided. How jarring it is, then, to be confronted in Godbeer's final chapter with the full-scale violence of the Salem witch hunt. In no way does Godbeer sympathize with this violence, but the reader is left without a way to understand how a harmless popular subculture could become so suddenly lethal.

The most detailed recent study of occult practices in seventeenth-century New England centers on the extraordinary career of John Winthrop Jr., alchemist, physician, entrepreneur, and governor of Connecticut in the 1660s and 1670s. In *Prospero's America: John Winthrop, Jr., Alchemy, and the Creation of New England Culture, 1606–1676* (2010), Walter W. Woodward persuasively argues for the limited presence of a subculture of learned alchemists, chiefly physicians, among the Puritan elite of New England (more prominent in Connecticut than Massachusetts), while offering no support for the existence of practicing witches. Woodward calls the persecution of alleged witches a "social pathology" on several occasions and characterizes those who were accused of witchcraft as "the deviant, the difficult, and the contentious persons" of a community. Significantly, those elite figures, such as Winthrop and Connecticut minister Gershom Bulkeley, who were drawn to alchemical ideas and practices, typically acted to moderate the impulse to prosecute witches. Woodward goes so far as to credit them with bringing an end to executions for witchcraft in Connecticut after 1663. In effect, men like Winthrop and Bulkeley had too much respect for the complicated, hidden ways that nature operated (what they called "natural magic") to be taken in by popular charges of witchcraft leveled at common people (*Prospero's America*, esp. chap. 7, quotations on 219, 224, 232).

12. Remarkably, in light of the power and endurance of the belief in witchcraft, there appears to be little evidence that practicing witches as such were ever present in the long history of the West. Excavated clay tablets and other textual sources from the Sumerian, Assyrian, and Babylonian civilizations of Ancient Mesopotamia reveal plenty of incantations and rituals aimed against presumed sorcery and demons, but "instructions for performing evil magic do not exist" (Thomsen, "Witchcraft and Magic in Ancient Mesopotamia" [2001], 1–95, quotation on 23). The same is true for ancient Israel. Biblical evidence exhibits a surprising number of magical elements "hidden" within Judaic practice (e.g., the Urim and Thummim, which may have been a binary form of oracle consulted by the priests to determine God's will) but offers nothing to indicate the presence of actual sorcerers. Prohibitions against divination, necromancy, and consulting with familiar spirits occur for the most part within the context of describing what the class of priests (the Levites) may and may not do. Even the notorious "Witch of Endor," who was supposed to have summoned the ghost of the dead prophet Samuel to give advice to King Saul—an incident cited during the Salem events both by magistrates and the accused in the argument over the meaning of spectral evidence (whether a specter could or could not impersonate an innocent person)—was in reality a diviner: "she is nowhere brought into relation with the actual practice of harmful magic, which is to say that she is hardly a 'witch' in the social-anthropological sense at all" (Cryer, "Magic in Ancient Syria-Palestine and in the Old Testament" [2001], 97–149, quotation on 141). Yet these characteristics of ancient Judaic magic did not

prevent the inclusion of the injunction, "Thou shalt not suffer a witch to live," among the Mosaic laws handed down to the people.

The more populous and complex societies of ancient Greece and Rome present a more complicated picture of magic and sorcery. The discovery of cursing tablets deposited throughout the Greco-Roman world provides the best evidence that harmful magic was carried out, a function of the highly competitive environment of these cultures. Individuals, typically men, seeking to harm occupational adversaries, rivals in love, opposing litigants, or perceived wrongdoers could inscribe these metal plates with curses and images aimed at "binding" or restraining their enemies, before placing the tablets in temples to invoke the help of a god or goddess in their cause. Aside from the cursing tablets (which seem to have involved few professional practitioners), however, nearly all the rest of the evidence concerning sorcerers or witches depicts proscribed practices aimed at harnessing supernatural forces to help clients in their daily lives, not bring injury to others. These practices, carried out by professionals ranging from well-to-do philosopher-magi to itinerant psychics, included divining the meaning of present and future events through a wide variety of techniques, supplying healing substances, providing protective amulets or love charms, offering incantations to aid in the growing of crops, and imparting learned systems of symbolic correspondences aimed at fostering a personal connection with the gods.

Yet, at the same time, the Greeks and Romans produced an elaborate literature that imagined a malign class of practitioners who manipulated a world of demons that grew increasingly menacing as the city-states of Greece and later the Roman republic and empire set forth ever clearer boundaries to mark off their own spiritual pantheons and official religious rituals. Significantly, this imaginative literature, through such figures as Medea, Canidia, and Erictho, overemphasized the role of women as witches compared to their actual presence among magicians (Ogden calls it a great "mismatch" ["Binding Spells," 65]), including in the invention of the exaggerated female figure of the "night witch," a clear sign of male prejudices among the literary elite. The result could be seen in one of the first recorded witch hunts in Western history, the execution of forty-five men and eighty-five women for practicing magic under the Roman emperor Tiberius around 20 CE. Mass executions for witchcraft seem to have begun even earlier (in the second century BCE), but I have no information on their gendered proportions. (In addition to Ogden's essay, this and the preceding paragraph rely on Luck, "Witches and Sorcerers in Classical Literature" [1999], 91–158; Gordon, "Imagining Greek and Roman Magic" [1999], 159–275; Graf, Magic in the Ancient World [1997]; and Flint, "Demonisation of Magic and Sorcery in Late Antiquity" [1999], 277–348.)

The rise of Christianity and the conversion of the Roman Empire to the new faith in the fourth century intensified the demonization of magic and witches. This stage in the process started gradually, with the first few centuries of Christian hegemony witnessing a measure of accommodation between many Christian leaders and what remained of pagan practices. But the emergence along with Christianity of the figure of Satan as the powerful leader of the demons meant that religious life in the West would be headed in a dualistic direction, absolute good arrayed against absolute evil, however much God was always placed on top. Moreover, the ascetic impulse in Christianity rendered misfortune increasingly a product of the individual's own piety or lack of it, making the relatively benign function of the pagan sorcerer as a manipulator of external spirits ever more irrelevant to daily life. In his or her place, the threatening figure of the witch grew in importance. He, and more often she, was now defined as an internal enemy, arising from within Christendom but having entered into a pact with the Devil, whose goal was nothing short of overturning Christian society.

In such a setting, it is fair to say that few, if any, people would have consciously practiced harmful magic, and even the continuation of such salutary practices as divination, occult healing, or exorcizing a demon would have been confined to those parts of Europe or sections of society that either had not yet come under strict Christian control or else housed individuals in positions influential enough to be safe from penalty. Whenever specific examples of harmful magic are cited in the historical record, the chief sources turn out to be homiletic works by Christian authors, aiming to show that calling upon spirits for help is apt to backfire. Even so-called manuals of necromancy (used for conjuring spirits from the dead) introduced a host of symbols, signs, chants, talismans, and other devices for a wide variety of purposes, all of which appear to have been protective. That some of these techniques may on rare occasion have been utilized to seek revenge on, say, a presumed adulterer or an abusive servant or master is certainly likely, but such practices can hardly have been widespread, nor would they have constituted a generalized threat to society. (This and the preceding paragraph rely on Peter Brown, "Sorcery, Demons, and the Rise of Christianity" [1970], 17–45; Flint, "Demonisation of Magic and Sorcery"; Jolly, "Medieval Magic" [2002], 1–71, esp. 58–66; and Peters, "Medieval Church and State on Superstition, Magic and Witchcraft" [2002], 173–245, esp. 223–237.)

In the early modern era, 1450–1700, European witch hunting, influenced by recurrent popular scares, the rise of increasingly efficient judicial systems, and the intellectual development of an elaborate Christian demonology, reached its most intense proportions, causing the executions of an estimated forty thousand people. However, the picture, as far as actual witchcraft goes, remains much the same. The English colonial outpost of New England fits easily into this historical construct, no less a part of Europe's periphery than Sweden, Scotland, Bermuda, or the Canary Islands, all places that witnessed virulent witch hunting during the mid- through later seventeenth century. In his summary of the overall subject, William Monter notes how "suspects were rarely caught with genuinely poisonous substances or bits of magical writings in their possession"—in fact, he offers not a single example for closer examination. As in earlier times, magical practices taken to be threatening by neighbors or demonic by the authorities turn out to have been protective in purpose, as when Normandy's shepherds, a group of men disproportionately targeted for acts of witchcraft that included "poisoning" their neighbors' animals, were found to use stolen consecrated Hosts to protect their own flocks. In Scandinavia accusations of *maleficia* (evil magical deeds) against neighboring farmers abounded in the era's legal proceedings, but how often were pouches of hair, bones, nails, or other putatively harmful substances actually found on neighbors' properties? Bengt Ankarloo implies that it happened quite frequently, yet he provides only one moderately persuasive example.

Stuart Clark's survey of popular magic during the same period offers no examples of harmful practices at all. Despite the nearly universal belief that those who possessed occult means to do good could just as easily use the same techniques to inflict harm, there is virtually no evidence of any such equivalence in actions. "The [just mentioned] idea crops up in many witchcraft trials," Clark observes, "where defendants charged with *maleficium* often returned the plea allegedly made by Ursley Kempe to Grace Thurlowe in the Essex village of St. Osyth sometime before 1582: that 'though shee coulde unwitche shee coulde not witche.'" In another sign of just how widely the belief in *maleficium* could diverge from its reality, Clark relates how the early seventeenth-century English physician Richard Napier recorded that "hundreds of his patients" thought themselves to have been bewitched. It is probably safe to say that not a single one was. (On Napier, a scientist and Anglican minister who was open to the possible workings of occult forces, and his enormous clientele, see also the discussion in Mac-Donald, *Mystical Bedlam* [1981], 106–110, 155–156, 198–217.) Even in the case of the Friulian peasants (the *benandanti*) studied by Carlo Ginzburg, sometimes said to provide the most striking evidence of actual witchcraft practiced in sixteenth-century Europe, one finds a shamanistic practice of dream travel aimed at protecting the crops from restless spirits of the dead. (This and the preceding paragraph rely on Monter, "Witch Trials in Continental Europe, 1560–1660" [2002], 1–52 [8 for the quotation; 42–43, 51 on shepherds]; Ankarloo, "Witch Trials in Northern Europe, 1450–1700" [2002], 53–95, esp. 57–68; Clark, "Witchcraft and Magic in Early Modern Culture" [2002], 97–169, esp. 99–105 [112 for the quotation, 114 for Napier example]; and Ginzburg, "Deciphering the Sabbath" [1990], 121–137.)

It should be evident from this brief survey that a strong belief in witchcraft scarcely requires the presence of any real witches at all.

CHAPTER 3:   John Demos's *Entertaining Satan* and the
Functionalist Perspective

1. Demos, *Entertaining Satan*, chap. 7, for the story of Elizabeth Garlick. The Puritan communities on Long Island at this time were part of Connecticut.

2. Ibid., 11, 401–409. The ninety-three indictments include seven legal "complaints" that did not reach the formal stage of indictment. For the Hartford witch hunt, see ibid., 351–352. The eight case studies cover the accusations against Rachel Clinton of Ipswich in 1692 (chap. 1), John Godfrey of Haverhill in the 1650s–70s (chap. 2), Elizabeth Morse of Newbury in 1679–80 (chap. 5), Elizabeth Garlick of Easthampton in 1658 (chap. 7), Mary Parsons of Northampton in the 1650s–70s (chap. 8), Eunice Cole of Hampton in the 1650s–80s (chap. 10), and Katherine Harrison of Wethersfield in 1668 (chap. 11), as well as the possession of Elizabeth Knapp of Groton in 1671–72 (chap. 4). Another way that witch-hunting panics differed from isolated prosecutions lay in the greater weight given in the latter cases to the testimonies of persons of high rank, who often played a protective role toward the accused. On this point compare Demos's findings on pp. 285–292 with the record of the Salem witch hunt, which disregarded the high rank of suspects and witnesses alike until the end. The similar ratios of executions to indictments presented in the text for witchcraft prosecutions excluding and including Salem are misleading, because at Salem there were no acquittals until the original witchcraft court was disbanded, after which all remaining suspects were acquitted, released before trial, or pardoned. In the non-Salem cases roughly 80% of the trials resulted in acquittals. Demos discusses how the functional implications of a witch hunt like Salem are likely to differ from those of more isolated prosecutions on pp. 277–278, 300–301.

One reviewer of Demos's book criticized its failure to integrate Salem into its inquiry (Michael MacDonald, "New England's Inner Demons," 325). Another reviewer implicitly called attention to its choice of the term "witchcraft" over "witch hunt" (Carol F. Karlsen, "On Witchcraft and Witch-Hunting," 613). Not all studies of colonial witchcraft accusations occurring apart from the 1692 Salem outbreak, however, have looked away from Salem. Frederick C. Drake's "Witchcraft in the American Colonies, 1647–62" (1968) argued that the prosecutions for witchcraft during the 1647–62 period (which included the Hartford panic) help explain the causes of the later Salem events by revealing a similar mix of religious (particularly Puritan) imperatives, external stimuli (especially the spike in witchcraft prosecutions in Essex, England, in 1645–47), and internal pressures (economic problems, crop failures, and epidemics), mostly valuable observations. Drake also thought he spotted a political pattern: the top governing official of the colony was often absent at the time of the greatest witch panics, allowing lesser officials to seize these opportunities to prove their worthiness to lead. This observation may fit the earlier Connecticut case but not that of Massachusetts in 1692. In truth, it mattered more what convictions a leader held concerning how the threat of witchcraft should be handled than whether he occupied the top colonial position or not. Karlsen's *Devil in the Shape of a Woman*, Konig's *Law and Society in Puritan Massachusetts*, Weisman's *Witchcraft, Magic, and Religion in 17th-Century Massachusetts*, and Godbeer's *Devil's Dominion* similarly aimed to integrate the pre-Salem cases of witchcraft prosecution with the 1692 trials.

3. Demos, *Entertaining Satan*, 368 ("continuous presence"). Karlsen, too, noted that Demos's book "discounts . . . the motives and interests of the witches themselves" ("On Witchcraft and Witch-Hunting," 618).

4. Demos, *Entertaining Satan*, chap. 3 (for the characteristics of accused witches), 275–298, 301–309, 312 (on the functions of witchcraft accusation).

5. Ibid.; for Rachel Clinton, see chap. 1, quotation on 34–35, italics in original; for John Godfrey, see chap. 2, quotation on 54; for Elizabeth Morse, see chap. 5, quotation on 152. For "met halfway" and "deep, though unacknowledged, bonds," see 197. For another statement of how accusers and accused "were joined by covert needs, or attraction, or affinity," see p. 303. One rare consideration of the devastating effect of a witchcraft conviction on the family of the accused appears on pp. 301–302. Carol Karlsen also questioned Demos's assertion of complicity in the case of Rachel Clinton and noted his general leanings toward blaming those accused for bringing the charge of witchcraft on themselves (*Devil in the Shape*, 310n3, 118). The functionalist approach did not necessarily require Demos to withdraw sympathy from the victims of witchcraft accusation, as witchcraft studies influenced by the functionalist tradition in the sociology of deviance indicate—Kai T. Erikson's *Wayward Puritans* and Richard Weisman's *Witchcraft, Magic, and Religion in 17th-Century Massachusetts*, discussed earlier, are two examples. But, as I explain in the succeeding paragraphs in the text, functionalist anthropology, which inspired Demos, and perhaps functionalism in general did contain a bias toward emphasizing the benefits, rather than the costs, of a social system operating rationally and efficiently.

6. On the shift in anthropological paradigms during these years and its relationship to witchcraft studies, see Lieberson, "Interpreting the Interpreter," 39–46; Midelfort, *Witch Hunting in Southwest Germany*, 2–5; Hutton, "Anthropological and Historical

Approaches to Witchcraft," 413–434; Rodgers, *Age of Fracture*, 98–102; Clifford, "Introduction: Partial Truths," 1–26; Geschiere, *The Modernity of Witchcraft*, 12–25, 215–221; Turner, "Witchcraft and Sorcery," chap. 5 in *The Forest of Symbols*, 112–127; Luhrman, "Anthropology," in *Encyclopedia of Witchcraft*, 43–45; and White, "Environmentalism and Indian Peoples," 129–130.

7. Demos discusses his relationship to functionalism in *Entertaining Satan*, 275–278, and his approach is especially visible throughout chap. 8. For Mary Douglas's nuanced critique of functionalism, see her "Introduction: Thirty Years after *Witchcraft, Oracles and Magic*," xiii–xxxviii, quotation on xxiii. Demos, too, cites Douglas's critique, but his assessment comes down on the side of her remarks that are favorable to some of the theoretical aims of functionalism (*Entertaining Satan*, 277–278), with which I also agree, although I highlight her insight into functionalism's political and moral stance.

Demos does not say which of the functionalist ethnographies may have been most influential to his study of New England witchcraft accusations, but I have chosen to single out Kluckhohn's because his was named first in Demos's original 1970 article ("Underlying Themes," 1312n4), in which the historian heralded the relevance of these studies to his own work on New England. Kluckhohn, who had come under the influence of psychoanalytic ideas in Vienna in 1931–32, also emphasized the psychological functions of witchcraft accusations through their projection and displacement of aggressive impulses, notions that would figure prominently in *Entertaining Satan*. See Kluckhohn, *Navaho Witchcraft*, esp. 76–128; the reference to "violently sadistic" executions appears on p. 98. Based on interviews with over 200 people during the 1920s and 1930s, Kluckhohn placed his observations on the functions of witchcraft accusation for the Navajos in the shadow of the extreme deprivation and cultural dislocation that befell their people following defeat at the hands of the American military just fifty years earlier (114–118).

The phrase "worlds we have lost" is a reference to the highly popular *The World We Have Lost*, by Peter Laslett, one of the first books in the era's new social history and one that went through many later editions after its initial publication in 1965.

8. Demos, *Entertaining Satan*, 298–300, 309–312, 399. On p. 309, Demos rephrases "neighborliness versus individualism" as "cooperative values *versus* individualistic ones, giving and sharing *versus* taking and accumulating—describe it as one may." Demos endorses Boyer and Nissenbaum's factional interpretation of the Salem witch hunt on 384–385. That the accused in Demos's account were more likely to exhibit aggressive, individualistic traits than the accusers is borne out by the frequency with which he calls them "grasping." In the case of accused witch John Godfrey, a perhaps revealing shift occurred between an earlier article that Demos published on Godfrey and his later account of the man in chapter 2 of *Entertaining Satan*. The accounts are nearly identical, but in the summaries that conclude each version, the word "grasping" (*Entertaining Satan*, 53) has taken the place of the word "greed" (John Demos, "John Godfrey and His Neighbors: Witchcraft and the Social Web in Colonial Massachusetts," 261). In changing this wording, Demos may have intended to soften his criticism of Godfrey. Still, the association of Godfrey with the new, capitalist values of "taking and accumulating" seems apparent.

The "neighborliness versus individualism" argument occupies the centerpiece of Keith Thomas's explanation for the upsurge in witchcraft prosecutions in early modern England (*Religion and the Decline*, chaps. 14–18, esp. 552–556, 561) and Alan Macfarlane's explanation for the same developments in Essex County, England (*Witchcraft in Tudor and Stuart England* [1970], esp. 161, 170, 197). In effect, both authors had applied the static functionalist principle of a social "safety valve" to a historical situation of social change. These same arguments are set forth more succinctly in Thomas, "The Relevance of Social Anthropology to the Historical Study of English Witchcraft," 62–63, and Macfarlane, "Witchcraft in Tudor and Stuart Essex," 92–95. The authors' sympathies are clearly aligned with the accused throughout these accounts, openly so in Thomas, more implicitly in Macfarlane (see, e.g., *Religion and the Decline*, 526–527, 530; and *Witchcraft in Tudor and Stuart England*, 240–241). Boyer and Nissenbaum note their own affinities with this British argument in *Salem Possessed*, 212, and in their introduction to *SWP*, 1:12–16, without acknowledging how the same argument, when brought to the American context, placed them sympathetically on the side of the accusers. Amanda Porterfield has also recognized how Boyer and Nissenbaum reversed the roles of participants in witchcraft accusations from the way they stood in Macfarlane's formulation, making those who felt left behind by the process of modernization into accusers, rather than the accused ("Witchcraft and the Colonization of Algonquian and Iroquois Cultures," 108).

Shortly after publishing *Witchcraft in Tudor and Stuart England*, Macfarlane seems to have moved away from the "neighborliness vs. individualism" argument, as he came to believe that individualism was both more pervasive and far older in English history than he had once thought. Without its "emergence" in the sixteenth and seventeenth centuries, the ethic of individualism could not have touched off witchcraft accusations stemming from its presumed conflict with an "older" ethic of neighborliness. So far as I have read, however, Macfarlane did not substitute a different mechanism for the one he discarded. On these changes in his position, see *The Origins of English Individualism* (1979), 1–2, 59–61, and throughout.

9. Demos, *Entertaining Satan*, 13, for the first quotation; for more on projection, see 195–196. For the part of his psychological argument that points toward Puritan child-rearing practices, see esp. 207–210, 395–398; the quotation on "core sense of self" is on 210.

10. For these themes, see ibid., chap. 6, esp. 162–165, and chap. 4.

11. Demos himself supplies excellent summary statistics for England, based on Alan Macfarlane's study of Essex County in East Anglia and Macfarlane's refinement of earlier work by C. L. Ewen for England as a whole (ibid., 12). These same statistics show that the incidence of indictments and executions for witchcraft in New England was on an exact par, proportionate to population, with that for Essex County, England, a point often missed by many scholars of New England's witch hunting, who assume the American phenomenon to be far less severe than its European counterparts. For a comparison of witchcraft prosecutions in New England with those in the other American colonies, see Frederick C. Drake, "Witchcraft in the American Colonies," 698–708. Drake lists fifty-seven trials for witchcraft that occurred in the American colonies from 1645 to 1662, all but six of which took place in New England. If the post-1662 cases, including

those from Salem, were added to this list, it seems certain that New England's share would be even more lopsided.

In their works from the early 1970s about England, Thomas and Macfarlane both minimized any special role played by Puritans (the "godly" wing of the Church of England) in the persecution of accused witches, although both (especially Thomas) stressed the more general contributions made by the Protestant Reformation to witch hunting through the removal of traditional, Catholic rituals that common people had regarded as a form of protection against black magic, along with an intensification of the idea that a personalized Satan was responsible for the many forms of evil in the world (see Thomas, *Religion and the Decline*, chaps. 2–4, 15; and Macfarlane, *Witchcraft in Tudor and Stuart England*, chaps. 14–15, and pp. 140–142). In keeping with their emphases on socioeconomic as opposed to religious factors, both historians thus found themselves arguing for the atypicality of England's greatest witch hunt, the campaign of 1645–47. Led by the "witch finders" Matthew Hopkins and John Stearne, it was carried out in the Puritan stronghold of East Anglia in the midst of the English Civil War and resulted in about one hundred hangings. More recent scholarship has brought the importance of absolutist religious ideology back into favor in understanding British witch hunting during the early modern period, allowing the East Anglia persecutions to be integrated more easily into the general picture of scapegoating on the village level. See, e.g., Larner, *Enemies of God: The Witch-hunt in Scotland* (1981), esp. chap. 12; Sharpe, *Instruments of Darkness: Witchcraft in Early Modern England* (1997), esp. intro., chap. 5; and Gaskill, *Witchfinders: A Seventeenth-Century English Tragedy* (2005), esp. chaps. 1–2, pp. 283–285. Nobody has put the lessons of this renewed emphasis on extreme religious ideology better than Keith Thomas himself when he observed, in reviewing Gaskill's study of the East Anglia panic, "The entire episode is a striking example of what can happen when popular prejudices are unrestrained by the strict rule of law. . . . Early modern England offers a salutary warning of the tragic consequences which follow when the world is envisaged as a cosmic battleground on which opposing forces of good and evil contend for supremacy" ("Speak of the Devil" [2006], 34).

12. In addition to the references in note 9 on Puritan childrearing practices, see *Entertaining Satan*, 309–311, for a strong statement of the relevance of Puritan beliefs to an understanding of witchcraft accusations. The problem with the latter statement, however, is that these few pages, although well expressed, constitute little more than a qualification of the principal arguments in the book, and even this qualification is undercut by the observations that immediate follow on pp. 311–312. Moreover, only two of the eight case studies include data about Puritan beliefs, yet there are incidents in nearly all of Demos's vignettes that cry out for religious explanations. One example is the case of Elizabeth Morse's grandson, John Stiles, a troubled and afflicted youth who believed himself to be guilty of allowing the Devil to influence him (150). Demos moves immediately to a psychological explanation, which may fit as well, but it surely must be significant that Puritan New Englanders, young and old, turned so quickly to Satan to explain their feelings of inadequacy, despite the often devastating consequences of doing so. The quotation about wolves appears on p. 344.

Two reviewers of *Entertaining Satan* made Demos's neglect of Puritan religious ideas central to their criticisms of the book: MacDonald, "New England's Inner Demons," and Morgan, "Witch Hunting," 39–41. Both also brusquely dismissed Demos's psychoanalytic interpretation. A similar but more respectful critique of *Entertaining Satan* appeared in David D. Hall's extensive review essay, "Witchcraft and the Limits of Interpretation" (1985). Hall, too, pointed to the need for greater inclusion of New England's religious beliefs in any understanding of witchcraft or witch hunting. He noted how thoroughly intermixed clerical ideas and popular conceptions had become at least by the 1640s, and he called attention to how the pervasive quality of spiritual guilt among New Englanders leant itself to the logic of witchcraft accusation and confession. (For these ideas, see Hall, "Witchcraft and the Limits of Interpretation," 275–281.) All this made great sense, and so it is curious to find that toward the beginning of his essay, Hall went out of his way to exonerate "Puritanism" of responsibility for the era of witch hunting, as if all critical inquiry into a Puritan connection to witchcraft accusation amounted to little more than old-fashioned and narrow-minded Puritan-bashing (261–263, 272–273). In the end Hall was left unpersuaded by any of Demos's sociological or psychological explanations. (He countered the "neighborliness versus individualism" argument by observing that there was no reason to regard colonial New Englanders, a people already embodying both individualistic and communal ideals and long prepared to adapt to change, as subject to any special degree of social strain.) Instead, Hall favored simpler notions of interpersonal conflict and the projection of anger to explain witch hunting (266–273). In his later book, *Worlds of Wonder, Days of Judgment*, Hall developed a somewhat stronger connection between witch hunting and Puritanism while still expressing a reluctance to implicate Reformed-based Protestantism with any special responsibility for generating attacks on presumed witches. See my discussion of this refinement in Hall's position in the conclusion.

13. Demos, *Entertaining Satan*, 311–312. For other examples of passages that evince nostalgia for the premodern community, see pp. 226–227, 232–233, 306–307, and the earlier references to the conflict between "neighborliness" and "individualism." A contrasting note, however, is sounded at the end of the case study of Katherine Harrison. Looking toward the changes in social life that brought an end to witchcraft accusations in Wethersfield, Connecticut, Demos writes, "In most respects the pace of change was quite modest; but, taken cumulatively, the effect was substantial. In a word, there was more variety, more openness, more *space* in every sense; the press of inner strains and conflicts was modified correspondingly. From all this, Wethersfield became by the end of the century a perceptibly different place. And—for eccentrics, for deviants, even for suspected witches—most probably a *better* place" (367, emphasis in original). In truth, however, the sharp decline in witchcraft accusations throughout New England by the early eighteenth century owed less to changes in small-town life and more to the fact that the judicial system would no longer support prosecutions. The Salem fiasco had undermined confidence in the courts' ability to prove that any given suspect had committed an act of witchcraft.

CHAPTER 4: Karlsen's *Devil in the Shape of a Woman* and Feminist Interpretations

1. Karlsen, *Devil in the Shape*, xii, 47.

2. Demos, *Entertaining Satan*, 60–64. For "systematic violence," see Karlsen, *Devil in the Shape*, xii. For examples of other recent historians, writing before Karlsen, who

downplayed the role of patriarchy or misogyny as important factors in understanding witch hunting, see Thomas, *Religion and the Decline*, 562, 568–569; Weisman, *Witchcraft, Magic, and Religion*, 37, 91; and Hall, "Witchcraft and the Limits of Interpretation," 274–275. Two works that did emphasize the role of women and gender relations in the history of New England witch hunting appeared a few years before Karlsen's book: Lyle Koehler, *A Search for Power: The "Weaker Sex" in Seventeenth-Century New England* (1980), and Ann Kibbey, "Mutations of the Supernatural: Witchcraft, Remarkable Providences, and the Power of Puritan Men" (1982). Both strongly sympathized with the female victims of witch hunting, and both implicated patriarchal principles upheld by the Puritans as critical to the accusations of witchcraft. Elizabeth Reis's *Damned Women: Sinners and Witches in Puritan New England* and Jane Kamensky's *Governing the Tongue: The Politics of Speech in Early New England*, two additional works containing interpretations of witch hunting in Puritan New England influenced by the new feminist scholarship, came out ten years after Karlsen's book. I discuss the arguments of these four works in the notes to this chapter. Still more recently, Marilynne K. Roach's *Six Women of Salem: The Untold Story of the Accused and Their Accusers in the Salem Witch Trials* (2013), has presented a chronological narrative of the intersecting lives of Rebecca Nurse, Bridget Bishop, Mary English, Ann Putnam Sr., Tituba, and Mary Warren. The account is filled with genealogical and descriptive detail by an author who knows the data intimately.

3. Karlsen, *Devil in the Shape*, chap. 2. Karlsen's data set of 344 accused persons is considerably larger than Demos's, which is composed of 114 accused suspects (producing 93 legal cases) from all of the non-Salem cases up through 1697. On top of that, Demos occasionally adds observations based on data from the Salem witch hunt (variously, a list of 141 accused individuals from 1692–1693, a roster of 165 accused individuals from Demos's 1970 article, and a select group of 14 Salem accused who had a prior history of suspicion). Karlsen is thus not quite accurate in asserting on pp. 280–281n1 that the difference in the size of their databases is small, 344 versus 234. (Karlsen has apparently added Demos's 93 legal cases to his 141 from Salem to arrive at this total.) The two data sets used to compile information on the age and marital status of accused individuals (as well as for all subsequent economic characteristics), unless Demos is specifically speaking about the Salem witch hunt, actually contain 344 and 114 records, respectively. The greatest proportion of this difference in size is due to Karlsen's inclusion of the accused from the Salem witch hunt. She also adds several accusations from the 1697–1725 period, four from earlier years missed by Demos, and an unspecified number of individuals accused of witchcraft but against whom a formal legal complaint had never been filed (although Demos, too, included some individuals who fell into this category).

The difference in their findings about older women versus women at midlife, however, is not due chiefly to the inclusion or exclusion of the Salem data. (Both historians agree that the Salem witch hunt brought in a greater number of women under the age of forty than was the case for non-Salem accusations.) Rather, the difference is due to the facts that Karlsen counts women aged sixty in her older category, while Demos counts them in his midlife category; Karlsen refrains from estimating ages where age data was only available for spouses; and Karlsen uses the age at the time of the accusation of her suspects, while Demos uses the age at the time accusers said their suspicions were first aroused. The first and third of these methodological decisions would certainly increase the number of women over sixty found in her data set compared to his; the second decision would likely reduce that number (since information about age has survived better for younger people). The net result would tend to explain why Karlsen finds a greater proportion of older women among the accused than Demos does. At stake, therefore, is less the divergence in findings than the divergence in interpretation noted in the text.

The same is true on the subject of marriage. Demos and Karlsen find approximately the same proportions of married women among the accused (higher proportions for the non-Salem cases, lower proportions for the Salem witch hunt). Only Karlsen, however, shows statistically that "women alone" were more likely to be accused than would be expected by their numbers in the population, although Demos does note separately that the absence of a husband increased a woman's vulnerability to prosecution as a witch. On these methodological points in conflict between the two historians, see Karlsen, *Devil in the Shape*, 47, 280–281n1, 292–293n86, 295n93; and Demos, *Entertaining Satan*, 11, 57, 401–409.

4. Karlsen, *Devil in the Shape*, chap. 4; the two quotations appear on p. 150 ("pride") and p. 131 ("ire"). The Sarah Good example may be found on p. 233, and for the detail of what Mercy Short did to provoke Sarah Good, see Cotton Mather, *A Brand Pluck'd Out of the Burning* [1693], in Burr, 260. Starkey, too, had described the Good-Short confrontation in this manner (*Devil in Massachusetts*, 151) and would surely have agreed with Karlsen's skeptical way of assessing most of the negative characterizations of the accused. Much like Starkey, Lyle Koehler portrayed New England's witch hunting as a form of scapegoating that relieved Puritan anxieties stemming from a sexually repressed and guilt-ridden society. Koehler anticipated Karlsen's view that women who broke with Puritan norms of femininity became the targets of attack, although he, like most male historians writing before Karlsen, was more willing than she to imagine that many of the accused had "objectively" contentious personalities. Koehler also accepted the likelihood that a number of the accused in the pre-Salem cases practiced actual witchcraft, although he had no evidence to support this assumption, apart from relying on confessions and accusations that otherwise contained wild fantasies. (See my discussion of this shortcoming in the Aside on Witchcraft Investigations at the end of chapter 2.) However, in the instance of the Salem panic, Koehler stated that there probably were no actual witches; scapegoating in response to a wide variety of stresses facing the communities of Essex County, in his view, accounted for the enormous flurry of accusations and prosecutions in 1692. See Koehler, *Search for Power*, 169–175, chaps. 10 and 13. A later article by Jane Kamensky elaborates on the ways in which accused witches were said to have violated the norms of speech set for women within Puritan New England. Kamensky compiles a long list of adjectives frequently used to describe the verbal styles of accused witches, including such terms as *boasting, chiding, complaining, cursing, disputing, foretelling, groaning, hectoring, jeering, mocking, quarreling, raging, scoffing, scolding, screeching, shrieking, slandering,* and *tattling*. See her "Words, Witches, and Woman Trouble" (1992), 286–307 (the list appears on 307).

Two articles appearing after Karlsen's book came out address the relative absence of explicitly sexual themes in the demonology of New England's witchcraft, compared to that of Continental Europe, in which wild orgies of women copulating with the Devil at "witches' Sabbaths" were commonplace. Citing the testimonies by Massachusetts men that the specters of female witches overpowered them in their beds at night and the prevalence of searches of suspects' bodies for "witches' teats," Louis J. Kern argues— unpersuasively, in my view—that roughly similar sexual themes could indeed be found in both places, with New England simply showing greater understatement in their expression. The problem with Kern's argument is that this type of male testimony typically comprised only a small portion of the evidence presented against female suspects, while searches for "teats," along with the "Devil's mark," were carried out equally for male as well as female suspects. I do not think that the geographic contrast in demonological themes can be dismissed so easily. See Kern, "Eros, the Devil, and the Cunning Woman: Sexuality and the Supernatural in European Antecedents and in the Seventeenth-Century Salem Witchcraft Cases" (1993), 3–38.

Richard Godbeer, on the other hand, accepts the geographic contrast and advances the explanation that the relative absence of torture in New England's prosecutions gave its witchcraft confessors and afflicted accusers the leeway to voice their covert rebellion against society. In their case doing so meant making Satan's domain mirror as closely as possible that of their own, Puritan churches. Rather than posit witches copulating with the Devil, as European suspects were coerced into doing, Godbeer suggests, it was both easier and more openly subversive for New England's confessors to imagine the Devil as a black-coated "minister," soliciting signatures to his secret covenant while administering perverse imitations of the Protestant sacraments. Problems exist with this reasoning, too. New England's witchcraft examinations, even without the common use of torture, felt plenty intimidating to suspects, who were typically forced to endure powerful cross-questioning, lengthy jailing, and the threat of possible execution. The large number of confessions (as opposed to assertions of innocence) at Salem, for example, testifies to how little leeway most suspects must have experienced. Nor is there much reason to think that rebellion or subversion chiefly motivated the typical New England witchcraft confessor or afflicted accuser (or her European counterparts, for that matter). These participants in the drama of witch hunting may have been nonconformists in certain respects, but they were not revolutionaries. Guilt over the perception that they lacked sufficient piety was the far more likely cause for their actions. Moreover, the symbolic content of their confessions and accusations could not have lain fundamentally within the control of the participants themselves, or else it would not have been instantly recognized as such a threat to the community. Greater variation in images would have developed, with the result that many such statements might have been passed off as merely eccentric. In truth, the demonology of witchcraft was no less a cultural construct in New England than it was in the British Isles or on the continent of Europe. A product of multiple influences arising from the clergy, the legal system, and the population at large, witchcraft lore showed unmistakable signs of being unconsciously "scripted" to reflect the distinctive yet often overlapping fears of Europe's socio-religious subcultures—Catholic, Lutheran, and Calvinist—with national and regional elements thrown in as well. See Godbeer's "Chaste and Unchaste Covenants: Witchcraft and Sex in Early Modern Culture" (1995), 53–72.

The strengths and weaknesses of both these articles, however, suggest that male sexual anxieties, though present in the phenomenon, do not hold a key to the understanding of witch hunting.

5. Karlsen, *Devil in the Shape*, chap. 3, quotation on 116.

6. In addition to the data supplied in Karlsen's accounts of the three woman discussed in this paragraph, see also, for Harrison, Demos, *Entertaining Satan*, chap. 11; for Martin and Carrier, SWP, 2:558, 560, and 1:190, respectively; and for Carrier, Norton, *In the Devil's Snare*, 235–236. Roger Toothaker likely had his own independent reasons to come under suspicion, since he was a medical doctor known also to practice counter-magic against presumed cases of witchcraft. In the Salem witch hunt, he was arrested even before his sister-in-law or wife (Norton, *In the Devil's Snare*, 172, 182).

7. The criticism concerning how briefly an "inheriting woman" might hold title to property appeared in Stephen Nissenbaum's otherwise favorable review of Karlsen's book in *William and Mary Quarterly*, 3rd ser. 46 (July 1989): 594. Karlsen's category, "women lacking either a brother or son," poses two additional problems. First, the author offers no estimate for a comparable proportion in the population at large, so it is difficult to evaluate the significance of her finding that *most* of the accused on her roster fit into it. Second, she expresses her category ambiguously, at first stating that it means "either/or" (101) but then sometimes implying that it means "both/and" (as in the formulation that these women had "no legitimate male heirs in their immediate families" [101] or in the titles to tables 11 and 12 [102–103]). John Murrin has criticized Karlsen's economic argument on still other grounds, noting that it failed to account for many of the well-known cases from the Salem witch hunt: at least six or seven of the fourteen women executed at Salem had sons. Karlsen's economic argument is based on an aggregate of all accused witches in New England over a one-hundred-year period and is not meant to explain any particular witch-hunting episode. Still, Murrin's criticism points to some of the argument's shortcomings. See Murrin, "Infernal Conspiracy of Indians and Grandmothers," 486, 493n1.

Also questionable is Karlsen's assumption that land pressures at the end of the seventeenth century would have made New England's sons especially resentful of their long-living mothers (and fathers, as she also maintains), from whom these potential witchcraft accusers are said to have displaced their anger onto other independent women in the local communities. She bases her assumption of mounting land pressures in part on the earlier argument set forth in *Salem Possessed*, which exaggerated the "declining" fortunes of the leading witchcraft accusers (see my discussion in chapter 2). Karlsen also cites an earlier town study of Dedham, Massachusetts, in support of her contention about land pressures, but later studies have moved in the opposite direction, depicting Dedham and other eastern Massachusetts towns as prosperous communities that functioned almost as "real estate developers" in spawning new settlements for their expanding populations. Dedham in particular gave rise to the four towns of Medfield, Natick, Wrentham, and Deerfield. See John Frederick Martin, *Profits in the Wilderness: Entrepreneurship and the Founding of New England Towns in the Seventeenth Century* [1991], 14–15, 34–37; for the Dedham example, see 294–304; for "real estate developers," see 301.

8. For the characteristics of the Salem outbreak, compared to the norms emphasized for witch hunting in general, see Karlsen, *Devil in the Shape*, 47–50, 66, 71.

9. Ibid., 242–243, 245–246 (on Procter, Jacobs, and Burroughs), 52–60 (on Godfrey). Karlsen shows particular bias in her treatment of George Jacobs Sr. She oddly interprets an anguished statement that Jacobs's servant, Sarah Churchill, made privately to a peer,

Sarah Ingersoll ("they thratened hur: and told hur thay would put her in to the dongin [dungeon]," Ingersoll recalled) as referring to Jacobs, when the word "they" almost certainly referred to the examining magistrates, who had just elicited from Churchill a forced confession of witchcraft (ibid., 242; SWP, 1:212). Karlsen also takes the charge that Jacobs's *specter* had beaten several of the afflicted girls and young women with his staff as equivalent to the accusation that Jacobs himself had done so (*Devil in the Shape*, 246; SWP, 2:481–483).

Later historians have similarly drifted too easily from fantasy to reality in their assessments of Jacobs. For example, see Baker, *Storm of Witchcraft*: "Jacobs or his specter had beaten them," when there is only evidence of the charge of spectral "beatings" (148). See also Schiff, *Witches*, 159–161, which additionally gives credence to the accusation made by the afflicted, sixteen-year-old nephew of Elizabeth Procter, John De Rich, that Jacobs had threatened to drown him. This same youngster also outlandishly accused Jacobs of murdering a Salem town couple and made equally fantastic charges against his aunt, uncle, and Procter cousins, all of whom, together with his mother, had already been arrested for witchcraft by this time (*Records*, #481, #482; Norton, *In the Devil's Snare*, 244). Schiff also mistakenly attributes to George Jacobs Sr. an earlier incident of neighborly conflict with Nathaniel Putnam over horses that actually involved George Jacobs Jr. See RFQCE, 5:428 for the incident. Jacobs Sr. was not a saint. He was fined in 1677 for violently striking a man, as Baker fairly notes (see also RFQCE, 6:292–293). But in 1692 there is evidence of nothing more than his anger against those who were accusing him of witchcraft.

10. Karlsen's discussion of the "non-possessed accusers" appears in *Devil in the Shape*, chap. 6, with her statistics about the proportions of men and women among them presented on pp. 183–185. The note to these statistics mentions the broad discrepancy between Demos's portrait of this group and her own but offers no satisfactory explanation. "Our differences on the non-Salem cases [for Demos roughly one-half of all non-possessed accusers were female, for Karlsen roughly one-third] are harder to account for," she writes, "but they may have to do with the fact that Demos's figures are based on the nine cases he researched most thoroughly, while mine are based on the information I could locate for all non-Salem cases" (324n2). Since she does not tell us how she compiled her database of 654 nonpossessed accusers, the reader is left to wonder whom to believe, the historian who examined nine cases in great detail or the historian who gathered the names of accusers from wider sources at a greater degree of distance from the events. I suspect Demos's findings are more trustworthy on this score.

The quotation in the text from Demos appears in "Underlying Themes," 1316. Richard Weisman made the same point that men were more likely than women to figure among the nonpossessed accusers because male heads of households typically took legal action on behalf of their families (*Witchcraft, Magic, and Religion*, 49). Like Karlsen, Ann Kibbey also minimized the role that women played as nonpossessed accusers when she suggested that in such a highly patriarchal society as that of Puritan New England, female accusers were often standing in for their husbands, who in turn sought to attack the husbands of the accused witches. Thus, for instance, Ann Putnam Sr. accused Rebecca Nurse of witchcraft because of a grudge Thomas Putnam Jr. held against Francis Nurse. But this scenario seems like only one (and not a frequent one) of many possible explanations for why women accused other women of witchcraft. See

Kibbey, "Mutations of the Supernatural," 147–148. Much more persuasively, Demos shows many instances in which witchcraft accusations originated in conflicts emerging out of the local sphere of women's activities. See, e.g., *Entertaining Satan*, chap. 5 (for accusations against Elizabeth Morse), chap. 7 (against Elizabeth Garlick), chap. 8 (against Mary Parsons of Northampton), and chap. 11 (against Katherine Harrison).

11. Strictly speaking, the term Karlsen employs, "possessed accusers" is a misnomer, since, as explained in chapter 1, note 20, Puritans regarded a person suffering such afflictions as a victim *either* of possession (suggesting an internal struggle over the destiny of the person's soul between the actions of the Devil and the person's allegiance to God) *or* of witchcraft (suggesting an attack by a demon in service to a witch, one of the Devil's human agents). To accuse someone else of initiating the afflictions was already to declare that the source of the problem lay not in possession but in witchcraft. As Karlsen demonstrates, however, a fine line existed between these two interpretations of the young women's suffering, and in this close relationship (and sometimes vacillation) between possession and accusation lay the key to understanding what was likely going on for the afflicted: a struggle between blaming oneself and blaming another.

12. Karlsen, *Devil in the Shape*, chap. 7. The quotations appear on 244, 242.

13. Ibid., 236–241, 246–247 (for long quotation, italics in original), 253–254, 40 (for the use of "subversion"). In another passage explaining the behavior of the possessed, Karlsen writes, "Witchcraft possession in early New England, then, was an interpretation placed upon a physical and emotional response to a set of social conditions that had no intrinsic relationship to witches or the Devil. These conditions were in some respect specific to Puritan New England, but they are also evident in other societies. Like women in other times and places, the New England possessed were rebelling against pressures to internalize stifling gender and class hierarchies" (250–251).

14. On Elizabeth Knapp, see also Demos's detailed description of her possession in *Entertaining Satan*, chap. 4. In an early article on the Salem witch hunt, Roger Thompson anticipated much of Karlsen's later placement of women at the center of the story, but he began this portion of his discussion by highlighting the courage of those who defiantly went to their deaths, before he acknowledged the rebellious undercurrents of the afflicted ("Salem Revisited," 324–329).

15. Karlsen's statistics on the possessed accusers appear in *Devil in the Shape*, 223–224. I discuss the number of accusations issuing from the core members of the afflicted group in chapter 5. Mary Walcott lived with her father, Capt. Jonathan Walcott, and stepmother, Deliverance Putnam Walcott, in a dwelling next to the village parsonage that housed the Parrises. (A number of secondary accounts of the Salem witch hunt, all the way up through Schiff's *Witches* [81, 138], state that Mary Walcott was living in the household of Thomas Putnam Jr. in 1692, but none of these accounts cites a primary source for this assertion.) At the outbreak of the Salem panic, Susannah Sheldon was living in Salem village with her mother, Rebecca Scadlock Sheldon, one brother, and four sisters. Her father, William Sheldon had just died in December 1691, at age sixty-eight. See Norton, *In the Devil's Snare*, 53–54 (on Walcott), 143 (on Sheldon). A map showing the location of the Walcotts' residence appears in S-VW, 408.

16. On the place of servants in Puritan families, see Edmund S. Morgan, *The Puritan Family*, chaps. 3 and 5; and John Demos, *A Little Commonwealth*, chaps. 6 and 7. Laurel Thatcher Ulrich captures some of the ways in which children and servants were

viewed similarly within the family when she writes, "Mothering in early New England was extensive rather than intensive. . . . Only in infancy were children simply children. As soon as they could pluck goose feathers or dry spoons, children were also servants. Hired servants, at the same time, were children, needing clothes of their own, firm discipline, and instruction in the Bible. Mothering meant generalized responsibility for an assembly of youngsters rather than concentrated devotion to a few" (*Good Wives: Image and Reality in the Lives of Women in Northern New England, 1650–1750*, 157).

17. On Knapp's parents, see Demos, *Entertaining Satan*, chap. 4. At one point in the midst of her distress, Elizabeth briefly left the Willards' home and went again to live with her parents. On the four Salem village servants, see Norton, *In the Devil's Snare*, 164–165, 374n22 (Warren), 22 (Hubbard), 160 (Churchill [Norton uses the spelling "Church-well"]), and 50 (Lewis). For examples of Abigail Williams's status, see Lawson, *Brief and True Narrative*, 153; Hale, *Modest Inquiry*, 413; and Calef, *More Wonders*, 344, all in Burr.

18. On Knapp, see Demos, *Entertaining Satan*, 114; on Churchill, see Karlsen, *Devil in the Shape*, 228; on Hubbard, Lewis, Warren, and Williams, see Norton, *In the Devil's Snare*, 310–311.

19. Richard Godbeer argues along these same lines in *Devil's Dominion*, 106–119.

20. Karlsen, *Devil in the Shape*, chap. 5. Much more enlightening is Elizabeth Reis's analysis of the connection between Puritanism and the tendency for New England's witch hunters, male and female alike, to focus on women as their victims. In her 1997 study, *Damned Women: Sinners and Witches in Puritan New England*, Reis explains that women were considered by the Puritans to be especially vulnerable to Satan's temptations. They were thought to have weaker bodies than men, and also the soul itself, whose capture and allegiance Satan aimed to win, was conceived of in feminine terms as longing for completion with either Christ or the Devil. As a result, even though Puritan women were more likely than men to undergo a conversion experience, they were also more likely than men to blame themselves for harboring an inner, sinful nature and, if they exercised appropriate scrutiny about their behavior, to believe they had already in a multitude of small ways invited Satan in. These gendered characteristics of Puritanism made states of diabolic possession, as well as witchcraft accusations and confessions, more frequent and more credible for women than for men. While one might regard these Puritan ideas simply as an elaboration of the Judeo-Christian myths of Adam and Eve, when one combines them with the Puritans' vivid beliefs in the physical reality of Satan, the terrors of Hell, and the imminence of the Day of Judgment, one comes away with a strong understanding of how Puritanism, notwithstanding its preaching about God's love and the duty of human beings to love one another, encouraged witch hunting and why women became the likely targets.

I find Ann Kibbey's interpretation of Puritanism and witch hunting considerably less persuasive. Writing in 1982, Kibbey held that Puritanism appropriated the occult powers of the medieval sorcerer into its own conception of an interventionist God and then indirectly granted much of this same power to Puritan men when it elevated, in patriarchal fashion, the male responsibility for sin (including sins committed by women) within God's providential design. Not only would it seem more accurate to say that Puritanism, like other forms of the Protestant Reformation, looked back to the early days of Christianity, rather than to medieval sorcery, to find its renewed sense of the supernatural, but also Kibbey's argument has a hard time explaining why women played most of the leading roles in seventeenth-century witch hunting: as accused witch, confessed witch, possessed accuser, and often nonpossessed accuser. The legal officials were strictly male, however, as Kibbey fairly notes. (See Kibbey, "Mutations of the Supernatural.")

On the connection between Puritanism and standards of male conduct in marriage, see Gildrie, *The Profane, the Civil, and the Godly*, 85–104, esp. 88, 95; Ulrich, *Good Wives*, 110, 187–189; Elaine Forman Crane, *Witches, Wife Beaters, and Whores: Common Law and Common Folk in Early America* (2011), 85–86, 115–117. Significantly, Mary Beth Norton finds that by far the greatest share of colonial prosecutions of husbands for spousal abuse, generally rare throughout the American colonies, took place in Puritan Massachusetts, "undoubtedly because of that colony's 1650 statute prohibiting either spouse from striking the other" (*Founding Mothers and Fathers: Gendered Power and the Forming of American Society* [1996], 78 [for the quotation], 426n57). But on the weakness of most of the punishments, see Koehler, *Search for Power*, 136–142.

Incisive comments about the interconnections of religion, gender, and witch hunting may be found in Elspeth Whitney, "International Trends: The Witch 'She'/The Historian 'He': Gender and the Historiography of the European Witch-Hunts" (1995), 77–101, esp. 86, 92. Puritanism's elevation of women's status is usefully discussed in Amanda Porterfield, *Female Piety in Puritan New England: The Emergence of Religious Humanism* (1992), 3–13. I cannot agree, however, with Porterfield's assessment of the Salem witch hunt, which relies too heavily on the late-seventeenth-century class-antagonism perspectives of Boyer and Nissenbaum and Karlsen (Porterfield, *Female Piety*, 143–153). I see greater continuities in the Puritan emphasis on female spiritual suffering (and related guilt) throughout the seventeenth century, culminating in the events of 1692, than Porterfield allows. If the identification of an elevated status for women within the context of continuing patriarchy were to hold up across Protestant and Catholic areas of early modern society, this might indicate just the sort of ambiguous or ill-defined status position that Mary Douglas has proposed for explaining which sorts of people get targeted in witch hunting at different times and places (see her "Thirty Years," xxv, xxx, xxxv). Suggestive comments along these lines (despite its title) may also be found in Allison P. Coudert, "The Myth of the Improved Status of Protestant Women: The Case of the Witchcraze" (1989), 60–89.

21. Jane Kamensky's chapter on witch hunting in *Governing the Tongue* (1997) does a better job than Karlsen's book at preserving the universal implications of the Salem events by stopping short of embracing "those poor, tormented souls," the young, female, afflicted accusers. Like Karlsen, Kamensky highlights the reversal in conventional power relations symbolized by the boldness and stridency of these accusers in the face of male authority figures. Again like Karlsen, Kamensky takes the instance of Elizabeth Knapp's possession as the norm and thus too readily dismisses the possibility of lethal outcomes resulting from the charges made by possessed accusers in the non-Salem cases. In fact, accusations emanating from the mouths of young, afflicted women led to executions at Hartford in the 1660s and at Boston in 1688. Yet when it comes to the Salem witch hunt, Kamensky includes in her account the terror faced by the targets of such accusations, including John Alden, one of the male suspects. She makes clear that the real heroes of 1692 were the women and men who proclaimed their innocence of

these charges, and in no way does she credit, as Karlsen does, Salem's extravagant accusers for bringing an end to witch hunting in the American colonies. See *Governing the Tongue*, chap. 6, quotation on 165.

CHAPTER 5: Norton's *In the Devil's Snare* and Racial Approaches I

1. Wabanakis are called Abenakis in some accounts. Wabanakis were one of many American Indian groups known to scholars as Algonquians, based on broad affinities in language.

2. Parris had come to Salem village with a third slave, a teenaged boy, who died early in 1689 (Roach, *Six Women*, 70). There is some dispute among historians about whether Tituba and Indian John were married, but at least two contemporary accounts of the witch hunt (John Hale's and Nathaniel Cary's) refer to them as husband and wife. Tituba's modern biographer, Elaine G. Breslaw, regards them as married at least by 1692 and possibly years earlier (*Tituba, Reluctant Witch of Salem: Devilish Indians and Puritan Fantasies* [1996], 82). For Hale's reference, see *Modest Inquiry*, in Burr, 413 (Burr changed "Enquiry" to "Inquiry" in the title to the edited version of Hale's book that he included in his widely used anthology); for Cary's, see Calef, *More Wonders*, in Burr, 351. Nathaniel Cary's wife, Elizabeth, was one of those accused at Salem. Tituba's confession may be found in *SWP*, 3:747–755.

3. Starkey, *Devil in Massachusetts*, 30. What makes the witch-cake incident enigmatic is that there are four contemporary accounts, three (by Deodat Lawson, John Hale, and Robert Calef) that mention Tituba and Indian John's involvement, and one (by Samuel Parris) that twice mentions only Indian John's. Parris's account (recorded in the church record book), which is also the only one to state that Mary Sibley had directed the minister's servant (or servants) to carry out the experiment in countermagic, appears to be the most reliable, since it was written by Parris himself only about one month after the incident. The other three accounts relied on second-hand reports, presumably coming originally from Parris, and were written at various intervals removed from the incident (Lawson's in April 1692, Hale's in 1697–98, and Calef's in 1697). It is possible, however, that Parris purposely omitted Tituba's name from his own two entries in the Salem village church records. By that date (March 27, 1692) Tituba was already in jail as a confessed witch, and Parris may have been embarrassed by her connection to his family. The minister's entries center instead on the scandal of church member Mary Sibley's direction of the illicit exercise. Nor were Lawson and Hale strangers to these early events, Hale having come to the village probably in late February and Lawson in mid-March, both to help Parris in dealing with the children's afflictions and for Lawson to learn more about the report that his wife and daughter's deaths in 1689 had been due to witchcraft. Their slightly later accounts of the witch-cake incident likely reflected what Parris told them at the time and may have included Tituba's name because she really had been involved. Hale's account also implies that he was present not long after the incident, when Tituba admitted her own participation in making the witch cake, although this admission may have been offered as a cover for her husband's and/or Mary Sibley's actions. (Nothing about the witch-cake incident appears in Tituba's formal confession, given to the Salem town magistrates on March 1 and 2. Lawson's and Calef's accounts add that the witch cake was fed to a dog.) There is probably no way to know which of these scenarios is the most accurate. For the four references, see Hale,

Modest Inquiry, 413–414; Lawson, *A Brief and True Narrative*, 162–163; Calef, *More Wonders*, 342, all in Burr; and Parris, "Records of the Salem-Village Church," entries for March 27 [1692], in *S-VW*, 278. On the conflicting reports of this incident as an example of the textual problems a Salem researcher faces, see Rosenthal, *Salem Story*, 25–27.

4. Hansen, "The Metamorphosis of Tituba, or Why American Intellectuals Can't Tell An Indian Witch from a Negro" (1974), 3–12; Rosenthal, *Salem Story*, 10–14. The earliest reference to Tituba and Indian John coming originally from "New Spain" appears to have been in Thomas Hutchinson, *History of the Colony and Province of Massachusetts-Bay* [1768], 2:20. An earlier draft of this portion of the colonial Massachusetts governor's history adopted a variation in phrasing: "Tituba, the name of the woman, who was a Spanish Indian, as some accounts tell us." It is not known to what "accounts" Hutchinson was referring. Nineteenth-century historian William Frederick Poole stated that the governor had access to documents that are no longer extant. See Poole, "The Witchcraft Delusion of 1692. By Gov. Thomas Hutchinson" (1870), 394 (for quotation), 381–382.

5. Rosenthal, "Tituba's Story" (1998), 190–203. Rosenthal did not emphasize the romantic component in the early versions of the "Tituba legend," but it can be detected even in the short excerpts he includes or references. Before Gaskell's short story, the American writer John Neal produced *Rachel Dyer* (1828), what Rosenthal calls the first novel written about the Salem witch hunt, which portrayed Tituba as "a woman of diabolical power" (Rosenthal, "Tituba's Story," 191). In Gaskell's story, note the following passage describing Nattee: "the poor old creature, herself believing and shuddering as she narrated her tale in broken English, took a strange, unconscious pleasure in her power over her hearers—young girls of the oppressing race, which had brought her down into a state little differing from slavery, and reduced her people to outcasts on the hunting-grounds which had belonged to her fathers" (quoted in Rosenthal, "Tituba's Story," 193). Starkey depicts Tituba's relationship to nine-year-old Betty Parris in strikingly similar terms:

> Betty was devoted to Tituba, whose special pet she was. The half-savage slave loved to cuddle the child in her own snuggery by the fire, stroke her fair hair and murmur to her old tales and nonsense rhymes. Never from her own mother had the child received such affection, for though godly parents loved their children as much as any heathen, they would not risk spoiling them. Basking in this warmth, Betty gave an almost hypnotic attention to the slurred Southern speech and tricksy ways of Tituba. Well she knew in her upright Puritan heart that she was tampering with the forbidden, but she could no more resist than she could lift a hand to free herself from the spell of an evil, thrilling dream. (Starkey, *Devil in Massachusetts*, 30–31)

Actually, it is hard to believe that Starkey could have developed her portrait of Tituba from reading Upham alone. Upham presents no details of the setting in which the supposed sessions of fortune-telling and other occult practices went on except to say that they occurred at the Parrises' house (Upham, *Salem Witchcraft*, 2:2–3), whereas Gaskell's story placed similar sessions in a kitchen, with its open fire, beneath the nose of an oblivious mother busy with her cooking, particulars that could all be found in Starkey's account. Starkey likely had Gaskell's story at hand when she wrote the pages on Tituba and Betty Parris, while Upham provided the legitimacy for her embellishments. Unlike the rest of her study, which was carefully based on the surviving records from 1692, Starkey drew this portion of her account, she clearly told her readers, only from "tradition" (*Devil in Massachusetts*, 272). Among the recent treatments of Tituba that tend to see her as an avenger, Rosenthal took note of Ann Petty's novel, *Tituba of Salem Village* (1964), Selma R. and Pamela J. Williams's study, *Riding the Night Mare: Women and Witchcraft* (1978), and Maryse Condé's novel, *I, Tituba, Black Witch of Salem* (1986, trans., 1992).

6. Rosenthal, *Salem Story*, chap. 1, quotation on 24. In this chapter Rosenthal argues that Sarah Good's examination, which came first among those of the three women questioned on March 1, provided more significant legitimacy to the initial charges of witchcraft than did Tituba's confession, because in implicating Sarah Osburn, Good confirmed one of the accusations before Tituba even took the stand. But this judgment seems misguided. Osburn, who went second, immediately denied the charge, and Tituba's questioning yielded not just renewed accusations but a *confession*, exactly the form of confirmation that seventeenth-century witch hunters considered solid. Plus, her confession was rich in detail and pointed to the involvement of at least six as-yet unidentified individuals. The contemporary participant John Hale wrote, "Her confession agreed exactly (which was afterwards verified in the other confessors) with the accusations of the afflicted. . . . And the success of Tituba's confession encouraged those in Authority to examine others that were suspected, and the event was, that more confessed themselves guilty of the Crimes they were suspected for. And thus was this matter driven on" (*Modest Inquiry*, in Burr, 415). Perhaps recognizing the problems with this line of reasoning, Rosenthal qualified his argument in his later article: "It is not my intention to shift blame from Tituba to Sarah Good; no scapegoat can account for the chaotic complexity of the witchcraft episode" ("Tituba's Story," 191n5).

7. John McWilliams, "Indian John and the Northern Tawnies" (1996), 580–604. On Tituba, see 586–588, quotation on 588; on Indian John, see 597–600, quotation on 599, where McWilliams uses the term "witch marks" loosely to mean physical injuries made to his body by a witch rather than this term's precise seventeenth-century meaning as a physical sign supernaturally placed on a witch so the Devil could readily recognize her or him. For the original data on Indian John's scars, also cited by McWilliams, see *SWP*, 1:208.

8. Breslaw, *Tituba*, esp. 5–6, 21–30, 38, 55–56, 62, 70–71, 73–75, 81. The statement that Tituba was not known for any occult activity prior to the witch hunt appears on p. 97 (on this point see also 90, 92); the comparison with Candy's confession appears on pp. 162–163. I have relied on *SWP*, 3:747–755, for the details of Tituba's confession, although Breslaw includes a copy from the same source in an appendix to her book. See also two articles by Breslaw that present portions of the same material found in her book: "The Salem Witch from Barbados: In Search of Tituba's Roots" (1992), 217–238, and "Tituba's Confession: The Multicultural Dimensions of the 1692 Salem Witch-Hunt" (1997), 535–556.

9. For Breslaw's treatment of the witch-cake episode, see *Tituba*, 95–97, 99. Some elements in Tituba's confession that Breslaw traces to Arawak roots include mentioning that the Devil came to her when she was in a dreamlike state before falling asleep (but

many Salem depositions spoke of witches approaching their targets at night in their beds), and asserting that the Devil could change his shape into the forms of various animals (such assertions are ubiquitous in the Salem depositions). Others are Tituba's describing witches' rides through the sky without detail as to the paths taken, trips thus more like "soul travel" (Mary Lacey Sr.'s testimony that she traveled by pole to Salem village and Newberry Falls similarly gives no details of her flight paths [*SWP*, 2:514]), and describing one of Satan's forms as a "hairy imp" (but many depositions refer to the Devil as a monster "all hairy," and Cotton Mather reported that "the Histories of the Witchcrafts beyond-sea [i.e., from Europe]" describe Satan as a short man [*Brand Pluck'd Out of the Burning* (1693), in Burr, 261]). For these references, see *Tituba*, 118, 126, 127, 128. Breslaw also maintains that Tituba's ending her own testimony by means of entering into a trance was more akin to the behavior of Arawak witches than English ones (122), but during her examination Tituba was acting as a victim of witchcraft as much as she was confessing to having (unwillingly) carried out the Devil's wishes; thus, her sudden silence fit with well-established English patterns of behavior for possession or torment at the hands of a witch. Breslaw acknowledges that the magistrates heard nothing alien in Tituba's confession in her article "Tituba's Confession," 549.

10. On Arawak witches as "outsiders," see *Tituba*, 18, 128; for the generalization about blood relations in English and American witchcraft accusations, see Demos, *Entertaining Satan*, 284. It is true that during the final, Andover phase of the Salem witch hunt, it became commonplace for children and other relatives of accused witches to confirm these accusations, but this was a new and exceptional development conditioned mainly by the contagion of confessions that broke out in mid-August, all influenced by the belief that confession was the only way to save oneself or one's close relatives. On this point, see Norton, *In the Devil's Snare*, 257–258. On evil as embodied in particular persons, see *Tituba*, 18, 126. The quotation from English witch lore is found in Norton, *In the Devil's Snare*, 343n33. For Breslaw's broader argument, see esp. xx, xxiv, 104, 106, 118, 132 (where the motive of "revenge" is floated as a possibility), 134–135, 178–181. The phrases "sophisticated manipulat[or]" and "passive victim" come from Breslaw, "Tituba's Confession," 541, 549.

11. In *Devil's Disciples*, Peter Charles Hoffer parallels almost exactly Breslaw's argument in regarding Tituba's actions as a heroic form of resistance to oppression, again using elements from Tituba's indigenous background (both through her participation in the witch-cake episode and in her confession) to cast off her English "mask" and "change her world." The main difference from Breslaw's account is that Hoffer believes Tituba came from the Yoruba-speaking region of the Niger River delta in West Africa. Hoffer's argument for Tituba's African origins is unpersuasive, however, relying solely on some resemblances in her name to certain Yoruba words, while ignoring virtually all of the many textual references in the Salem primary sources to her as an "Indian." See esp. 1–16 (the quotations come from 2, 15), 114–117, 205–210. See also Rosenthal's criticism of Hoffer's argument for Tituba's African origins in "Tituba's Story," 199–201.

Most historians place the emergence of racial labels to distinguish English people from Native Americans within a range of years stretching from the late seventeenth through the mid-eighteenth centuries. Prior to that development, the English typically described American Indians in cultural or religious terms, often but not wholly pejorative. When naturalistic explanations were offered, native people were said by the English to have been "born white," with their skins darkened by environmental factors. Some English observers linked the Indians genealogically to the "lost tribes of ancient Israel." In New England the Puritans undertook efforts to bring Christianity to Indian people, including through the translation of the Bible into the Massachusett language. However, the widespread and intense violence of King Philip's War in the 1670s seems to have all but halted such missionizing endeavors, beginning the process by which the English came to regard Native Americans as fundamentally different from themselves, based increasingly on immutable biological traits. Perhaps in response to these and similar developments elsewhere in North America, some Indian people by the middle-1700s also took up this distinction. As one mid-eighteenth-century Cherokee prophet put it, "You yourselves can see that the white people are entirely different beings from us; we are made of red clay; they, out of white sand." (This paragraph draws on Vaughan, "From White Man to Redskin," 917–953; Salisbury, "Red Puritans," 27–54; Davis, "Constructing Race," 7–18; and Joel Martin, *Sacred Revolt*, 183, for the Cherokee quotation.)

12. In *Regeneration Through Violence: The Mythology of the American Frontier, 1600–1860* (1973), chap. 5, Richard Slotkin regarded the Salem witch hunt as ironic punishment for the Puritans' refusal to recognize a common humanity with their Native American neighbors. According to Slotkin, the Puritans were actually attracted to the greater sexual freedom and violent ways of the Algonquian and Iroquoian peoples, but because the Puritans could not accept these impulses in themselves, they demonized their adversaries and embarked on a course of exterminating them. Indian bands murdered settlers and took captives in retaliation, and one of these captives, seventeen-year-old Mercy Short, on returning to New England, spread the "virus" of Indian hating and demonization to her fellow young people of Salem village in the form of imagined "captivity" at the hands of witches and their specters. Cotton Mather and other Puritan ministers, Slotkin added, nurtured this imaginary connection between Indians and witches in their sermons and teachings, thus fostering a parallel drive to exterminate witches. The choice of a few of the targets of the witch hunt, like George Burroughs and John Alden (who was accused but escaped), also pointed, for Slotkin, to the same connection with Indian conflict, because these people were thought by many New Englanders to have become too friendly with the Indians.

Slotkin's interpretation, however, suffered from a number of shortcomings. As a literary rather than a historical analysis, it highlighted Mercy Short's role in the Salem witch hunt chiefly because she became the focus of a treatise on possession by Cotton Mather. In reality, Short, who lived in Boston, played only a minimal role in the witch hunt, which was centered in Essex County to the north. She intersected with the events of the witch hunt only through her brief, private confrontation with the accused witch Sarah Good at the Boston jail in late May or June (when she threw wood shavings into Good's cell and elicited an angry curse in return). Afterward, she suffered from afflictions, according to Cotton Mather, for "diverse weeks" and then recovered. Her well-known case of possession and Mather's ministering to her occurred from late November 1692 to March 1693, after the witch hunt was essentially over. During the active time of the panic, she may have publicly accused only one person (besides Sarah Good) of witchcraft, her likely mistress, Margaret Thacher, a woman of high social standing and the mother-in-law of Salem magistrate Jonathan Corwin, but this accusation was dismissed as improbable. (See Mather, *Brand Pluck'd Out of the Burning*, in Burr, 259–260, and Norton, *In the Devil's Snare*, 176–181.) Slotkin's perspective also exaggerated the "hidden" affinities between Puritan and Native American cultures, especially in the characteristics of violence found in each. In terms of its sympathies, Slotkin's argument showed some respect for men like Burroughs and Alden, presumed friends of the Indian who became victims of the witch hunt, although they were accorded only brief space in his chapter. Overall, the reader is left to feel that the Puritans got what they deserved at the hands of "Fur[ies]" (Slotkin, *Regeneration through Violence*, 117) like Mercy Short.

James E. Kences's influential article, "Some Unexplored Relationships of Essex County Witchcraft to the Indian Wars of 1675 and 1689" (1984), similarly held Puritans responsible for bringing the Salem witch hunt (and some previous, smaller witchcraft scares) on themselves through their mistreatment of Native Americans and their determination to view acts of Indian retaliation through the self-aggrandizing lens of their providential outlook, uniting Satan, the Catholic French, and the latter's Indian allies in a monstrous conspiracy to bring down God's chosen people. Just as Norton's book would later do, Kences's article focused on the residual fears of the young accusers at Salem who had previously suffered family losses or dislocation at the hands of Indian attacks in New Hampshire or Maine. He explained their later "hallucinati[ons]" (211) about witches, given Puritan beliefs, as predictable, posttraumatic responses to these Indian raids in the context of resumed fighting in the northern parts of the colony. It was less painful, in effect, for the accusers to imagine being attacked by witches than to fear being set upon once again by real Indians. Kences also noted how the accusations often fell on people (like George Burroughs) who had had contact with Native Americans but had survived the wars, as if only the power of witchcraft could explain their seeming good fortune, an interpretation that would find an equally prominent place in Norton's account.

Unlike Slotkin, Kences was sympathetic to the plight of the young accusers in the witch hunt, their misdirected fears and "hallucinations" notwithstanding. He rather blamed the adults in the Puritan colony for failing to recognize the true source of the anxiety gripping their young people and to provide solace to them. The adults could not do so, in his view, because they shared the same beliefs about Indian people as their children and servants. In the end, Kences implied that the Salem witch hunt allowed the Puritans to reap what they had sown as a result of their intolerance toward Native American life, which stemmed, just as Slotkin believed, from a covert and forbidden "Puritan ambivalence toward the Indian" (Kences, "Some Unexplored Relationships," 186). There is no call to sympathize with the witch hunt's victims. Kences concluded his article by noting how ingrained among Puritans, of high stature and low, was the "grisly analogy" (212) of likening Indian warfare to the diabolical barbarities of bears and wolves. There is little in his article to suggest that there was truth in this Puritan perception—it would take Norton's book to bring out this crucial fact—even if Puritans, too, could act like bears or wolves on occasion. And if the two cultures really did show substantial differences in the forms of violence they sanctioned, then the problem of Puritan intolerance toward native people is not so easily explained away by the assumption that the Puritans simply became the victims of their own hypocrisy.

John McWilliams carried forward this line of thinking in his 1996 article, "Indian John and the Northern Tawnies." As Kences had done, McWilliams showed that there were real grounds for Essex County residents to fear Indian attack during the late 1680s and early 1690s, based on occasional Indian raids on the northern towns of the county and the far more devastating strikes, often with French support, on Puritan outposts in New Hampshire and Maine. McWilliams went on to list as many cases of witchcraft accusation throughout the county as he could find from the misnamed "Salem" witch hunt that bore the imprint of these fears of Indian attack. Some of his examples are well substantiated, but many seem far-fetched and susceptible to other, less remote explanations. (Norton would repeat all of these incidents and add more, with similarly mixed results.) As Slotkin and Kences had done, McWilliams emphasized how Puritan demonology easily equated the "tawny" Indian with the Englishmen's "black" Devil, although he implied this was a racial identification when it was really more of a religious marker, taking in the Catholic French among Satan's forces as well. For McWilliams, as for Slotkin and Kences, underneath the Puritans' fear of Native Americans lay "forbidden desires" to live more as Indians did in "a new life of bravery and equality, free of the last judgment" ("Indian John and the Northern Tawnies," 594), desires that were swiftly repudiated by turning Indians into demons. This understanding of the Puritans' purported intolerance and hypocrisy left little room for readers to sympathize even with victims of the witch hunt like John Alden and George Burroughs, who might have been more receptive to Native Americans than most New Englanders. In this rendering, the Puritan enterprise appeared far too flawed to deserve moral discriminations between the witch hunt's accusers and accused.

13. Norton published two article-length versions of her subject at about the same time that her book appeared: "George Burroughs and the Girls from Casco: The Maine Roots of Salem Witchcraft" (2001–02), 259–277; and "The Refugee's Revenge" (2002). The first of these articles, due to its brevity, is perhaps susceptible to a pro-Indian, anti-English interpretation, but the second, like the book itself, is not. At least one reviewer mistakenly placed Norton's study in an anti- (or post-) colonial context: Jane Kamensky, "Salem Obsessed," 394. Similarly, Emerson W. Baker, citing Norton's book, retells the story of witchcraft accuser Mercy Short but omits the critical element in Norton's account describing the prior cruelty Short witnessed at the hands of her Native American captors (*Storm of Witchcraft*, 104). This observation gets ahead of our story (see chapter 6), but I suspect Norton's book will be subject to many more such pro-Indian misreadings in the future.

14. For critical reviews of *In the Devil's Snare*, see Karlsen, "Devils in the Shape of Good Men"; Alan Taylor, "Crucibles"; and untitled reviews by Chaplin, Godbeer, and Salisbury. For favorable reviews, see Murrin, "The Infernal Conspiracy of Indians and Grandmothers"; Lepore, "The Red Scare"; and the untitled review by Minkema.

Evidence of the current influence of Norton's book may be found in the prominent place its arguments occupy in the most recent accounts of the witch hunt. Marilynne K. Roach's *Salem Witch Trials* (2004) and Gretchen A. Adams's *Specter of Salem* (2008), for example, draw on Norton's reasoning while ignoring entirely the older explanation based on economic factionalism within the village (Roach, intro.; Adams, chap. 1), even while each book maintains that no single cause adequately accounts for the outbreak of the witch hunt. Still more recently (2009), Bernard Rosenthal highlights Norton's argument above all others when he writes, "the heart of understanding the causes of the Salem witch trials rests in finding out why those in power chose to depart from the New

England tradition of not encouraging such charges [of witchcraft]," adding in a footnote that the effort to do so "has so far reached its fullest expression with Mary Beth Norton's landmark book, *In the Devil's Snare*" (Rosenthal, "General Introduction" to *Records*, p. 17). In a lengthy introduction to her anthology of primary sources, *Witchcraft in Early North America* (2010), Alison Games similarly regards Norton's emphasis on European-Indian conflict as the most valuable among a variety of contexts (which include Boyer and Nissenbaum's economic argument and Karlsen's feminist approach) for explaining the Salem witch hunt (55–71, esp. 59–62). (Quite apart from her reliance on Norton's argument, Games also tries to link the Salem events less to early modern European witch hunting than to other North American witchcraft persecutions, including those carried out within Native American groups in the seventeenth, eighteenth, and early nineteenth centuries, all owing to their colonial settings [76, 91]. This approach seems misguided. Witch beliefs everywhere showed certain local influences— e.g., a connection to presumed American Indian "devil worship" in New England or a tie to the prevalence of wolf attack, including attack by half-human werewolves, in forested parts of Europe—but the underlying mechanism behind the heightened persecution of "witches" during the 1450–1750 period in Europe and its colonial settlements showed broadly homogeneous characteristics having nothing to do with colonialism. Witch hunts within indigenous societies coming under colonial pressures, however, are another story.) Emerson Baker's *Storm of Witchcraft* (2015), a synthesis of the existing historical literature on the Salem witch hunt, also places Norton's explanations first among the witch hunt's multiple causes, and the author acknowledges that he relies most on *In the Devil's Snare* for answering "questions of fact or interpretation" (6, 9, 299).

15. Previous historians of the witch hunt who had devoted substantial space to discussing the context of the northern Indian war included Richard Slotkin, James E. Kences, John McWilliams, Carol F. Karlsen, Richard Godbeer, Christine Leigh Heyrman, and David T. Konig. The subject received at least a mention in nearly all accounts, including Marion Starkey's and Perry Miller's. Note particularly T. H. Breen's brief placement of the Salem witch hunt squarely within the context of the fears generated by the northern Indian war. Breen anticipated Norton's argument exactly when he wrote, "If the Massachusetts government had been able to defend the colonists from the French and Indians, the witch hunting episode might never have occurred, much less gotten out of hand" (*Puritans and Adventurers* [1980], 105).

16. See Norton's summary in *In the Devil's Snare*, 298–299, quotation on 298. For similar formulations, see 30, 78, and the following statement from the introduction: "*In the Devil's Snare*, then, contends that the witchcraft crisis of 1692 can be comprehended only in the context of nearly two decades of armed conflict between English settlers and the New England Indians in both southern and northern portions of the region. The ongoing frontier war, and the multiple fears it generated—in Maine and New Hampshire, in Essex County, and in Boston itself—thus supplies the answer to the question I posed earlier: why was Salem so different from all previous witchcraft episodes in New England?" (12).

17. Several of the critical reviews cited above in note 14 called attention to the relatively small number of victims and accusers with ties to the frontier. I have brought these separate, similar criticisms together in a composite statement. The observation concerning the late date at which Sheldon and Churchill joined the accusers and the

statistical comparison of the total number of accusations emanating from frontier-related accusers versus non-frontier-related accusers (based on data found in S-VW, 379–380) are my own. Admittedly, Norton places Mary Walcott (responsible for some 16 accusations) in the frontier-related group, because her older brother, John Walcott, was a militia sergeant who served in the war in Maine during 1689 and again in 1690. The Walcott family was also related to the Ingersoll family, some of whose members had lived in Falmouth, Maine, during the 1670s and 1680s. "Although Mary had not herself lived in Maine," Norton writes, "she must have heard many stories of the frontier and the Indian war from her brother and her Ingersoll relatives" (*In the Devil's Snare*, 54–55). No doubt Mary Walcott did, but this indirect experience at least places her in a different category from those accusers who Norton will argue likely suffered posttraumatic anxiety stemming from direct exposure to frontier violence. In addition, grouping Walcott with the frontier-related accusers suggests, without evidence, that whatever she may have heard about the frontier did more to shape her accusations than all of the local influences on the seventeen-year-old girl. (Norton spells Sarah Churchill as Sarah Churchwell throughout her book, because Sarah's surname appears in that form in the documentary record from Maine, where the family lived for a number of years. I use "Churchill" in my study, because that spelling is more commonly used in the witch hunt's secondary literature and published documentary sources, including the authoritative *Records*.)

18. These critical observations come from the reviews cited above in note 14, where many of the same points are made in several of the reviews. I added the final observation about the likelihood that Salemites felt safer, not more threatened, in the immediate aftermath of Bridget Bishop's execution. The lull in accusations after Bishop's hanging actually lasted for close to a month, as I demonstrate later in this chapter. Norton's linkage between Bishop's execution and the attack on Wells appears in *In the Devil's Snare*, 210–211.

19. Ibid., 222.

20. SWP, 2:564–566. In another instance of unpersuasive reasoning, Norton argues that the absence of a larger outbreak of witchcraft accusations in southwestern Connecticut during 1692, where a female servant, Katherine Branch, was afflicted in mid-April in a manner similar to the first girls and young women at Salem, suggests the importance of the northern Indian war to the development of the Essex County witch hunt. In the Connecticut case, Branch's afflictions led to accusations against six local women, three indictments, two trials, and one conviction but no executions. "Of course, the absence of a Connecticut crisis comparable to that in Essex County does not by itself prove that the looming presence of the war on the northeastern frontier was *the* crucial factor in creating the contrast between the two regions," Norton writes. "Yet at the same time it is highly suggestive that a teenage maidservant could experience severe and prolonged fits in 1692 in southern New England and not set off a regionwide panic like that which occurred simultaneously two hundred miles north in Massachusetts" (*In the Devil's Snare*, 78, italics in original). Actually, Indian violence was not as removed from southwestern Connecticut as Norton's comparison suggests. An Indian raid up the Connecticut River on Northfield, Massachusetts, had taken five English lives in August 1688, and a major attack on nearby Schenectady, New York, in February 1690, resulted in the deaths of sixty English men, women, and children. French

forces also attacked the Connecticut coast in mid-July 1690, causing the loss of houses and livestock, just as Connecticut militiamen were joining New Yorkers in a failed campaign to attack the French at Montreal (94, 102, 348n76). Thus, the same factors that Norton emphasizes for Essex County (the dangers of a grisly and widening war nearby, together with the inability of the colony's leadership to put a quick end to the conflict) were present in Connecticut. Richard Godbeer's later study of the same Connecticut witch hunt accepts Norton's dubious reasoning for why it never rivaled the magnitude of Salem's, adding the additional factor of the absence of a heretical Quaker minority in the southwestern Connecticut region (*Escaping Salem*, 165–166). Yet most historians doubt that the Quaker presence in eastern Massachusetts, though threatening to the Puritans in the 1650s and 1660s, played much of a role in generating anxieties by the early 1690s. On the Quaker factor, see my discussion in chapter 2, notes 28 and 29. A more persuasive explanation than either Norton's or Godbeer's for the failure of Branch's afflictions to produce a wider or more lethal witch hunt lies in the ascendancy of more liberal Puritan values among Connecticut's elite, beginning in the late 1660s under the influence of its governor, John Winthrop Jr., and prominent minister Gershom Bulkeley (see Woodward, *Prospero's America*, chap. 7, esp. 226–252).

Despite the strained reasoning involved in most of Norton's attempts to link fear of Indian attack to specific accusations or confessions of witchcraft, she did include occasional instances where the two fears appear directly related. The case of Mary Allen Toothaker, who on July 30, 1692, confessed to signing the Devil's "burch bark" in order to be protected from Indian attack in the outlying Essex County community of Billerica, provides a strong, though unusual, example. Remarkably, just two days after Toothaker was jailed, an Indian raid on the town killed the occupants of two households near hers (*In the Devil's Snare*, 239–241).

21. It is worthwhile at this point to dismiss attempts at arguing for an external biological cause of the afflictions. The two proposed candidates are ergot, a fungus that infects the rye plant, and the unidentified agent (most likely a virus) that causes encephalitis lethargica. Both of these proposed explanations, however, founder on the fact that the afflicted moved in and out of their torments seemingly on cue, utterly dependent on the social situations they were facing, thus suggesting a psychosocial mechanism. In addition, the conditions said to be conducive to the spread of such biological agents were in no way restricted to Puritan areas of the American colonies, yet such symptoms developed nearly exclusively in this region, again pointing to cultural rather than biological factors at work. See Caporael, "Ergotism" (1976), 21–26; Spanos and Gottlieb, "Ergotism and the Salem Village Witch Trials" (1976), 1390–1394, for a refutation of Caporael's argument; Matossian, "Ergot and the Salem Witchcraft Affair" (1982), 355–357; and Carlson, *A Fever in Salem* (1999).

22. Norton, *In the Devil's Snare*, 23; Cotton Mather, *Pietas in Patriam*, 326–327.

23. Norton, *In the Devil's Snare*, 23–24, 307, 336n30. Baker accepts Norton's dismissal of fortune-telling in *Storm of Witchcraft*, 15, 108–109, 123.

24. Hale, *A Modest Enquiry into the Nature of Witchcraft* (1702; 1973, facsimile reproduction). The two paragraphs in question read as follows:

I fear some young persons through a vain curiosity to know their future condition, have tampered with the Devils tools, so far that thereby one door was opened to

Satan to play those pranks; *Anno* 1692. I knew one of the Afflicted persons, who (as I was credibly informed) did try with an egg and a glass to find her future Husbands Calling; till there came up a Coffin, that is, a Spectre in likeness of a Coffin. And she was afterward followed with diabolical molestation to her death; and so dyed a single person. A just warning to others, to take heed of handling the Devils weapons, lest they get a wound thereby.

Another, I was called to pray with, being under sore fits and vexations of Satan. And upon examination I found she had tried the same charm: and after her confession of it and manifestation of repentance for it, and our prayers to God for her, she was speedily released from those bonds of Satan. This iniquity, though I take it not to be the Capital crime condemned, *Exod.* 22. Because such persons act ignorantly, not considering they hereby go to the Devil; yet borders very much upon it: and is too like Sauls going to the Witch at *Endor*, and *Ahaziah* sending to the God of *Ekron* to enquire. (132–133)

The six other references to the 1692 Salem events may be found on pp. 46, 53, 76, 80, 86, 156.

25. Lawson's observations came in his sermon, "Christ's Fidelity the Only Shield Against Satan's Malignity," delivered at Salem village, March 24, 1692. Norton states that Lawson made only "a very brief and unspecific reference to fortune-telling" in his coverage of what might have brought on the flurry of witchcraft, placing his emphasis on contentions within the village and the villagers' use of countermagic, as in the instance of the witch cake (*In the Devil's Snare*, 336n30). But in his lengthy discussion of this subject, Lawson presented three likely explanations: (1) neighborly contentiousness, (2) "using indirect means to prevent or remove this affliction; and trying unwarrantable projects, to reveal Secrets, or discover future events," and, interestingly, (3) accusing people of witchcraft falsely or "without sufficient grounds." Under the second heading, he went on to include a substantial assertion about fortune-telling.

> But I must not conclude this particular, without testifing against some other practises amongst us Condemned by the Rule of God, and writings of learned and judicious men as yielding to, and tampering with the Divel, Viz the sieve and scyssers; the Bible and Key; The white of an Egge in a Glass; The horse shooe nailed on the threshold; A stone hung over the Rack in a stable with many more . . . and if in the use of them Discoveryes are made; or Effects produced, to the gratifying their sinful Curiosity in any degree, it must be from the Devil, and not from GOD; who never instituted any such ways, by and in which, to discover secret things or future Events to the Children of Men.

Lawson's sermon is reprinted in Trask, ed., *"The Devil hath been raised."* For his discussion of the actions that may have provoked God's displeasure, see pp. 98–101, with the quotation on pp. 99–100. The phrase about the Roaring Lion (Satan) appears on p. 91.

Brattle observed,

> Now I am writing concerning Andover, I cannot omit the opportunity of sending you this information; that Whereas there is a report spread abroad the country, how that they were much addicted to Sorcery in the said town, and that there were fourty men in it that could raise the Devill as well as any astrologer, and the like; after the best search that I can make into it, it proves a mere slander, and a very

unrighteous imputation. The Rev'd Elders of the said place were much surprized upon their hearing of the said Report, and faithfully made inquiry about it; but the whole of naughtiness, that they could discover and find out, was only this, that two or three girls had foolishly made use of the sieve and scissors, as children have done in other towns. ("Letter of Thomas Brattle, F.S.M." in Burr, 181)

While Lawson's remarks are more general and Brattle's more specific (for Andover), together they add support for Hale's and Mather's observations about Salem. There is additional evidence of illicit fortune-telling by adults in the communities of Essex County, including by some individuals who became the victims of the witch hunt (e.g., Dorcas Hoar, Roger Toothaker, and Samuel Wardwell). On one such adult fortune-teller, see Dailey, " 'Where Thieves Break Through and Steal': John Hale versus Dorcas Hoar, 1672–1692" (1992), 257, 262.

26. Norton, *In the Devil's Snare*, 81, 122. In another statement of the turning point, she writes, "The talk about local witches, fortune-tellers, and the like spread all the more widely and intensely through the region because Abigail Hobbs's confession on April 19 caused Essex County residents to connect their fears of neighbors long suspected of malefic acts with their newer concerns about the consequences of the Second Indian War" (114). Baker endorses Norton's argument for Abigail Hobbs's confession as the turning point in *Storm of Witchcraft*, 23.

27. For turning points, see Karlsen, *Devil in the Shape*, 37; Starkey, *Devil in Massachusetts*, 72–75; Breslaw, *Tituba*, 114; and Rosenthal, *Salem Story*, 109.

28. Data for construction of figure 7 comes from the chronological list of titles of the 977 legal documents included in *Records*, pp. 101–124. The full list of named suspects, together with their precise dates of legal action, may be found in my appendix 2. I discuss my procedure for forming this list of 138 usable names in the note at the end of the appendix. Richard Latner has also called attention to the witch hunt's two waves ("The Long and the Short of Salem Witchcraft" [2008], 139 and throughout). I discuss Latner's article in the conclusion, note 11.

Norton presents her own illustration of the trajectory of the witch hunt in the form of two graphs (*In the Devil's Snare*, 121, 253). She does not say where her data comes from, but the titles of her two graphs ("Chart 2: Cumulative Total of New Formal Witchcraft Complaints, February–June 1692" and "Chart 3: Cumulative Total of New Complaints, Examinations, and Confessions, July–September 1692") suggest that her initial source was probably the "List of All Persons Accused of Witchcraft in 1692" from S-VW, 376–378, since the term "complaints" appears prominently in the original list and her two graphs. Norton likely added data of her own collection to Boyer and Nissenbaum's list, ending up with a total of 136 names. Because Norton's two graphs display the change in the number of accusations only cumulatively (and in the first chart using irregular intervals on the x-axis), it is hard to get from her illustrations a true picture of the wavelike trajectory that the witch hunt followed. In addition, the separation of her data into two distinct graphs, the first one ending at June 6 and the second one commencing at July 15, obscures the lull between the two waves lasting from June 10 until mid-July.

29. Technically, five-year-old Dorothy (often misnamed as Dorcas) Good, Sarah Good's daughter, became the second person to confess to the crime of witchcraft in late March, but her admission did not carry the weight of an adult's or teenager's confession.

30. Norton, *In the Devil's Snare*, 78–81, 118–119, quotation on 81.

31. I list the names and dates of accusation for everyone mentioned in this and the next two paragraphs in appendix 2. Born Philippe L'Anglois on the Channel Isle of Jersey, Philip English emigrated to Essex County around 1670. Although ethnically mostly French, Jerseyans were considered of English nationality, as the island had remained under English control since the eleventh-century Norman conquest. Most residents, including Philip English's family, however, were Anglican in religious affiliation, a source of suspicion for many Puritans. The Massachusetts Jerseyans also tended to support the authoritarian regime (discredited after its collapse in 1689) of Edmund Andros, who himself hailed from the channel islands. For Norton's discussion of the accusations against the Englishes, see *In the Devil's Snare*, 137, 140, 143–146. For more on the French community in Essex County at the time of the witch hunt, see Konig, "A New Look at the Essex 'French,'" 167–180. The most extensive treatment of Philip English's place in the merchant world of colonial Salem, emphasizing his outsider status despite his great wealth and achievements, may be found in Phyllis Whitman Hunter, *Purchasing Identity in the Atlantic World: Massachusetts Merchants, 1670–1780* (2001), esp. chap. 2. Carol Karlsen helpfully emphasizes the greater vulnerability and prior accusation of Philip English's wife, Mary Hollingsworth English, due to the earlier charge of witchcraft leveled against her mother, the "aggressive and outspoken" Eleanor Hollingsworth (*Devil in the Shape*, 106–107).

32. Data on William Hobbs may be found in SWP, 2:425–431; for Deliverance Hobbs's confession, see SWP, 2:419–422. Ann Pudeator had two sons who continued to live in Falmouth, Maine, long after she returned to Salem town, but the charges against her apparently stemmed from her long reputation as a witch in Salem, including the belief that she had murdered her second husband and his first wife (*In the Devil's Snare*, 164–165). Some historians consider Deliverance Hobbs to be the fourth adult or teenager to confess, because on April 20, after Abigail Hobbs's confession but before her mother's, Mary Warren, John Procter's servant, briefly switched from accuser to confessed witch, before returning to her earlier position as an afflicted accuser. Warren, however, did not function chiefly as one of the confessed witches in the witch hunt.

33. For Ann Putnam Jr.'s vision, see *In the Devil's Snare*, 119–120. The addition of Rev. George Burroughs to the ranks of the accused certainly was important for propelling the witch hunt forward, yet it is still possible to overrate the influence of Ann Putnam's vision on the subsequent number of accusations. The next nine formal accusations came on April 21, just one day after Putnam's vision, too soon to have been affected by it. By the end of that day, twenty-three individuals had been formally accused of witchcraft before the naming of George Burroughs would have registered with the community.

34. Abigail Hobbs's confession may be found in SWP, 2:405–408. Significantly for a psychological understanding of what prompted confessions of witchcraft, Hobbs began hers with the following words: "I will speak the truth. I have seen sights and been scared. I have been very wicked. I hope I shall be better, if God will help me." Exactly what caused this fourteen-year-old to believe she had "been very wicked" is not clear, but other depositions entered into evidence at her later trial spoke of her lying out at nights alone in the Topsfield woods, being disobedient to her father and mother, pretending to baptize her mother, and not caring what anybody said to her (2:413, 415).

35. *In the Devil's Snare*, 120–132; for all of the accusations against Burroughs, see SWP, 1:151–178. Burroughs's first wife, Hannah Fisher Burroughs, died in September 1681 at Salem village, as Norton notes, "perhaps from complications following the birth of her fourth (and third surviving) child" (*In the Devil's Snare*, 125). The following year Burroughs married Sarah Ruck Hathorne, who had been recently widowed when her first husband, William, John Hathorne's brother, died suddenly. The Burroughs family moved in 1683 to Falmouth, where they seem to have lived until the winter of 1689–90, although Burroughs himself traveled to other Maine communities to preach, especially the nearby settlement at Black Point, where by 1686 land had already been donated to him for his support and he had begun to plant crops. Sarah died during that winter (I have not seen an explanation for the cause of her death), and soon after Burroughs moved with his seven children to Wells, Maine. There he was married for a third time, to a woman named Mary (maiden name unknown) (Robinson, *Devil Discovered*, 90–96).

As for the deaths of Lawson's wife and daughter, Charles Upham simply stated, "While Mr. Lawson was at the village [1684–88], he lost his wife and daughter" (*Salem Witchcraft*, 1:282). Cotton Mather in late 1692 had commented, "there were some odd circumstances about them [the deaths], which made some of the Attendents there suspect something of witchcraft, tho' none Imagined from what Quarter it should come" (*Wonders of the Invisible World*, in Burr, 218). Rosenthal argues that Burroughs's vulnerability arose chiefly from his unorthodox religious views, which may have leaned toward the Baptist perspective (*Salem Story*, chap. 7). While all of the murder charges against Burroughs appear wholly imagined, it is plausible that he subjected his wives to verbal abuse and boasted about his physical strength.

In a clear statement of her intention to combine Hobbs's confession with Ann Putnam's vision, and illustrating her undue emphasis on the northern war, Norton writes, "Abigail Hobbs's confession of April 19, coupled with Ann Jr.'s spectral encounter with George Burroughs on the evening of April 20, transformed the 1692 witchcraft crisis from a serious but not wholly unprecedented set of incidents into the extraordinary event that played out over the next six months. Immediately after Abigail confirmed the Devil's presence in Falmouth and Ann Jr. revealed that Burroughs, his minion, had worked in concert with the Wabanakis by bewitching Sir Edmund Andros's troops, the number of accusations skyrocketed" (*In the Devil's Snare*, 120–122).

36. For Mather's account, see his *Wonders of the Invisible World*, in Burr, 215–222. Norton's speculation about Burroughs's hypothetical motives for wishing to hurt Lawson's child—that he envied Lawson's selection as minister on Andros's mission during the winter of 1688–89—is unpersuasive. She cites a September 1689 statement by militia commander Benjamin Church, offering to keep Burroughs in Falmouth by hiring him as an army chaplain, as supporting the notion that Burroughs might have sought the earlier chaplaincy on Andros's military expedition (*In the Devil's Snare*, 129–130). But there is no logical connection between Church's plan and Burroughs's previous hopes for himself. Church's statement accurately noted Burroughs's financial straits in Falmouth, due to the community's poverty, and the minister's "thoughts of removeing," but with a family of seven children and land already purchased for him in Black Point, Burroughs was much more likely during the winter of 1688–89 to have been contemplating relocating to Black Point than angling to serve as an army minister on a temporary

campaign. An alternate explanation for Putnam's two charges against Burroughs concerning the Indian war—if Mather's explanation is thought inadequate—would be that they both reflected the readiness of Salemites to blame Burroughs for any misfortunes to which he could be even implausibly linked, in this case the setbacks suffered by Andros's forces in Maine.

37. Norton, *In the Devil's Snare*, 48–49, 128–130.

38. For Abigail Williams's vision (as reported by Benjamin Hutchinson), see *SWP*, 1:171–172; for Lewis's vision, 1:168–169. The biblical verses (King James Version) read, "Again, the devil taketh him [Jesus] up into an exceeding high mountain, and sheweth him all the kingdoms of the world, and the glory of them; And saith unto him, All these things will I give thee, if thou wilt fall down and worship me" (Matt 4:8–9). "And the devil, taking him up into an high mountain, shewed unto him all the kingdoms of the world in a moment of time. And the devil said unto him, All this power will I give thee, and the glory of them: for that is delivered unto me; and to whomsoever I will I give it. If thou therefore wilt worship me, all shall be thine" (Luke 4:5–6).

39. "Selected List of Accusers and Persons Against Whom They Testified," *S-VW*, 379–380. The numbers given in my text include overlapping accusations against targeted individuals, since a legal complaint required more than one accusation of witchcraft. Norton provides her own list of accusers (*In the Devil's Snare*, 321), giving the "number of legal complaints" and the "number of cases with formal testimony" for each. Her numbers for legal complaints by the same group of accusers cited in my text are Ann Putnam Jr. (53), Elizabeth Hubbard (40), Mary Walcott (69), Mary Warren (40), Mercy Lewis (54), Susannah Sheldon (24), and Abigail Williams (41). For formal testimony, she gives these numbers: Ann Putnam Jr. (28), Elizabeth Hubbard (32), Mary Walcott (28), Mary Warren (16), Mercy Lewis (12), Susannah Sheldon (3), and Abigail Williams (7). I find Norton's category of "legal complaints" less useful than Boyer and Nissenbaum's data, because Norton adds to the number of accusations for which a written record survives a sum corresponding to admissions by confessors that they had afflicted the accuser. If, for example, the confessed witch Abigail Hobbs said that she tormented Mercy Lewis, then Norton would add one more "legal complaint" to Mercy Lewis's total, even if there is no surviving record that Lewis accused Hobbs. The data shown under Norton's category of "formal testimony" does look roughly similar, in relative numbers, to that provided in Boyer and Nissenbaum's list, which, in any case, Boyer and Nissenbaum tell us, is a "Selected List."

40. On legal age requirements for testimony and for the observation about the omission of Ann Putnam Jr.'s and Abigail Williams's ages from legal documents, see *In the Devil's Snare*, 21, 335n24. The comparison in the number of appearances of Ann Putnam Jr.'s and Mercy Lewis's names on indictments, depositions, or complaints against the twenty people executed comes from my own survey of the documents gathered for Bridget Bishop, George Burroughs, Martha Carrier, Giles Cory, Martha Cory, Mary Esty, Sarah Good, Elizabeth How, George Jacobs Sr., Susannah Martin, Rebecca Nurse, Alice Parker, Mary Parker, John Procter, Ann Pudeator, Wilmot Redd, Margaret Scott, Samuel Wardwell, Sarah Wilds, and John Willard, arranged alphabetically in *SWP*.

41. *In the Devil's Snare*, 305–308.

42. On Esty, see ibid., 172–173. On Cory, ibid., 277; *SWP*, 1:246; Sewell, *Diary of Samuel Sewall*, 1674–1729, 295–296. On Abbott, see Norton, *In the Devil's Snare*, 136–137. Sewall was the witchcraft trial judge to whom Thomas Putnam Jr. addressed his letter. The timing of the two events (Ann's vision and Cory's ordeal) is reported variously by different historians, but the two relevant primary sources suggest the sequence described in my text, the same sequence that Norton offers. There is no strong evidence that Cory's punishment went on for two or three days (as suggested in Schiff, *Witches*, 315, 465n, and some other accounts), which would have contradicted Thomas Putnam's letter and Sewall's diary entry, nor are the descriptive details of the ordeal known for sure. Confusion about the timing seems to have stemmed from a likely misdating of Cory's death by Robert Calef as September 16 instead of September 19 (*More Wonders*, in Burr, 366) and a backdating by one day (from September 19 to September 18) of the action taken by the Salem town church to excommunicate Cory for either witchcraft or "suicide." Charles Upham's account is helpful in making the sequence clearer (Upham, *Salem Witchcraft*, 2:334–344, esp. 343–344).

Halsey Thomas, the editor of Sewall's diary, adds in a note that in 1676, after the death of his servant Jacob Goodale, Cory had been tried in the county court for physically abusing him and had received a fine for his responsibility (*Diary of Samuel Sewall*, 296n14). Clearly, some in the community felt that Cory had not received adequate punishment. In the same letter from Thomas Putnam to Sewall, Putnam wrote of the jury in that earlier case, "The Jury, whereof several are yet alive [John Procter had sat on that jury, but he had been executed as of the date of Putnam's letter], brought in the man [i.e., Goodale] Murdered; but as if some Enchantment had hindred the Prosecution of the Matter, the Court Proceeded not against Giles Cory, tho' it cost him a great deal of Mony to get off" (*SWP*, 1:246). A more likely cause than either "enchantment" or the payment of money for Cory's relatively lenient sentence, however, was that the trial brought out conflicting reports about the source of young Goodale's injuries. Apparently mentally disabled, Goodale seems to have been beaten by his brother and by a son-in-law of Cory's, as well as by Giles Cory himself, against whom there was strong and shocking evidence (*RFQCE*, 6:190–191). Despite the likelihood of multiple sources for Goodale's injuries, it is not surprising that staunch Puritans in the village might have seen the Devil's hand behind Cory's part in such acts of physical abuse. Later, so, too, might have "an Ancient Woman, named Goodall," an unidentified relative of Jacob Goodale, who was reported to be among four afflicted adults at the examination of Martha Cory in March 1692 (*Records*, #17). Evidently, it did not sufficiently help Giles Cory at the time of his arrest for witchcraft that, "having been a scandalous person in his former time," in the words of the church's record-keeper, he had joined the Salem town church just the previous year at the age of about seventy-two (*Records of the First Church in Salem*, 170–171).

43. See Norton, *In the Devil's Snare*, 133–134 (on Hobbs), 228 (on Bradbury), 185–186 (on Alden). Norton argues that even though Ann Putnam Jr. was the only one to identify Deliverance Hobbs when the afflicted girls were tested in this way by the presiding magistrates (while Lewis and another girl were "struck dumb," in Samuel Parris's words), Mercy Lewis must have been "the source of the little girl's information" because Lewis had likely lived close to the Hobbs family in Falmouth and because there was no

known feud between the Hobbs family in Topsfield and the Putnams in Salem, making it unlikely that Ann Jr. would have known Deliverance (133–134). But a simpler explanation presents itself from evidence Norton provides elsewhere. Deliverance had attended church in Salem village just the previous Sunday, and she likely attended the examination of her stepdaughter, Abigail Hobbs, three days earlier. In either or both instances, Ann Putnam Jr. might have taken note of her. Besides, it is not known exactly when Abigail's mother, Avis Hobbs, died, and when her father, William, was remarried to Deliverance. It could be that during most of the time that the Hobbs and Lewis families were neighbors in Falmouth, Avis, not Deliverance, was present in the Hobbs household.

Peter Charles Hoffer also argues for Mercy Lewis's leadership among the afflicted girls, but his discussion is largely theoretical (based on knowledge of modern youth gangs), speculative (based on the ages and circumstances of the participants), and contradictory. He writes on one page, "Perhaps the Salem girls had no leader, or rather, leadership shifted from one to another of the girls. 'Diffuse' packs of adolescents and near adolescents are more common than structured gangs" (*Devil's Disciples*, 97). But on the next page he states, "Once constituted, the Salem girls developed their own ranking system. Packs and gangs have hierarchies that are internal as well as external, and often the two do not match" (98). He suggests that Lewis was the leader because of her wide and painful experiences in the world, producing intense anger and alienation from her community. He adds, "Of all the girls, she was far and away the most forceful, imaginative, and compelling in her accusations." Hoffer, however, provides no evidence to back up this last assertion.

CHAPTER 6: Norton's *In the Devil's Snare* and Racial Approaches II

1. Norton, *In the Devil's Snare*, 211.

2. For the quotations, see ibid., 15 (the internal quotation comes from an account by Cotton Mather) and 43. I do not recall a single usage of the term "witch hunt" in Norton's book, and I have found only one instance of the term "panic" used to describe the events of 1692, in a side comparison with the much smaller, concurrent witch hunt in Fairfield, Connecticut (78). I use the phrase "circle of accusers" loosely, since Mercy Short, who lived in Boston, participated in the witch hunt only tangentially during the summer, adding her voice to the accusations against Sarah Good, and then again as an afflicted young person in November, after the witch hunt was nearly over. For more on Short, see below in the text and chapter 5, note 12. I describe the devastating effects on Mercy Lewis's extended family of the Wabanakis' 1676 raid on Falmouth in chapter 5.

3. Norton, *In the Devil's Snare*, 141–143, quotation on 142.

4. Ibid., 135, 178–179. Norton presents Short's captivity at two points in her account; I have combined the two in my quotation. The phrase "Invisible Furies," which Norton quotes, was Cotton Mather's to describe the witches that beset Short and the other afflicted people during the witch hunt.

5. Ibid., 159–160. Given the absence of evidence about Churchill's life between 1676 and 1692, it is surprising that Norton is so ready to attribute Sarah's "unenviable existence" at the time of the witch hunt to the family's earlier "wartime losses." Not all families who chose to move from Maine to Massachusetts to escape the Indian danger would necessarily have entered into a downward path. The death of her mother must

have been the single biggest factor in accounting for Sarah's condition of servitude in 1692, yet this loss might have had nothing to do with the frontier or the war. Norton also reveals in a note that Sarah was likely to have been a child born to her mother out of wedlock with another man, before her mother married Arthur Churchill (373n11). If so, that fact might help explain why Sarah became separated from her father after her mother's death, which in turn contributed to her drop in social status.

Ibid., 10, for the quotation "As daughters and servants," and 51, for another statement along the same lines. Among her tributes to the afflicted accusers, Norton heralds their ability to extract confessions, spectral though they might be, from alleged witches, while the magistrates failed so miserably at the same efforts in the weeks following Tituba's initial admission.

> Time and again Hathorne had done his best to interrogate suspects carefully in order to expose the contradictions and falsehoods in their stories that would reveal their involvement with the devil. Yet he rarely succeeded. Instead of being uncovered by the magistrates' questioning, even before May 9 [at the examination of George Burroughs] witches were being revealed by the fits, visions, and mimicking movements of the afflicted Villagers. In the weeks and months after the examination of George Burroughs, the process moved even farther along the same path, as spectral confessions to the bewitched and appearances of the dead turned into witch-finding, and as the magistrates ceased all attempts to conduct meaningful examinations of the accused. (154)

6. Norton, *In the Devil's Snare*, quotation on 86–87. On the clash in fighting norms between seventeenth-century British Americans and Native Americans, see Donagan, "Atrocity, War Crime, and Treason in the English Civil War" (1994), esp. 1142, 1146–1149; Drake, "Restraining Atrocity: The Conduct of King Philip's War" (1997), 33–56, which does not seem quite to grapple with the military fierceness of the Wabanakis in the northern theater of the war; and Hirsch, "The Collision of Military Cultures in Seventeenth-Century New England" (1988), 1187–1212, esp. 1192, 1207n57, which acknowledges, though underplays, Indian use of torture on captives. Hirsch argues that the Puritans' infamous slaughter in 1637 of native noncombatants (including women and children) at the Pequots' Fort Mystic settlement during the Pequot War set a precedent for future warfare during the colonial era (1204), but Alfred A. Cave shows that the massacre was not a premeditated aspect of Puritan military policy but arose in the heat of battle, even though it was justified thereafter on the basis of Old Testament analogies (*The Pequot War* [1996], 144–178). See also the valuable final remarks about Native American torture and cruelty in Abler, "Iroquois Cannibalism: Fact Not Fiction" (1980), 314–315.

Examples of historical accounts of American Indian warfare (restricted to New England bands) that omit, minimize, or explain away Indian violence include Jennings, *The Invasion of America: Indians, Colonialism, and the Cant of Conquest* (1975); Salisbury, *Manitou and Providence: Indians, Europeans, and the Making of New England, 1500–1643* (1982); Morrison, *The Embattled Northeast: The Elusive Ideal of Alliance in Abenaki-Euramerican Relations* (1984); Calloway, *The Western Abenakis of Vermont, 1600–1800: War, Migration, and the Survival of an Indian People* (1990); Lepore, *The Name of War: King Philip's War and the Origins of American Identity*

(1998); Calloway and Salisbury, eds., *Reinterpreting New England Indians and the Colonial Experience* (2003); and Pulsipher, *Subjects unto the Same King: Indians, English, and the Contest for Authority in Colonial New England* (2005). See the sharp critique of Lepore's book on this issue by Wood, "The Bloodiest War." On the other side of the ledger remains the older account by Vaughan, *New England Frontier: Puritans and Indians, 1620–1675* (1965; 3rd ed., 1995); see Vaughan's historiographical discussions in the introductions to the 2nd and 3rd editions. Outside the confines of New England's history, one can find a number of modern historians of the Native American experience, including James Merrell, Richard White, Daniel Richter, James F. Brooks, and Peter Silver, who, like Norton in *In the Devil's Snare*, include American Indian strategies of cruelty and terror in their discussions of traditional warfare. Meanwhile, virtually all historians writing after the 1960s are not shy about including descriptions of atrocities committed in wartime by Anglo-American settlers and militias.

7. *In the Devil's Snare*, 82–83, 89–91, 86, 92 (for the long quotation).

8. Ibid., 89–90 (on Waldron), 93 (on the Marblehead women, including the quotation). On the violent Saco River harassment incident, see Hubbard, *History of the Indian Wars in New England*, 2:135. Two other historians of the Indian wars in Maine interpret Hubbard's "Seamen" to mean local fisherman: Baker, in "Trouble to the Eastward: The Failure of Anglo-Indian Relations in Early Maine" (1986), 190; and Pulsipher, in *Subjects unto the Same King*, 223. (Pulsipher misdates the drowning incident as occurring in the summer of 1676 instead of the summer of 1675, as Hubbard states.) For more on the Marblehead incident, see Axtell, "The Vengeful Women of Marblehead" (1974), 647–652.

9. Norton, *In the Devil's Snare*, chap. 3, quotations on 90, 101–102.

10. Ibid., 86 (on Sylvanus Davis's decision), 356n57 (on settlers trading guns with Indians). Davis was not acting alone but in concert with other traders in the Kennebec region. Puritan historian William Hubbard called him an agent for Thomas Clarke and Thomas Lake, whose fur-trading interests on the Kennebec dated back to 1654 (Hubbard, *History of the Indian Wars*, 2:148; Baker and Reid, *The New England Knight: Sir William Phips, 1651–1695* [1998], 12). More extensive accounts of the role played by Maine residents in provoking hostilities with the Wabanakis may be found in Pulsipher, "'Dark Cloud Rising from the East': Indian Sovereignty and the Coming of King William's War in New England" (2007), esp. 600, 605–606, 608; Pulsipher, *Subjects unto the Same King*, esp. 209–210, 223–225; and Morrison, *Embattled Northeast*, esp. 89, 109, 113, 115.

11. Norton, *In the Devil's Snare*, 103–104 (on the councilors' complaints about the frontier settlements), 103 ("grandiose strategies"), and 100 ("For once"). Norton is more even-handed in her treatment of Andros's frontier policies than she is about the post-Andros provisional government's, but in summary statements (97–98, 101–102, 103–104) she still resorts to hostile characterizations of both sets of policies. For a more positive assessment of Andros's policies, see Morrison, *Embattled Northeast*, 113–117; for a more negative one, see Pulsipher, *Subjects unto the Same King*, 253–255.

12. Norton, *In the Devil's Snare*, quotations on 300, 299.

13. On Stoughton's actions, see ibid., 95. In fact, a miscommunication seems to have ruined Stoughton's efforts at the hostage exchange in this instance (Barnes, *The Dominion of New England* [1923], 225). On Hathorne and Corwin's mission to Maine,

see *In the Devil's Snare*, 104–105, 357n66. In the latter note Norton acknowledges, "Some of those who talked to Hathorne and Corwin thought that the two men had been convinced of the need for the soldiers [to remain at Fort Loyal]." If so, then there is even some direct evidence to undermine the claim that the two Salem magistrates would have felt personally responsible for the council's decision to withdraw the militia unit.

14. *In the Devil's Snare*, 105, 357n66 ("it seems that Willard's men"), 299 ("had most likely caused"). On Gedney, Sewall, and the 1690 expeditions to Port Royal and Quebec, see ibid., 103, 104, 106, and 108 (for Bradstreet's quotation). Although the initial proposal for the expeditions conformed to the common public-private financing formula, the Massachusetts Council decided to finance the two naval campaigns through tax revenues alone, although plunder was still taken for purposes of rewarding the crew and its captain, William Phips. On this point, see Richard R. Johnson, *Adjustment to Empire: The New England Colonies, 1675–1715* (1981), 193; and John Nelson, *Merchant Adventurer: A Life Between Empires* (1991), 58–61, 64.

15. For Brattle's observation about Stoughton, see "Letter of Thomas Brattle," in Burr, 183–184. On the judges in the Glover trial, see *In the Devil's Snare*, 382n17. On Bridget Bishop, see *S-VW*, 162, 157–158. The earlier accusation of witchcraft against Bishop occurred in 1680, resulting in an order that the suspicion be presented to the Massachusetts Court of Assistants. Nothing is known about the further disposition of that case. Background on Hathorne and Corwin is provided in Robinson, *Devil Discovered*, 25–26, 32–35. For more on Hathorne's religious conservatism and Winthrop's growing conservatism from the time of the overthrow of Andros (April 1689) until the end of his life (1717), see references in my chapter 2, note 30. Adding still further plausibility to the charges of witchcraft at Salem would have been the arrest and jailing of an accused witch (Martha Sparks) from Chelmsford, northwest of Andover, in late October 1691, and the likely case of a girl (Mary Knowlton) suffering the afflictions of apparent witchcraft in nearby Ipswich during the month just preceding the outbreak in Salem village. Word of these instances would likely have reached Hathorne and Corwin. On these two cases, see Rosenthal, "General Introduction," *Records*, p. 16.

16. Sewall, *Diary of Samuel Sewall*, 1:289; *In the Devil's Snare*, 191 (on Newton and Alden).

17. *In the Devil's Snare*, 302 (for "ordinary Essex folk" and for just one example among many of the use of "stories" and "gossip"). Free acquisition of land for speculative purposes by the colony's officials is the one form of corruption that many historians allude to in their discussions of Puritan political practices in seventeenth-century Massachusetts. However, given the Puritans' acceptance of social hierarchy and their belief that the godly would be rewarded by material signs of a sanctified life, it is questionable to what extent the common people of New England objected to such acquisitions. "Government was not a source of profit in early Massachusetts, which could compensate its magistrates for the costs of their office only by large grants of land," Stephen Foster writes: "These in turn could not be developed without capital, just what governors and government did not have. Nor did the grants have much speculative value while other land was still available for free: many magistrates ended up, in effect, land poor" (*Their Solitary Way: The Puritan Social Ethic in the First Century of Settlement in New England* [1971], 37). In later decades, when speculation did lead to profits through the sale of subdivisions, most, though not all, residents of the New England colonies

seem to have regarded this process as an acceptable way for the countryside to be developed and the growing population accommodated. On this subject, see Bailyn, *New England Merchants*, 174–175; Lewis, "Land Speculation and the Dudley Council of 1686" (1974), 255–272; Martin, *Profits in the Wilderness*, 118–128. As William Cronon has pointed out, speculative returns from land were integrated into virtually all New England property holders' expectations for their future prosperity (*Changes in the Land: Indians, Colonists, and the Ecology of New England* [1983], 74–81, 167–170.

At least two earlier historians, William Pencak and Timothy H. Breen, both emphasizing the return of Indian warfare amid the chaos of the period 1689–1691 following the ouster of Edmund Andros, anticipated Norton's argument for hidden political motives behind the justices' support for the witch hunt. Pencak suggested that the trials offered officials like Stoughton an opportunity to reestablish authority after having served in the discredited Andros regime by "convinc[ing] themselves that they truly believed in their religious and political ideals" through the zealous prosecution of witches (*War, Politics, and Revolution in Provincial Massachusetts*, 14–28, quotation on 24). T. H. Breen stressed the convenience of blaming witches for the failure of the colony's government to defend the frontier from enemy attack (*Puritans and Adventurers*, 104–105, and see my chapter 5, note 15, for the direct quotation). Writing just after the appearance of Norton's book, John M. Murrin also endorsed its political argument, placing his emphasis on the need for political figures, including Stoughton, Gedney, Winthrop, Richards, Hathorne, and Corwin, who had "compromised" their credentials through their support of the Andros regime, to pander to the will of the people in their witch hunting. "As a group," Murrin wrote, "they could not afford to appear soft on witches" ("Coming to Terms," 322–23, 333–334, 344–345, quotation on 323; "Infernal Conspiracy," 490). Emerson W. Baker parallels Norton's argument in placing the lion's share of blame for the witch hunt on the trial judges, due to their relationship with Native Americans. Baker agrees with Norton that the justices embraced witch hunting in part as a means to deflect public anger about the dismal conduct of the war, but he believes their motivation stemmed even more acutely from a need to purify themselves and the colony from a sense of moral and spiritual contamination resulting from the elite's greedy land transactions with the "devilish" Indians. See Baker, *Storm of Witchcraft*, chap. 6; Baker and Kences, "Maine, Indian Land Speculation, and the Essex County Witchcraft Outbreak of 1692" (2001), esp. 167, 177, 179–181.

While one should probably never underestimate the instinct of politicians to pander to the prejudices of their constituencies, the problem with these variants of Norton's argument, like her own, is the lack of evidence to suggest that these political officials saw themselves as vulnerable or in need of political strengthening as a result of their leadership (or land purchases) during the eight years preceding the witch hunt. All, with the possible exception of Stoughton, had served the Andros regime with considerable reserve; all, Stoughton included, had participated in Andros's removal; all, except Stoughton briefly, remained popular during the several years of the post-Andros provisional government. All equally benefited from the renewed sense of colonial unity brought to Massachusetts by the resumption of hostilities with the northern Indians, and all would have regarded their land acquisitions as fully their due and as undertaken for the best interests of the colony. The most critical observation one can make with confidence is that the colony's leaders in the summer of 1692 would not have wanted their newly chartered government to appear weak either to local rivals (urging greater independence from England) or to ones across the Atlantic (pushing for tighter imperial control), a point made in a number of accounts (including Roger Thompson, "Review Article: Salem Revisited," 322–323). Moreover, as my text argues, there is no need to posit a hidden motive. The civil and religious convictions of the judges, combined with the circumstances of what they took to be an extraordinary outbreak of the Devil's intervention, provide ample explanation for their actions. One advantage of Pencak's, T. H. Breen's, and Murrin's formulations over Norton's and Baker's, however, is that the former do not seek to exonerate the common people for responsibility in the witch hunt, while the latter do.

Baker's populist leanings extend even to the point of alleging a "cover-up" on the part of Massachusetts officials, with Governor Phips in the lead, in the immediate aftermath of the witch hunt, as a way of shielding the governing elite from popular sentiment said to have turned against the persecutions (*Storm of Witchcraft*, 8, 38–42, chap. 7, esp. 195). In reality, the population, locally and in the colony at large, remained deeply divided for years about the propriety of the witch hunt. This division was indicated by the closeness of the vote (33–29) in the elected Massachusetts House of Representatives (formerly House of Deputies) in October 1692 to disband the special witchcraft court (Sewall, *Diary*, 1:299); the large number of names on Salem village's 1695 "pro-Parris" petition, larger than the number on the same year's anti-Parris petition (see my discussion in chapter 2); and the slowness with which public figures in the colony came forward to express remorse for what had happened, beginning only tentatively in 1697 with Judge Samuel Sewall's notable apology. (For a sensitive treatment of Sewall's courageous and lonely statement, see Francis, *Judge Sewall's Apology*, introduction, part 1, esp. chaps. 8 and 9.) No deliberate cover-up was needed for a set of actions that the people and leaders of Massachusetts only gradually came to realize had been an immense miscarriage of justice. Phips did prevent publication of opinions about the witch hunt (with the exception of writings by Increase and Cotton Mather) in the first two years after the panic ended, but this ban was motivated by the governor's fear that extended public debate about the events might unsettle English confidence in the colony's government under the new charter. In the long run, many records and contemporary personal accounts of the persecutions were lost to history, but this was due to the voluntary actions of participants themselves.

18. *In the Devil's Snare*, 184; SWP, 3:872; Johnson, *Adjustment to Empire*, 88–90; David S. Lovejoy, *The Glorious Revolution in America* (1974), 240. Ex-governor Andros later listed desertions at New Dartmouth, Newcastle, Sagadahoc, Newtown, Fort Anne, Pejebscot, and Saco ("The officers and soldiers at Saco all deserted, as did others afterwards") in a pamphlet aimed at defending his regime's actions in the Northeast. The reconstituted Massachusetts government replied that the desertions were fewer in number and occasioned by the severity of some of Andros's chosen officers, adding, "Sacoe River fort was deserted in Sir Edmond's time for want of necessaryes and privisions for the soldiers, and Capt. Floyd himself made a prisoner by Sir Edmond upon his coming to ask provision for the necessarye subsistence of that Garrison" (*Andros Tracts*, 3:31–33, quotation on 32; 34–38, quotation on 36). Norton cites the *Documentary History of the State of Maine* (1900), 6:473–475, in support of her interpretation of the April 1689 mutiny, but here she was probably misled by Andros's early statement (dated April 12,

1689) that some of Flood's men had deserted their posts against the captain's orders. It is possible that the abandonment of the Saco station had begun that way, but if so, the later accounts by Andros and the Massachusetts Council indicate that Flood quickly made common cause with his men.

19. *In the Devil's Snare*, 184–185. Norton's principal source for the Exeter incident, a 1699 account by Cotton Mather, provides a more even-handed description of Flood's actions than her own.

> About this Time a Council of War was called at Portsmouth, by which 'twas thought adviseable to send out Captain Wiswel, with a considerable Scout, for to Scour the Woods [for enemy Wabanakis] as far as Casco; and it being Resolved, That one of the other Captains with about Fourscore Stout men should accompany Captain Wiswel in this action, they All with such a Generous Emulation offered it, that it was necessary to determine it by a Lot, which fell upon Captain Floyd. On July 4 [1690], assisted with Lieut. Andrews, and a Detachment of Twenty-two men from Wells, they took their March from Quochecho into the Woods. But the Day following, the Enemy set upon Captain Hilton's Garrison in Exeter, which Lieutenant Bancroft, then posted at Exeter, with the loss of a few of his men Relieved. . . . On July 6. Lord's Day, Captain Floyd, and Captain Wiswel, sent out their Scouts before their Breakfast, who immediately returned, with Tydings . . . of a considerable Track of the Enemy, going to the Westward. Our Forces vigorously followed the Track, till they came up with the Enemy, at a place call'd Wheelwright's Pond; where they engaged 'em in a Bloody Action for several Hours. . . . Fifteen of ours [including Capt. Wiswel] were Slain, and more Wounded; . . . Captain Floyd maintained the Fight, after the Death of Captain Wiswel, several Hours, until so many of his Tired and Wounded men Drew off, that it was Time for him to Draw off also; for which he was blamed perhaps, by some that would not have continued at it so long as he. (*Decennium Luctuosum* 221, 223–224)

Exactly how Norton formed the impression that Captain Flood had left Exeter "in order to destroy some Indian cornfields" is unclear, since no reference to that effect appears in the documents cited in her notes to this paragraph. But such a reference does appear in another, briefer account of the Indian raid on Exeter, which asserted, "Capt. Flood & Capt. Wizwell was sent outt with a design to destroy the Indians corne," an assessment of Flood's and Wiswel's mission at odds with Mather's account yet still not one that implies any failing on Flood's part, as Norton suggests (abstract of letter from [Lieutenant Governor of New Hampshire John?] Usher to unknown recipient, July 7, 1690, *Documentary History of the State of Maine*, 5:133).

Norton's sources also offer no justification for siding with the men who abandoned Flood's unit in the midst of their fight with the Wabanakis outside of Exeter. Norton writes that Cotton Mather's choice of words ("until so many of his Tired and Wounded men Drew off, that it was Time for him to Draw off also; for which he was blamed perhaps, by some that would not have continued at it so long as he") "downplay[ed] the seriousness of what had happened. Floyd's men, suffering significant casualties, had deserted him in the field of battle . . . [due to his] futile persistence" (*In the Devil's Snare*, 185). But there is no account of this aspect of the fighting except Mather's; thus, there is no way to know whether Flood or his men (or neither) were at fault in this engagement from a brutal war in which men commonly drew back from fighting. Norton tries to buttress her interpretation of Flood's unpopularity with his men by adding that when the captain later questioned one of the men who had abandoned his company, "the deserter replied (in Floyd's words), 'he woold sarve [serve] me woors [worse] before he had dun with me for sayd he I care nott for you nor for none and sayd that he hopt that he shoold wash his hands In my blood'" (185). Norton breaks off her quotation after the word "blood," but the original sentence continues, "and In thoas [those] that ded geve me my powar," a phrase that picks up on the earlier expression "nor for none." Both references point to the more generalized anger that this man evidently felt for the policy makers who had brought on the war. Indeed, this same deserter told Flood that "he had Rathar brak [break] his goon [gun] then too Kel [kill] ani of the Enimy as I cald them boot [but] Rathar Kel me or any that ded send me or him out" (*Documentary History of the State of Maine*, 5:141).

It is also noteworthy that Flood was not one of those militia officers who was forced out of a commission by the local men of his native community, Rumney Marsh, as a number of other Massachusetts militia officers were, amid the political upheavals following the overthrow of the Andros regime. On these developments, see T. H. Breen, *Puritans and Adventurers*, chap. 5.

20. Norton, *In the Devil's Snare*, 185.

21. Ibid., 185–188. For useful background on Alden's activities, see Johnson, *John Nelson*, 22–29, 35–36; Baker and Reid, *New England Knight*, 92, 157–161; Louise A. Breen, *Transgressing the Bounds: Subversive Enterprises among the Puritan Elite in Massachusetts, 1630–1692* (2001), 197–206.

22. Norton, *In the Devil's Snare*, 186–189. For Ravenscroft's role in transmitting Emerson's affidavit, see Louise Breen, *Transgressing the Boundaries*, 203. Norton similarly biases her account of Alden's actions by presenting a report conveyed from a New Hampshire official to the authorities in Boston about Alden's last trip to Maine before he was accused of witchcraft, as if this piece of seemingly incriminating information spoke for itself. The New Hampshire official, Maj. Elisha Hutchinson, reported that two recent escapees from French captivity stated that the French leader, Castine, was angered when goods Alden had promised to bring him in March 1692 had not arrived at Port Royal with the merchant. But this "promise," Norton fails to explain, was simply the latest development in a complicated line of exchanges, all known to the Massachusetts Council, that Alden was pursuing with the French, stemming from William Phips's rash act of taking some sixty French prisoners when he gained control of Port Royal in May 1690. A number of these prisoners had already been sold into slavery in the Caribbean, and in retaliation for this violation of the surrender agreement, as the French saw it, several Englishmen, including Alden's son, John Jr., had been taken prisoner in 1691. The promise to deliver supplies to Castine in March 1692 was part of Alden's continuing efforts to return both sets of prisoners. On this incident, see *In the Devil's Snare*, 190, 192–193; Johnson, *John Nelson*, 72, 76; Baker and Reid, *New England Knight*, 157–158.

23. Norton, *In the Devil's Snare*, 189 (for the three quotations). The historical literature on the Alger Hiss case is extensive. My understanding comes from Tanenhaus, *Whittaker Chambers* (1997), Jacoby, *Alger Hiss and the Battle for History* (2009), Weinstein,

Perjury: The Hiss-Chambers Case, 3rd ed. (2013), and Judt, "An American Tragedy? The Case of Whittaker Chambers" (2008). Hiss was convicted of perjury and served five years in prison; the statute of limitations prevented a trial for espionage.

24. Norton, *In the Devil's Snare*, 130, for first quotation; 132, for second quotation; 122–123, for previous hunch; 100 and 110, for Burroughs's actions at Falmouth and Wells. In another instance of ambiguous language, Norton writes of the September 1689 attack on Falmouth, "The English lost eleven soldiers killed and ten wounded, some of whom died later. How many townspeople were among the casualties is uncertain. But the Reverend George Burroughs again survived an attack on Falmouth" (100). Since most of the town's residents survived this attack, as they had the one thirteen years before, there is no reason to single out Burroughs's good fortune. The missing context serves to make Burroughs's survival in both instances seem unusual, which it was not.

25. Ibid., 124, 128–130. Provincial records from Maine, dated March 30, 1686, even refer to the minister as "Mr. Burrows, Minister of Bla: Poynt [Black Point]" ("George Burroughs," *Sibley's Harvard Graduates*, 2:326).

26. Norton, *In the Devil's Snare*, 129, for the first three quotations; Breen, *Transgressing the Bounds*, 204, for the quotation from the petition. The nineteenth-century historian of Portland (formerly Falmouth), William Willis, while clearly sympathetic to the petitioners' claims, cast doubt on how truly representative of Falmouth residents the petitioners actually were: "Although these persons in the petition [he lists sixty-seven signers], style themselves inhabitants of Falmouth, I have met with the names of many of them on no other occasion; I have therefore thought that the names of persons who were on service here for a temporary period may have been enlisted in the cause to give a show of strength. It is very evident that we do not find among the subscribers, the names of many persons of known respectability and property in town" (*History of Portland*, 267n1). Since the petition centered on grievances against Tyng, Davis, and one other man in their capacity as officers of the town's militia, Willis's comment about the petition attracting the names of "persons who were on service here for a temporary period" makes sense. Yet solely on the basis of her discussion of this petition, Norton later identifies Edward Tyng in passing as "the magistrate and wealthy landowner with whom George Burroughs was aligned in Casco" (*In the Devil's Snare*, 201). Throughout his lengthy discussion of the history of Falmouth during the 1670s and 1680s, Willis gave no indication at any point of George Burroughs's alignment with either Tyng or Davis (*History of Portland*, 194–308).

The land dispute between Lawrence and Davis (and to a lesser extent Tyng) is complicated and not one in which blame can be easily assigned to one side or the other. Viola F. Barnes, a historian whose sympathies lay with the Andros regime, stated that Robert Lawrence's grievance over some of his land having been regranted to Edward Tyng stemmed from the land policies of the Massachusetts government before the Dominion period, even though it was fought out in the courts under the Andros regime. She also argued that Maine residents in general approved of Andros's land policy as a way to provide security against conflicting claims (*Dominion of New England*, 189n43, 201–202, 205). Willis, although an obvious critic of Andros's policies, nevertheless pointed out that Lawrence was the largest landholder in the Casco Bay area and had acquired much of his holdings through his marriage to a widow (Mary Munjoy), whose substantial property had come into her first husband's hands through an agreement with a local

Indian leader whose power to sell this land was later questioned by Davis and others. Davis himself had been welcomed to Falmouth in 1680 by town residents and Massachusetts officials with the gift of substantial land grants (some of which conflicted with Lawrence's claims), in order to attract his enterprise and capital connections to the area as it was being resettled with English residents following King Philip's War. Concerning the dispute that ensued between the two men, Willis concluded,

> Davis certainly settled here with the approbation of the town, from which he received large grants of land and extensive privileges; those undoubtedly excited the envy and jealousy of some who took advantage of the political changes [with the fall of the Andros regime] to ruin him in public favor. Lawrence was undoubtedly stimulated in his pursuit of him by motives of private interest and revenge, and was able by his standing and property to rally a party in his service. There is, we think, no good reason to pronounce an unqualified condemnation against such men as Davis and Tyng, whose capital and enterprise for several years promoted the prosperity of the place. It must not however be denied that in the time of Andros, their ambition prompted them to support the cause of arbitrary power against the rights and interests of the people. (*History of Portland*, 269, for the quotation; 222–269)

27. Norton, *In the Devil's Snare*, 163. For Hobbs's examination of May 12, 1692, see *SWP*, 2:410–412, and for her earlier confession of April 19, 1692, see ibid., 2:405–408. The testimony by Simon Willard may be found at ibid., 1:161.

28. *In the Devil's Snare*, 141–143, quotations on 143; 88. For different perspectives on Scottow's history in Maine, see Pulsipher, *Subjects unto the Same King*, 213–219; and Baker, "Trouble to the Eastward," 203–205, 217–218. Baker notes that Scottow's trading interests in Maine went back even further than the 1660s to his involvement in the Penobscot River fur trade in the late 1650s (118). Meanwhile, the Alger brothers seem to have arrived in the Black Point area sometime after 1659, the date of the deed to a land sale bearing their names (156). Scottow and the Algers came into conflict well before the events of the 1675 raid that took the brothers' lives, but at least in this case there is little to the distinction Norton wishes to draw between Maine's "old settlers" and "newcomers" to explain their antagonism.

29. My generalizations about Maine's seventeenth-century history rely on Baker, "Trouble to the Eastward," 89–93, on the intermarriage of old and new residents in the Sagadahoc area; and throughout; Baker and Reid, *New England Knight*, chap. 1; Pulsipher, *Subjects unto the Same King*, 39–43, 52–54, 63–64, 83–85, 195–196, chap. 9. John Alden's marriage to Elizabeth Phillips, daughter of William Phillips of Saco, Maine, provides another instance of the blurring of Norton's distinction between the Massachusetts merchant elite and Maine's "old settler" families. Sylvanus Davis was also hardly a newcomer to Maine, nor does he appear to have arrived with money. Davis came to Maine "sometime after 1665" to serve as an agent for the Clarke & Lake Company, fur traders on the northern Kennebec River (Baker, *The Clarke & Lake Company* [1985], 10). He moved to Falmouth after King Philip's War. Scottow's conservative Puritan outlook is described in Bailyn, *New England Merchants*, 122–123, 135, while Burroughs's brand of Puritanism is thought to have lain close to the Baptists, a stance which I consider "conservative" in the sense of its opposition to the Halfway Covenant and other developments taken to broaden church membership in the second half of the seventeenth century.

For Scottow's attendance at a day of fasting and prayer for John Alden, see *In the Devil's Snare*, 230.

30. *In the Devil's Snare*, 301, 303. See also the quotation in note 5 above, lauding the afflicted accuser's competence as surrogate magistrates.

Conclusion

1. Paul Boyer received a doctorate from Harvard in 1966, Stephen Nissenbaum from University of Wisconsin in 1968, Mary Beth Norton from Harvard in 1969, and Carol Karlsen from Yale in 1980. John Demos completed his graduate work at Harvard and other institutions around 1970.

2. On the New Left's hostility to liberalism, see Matusow, *The Unraveling of America* (1986), chap. 11; Brinkley, *Liberalism and Its Discontents* (1998), chap. 12; Isserman and Kazin, *America Divided* (2000), esp. chaps. 9 and 12; and Gitlin, *The Sixties* (1987). A particularly succinct treatment of the subject is E. J. Dionne Jr.'s chapter, "Freedom Now: The New Left and the Assault on Liberalism," in his *Why Americans Hate Politics* (1991), 331–354.

George M. Marsden offers a slightly different list of midcentury liberal values: "individual freedom, free speech, human decency, justice, civil rights, community responsibilities, equality before the law, due process, balance of powers, economic opportunity, and so forth" (quoted in Worthen, "Faithless" [2014], 80).

3. I am aware that *In the Devil's Snare*, unlike the other three main post-1960s books highlighted in my text, fits uneasily under the rubric of a "New Left"–influenced book. Nearly all left-leaning academic works published after 1969 adopt a critical stance when the subject matter concerns anything to do with Euro-American colonialism (these works call themselves "postcolonial," by which they mean anticolonial), while Norton's study champions the perspective of the English colonial settlers (and their war-refugee children) in relation to the indigenous Wabanakis. The common element to be found in all four Salem books, however, resides in their underlying populism, the central ideological component of late-1960s radicalism. Loose as this ideology was, consisting of little more than a belief in the goodness of ordinary people (variously defined) and anger toward an elite (variously defined) said to have stolen the fruits of other people's labor and otherwise oppressed them, this homegrown variant of anarchism and small-scale communalism came to dominate the groups and less formal movements of young people on the fringes of the antiwar and civil rights movements and in the era's counter-culture. Because left-wing organizations (e.g., Students for a Democratic Society) attracted the largest number of these young people, it makes sense to speak of the overall phenomenon as the New Left, just as people did at the time. But radicalized individuals during the 1960s and in subsequent decades sometimes traveled back and forth between populist groups on the left and on the right. *In the Devil's Snare*'s right-leaning populism unites it with an older tradition in American literature and popular culture that depicts heroic stories of self-reliant frontier settlers surviving brutal captivity at the hands of Native American raiders and freeing themselves with minimal help from metropolitan elites, government officials, or the army. (One thinks of the classic 1955 John Ford film, *The Searchers*.) If this particular ideological shading, which helped Norton's study gain insight into what motivated a subset of the accusers at Salem, distinguishes her work from that of the rest of her left-leaning cohort, all four books nevertheless com-

prise a family whose shared populist assumptions account for the analytical and ethical shortcomings of an entire era in the historiography of the witch hunt. (For this paragraph, see, in addition to the sources listed in the previous note, Kazin, *The Populist Persuasion* [1995], intro. and chap. 8.)

Much the same illiberal populism (of the left-wing sort) appears to inform Gretchen A. Adams's *The Specter of Salem* (2008). *The Specter of Salem* focuses not on the events of 1692 but rather on how "the Salem witch hunt" was used as a political metaphor by various segments of the American population during the nineteenth century. Adams recognizes that the roots of the metaphor lay in the witch hunt's violation of its victims' due-process rights by the "zeal" and "folly"—two pejorative terms first applied to the witch hunt by its leading contemporary critics, Thomas Brattle and Robert Calef—of the Puritan crowd and officials. However, she fails to point out the distortion involved as the metaphor quickly became used by powerful groups in the nation to tar less powerful opponents with charges of "fanaticism" or "intolerance," much as some present-day politicians allege a "witch hunt" when faced with legitimate questioning of their actions. Adams adopts a mostly cynical posture as she relates how early national Federalists cried, "Salem!" as a means of countering democratic interpretations of the Revolution that credited "passions" or "excitement" in the founding of the United States; how antebellum Protestants branded their Roman Catholic, Spiritualist, and Mormon antagonists as incipient "tyrants" and "witch hunters"; how white Southern defenders of slavery did the same toward their abolitionist enemies; and how Gilded Age Northerners traded the term "Puritan" for "Pilgrim" as a reference point for their revered forbears in order to distance themselves from the "fanatical" legacy of the Reconstruction-era Radical Republicans—all as if nothing more could have been expected from the meaning of the original Salem events or even as if there might not be grains of truth in each of these exaggerated Salem-based critiques. Only when the metaphor became centered more narrowly on *government* intolerance, which, she argues, occurred in the late nineteenth century, does Adams show some interest in the ethical value that "Salem" might have for readers today, as when this meaning of the Salem metaphor was later adopted by opponents of the impeachment of President Bill Clinton. The problem with this perspective, however, is that Adams provides no evidence that such a shift in the meaning of the "Salem" symbol ever occurred. Her own evidence suggests that the symbol always signified the intolerance of the crowd as well as that of officials authorized by the crowd, a meaning that emerged again in the twentieth century during Prohibition, the Scopes anti-evolution trial, and McCarthyism. Like the New Left historians of the Salem witch hunt, whose work seems to have influenced her own study of the event's cultural memory, Adams appears unable to recognize the genuine dangers posed by extremist popular ideologies and the reasons why Americans might have sought in the lessons of the colonial past a means of identifying such threats.

4. My summary of the older historiographical debate among witchcraft scholars between "rationalists" and "romantics" draws on Monter, "The Historiography of European Witchcraft" (1972), 435–451; Karlsen, "On Witchcraft and Witch-Hunting," 617–619; Hall, "Witchcraft and the Limits of Interpretation," 253–262; and Behringer, "Historiography," in *Encyclopedia of Witchcraft: The Western Tradition* (2006), 492–498. In most ways that debate has been superseded by the scores of detailed studies of

witch hunting in Europe that have appeared over the past four decades, studies that have added much precision to generalizations about the chronology, geography, sociology, political circumstances, legal conditions, and religious foundations of witch hunting. One particularly important finding of these studies, relevant to Salem, is that the rise in witch hunting in the early modern period went hand-in-hand with a "judicial revolution" that brought, on the one hand, more thorough means of investigating crimes and more severe inquisitorial techniques (including the use of torture) but, on the other hand, more careful procedures of judicial review in the more centralized states, a review process that worked ultimately to encourage officials to regard witchcraft accusations with skepticism. Everywhere, witch hunting arose "from below" in society and was greatly intensified by zealous local officials and clerics, but the most developed legal opinion of the day, located in a few metropolitan centers, was starting to put the brakes on these persecutions. New England's witch hunting, occurring in an outpost of the English empire under homogeneously Puritan control, with criminal procedures not subject to any judicial review in the mother country, was able to cause greater damage than would have been the case in England or many parts of the European continent by the late seventeenth century. For a respected survey of this recent historical scholarship, see Levack, *The Witch-Hunt in Early Modern Europe* (2006), along with the essays in Ankarloo and Clark, *Witchcraft and Magic in Europe*, vol. 5, *The Period of the Witch Trials*. Nevertheless, when considering the shifting eras in the historiography of Salem, I am struck by the continuing utility of the rationalist-romantic dichotomy. Kittredge's treatment of Salem may be found in *Witchcraft in Old and New England*, chap. 18 (the quotation appears on 338).

5. Perry Miller, *New England Mind*, 191. H. C. Erik Midelfort has recently argued for a shift in the historiography of European witch hunting away from a preoccupation with large-scale "panics" toward a greater appreciation for the "ordinary" manifestations of small-scale witchcraft accusations under nonpanic circumstances ("Witch Craze? Beyond the Legends of Panic" [2011], 11–33). While Midelfort's suggestion doubtless has value for furthering the understanding of witch hunting in Europe, where panics have dominated the subjects of inquiry, it probably should not be extended to the study of American witch hunting, where investigations into the Salem witch hunt have not yet yielded diminishing returns and the Hartford panic has barely been looked at. Exactly what to call the large-scale outbreaks is perhaps another matter—Midelfort is critical of latter-day biases contained in such terms as "craze" or "panic"—but again, in the American context, the extremism of the persecutions has been too readily obscured by American scholars of the post-1960s generation.

Unlike the New Left historians of American witch hunting, most historians of the European experience writing during the last three decades of the twentieth century never lost sight of the importance of religious fervor and communal scapegoating in generating witch hunts, even as their interests turned toward discovering the political and legal determinants of witchcraft panics. New Left romanticism, stemming from "the wish of most witchcraft historians," in the words of Willem de Blécourt, "to write a history of people previously neglected," seems to have affected these scholars chiefly by producing a renewed interest (brought forward from the discredited work of the early twentieth-century English historian Margaret Murray) in looking for the persistence into the early modern period of popular forms of pre-Christian spirituality that could encompass what fearful officials took to be witchcraft. An analogous strain of romanticism affected some American witchcraft scholars as well, those in search of actual witches in seventeenth-century New England. (See my discussion of the works of these scholars in the Aside that follows chapter 2.) But overall, New Left romanticism in American studies produced a far more profound rejection of the ideological and communal causes of witchcraft persecutions than anything that could be found in the works of those who studied the European record. Significantly, these differences in approach help explain why historians of European witchcraft appear never to have withdrawn their sympathies from the victims of witch hunting, while the post-1960s scholars of the American phenomenon did. (For a critical look at one romantic strain of post-1960s European witchcraft historiography, see de Blécourt, "The Return of the Sabbat" [2007], 125–145, quotation on 126.)

6. Evidence in support of a religious interpretation of the Hartford panic, suggesting many resemblances to the Salem witch hunt, including the leading prosecutorial role played by local conservative Puritans, may be found in Woodward, *Prospero's America*, 230–235.

7. There is a tendency in some very recent accounts of the Salem witch hunt to employ the metaphor "a perfect storm" to describe the convergence of a great many peculiar factors said to be needed to account for such a catastrophe. But, as I have tried to show throughout my study, the 1692 witch hunt was not such an unusual or surprising event, given the dominant presence of Puritanism in colonial New England, the ubiquity of the belief in witchcraft, and storehouses of common enmities and resentments in the small towns of the region. The Hartford panic of the 1660s likely had the potential to reach similar proportions. When both these incidents, together with the remaining individual witchcraft prosecutions carried out in seventeenth-century Massachusetts and Connecticut, are placed within the wider context of witch hunting throughout Europe and its colonial domains during the 1450–1700 period, the magnitude of such persecution in New England measures up to just about what one would expect, given the region's population size. The "perfect storm" metaphor applied to Salem appears in Gary Jensen, *The Path of the Devil: Early Modern Witch Hunts* (2007), title of chap. 7; Baker, *Storm of Witchcraft*, 6; Ray, *Satan and Salem*, 6; and Games, *Witchcraft in Early North America*, 62 (which sets forth the same idea without the phrase).

8. Writing of the intellectual basis for Christian anti-Semitism, David Nirenberg observes, "One consequence of this way of thinking [labeling as "Judaizing" what the Apostle Paul called any attachment to law, letter, and flesh, as opposed to the spirit] is that every Christian is potentially 'Jewish.' Since no one in this world can do entirely without letters, laws, or things of the flesh, no one is entirely immune to the charge of Judaizing" ("Dark Counterpoint," review of *The Music Libel Against the Jews*, by Ruth HaCohen [2013], 48). In a similar way, antiblack scapegoating in American history probably acquired added potency from the fear among whites that their own doubts about the presumed rigid distinction between the races might be discovered.

9. John Demos describes the 1885 monument to Rebecca Nurse in *The Enemy Within: 2,000 Years of Witch-Hunting in the Western World* (2008), 154–155. At the conclusion of his article, "Defending against the Indefensible: Spectral Evidence at the

Salem Witchcraft Trials" (1993), Daniel G. Payne suggests that the miscarriage of justice at Salem may have contributed to the later development of legal protections for defendants, pointing toward their embodiment in the Constitution's Fifth and Sixth Amendments (82–83). Peter Charles Hoffer advances the same general idea in *The Salem Witchcraft Trials: A Legal History* (1997), ix. Another hint at the possible legal consequences of the Salem trials may perhaps be derived from the observation that the introduction of defense counsel into English criminal proceedings began with trials for treason in the 1690s (Langbein, *The Origins of Adversary Criminal Trial* [2003], 1–7). If the capital crime of treason was the first in Anglo-American criminal law for which defense counsel was thought necessary to provide defendants, perhaps the related capital crime of witchcraft, where abuses in trial proceedings were equally apparent at just around the same time, played a supportive role in spawning the need for this sort of protection.

The New Left historians' disinterest in the heroism of the executed victims at Salem persists in an otherwise valuable article by Margo Burns ("'Other Ways of Undue Force and Fright': The Coercion of False Confessions by the Salem Magistrates" [2012], 24–39). Burns wants to emphasize that most of the some fifty-five confessions in the witch hunt were brought on by physical and psychological intimidation by colonial officials rather than by any facile assumption on the part of suspects that they could be assured of their survival by confessing. While there is truth to both halves of this judgment when taken separately, the formulation as a whole, in populist fashion, overlooks the role of an aroused population in supporting the persecutions and dismisses the courage displayed by many suspects in resisting all of these pressures. "Assumptions that the confessions were produced simply as defense ploys to avoid the death penalty miss the point," Burns writes in her conclusion, "and put the focus on the victims—suggesting that those who were executed actually had a choice to confess or die, thus ennobling the deaths of those who were executed maintaining their innocence—and diverts attention from the people who actually had the power and agency to exert discretion and mercy in the proceedings and possibly avert the entire episode: the justices of the Court" (37; see also 26). In fact, the twenty executed victims repeatedly said that they held the truth in such high regard that they could not in good conscience "belie themselves" and would rather go to their deaths than do so. These victims did exercise choice and deserve ennobling, even if we can surely sympathize with the majority of suspects who were unable to follow their example.

In a sharp rebuttal to what he sees as a populist tendency in the historiography of European witch hunting—to which I'd add the Salem example—Marco Nenonen decries the "fake" history of "innocent people always merely being subjugated by the state, army and the rich. What one needs is the history of evil [common] people—the history of humans." Nenonen does not discount the ideological, political, and social factors involved in witch hunting, but he wishes to remind scholars that "ordinary people" (a reference to *Ordinary Men*, the title of Christopher R. Browning's study of a Nazi reserve police battalion) participated in these persecutions, sometimes becoming accusers for all sorts of personal reasons that took advantage of the ongoing means to bring others down. See Nenonen, "Who Bears the Guilt for the Persecution of Witches?" (2012), 70–87, quotation on 82.

10. Foster, *Long Argument*, 250–264. In summary of his argument, Foster writes, "But [the ministers] had done their work badly [in acquiescing to the witchcraft trials],

palpably so, following Increase Mather's lead in his desperate attempt to avoid rocking the fragile craft he had constructed for Massachusetts [under the new charter]. Conscience had been subordinated to a worldly consideration more relevant to politicians because the ministry had been led since the mid-1680s into a more nakedly political role than anything they had been accustomed to" (263). Hall, *Faithful Shepherd*, 244–247; Hall, *Worlds of Wonder*, chap. 4, esp. 189–196. One other Puritan scholar, Larzer Ziff, addressed the Salem witch hunt in his 1973 study, *Puritanism in America: New Culture in a New World*, 242–250, but his more sharply critical treatment of Puritanism may be regarded as an exception that proves the rule concerning religious historians. Ziff followed Perry Miller and Starkey in his open hostility to the temporary rule exercised by the Puritan "folk" during the panic, regarding this outbreak of scapegoating as a last gasp of the powerless in New England society, as they perceived its transition from a confident outpost of God's vanguard to a subordinate province within the broader British empire. But Ziff, whose training was in literary studies, is a cultural rather than religious historian, and the early date of his work reflected its affinities with the works of the older generation of Salem scholars.

11. The two journal articles are Ray, "Geography of Witchcraft Accusations in 1692 Salem Village," and Latner, "Salem Witchcraft, Factionalism, and Social Change Reconsidered." The commentary is Sarah Rivett, "Our Salem, Our Selves," 495–502. For Ray's and Latner's contributions, see my discussion of their articles in chapter 2, notes 25, 27, 29, 30, where I also cover Ray, "Satan's War against the Covenant," Latner, "Here Are No Newters," and Ray's later book, *Satan and Salem*.

Rivett's commentary argues persuasively for the modernity of the Puritans' embrace of evidences of witchcraft, including spectral evidence. (Her ideas are developed more fully in her book, *The Science of the Soul in Colonial New England* [2011], intro. and chap. 5.) Rivett shows that by the late seventeenth century, religious figures like Increase and Cotton Mather held to an empirical epistemology that closely resembled that employed by contemporary thinkers we tend to regard as nascent scientists, people who were starting to make a sharper differentiation between what could be known of the natural and the spiritual worlds. This insight helps explain why it was so difficult for intellectual opposition to the witchcraft accusations to arise during the early and middle phases of the witch hunt. To my mind, however, Rivett's argument does not adequately account for why the consensus behind the truth of the accusations rapidly broke down once the magnitude of the witch hunt's results began to appear improbable to many of these same religious people. At that point it would seem that more experimentally inclined observers than the Mathers, including the Boston scientist Thomas Brattle, moved into position to become influential in bringing the witch hunt to a close. Empiricism itself, in other words, may have been coming to signify different sorts of methods to different people.

As a work that stands somewhere between a popular and academic account, Schiff's *Witches* (2015) occupies a slightly different place from most of the books and articles discussed in my study. While serious-minded readers may be put off by the author's frequent resort to irony and occasional references to elements in modern popular culture, *Witches* nevertheless deserves to be taken as a serious contribution to the Salem literature. The book utilizes all of the known primary sources to tell its story, and for its explanations it draws heavily on the major secondary studies of New England witch hunting, which are listed in a brief bibliography. Unfortunately for scholars, specific references to these secondary works have been omitted, while only the book's more narrow assertions receive detailed citations. Of the secondary accounts, after David D. Hall's study of Puritanism, *Worlds of Wonder, Days of Judgment*, Norton's *In the Devil's Snare* probably exerts the greatest influence on Schiff's book, including for explaining why George Burroughs was targeted as the principal suspect. Still, as noted in my text, Schiff clearly places religious anxiety—what she calls Puritanism's "insecure-making creed" (*Witches*, 68)—above the Indian wars among the leading causes of the Salem events. Vague references to Salem village "church factions" and "party lines" make a fleeting appearance at the book's beginning (30–31), but these references are quickly subsumed into a more general portrait of the Puritans' contentious ecclesiastical life, helpfully deemphasizing Salem's uniqueness in this respect. Boyer and Nissenbaum's economic interpretation of the witch hunt is thus nowhere to be found. Oddly, Starkey's study, the book that Schiff's account most closely resembles, is not listed in her bibliography. *The Witches'* sensationalism—at places it reads like a "Puritan freak show," in service of which one might add the hype connected to the book's release just before Halloween—is regrettable, because the work might otherwise have more successfully achieved one of its presumed goals, that of presenting a logically comprehensible set of religious beliefs remote from the modern world. Nevertheless, *The Witches* is significant historiographically for its return to the recognition that the Salem witch hunt constitutes an episode in the history of ideological extremism, where, as Schiff puts it, "extreme right can blunder into extreme wrong" (13). Neither Tituba nor any of the other accusing girls and young women are romanticized. New Left interpretations have been left behind. (The sensationalism of Schiff's approach is on even greater display in a *New Yorker* essay, "The Witches of Salem," which she published to herald the coming of her book.)

Three historians whose earlier studies also deserve mention as pointing toward this emerging religious interpretation of the witch hunt are Larry Gragg, Elizabeth Reis, and Richard Gildrie. Like Ray, Gragg focused on Samuel Parris, the Salem village minister. See chapter 2, note 29, for my discussion of his two books. I summarize Reis's observations on women's religious vulnerabilities under Puritanism in chapter 4, note 20. In his article, "The Salem Witchcraft Trials as a Crisis of Popular Imagination" (1992), 270–285, and subsequent book, *The Profane, the Civil, and the Godly: The Reformation of Manners in Orthodox New England, 1679–1749* (1994), Gildrie followed the lead of European witchcraft historian Stuart Clark in interpreting New England's witch lore as representative of a set of social and religious ideals (e.g., personal autonomy, material comfort, egalitarianism, and immediate salvation) that resided within the popular culture in a suppressed state because it contradicted established Puritan values, values that were also widely shared. According to this view—although Gildrie does not take his argument quite this far—witch hunts could be seen as times of purging the Puritan community of any competing set of values. I briefly discuss Gildrie's still earlier article, "Visions of Evil," in chapter 2, note 30.

In a separate, new approach to the study of the Salem witch hunt (not centered on religion), Richard Latner has applied Charles Tilly's sociological analysis of collective violence to the events of 1692. While the results have yielded valuable precision in charting the chronology and geography of the panic, allowing all of the affected communities in Essex County to become more visible in the process, I fear that a new kind of functionalism has crept into this approach, in which now a succession of smaller witch hunts are imagined (first in Salem village, then Salem town, then Andover, then Gloucester, etc.), with each running its seemingly natural course according to paths that are "logical," "coherent," and "limited," all terms that Latner employs. This approach would seem to allow little room for the actions of individuals to affect the course of these witch hunts—as, for example, happened at Salem with the accumulation of unexpected denials of guilt (or at Andover with the startlingly high number of confessions), gradually inducing skepticism about the legitimacy of the entire process. We need to remember that the outcome of the Salem witch hunt could have been worse. See Latner, "The Long and the Short of Salem Witchcraft: Chronology and Collective Violence in 1692" (2008), 137–156. I agree with Latner that Tilly's *The Politics of Collective Violence* (2003) offers much that is relevant to the understanding of witch hunting (even while the book downplays the critical factor of ideology), provided Tilly's openendedness about the pace, frequency, and specific outcomes of the processes he describes is preserved.

12. Gragg, *Salem Witch Crisis*, chap. 6; Rosenthal, *Salem Story*, chaps. 4, 5, 6, and 8; Hoffer, *Devil's Disciples*, esp. chaps. 6 and 7; Hoffer, *Salem Witchcraft Trials*, xi (for the dedication). Other narratives of the Salem witch hunt appearing in the 1990s include Enders A. Robinson, *Devil Discovered* (1991), which strongly defends the witch hunt's victims against what the author terms a "conspiracy" of envious local people and the colony's "Old Guard Puritan leaders" (see, e.g., xiv, chap. 7); Frances Hill, *A Delusion of Satan: The Full Story of the Salem Witch Trials* (1995), which is also strongly sympathetic to the victims and critical of Puritanism in a manner that recalls Starkey's account; and Bryan F. Le Beau, *The Story of the Salem Witch Trials* (1998), again thoroughly sympathetic to the victims and which draws directly on Starkey's account, while at the same time downplaying the role of Puritanism and accepting the ordinariness of witch hunting in the seventeenth-century world.

13. The 1983 McMartin Preschool case touched off the series of child-abuse scares at daycare centers and schools, leading to some forty legal cases and one hundred convictions (Mintz, *Huck's Raft*, 335–336). Mintz adds that "in virtually every case the prosecution claims were eventually overturned" (336). The six Salem works that noted the modern context of the child-abuse scares or similar events were Rosenthal, *Salem Story* (1993), 213; Hill, *Delusion of Satan* (1995), xv; Hoffner, *Devil's Disciples* (1996), 57, 91–93; Reis, *Damned Women* (1997), 10; Roach, *Salem Witch Trials* (2002), 585; and Demos, *Enemy Within* (2008), xi. Even as late as 2015, Stacy Schiff referred to the same modern panic in *The Witches*, 401, 477.

Apart from the works that mentioned these current events, one important scholarly article and four additional books appeared during the first two decades of the twenty-first century that shared in the rediscovered sympathy for Salem's victims. John Murrin's essay "Coming to Terms with the Salem Witch Trials" (2000) pays tribute to the extraordinary Christian courage of the victims (338–339). Richard Godbeer's *Escaping Salem: The Other Witch Hunt of 1692* (2005), a study of the small Fairfield, Connecticut, witch scare that occurred in the midst of the Salem panic, openly condemns the practice of "demoniz[ing] those whom we dislike" (169) in its scholarly afterword, and Godbeer dedicated the book to "all those falsely accused" (v). Richard Francis's *Judge*

Sewall's Apology (2005) similarly acknowledges the victims of the witch hunt's "twisted no-win logic" (137). Even more significantly, Bernard Rosenthal and a team of researchers came out in 2009 with a new compilation of all the documents related to the Salem examinations and trials. The title of this important reference work, *Records of the Salem Witch-Hunt*, offers a striking contrast to that of the standard reference work that preceded it, the three-volume *Salem Witchcraft Papers*, edited by Boyer and Nissenbaum in 1977. No better symbol than this shift in titles is needed to express the renewed legitimacy of the concept of a "witch hunt" to describe the Salem events. Emerson Baker also dedicated his book, *Storm of Witchcraft* (2015) to the witch hunt's victims and included a number of passages describing the suffering they endured.

14. Demos, *The Enemy Within*, xi and 14 ("injustice," "innocent targets," and "scapegoating"); 143–156 (for the ordeal of Rebecca Nurse, with "persecution" on 149 and "cornered" on 153); and 228 ("history will not easily forgive him"). The irony in his treatment of the causes of the Salem witch hunt comes from Demos's repeated use of his invented term, "Salemwitchcraft," to outline the great many theories that have been put forward over the years to explain this event. One senses a small remnant of the same "embarrassment" here that the author expressed in his 1970 article over being forced to deal with such a well-worked topic.

15. Bernard Rosenthal replied in a similar way to Demos's 1970 lament when he wrote, "Yet no matter how frequently the issue of guilt at Salem is posed and reposed, it will not go away" (*Salem Story*, 78).

16. I have been guided in these final remarks by Thomas L. Haskell, *Objectivity is Not Neutrality: Explanatory Schemes in History* (1998), intro. (the quotation that I took as the epigraph for my study appears on p. 11) and chap. 6; Richard S. Taylor, "Telling Lincoln's Story," 44–68; and George Cotkin, "History's Moral Turn" (2008), 293–315.

Bibliography

Abler, Thomas S. "Iroquois Cannibalism: Fact Not Fiction." *Ethnohistory* 27 (Fall 1980): 309–316.

Adams, Gretchen A. *The Specter of Salem: Remembering the Witch Trials in Nineteenth-Century America*. Chicago: University of Chicago Press, 2008.

The Andros Tracts, Being a Collection of Pamphlets and Official Papers Issued during the Period between the Overthrow of the Andros Government and the Establishment of the Second Charter of Massachusetts. With notes by W. H. Whitmore. First published as vol. 7 of *Publications of the Prince Society*, Boston, 1874. Reprint, *Burt Franklin Research and Source Works Series*, no. 131, *American Classics in History and Social Science* 3, no. 2.

Ankarloo, Bengt. "Witch Trials in Northern Europe, 1450–1700." In Ankarloo and Clark, *Witchcraft and Magic in Europe*, vol. 4, *The Period of the Witch Trials*, 53–95.

Ankarloo, Bengt, and Stuart Clark, eds. *Witchcraft and Magic in Europe*. 6 vols. Philadelphia: University of Pennsylvania Press, 1999–2002.

Axtell, James. "The Vengeful Women of Marblehead: Robert Roules's Deposition of 1677." *William and Mary Quarterly*, 3rd ser., 31 (October 1974): 647–652.

Bailyn, Bernard. *The New England Merchants in the Seventeenth Century*. 1955. New York: Harper Torchbooks, 1964.

——. *The Ordeal of Thomas Hutchinson*. Cambridge, MA: Harvard University Press, 1974.

Baker, Emerson W. *The Clarke and Lake Company: The Historical Archaeology of a Seventeenth-Century Maine Settlement*. Augusta: Maine Historic Preservation Commission, 1985.

——. *A Storm of Witchcraft: The Salem Trials and the American Experience*. New York: Oxford University Press, 2015.

——. "Trouble to the Eastward: The Failure of Anglo-Indian Relations in Early Maine." PhD diss., College of William and Mary, 1986.

Baker, Emerson W., and James Kences. "Maine, Indian Land Speculation, and the Essex County Witchcraft Outbreak of 1692." *Maine History* 40 (Fall 2001): 159–189.

Baker, Emerson W., and John Reid. *The New England Knight: Sir William Phips, 1651–1695*. Toronto: University of Toronto Press, 1998.

Barnes, Viola. *The Dominion of New England: A Study in British Colonial Policy*. New Haven: Yale University Press, 1923.

Behringer, Wolfgang. "Historiography." In Golden, *Encyclopedia of Witchcraft: The Western Tradition*, vol. 2, *E–J*, 492–498.

Bigsby, Christopher. *Arthur Miller, 1915–1962*. Vol. 1 of *Arthur Miller*. Cambridge, MA: Harvard University Press, 2009.

Blécourt, Willem de. "The Return of the Sabbat: Mental Archaeologies, Conjectural Histories or Political Mythologies?" In *Palgrave Advances in Witchcraft Historiography*, edited by Jonathan Barry and Owen Davies, 125–145. Houndmills, Basingstoke, UK: Palgrave Macmillan, 2007.

Boyer, Paul, and Stephen Nissenbaum. "*Salem Possessed* in Retrospect." *William and Mary Quarterly*, 3rd ser., 65 (July 2008): 503–534.

——. *Salem Possessed: The Social Origins of Witchcraft*. Cambridge, MA: Harvard University Press, 1974.

——, eds. *Salem-Village Witchcraft: A Documentary Record of Local Conflict in Colonial New England*. Belmont, CA: Wadsworth, 1972.

——, eds. *The Salem Witchcraft Papers: Verbatim Transcripts of the Legal Documents of the Salem Witchcraft Outbreak of 1692*. 3 vols. New York: Da Capo, 1977.

Brattle, Thomas. "Letter of Thomas Brattle, F.S.M." In Burr, *Narratives of the Witchcraft Cases*, 165–190.

Breen, Louise A. *Transgressing the Bounds: Subversive Enterprises among the Puritan Elite in Massachusetts, 1630–1692*. Cary, NC: Oxford University Press, 2001.

Breen, T. H. *Puritans and Adventurers: Change and Persistence in Early America*. New York: Oxford University Press, 1980.

Breslaw, Elaine G. "The Salem Witch from Barbados: In Search of Tituba's Roots." *Essex Institute Historical Collections* 128 (1992): 217–238.

——. "Tituba's Confession: The Multicultural Dimensions of the 1692 Salem Witch-Hunt." *Ethnohistory* 4 (Summer 1997): 535–556.

——. *Tituba, Reluctant Witch of Salem: Devilish Indians and Puritan Fantasies*. New York: New York University Press, 1996.

Brown, David C. "The Case of Giles Cory." *Essex Institute Historical Collections* 121 (1985): 282–299.

——. "The Forfeitures at Salem, 1692." *William and Mary Quarterly*, 3rd ser., 50 (January 1993): 85–111.

Brown, Peter. "Sorcery, Demons, and the Rise of Christianity from Late Antiquity into the Middle Ages." In Douglas, *Witchcraft Confessions and Accusations*, 17–45.

Brinkley, Alan. *Liberalism and Its Discontents*. Cambridge, MA: Harvard University Press, 1998.

Burns, Margo. "'Other Ways of Undue Force and Fright': The Coercion of False Confessions by the Salem Magistrates." *Studia Neophilologica* 84 (2012): 24–39.

Burns, Margo, and Bernard Rosenthal. "Examination of the Records of the Salem Witch Trials." *William and Mary Quarterly*, 3rd ser., 65 (July 2008): 401–422.

Burr, George Lincoln, ed. *Narratives of the Witchcraft Cases, 1648–1706*. New York: Charles Scribner's Sons, 1914.

"Burroughs, George." In *Biographical Sketches of Graduates of Harvard University*, by John L. Sibley, 3 vols., 2:323–334. Cambridge, MA: Charles William Sever, 1873–1885.

Butler, Jon. *Awash in a Sea of Faith: Christianizing the American People*. Cambridge, MA: Harvard University Press, 1990.

———. "Magic, Astrology, and the Early American Religious Heritage, 1600–1760." *American Historical Review* 84 (April 1979): 317–346.

———. "Witchcraft, Healing, and Historians' Crazes." *Journal of Social History* 18 (1984): 111–118.

Calef, Robert. *More Wonders of the Invisible World.* 1700. In Burr, *Narratives of the Witchcraft Cases*, 289–393.

———. *More Wonders of the Invisible World.* 1700. Facsimile reprint with an introduction by Chadwick Hansen. Bainbridge, NY: York Mail Print, 1972.

Calloway, Colin G. *The Western Abenakis of Vermont, 1600–1800: War, Migration, and the Survival of an Indian People.* Norman: University of Oklahoma Press, 1990.

Calloway, Colin G., and Neal Salisbury, eds. *Reinterpreting New England Indians and the Colonial Experience.* Boston: Colonial Society of Massachusetts; distributed by the University of Virginia Press, 2003.

Caporael, Linnda R. "Ergotism: The Satan Loosed in Salem?" *Science*, April 2, 1976.

Carlson, Laurie Winn. *A Fever in Salem: A New Interpretation of the New England Witch Trials.* Chicago: Ivan R. Dee, 1999.

Cave, Alfred A. "Indian Shamans and English Witches in Seventeenth-Century New England." *Essex Institute Historical Collections* 128 (1992): 239–254.

———. *The Pequot War.* Amherst: University of Massachusetts Press, 1996.

Chaplin, Joyce E. Review of *In the Devil's Snare: The Salem Witchcraft Crisis of 1692,* by Mary Beth Norton. *William and Mary Quarterly*, 3rd ser., 60 (April 2003): 427–430.

Chowning, Margaret. *Rebellious Nuns: The Troubled History of a Mexican Convent, 1752–1863.* New York: Oxford University Press, 2006.

Chu, Jonathan M. *Neighbors, Friends, or Madmen: The Puritan Adjustment to Quakerism in Seventeenth-Century Massachusetts Bay.* Westport, CT: Greenwood, 1985.

Clark, Stuart. "Witchcraft and Magic in Early Modern Culture." In Ankarloo and Clark, *Witchcraft and Magic in Europe,* vol. 4, *The Period of the Witch Trials,* 97–169.

Clifford, James. "Introduction: Partial Truths." In *Writing Culture: The Poetics and Politics of Ethnography,* edited by James Clifford and George E. Marcus, 1–26. Berkeley: University of California Press, 1986.

Cooper, James F., Jr. *Tenacious of Their Liberties: The Congregationalists of Colonial Massachusetts.* New York: Oxford University Press, 1999.

Cooper, James F., and Kenneth P. Minkema, eds. *The Sermon Notebook of Samuel Parris, 1689–1694.* Boston: The Colonial Society of Massachusetts, 1993.

Cotkin, George. "History's Moral Turn." *Journal of the History of Ideas* 69 (April 2008): 293–315.

Coudert, Allison P. "The Myth of the Improved Status of Protestant Women: The Case of the Witchcraze." In *The Politics of Gender in Early Modern Europe,* edited by Jean R. Brink, Allison P. Coudert, and Maryanne C. Horowitz, 60–89. Kirksville, MO: Sixteenth Century Journal, 1989.

Cowing, Cedric B. *The Saving Remnant: Religion and the Settling of New England.* Urbana: University of Illinois Press, 1995.

———. Review of *Salem Possessed: The Social Origins of Witchcraft,* by Paul Boyer and Stephen Nissenbaum. *American Historical Review* 80 (December 1975): 1381–1382.

Craker, Wendel D. "Spectral Evidence, Non-spectral Acts of Witchcraft, and Confession at Salem in 1692." *Historical Journal* 40 (1997): 331–358.

Crane, Elaine Forman. *Witches, Wife Beaters, and Whores: Common Law and Common Folk in Early America.* Ithaca: Cornell University Press, 2011.

Cronon, William. *Changes in the Land: Indians, Colonists, and the Ecology of New England.* New York: Hill and Wang, 1983.

Cryer, Frederick H. "Magic in Ancient Syria-Palestine and in the Old Testament." In Ankarloo and Clark, *Witchcraft and Magic in Europe,* vol. 1, *Biblical and Pagan Societies,* 97–149.

Dailey, Barbara Ritter. "'Where Thieves Break Through and Steal': John Hale versus Dorcas Hoar, 1672–1692." *Essex Institute Historical Collections* 128 (1992): 255–269.

Davis, David Brion. "Constructing Race: A Reflection." *William and Mary Quarterly,* 3rd ser., 54 (January 1997): 7–18.

Demos, John. *The Enemy Within: 2,000 Years of Witch-Hunting in the Western World.* New York: Viking Penguin, 2008.

———. *Entertaining Satan: Witchcraft and the Culture of Early New England.* 1982. New York: Oxford University Press, 1983.

———. "John Godfrey and His Neighbors: Witchcraft and the Social Web in Colonial Massachusetts." *William and Mary Quarterly,* 3rd ser., 33 (April 1976): 242–265.

———. *A Little Commonwealth: Family Life in Plymouth Colony.* New York: Oxford University Press, 1970.

———. "Underlying Themes in the Witchcraft of Seventeenth-Century New England." *American Historical Review* 75 (June 1970): 1311–1326.

Dionne, E. J., Jr. "Freedom Now: The New Left and the Assault on Liberalism." Chap. 1 in *Why Americans Hate Politics.* New York: Simon and Schuster, Touchstone, 1991.

Documentary History of the State of Maine. Edited by James Phinney Baxter. In *Collections of the Maine Historical Society,* 2nd ser., 5 (1897), 6 (1900).

Donagan, Barbara. "Atrocity, War Crime, and Treason in the English Civil War." *American Historical Review* 99 (October 1994): 1137–1166.

Douglas, Mary. "Introduction: Thirty Years after *Witchcraft, Oracles and Magic.*" In Douglas, *Witchcraft: Confessions and Accusations,* xiii–xxxviii.

Douglas, Mary, ed. *Witchcraft Confessions and Accusations.* London: Tavistock, 1970.

Dow, George Francis, ed. *Records and Files of the Quarterly Courts of Essex County, Massachusetts.* 9 vols. Salem, Massachusetts: Essex Institute, 1911–1975. http://salem.lib.virginia.edu/Essex/index.

Drake, Frederick C. "Witchcraft in the American Colonies, 1647–62." *American Quarterly* 20 (Winter 1968): 694–725.

Drake, James. "Restraining Atrocity: The Conduct of King Philip's War." *New England Quarterly* 70 (March 1997): 33–56.

Drake, Samuel G., ed. *The Witchcraft Delusion in New England.* 3 vols. 1866. Facsimile reprint by New York: Burt Franklin, 1970.

Dunn, Richard S. *Puritans and Yankees: The Winthrop Dynasty of New England, 1630–1717.* New York: Norton, 1962.

Erikson, Kai T. *Wayward Puritans: A Study in the Sociology of Deviance.* New York: John Wiley, 1966.

Flint, Valerie. "The Demonisation of Magic and Sorcery in Late Antiquity: Christian Redefinitions of Pagan Religion." In Ankarloo and Clark, *Witchcraft and Magic in Europe*, vol. 2, *Ancient Greece and Rome*, 277–348.

"Forum: Salem Repossessed." *William and Mary Quarterly*, 3rd ser., 65 (July 2008).

Foster, Stephen. *The Long Argument: English Puritanism and the Shaping of New England Culture, 1570–1700.* Chapel Hill: University of North Carolina Press, 1991.

———. *Their Solitary Way: The Puritan Social Ethic in the First Century of Settlement in New England.* New Haven: Yale University Press, 1971.

Fowler, Samuel P. "Account of the Life and Character of Samuel Parris." In Samuel G. Drake, *The Witchcraft Delusion in New England*, 3:198–122.

Fox, Sanford J. *Science and Justice: The Massachusetts Witchcraft Trials.* Baltimore: Johns Hopkins University Press, 1968.

Francis, Richard. *Judge Sewall's Apology: The Salem Witch Trials and the Forming of an American Conscience.* 2005. New York: Harper Perennial, 2006.

Games, Alison, ed. *Witchcraft in Early North America.* Lanham, MD: Rowman and Littlefield, 2010.

Gaskill, Malcolm. *Witchfinders: A Seventeenth-Century English Tragedy.* Cambridge: Harvard University Press, 2005.

Geschiere, Peter. *The Modernity of Witchcraft: Politics and the Occult in Postcolonial Africa.* Charlottesville: University of Virginia Press, 1997.

Gildrie, Richard P. "Contention in Salem: The Higginson-Nicholet Controversy, 1672–1676." *Essex Institute Historical Collections* 113 (1977): 117–139.

———. *The Profane, the Civil, and the Godly: The Reformation of Manners in Orthodox New England, 1679–1749.* University Park: Pennsylvania State University Press, 1994.

———. *Salem, Massachusetts, 1626–1683: A Covenant Community.* Charlottesville: University Press of Virginia, 1975.

———. "The Salem Witchcraft Trials as a Crisis of Popular Imagination." *Essex Institute Historical Collections* 128 (1992): 270–285.

———. "Visions of Evil: Popular Culture, Puritanism and the Massachusetts Witchcraft Crisis of 1692." *Journal of American Culture* 8 (1985): 17–35.

Ginzburg, Carlo. "Deciphering the Sabbath." In *Early Modern European Witchcraft: Centres and Peripheries*, edited by Bengt Ankarloo and Gustav Henningsen, 121–137. Oxford: Clarendon, 1990.

Gitlin, Todd. *The Sixties: Years of Hope, Days of Rage.* Toronto: Bantam, 1987.

Godbeer, Richard. "Chaste and Unchaste Covenants: Witchcraft and Sex in Early Modern Culture." In *Wonders of the Invisible World: 1600–1900*, edited by Peter Benes, 53–72. Boston: Boston University Press, 1995.

———. *The Devil's Dominion: Magic and Religion in Early New England.* New York: Cambridge University Press, 1992.

———. *Escaping Salem: The Other Witch Hunt of 1692.* New York: Oxford University Press, 2005.

———. "Folk Magic in British North America." In *The Cambridge History of Magic and Witchcraft in the West: From Antiquity to the Present*, edited by David J. Collins, S.J. New York: Cambridge University Press, 2015.

———. Review of *In the Devil's Snare: The Salem Witchcraft Crisis of 1692*, by Mary Beth Norton. *New England Quarterly* 76 (September 2003): 484.

———, ed. *The Salem Witch Hunt: A Brief History with Documents*. Boston: Bedford/
St. Martin's, 2011.

Golden, Richard M., ed. *Encyclopedia of Witchcraft: The Western Tradition*. 4 vols.
Santa Barbara, CA: ABC-CLIO, 2006.

Gordon, Richard. "Imagining Greek and Roman Magic." In Ankarloo and Clark,
Witchcraft and Magic in Europe, vol. 2, *Ancient Greece and Rome*, 159–275.

Graf, Fritz. *Magic in the Ancient World*. Translated by Franklin Philip. Cambridge,
MA: Harvard University Press, 1997.

Gragg, Larry. *A Quest for Security: The Life of Samuel Parris, 1653–1720*. New York:
Greenwood, 1990.

———. *The Salem Witch Crisis*. New York: Praeger, 1992.

Greene, David L. "Bray Wilkins of Salem Village MA and His Children." *American
Genealogist* 60 (January 1984): 1–18, 101–113.

———. "Salem Witches II: George Jacobs." *American Genealogist* 58 (April 1982):
65–76.

Hale, John. *A Modest Enquiry into the Nature of Witchcraft*. 1702. Facsimile reprint by
Bainbridge, NY: York Mail-Print, 1973.

———. *A Modest Inquiry into the Nature of Witchcraft*. 1702. In Burr, *Narratives of the
Witchcraft Cases*, 395–432.

Hall, David D. *The Faithful Shepherd: A History of the New England Ministry in the
Seventeenth Century*. Chapel Hill: University of North Carolina Press, 1972.

———. "Middle Ground on the Witch-Hunt Debate." *Reviews in American History* 26
(June 1998): 345–352.

———. "Religion and Society: Problems and Reconsiderations." In *Colonial British
America: Essays in the New History of the Early Modern Era*, edited by Jack P.
Greene and J. R. Pole, 317–344. Baltimore: Johns Hopkins University Press, 1984.

———. "Witchcraft and the Limits of Interpretation." *New England Quarterly* 58
(June 1985): 253–281.

———, ed. *Witch-Hunting in Seventeenth-Century New England: A Documentary
History, 1638–1692*. Boston: Northeastern University Press, 1991.

———. *Worlds of Wonder, Days of Judgment: Popular Religious Belief in Early New
England*. 1989. Cambridge: Harvard University Press, 1990.

Hall, David D., John M. Murrin, and Thad W. Tate, eds. *Saints and Revolutionaries:
Essays on Early American History*. New York: Norton, 1984.

Hansen, Chadwick. "Andover Witchcraft and the Causes of the Salem Witchcraft
Trials." In *The Occult in America: New Historical Perspectives*, edited by Howard
Kerr and Charles L. Crow, 38–57. Urbana: University of Illinois Press, 1983.

———. "The Metamorphosis of Tituba, or Why American Intellectuals Can't Tell an
Indian Witch from a Negro." *New England Quarterly* 47 (March 1974): 3–12.

———. *Witchcraft at Salem*. New York: George Braziller, 1969.

Harley, David. "Explaining Salem: Calvinist Psychology and the Diagnosis of
Possession." *American Historical Review* 101 (April 1996): 307–330.

———. "Historians as Demonologists: The Myth of the Midwife-witch." *Social History
of Medicine* 3 (1990): 1–26.

Haskell, Thomas L. *Objectivity Is Not Neutrality: Explanatory Schemes in History*.
Baltimore: Johns Hopkins University Press, 1998.

Heinze, Andrew R. *Jews and the American Soul: Human Nature in the Twentieth Century.* Princeton: Princeton University Press, 2004.

Heyrman, Christine Leigh. *Commerce and Culture: The Maritime Communities of Colonial Massachusetts, 1690–1750.* New York: Norton, 1984.

———. "Specters of Subversion, Societies of Friends: Dissent and the Devil in Provincial Essex County, Massachusetts." In Hall, Murrin, and Tate, *Saints and Revolutionaries: Essays on Early American History,* 38–74.

Hill, Frances. *A Delusion of Satan: The Full Story of the Salem Witch Trials.* New York: Doubleday, 1995.

Hirsch, Adam. "The Collision of Military Cultures in Seventeenth-Century New England." *Journal of American History* 74 (March 1988): 1187–1212.

Hobsbawm, E. J. *Bandits.* New York: Delacorte, 1969.

———. *Primitive Rebels: Studies in Archaic Forms of Social Movement in the 19th and 20th Centuries.* 1959. New York: Norton, 1965.

Hoffer, Peter Charles. *The Devil's Disciples: Makers of the Salem Witchcraft Trials.* 1996. Baltimore: Johns Hopkins University Press, 1998.

———. *The Salem Witchcraft Trials: A Legal History.* Lawrence: University Press of Kansas, 1997.

Hubbard, William. *The History of the Indian Wars in New England from the First Settlement to the Termination of the War with King Philip, in 1677.* 1677. Revised and annotated in two volumes by Samuel G. Drake in 1865. Facsimile reprint, with vols. 1 and 2 published together. New York: Burt Franklin, 1971.

Hunter, Phyllis Whitman. *Purchasing Identity in the Atlantic World: Massachusetts Merchants, 1670–1780.* Ithaca, NY: Cornell University Press, 2001.

Hutchinson, Thomas. *History of the Colony and Province of Massachusetts-Bay.* 1765, 1768, and 1828. Edited by Laurence Shaw Mayo. 3 vols. Boston: Harvard University Press, 1936.

Hutton, Ronald. "Anthropological and Historical Approaches to Witchcraft: Potential for a New Collaboration?" *Historical Journal* 47 (2004): 413–434.

Huxley, Aldous. *The Devils of Loudun.* New York: Harper Torchbooks, 1952.

———. Introduction to *The Devil in Massachusetts: A Modern Inquiry into the Salem Witch Trials,* by Marion L. Starkey. Alexandria, VA: Time-Life Books, 1963.

Isserman, Maurice, and Michael Kazin. *America Divided: The Civil War of the 1960s.* New York: Oxford University Press, 2000.

Jacoby, Susan. *Alger Hiss and the Battle for History.* New Haven: Yale University Press, 2009.

Jennings, Francis. *The Invasion of America: Indians, Colonialism, and the Cant of Conquest.* Chapel Hill: University of North Carolina Press, 1975.

Jenson, Gary. *The Path of the Devil: Early Modern Witch Hunts.* Lanham, MD: Rowman and Littlefield, 2007.

Johnson, Richard R. *Adjustment to Empire: The New England Colonies, 1675–1715.* New Brunswick, NJ: Rutgers University Press, 1981.

———. *John Nelson, Merchant Adventurer: A Life between Empires.* New York: Oxford University Press, 1991.

Jolly, Karen. "Medieval Magic: Definitions, Beliefs, Practices." In Ankarloo and Clark, *Witchcraft and Magic in Europe,* vol. 3, *The Middle Ages,* 1–71.

Judt, Tony. "An American Tragedy? The Case of Whitakker Chambers." Chap. 18 in
    Reappraisals: Reflections on the Forgotten Twentieth Century. New York: Penguin, 2008.
Kamensky, Jane. *Governing the Tongue: The Politics of Speech in Early New England.*
    New York: Oxford University Press, 1997.
———. "Salem Obsessed; Or, *Plus Ça Change*: An Introduction." *William and Mary
    Quarterly*, 3rd ser., 65 (July 2008): 391–400.
———. "Words, Witches, and Woman Trouble: Witchcraft, Disorderly Speech, and
    Gender Boundaries in Puritan New England." *Essex Institute Historical Collections*
    128 (1992): 286–307.
Karlsen, Carol F. *The Devil in the Shape of a Woman: Witchcraft in Colonial New
    England.* New York: Norton, 1987.
———. "Devils in the Shape of Good Men." *Common-place: The Interactive Journal of
    Early American Life* 3, no. 2 (January 2003). www.common-place.org.
———. "On Witchcraft and Witch-Hunting." *Yale Review* 72 (July 1983): 612–619.
Kazin, Michael. *The Populist Persuasion: An American History.* New York: Basic
    Books, 1995.
Kences, James E. "Some Unexplored Relationships of Essex County Witchcraft to the
    Indian Wars of 1675 and 1689." *Essex Institute Historical Collections* 120 (1984):
    179–212.
Kern, Louis J. "Eros, the Devil, and the Cunning Woman: Sexuality and the Super-
    natural in European Antecedents and in the Seventeenth-Century Salem Witch-
    craft Cases." *Essex Institute Historical Collections* 129 (1993): 3–38.
Kibbey, Ann. "Mutations of the Supernatural: Witchcraft, Remarkable Providences,
    and the Power of Puritan Men." *American Quarterly* 34 (Summer 1982): 125–148.
Kirsch, Adam. "The Great Disconcerting Wipeout." *New Republic*, October 7, 2009.
Kittredge, George Lyman. *Witchcraft in Old and New England.* Cambridge: Harvard
    University Press, 1929.
Kloppenberg, James T. *The Virtues of Liberalism.* New York: Oxford University Press,
    1996.
Kluckhohn, Clyde. *Navaho Witchcraft.* Boston: Beacon, 1944.
Koehler, Lyle. *A Search for Power: The "Weaker Sex" in Seventeenth-Century New
    England.* Urbana: University of Illinois Press, 1980.
Konig, David Thomas. *Law and Society in Puritan Massachusetts: Essex County,
    1629–1692.* Chapel Hill: University of North Carolina Press, 1979.
———. "A New Look at the Essex 'French': Ethnic Frictions and Community Tensions
    in Seventeenth-Century Essex County, Massachusetts." *Essex Institute Historical
    Collections* 110 (1974): 167–180.
Langbein, John H. *The Origins of Adversary Criminal Trial.* New York: Oxford
    University Press, 2003.
Larner, Christina. "Crimen Exceptum? The Crime of Witchcraft in Europe." In
    Crime and the Law: The Social History of Crime in Western Europe Since 1500,
    edited by V. A. C. Gatrell, Bruce Lenman, and Geoffrey Parker, 49–75. London:
    European Publications, 1980.
———. *Enemies of God: The Witch-hunt in Scotland.* Baltimore: Johns Hopkins
    University Press, 1981.

——. *Witchcraft and Religion: The Politics of Popular Belief.* Edited by Alan Macfarlane. Oxford, UK: Basil Blackwell, 1984.

Latner, Richard. "'Here Are No Newters': Witchcraft and Religious Discord in Salem Village and Andover." *New England Quarterly* 79 (March 2006): 92–122.

——. "The Long and the Short of Salem Witchcraft: Chronology and Collective Violence in 1692." *Journal of Social History* 42 (Fall 2008): 137–156.

——. "Salem Witchcraft, Factionalism, and Social Change Reconsidered: Were Salem's Witch-Hunters Modernization's Failures?" *William and Mary Quarterly*, 3rd ser., 65 (July 2008): 423–448.

Lawson, Deodat. *A Brief and True Narrative of Witchcraft at Salem Village.* 1692. In Burr, *Narratives of the Witchcraft Cases*, 145–164.

——. "Christ's Fidelity the Only Shield against Satan's Malignity." In Trask, *"The Devil Hath Been Raised,"* 64–114.

Le Beau, Bryan F. *The Story of the Salem Witch Trials.* Upper Saddle River, NJ: Prentice-Hall, 1998.

Lepore, Jill. *The Name of War: King Philip's War and the Origins of American Identity.* New York: Alfred A. Knopf, 1998.

——. "The Red Scare." *New York Times Book Review*, November 3, 2002.

Levack, Brian P. *The Devil Within: Possession and Exorcism in the Christian West.* New Haven: Yale University Press, 2013.

——. *The Witch-Hunt in Early Modern Europe.* 3rd ed. Harlow, UK: Pearson Education, 2006.

Levin, David. *Cotton Mather: The Young Life of the Lord's Remembrancer, 1663–1703.* Cambridge, MA: Harvard University Press, 1978.

——. *In Defense of Historical Literature: Essays on American History, Autobiography, Drama, and Fiction.* New York: Hill and Wang, 1967.

——, ed. *What Happened in Salem? Documents Pertaining to the Seventeenth-Century Witchcraft Trials.* 2nd ed. New York: Harcourt, Brace, and World, 1960.

Lewis, Theodore B. "Land Speculation and the Dudley Council of 1686." *William and Mary Quarterly*, 3rd ser., 31 (April 1874): 255–272.

Lieberson, Jonathan. "Interpreting the Interpreter." Rev. of *Local Knowledge: Further Essays in Interpretive Anthropology*, by Clifford Geertz. *New York Review of Books*, March 15, 1984.

Longbein, John H. *The Origins of Adversary Criminal Trial.* Oxford: Oxford University Press, 2003.

Lovejoy, David S. *The Glorious Revolution in America.* New York: Harper Torchbooks, 1974.

——. "Between Hell and Plum Island: Samuel Sewall and the Legacy of the Witches, 1692–97." *New England Quarterly* 70 (September 1997): 355–367.

Luck, Georg. "Witches and Sorcerers in Classical Literature." In Ankarloo and Clark, *Witchcraft and Magic in Europe*, vol. 2, *Ancient Greece and Rome*, 91–158.

Luhrman, T. M. "Anthropology." In Golden, *Encyclopedia of Witchcraft: The Western Tradition*, vol. 1, A-D, 43–45.

MacDonald, Michael. *Mystical Bedlam: Madness, Anxiety, and Healing in Seventeenth-Century England.* Cambridge: Cambridge University Press, 1981.

——. "New England's Inner Demons." *Reviews in American History* 11 (September 1983): 321–325.

Macfarlane, Alan. *The Origins of Individualism: The Family, Property, and Social Transition.* 1978. New York: Cambridge University Press, 1979.

——. *Witchcraft in Tudor and Stuart England: A Regional and Comparative Study.* London: Routledge and Kegan Paul, 1970.

——. "Witchcraft in Tudor and Stuart Essex." In Douglas, *Witchcraft Confessions and Accusations,* 81–99.

Maier, Pauline. "Popular Uprisings and Civil Authority in Eighteenth-Century America." *William and Mary Quarterly,* 3rd ser., 27 (1970): 3–35.

Martin, Joel. *Sacred Revolt: The Muskogees' Struggle for a New World.* Boston: Beacon, 1991.

Martin, John Frederick. *Profits in the Wilderness: Entrepreneurship and the Founding of New England Towns in the Seventeenth Century.* Chapel Hill: University of North Carolina Press, 1991.

Mather, Cotton. *A Brand Pluck'd Out of the Burning.* 1693. In Burr, *Narratives of the Witchcraft Cases,* 253–287.

——. *Decennium Luctuosum [Sorrowful Decade].* 1699. In *Narratives of the Indian Wars, 1675–1699,* edited by Charles H. Lincoln, 169–300. New York: Charles Scribner's Sons, 1913.

——. *Pietas in Patriam [Love to One's Country]: The Life of His Excellency Sir William Phips.* 1697. In *Magnalia Christi Americana, Books I and II,* edited by Kenneth B. Murdock with the assistance of Elizabeth W. Miller, 272–359. Cambridge: Harvard University Press, 1977.

——. *The Wonders of the Invisible World.* 1693. In Samuel G. Drake, *The Witchcraft Delusion in New England,* 1:1–247.

——. *The Wonders of the Invisible World.* 1693. In Burr, *Narratives of the Witchcraft Cases,* 203–251.

Mather, Increase. *Cases of Conscience Concerning Evil Spirits Personating Men* (excerpts). 1692. In *What Happened in Salem?,* edited by David Levin, 117–126. 2nd ed. New York: Harcourt, Brace, and World, 1960.

Matossian, Mary K. "Ergot and the Salem Witchcraft Affair." *American Scientist* 70 (July–August 1982): 355–357.

Matusow, Allen J. *The Unraveling of America: A History of Liberalism in the 1960s.* New York: Harper Torchbooks, 1986.

McManus, Edgar J. *Law and Liberty in Early New England: Criminal Justice and Due Process, 1620–1692.* Amherst: University of Massachusetts Press, 1993.

McWilliams, John. "Indian John and the Northern Tawnies." *New England Quarterly* 69 (December 1996): 580–604.

Micale, Mark S. *Hysterical Men: The Hidden History of Male Nervous Illness.* Cambridge: Harvard University Press, 2008.

Middlekauff, Robert. *The Mathers: Three Generations of Puritan Intellectuals, 1596–1728.* New York: Oxford University Press, 1971.

Midelfort, H. C. Erik. *A History of Madness in Sixteenth-Century Germany.* Stanford: Stanford University Press, 1999.

———. "Were There Really Witches?" In *Transition and Revolution: Problems and Issues of European Renaissance and Reformation History*, edited by Robert M. Kingdon, 189–205. Minneapolis: Burgess, 1974.

———. "Witch Craze? Beyond the Legends of Panic." *Magic, Ritual, and Witchcraft* 6 (Summer 2011): 11–33.

———. *Witch Hunting in Southwest Germany, 1562–1684: The Social and Intellectual Foundations*. Stanford: Stanford University Press, 1972.

Miller, Arthur. "Again They Drank from the Cup of Suspicion." *New York Times*, November 26, 1989.

———. *The Crucible: Text and Criticism*. Edited by Gerald Weales. New York: Viking, 1971.

———. "Journey to 'The Crucible.'" *New York Times*, February 8, 1953.

———. *Timebends: A Life*. New York: Grove, 1987.

Miller, Perry. *The New England Mind: From Colony to Province*. Vol. 2 of *The New England Mind*. 1953. Boston: Beacon, 1961.

Minkema, Kenneth P. Review of *In the Devil's Snare: The Salem Witchcraft Crisis of 1692*, by Mary Beth Norton, and *The Salem Witch Trials: A Day-by-Day Chronicle of a Community under Siege*, by Marilynne K. Roach. *Christian Century*, April 19, 2003.

Mintz, Steven. *Huck's Raft: A History of American Childhood*. Cambridge: Belknap Press of Harvard University Press, 2004.

Monter, E. William. "The Historiography of European Witchcraft: Progress and Prospects." *Journal of Interdisciplinary History* 2 (Spring 1972): 435–451.

———. "Witch Trials in Continental Europe, 1560–1660." In Ankarloo and Clark, *Witchcraft and Magic in Europe*, vol. 4, *The Period of the Witch Trials*, 1–52.

Morgan, Edmund. "Arthur Miller's *The Crucible* and the Salem Witch Trials: A Historian's View." In *The Golden and Brazen World: Papers in Literature and History, 1650–1800*, edited by John M. Wallace, 171–186. Berkeley: University of California Press, 1985.

———. *The Puritan Family: Religion and Domestic Relations in Seventeenth-Century New England*. 1944. New York: Harper Torchbooks, 1966.

———. Review of *The Devil in Massachusetts: A Modern Enquiry into the Salem Witch Trials*, by Marion L. Starkey. *American Historical Review* 55 (April 1950): 616–617.

———. "Witch Hunting." *New York Review of Books*, November 4, 1982.

Morrison, Kenneth M. *The Embattled Northeast: The Elusive Ideal of Alliance in Abenaki-Euramerican Relations*. Berkeley: University of California Press, 1984.

Murrin, John M. "Coming to Terms with the Salem Witch Trials." *Proceedings of the American Antiquarian Society* 110 (2000): 309–347.

———. "The Infernal Conspiracy of Indians and Grandmothers." *Reviews in American History* 31 (2003): 485–494.

———. "Magistrates, Sinners, and a Precarious Liberty: Trial by Jury in Seventeenth-Century New England." In Hall, Murrin, and Tate, *Saints and Revolutionaries: Essays on Early American History*, 152–206.

Nenonen, Marco. "Who Bears the Guilt for the Persecution of Witches?" *Studia Neophilologica* 84 (2012): 70–87.

Nirenberg, David. "Dark Counterpoint." Review of *The Music Libel against the Jews*, by Ruth HaCohen. *New Republic*, December 31, 2013.

Nissenbaum, Stephen. Review of *The Devil in the Shape of a Woman: Witchcraft in Colonial New England*, by Carol Karlsen. *William and Mary Quarterly*, 3rd ser., 46 (July 1989): 593–596.

Norton, Mary Beth. *Founding Mothers and Fathers: Gendered Power and the Forming of American Society.* New York: Alfred A. Knopf, 1996.

———. "George Burroughs and the Girls from Casco: The Maine Roots of Salem Witchcraft." *Maine History* 40 (Winter 2001–2): 259–277.

———. *In the Devil's Snare: The Salem Witchcraft Crisis of 1692.* New York: Alfred A. Knopf, 2002.

———. "The Refugee's Revenge." *Common-place: The Interactive Journal of Early American Life* 2, no. 3 (April 2002). www.common-place.org.

Ogden, Daniel. "Binding Spells: Curse Tablets and Voodoo Dolls in the Greek and Roman Worlds." In Ankarloo and Clark, *Witchcraft and Magic in Europe*, vol. 2, *Ancient Greece and Rome*, 1–90.

Parris, Samuel. "A general account of the transactions between the inhabitants of Salem village and my self Samuel Parris." Handwritten manuscript, Gold Star Collection, William L. Clements Library, University of Michigan.

Patterson, James T. *Grand Expectations: The United States, 1945–1974.* New York: Oxford University Press, 1996.

Payne, Daniel G. "Defending against the Indefensible: Spectral Evidence at the Salem Witchcraft Trials." *Essex Institute Historical Collections* 129 (1993): 62–83.

Pencak, William. *War, Politics, and Revolution in Provincial Massachusetts.* Boston: Northeastern University Press, 1981.

Perley, Sidney. *The History of Salem, Massachusetts.* 3 vols. Salem: Sidney Perley, 1924–28.

Pestana, Carla Gardina. *Quakers and Baptists in Colonial Massachusetts.* New York: Cambridge University Press, 1991.

Peters, Edward. "The Medieval Church and State on Superstition, Magic and Witchcraft: From Augustine to the Sixteenth Century." In Ankarloo and Clark, *Witchcraft and Magic in Europe*, vol. 3, *The Middle Ages*, 173–245.

Pierce, Richard D., ed. *The Records of the First Church in Salem, Massachusetts, 1629–1736.* Salem, MA: Essex Institute, 1974.

Poole, William Frederick. "The Witchcraft Delusion of 1692. By Gov. Thomas Hutchinson." *New England Historical and Genealogical Register* 24 (1870): 381–414.

Pope, Robert G. *The Half-Way Covenant: Church Membership in Puritan New England.* Princeton: Princeton University Press, 1969.

Porterfield, Amanda. *Female Piety in Puritan New England: The Emergence of Religious Humanism.* New York: Oxford University Press, 1992.

———. "Witchcraft and the Colonization of Algonquian and Iroquois Cultures." *Religion and American Culture: A Journal of Interpretation* 2 (Winter 1992): 103–124.

Pulsipher, Jenny Hale. "'Dark Cloud Rising from the East': Indian Sovereignty and the Coming of King William's War in New England." *New England Quarterly* 80 (December 2007): 588–613.

———. *Subjects unto the Same King: Indians, English, and the Contest for Authority in Colonial New England.* 2005. Philadelphia: University of Pennsylvania Press, 2007.

Ray, Benjamin C. "The Geography of Witchcraft Accusations in 1692 Salem Village." *William and Mary Quarterly*, 3rd ser., 65 (July 2008): 449–478.

———. "'The Salem Witch Mania': Recent Scholarship and American History Textbooks." *Journal of the American Academy of Religion* 78 (March 2010): 40–64.

———. *Satan and Salem: The Witch-Hunt Crisis of 1692.* Charlottesville: University of Virginia Press, 2015.

———. "Satan's War against the Covenant in Salem Village, 1692." *New England Quarterly* 80 (March 2007): 69–95.

"Records of the Topsfield Church." *Historical Collections of the Topsfield Historical Society* 14 (1909).

Reis, Elizabeth. *Damned Women: Sinners and Witches in Puritan New England.* Ithaca: Cornell University Press, 1997.

Rivett, Sarah. "Our Salem, Our Selves." *William and Mary Quarterly*, 3rd ser., 65 (July 2008): 495–502.

———. *The Science of the Soul in Colonial New England.* Chapel Hill: University of North Carolina Press, 2011.

Roach, Marilynne K. *The Salem Witch Trials: A Day-by-Day Chronicle of a Community under Siege.* 2002. Lanham, MD: Taylor Trade, 2004.

———. *Six Women of Salem: The Untold Story of the Accused and Their Accusers in the Salem Witch Trials.* Boston: Da Capo, 2013.

———. "'That Child, Betty Parris': Elizabeth (Parris) Barron and the People in Her Life." *Essex Institute Historical Collections* 124 (January 1988): 1–27.

Robinson, Enders A. *The Devil Discovered: Salem Witchcraft 1692.* New York: Hippocrene Books, 1991.

———. *Salem Witchcraft and Hawthorne's House of the Seven Gables.* Bowie, MD: Heritage Books, 1992.

Rodgers, Daniel T. *Age of Fracture.* Cambridge, MA: Belknap Press of Harvard University Press, 2011.

Rosenthal, Bernard. "General Introduction." In *Records of the Salem Witch-Hunt,* edited by Rosenthal et al., 15–43. New York: Cambridge University Press, 2009.

———. *Salem Story: Reading the Witch Trials of 1692.* 1993. Cambridge: Cambridge University Press, 1995.

———. "Tituba's Story." *New England Quarterly* 71 (1998): 190–203.

Rosenthal, Bernard, et al., eds. *Records of the Salem Witch-Hunt.* New York: Cambridge University Press, 2009.

Rudé, George. *The Crowd in History: A Study of Popular Disturbances in France and England, 1730–1848.* New York: Wiley, 1964.

Salisbury, Neal. *Manitou and Providence: Indians, Europeans, and the Making of New England, 1500–1643.* 1982. New York: Oxford University Press, 1984.

———. "Red Puritans: The 'Praying Indians' of Massachusetts Bay and John Eliot." *William and Mary Quarterly*, 3rd ser., 31 (January 1974): 27–54.

———. Review of *In the Devil's Snare: The Salem Witchcraft Crisis of 1692,* by Mary Beth Norton. *Journal of American History* 91 (June 2004): 201–202.

Schiff, Stacy. "The Witches of Salem." *New Yorker,* September 7, 2015.

———. *The Witches: Salem, 1692.* New York: Little, Brown, 2015.

Sewall, Samuel. *The Diary of Samuel Sewall, 1674–1729,* edited by M. Halsey Thomas. Vol. 1, 1674–1708. New York: Farrar, Straus and Giroux, 1973.

Shapiro, Laura. "The Lessons of Salem." *Newsweek,* August 31, 1992.

Sharpe, James. *Instruments of Darkness: Witchcraft in Early Modern England.* 1996. Philadelphia: University of Pennsylvania Press, 1997.

Silverman, Kenneth. *The Life and Times of Cotton Mather.* New York: Columbia University Press, 1985.

Slotkin, Richard. *Regeneration through Violence: The Mythology of the American Frontier, 1600–1860.* Middletown, CT: Wesleyan University Press, 1973.

Smith-Rosenberg, Carroll. "The Hysterical Woman: Sex Roles and Role Conflict in 19th-Century America." *Social Research* 39 (Winter 1972): 652–678.

Spanos, Nicholas P., and Jack Gottlieb. "Ergotism and the Salem Village Witch Trials." *Science,* December 24, 1976.

Starkey, Marion L. *The Devil in Massachusetts: A Modern Enquiry into the Salem Witch Trials.* 1949. Garden City, NY: Anchor Books, 1969.

Tanenhaus, Sam. *Whittaker Chambers: A Biography.* New York: Random House, 1997.

Taylor, Alan. "Crucibles." Chap. 7 in *Writing Early American History.* Philadelphia: University of Pennsylvania Press, 2005.

Taylor, Richard S. "Telling Lincoln's Story." *Journal of the Abraham Lincoln Association* 21 (Summer 2000): 44–68. http://quod.lib.umich.edu/j/jala/2629860.0021.206.

Thomas, Keith. "The Relevance of Social Anthropology to the Historical Study of English Witchcraft." In Douglas, *Witchcraft Confessions and Accusations,* 47–79.

———. *Religion and the Decline of Magic.* New York: Charles Scribner's Sons, 1971.

———. "Satan in Salem." *New York Review of Books,* August 8, 1974.

———. "Speak of the Devil." *New York Review of Books,* April 27, 2006.

Thompson, E. P. "The Moral Economy of the English Crowd in the Eighteenth Century." *Past and Present* 50 (1971): 76–136.

Thompson, Roger. "Review Article: Salem Revisited." *Journal of American Studies* 6 (1972): 317–336.

Thomsen, Marie-Louise. "Witchcraft and Magic in Ancient Mesopotamia." In Ankarloo and Clark, *Witchcraft and Magic in Europe,* vol. 1, *Biblical and Pagan Societies,* 1–95.

Tilly, Charles. *The Politics of Collective Violence.* Cambridge: Cambridge University Press, 2003.

Tomlin, R. S. O. "'Paedagogium and Septizonium': Two Roman Lead Tablets from Leicester." *Zeitschrift fur Papyrologie und Epigraphik* 167 (2008): 207–218.

Trask, Richard B., ed. *"The Devil Hath Been Raised": A Documentary History of the Salem Village Witchcraft Outbreak of March 1692.* Rev. ed. Danvers, MA: Yeoman, 1997.

Turner, Victor. "Witchcraft and Sorcery: Taxonomy versus Dynamics." Chap. 5 in *The Forest of Symbols: Aspects of Ndembu Ritual.* 1967. Ithaca: Cornell University Press, 1970.

Ulrich, Laurel Thatcher. *Good Wives: Image and Reality in the Lives of Women in Northern New England, 1650–1750.* 1980. New York: Vintage Books, 1991.

Upham, Charles W. *Salem Witchcraft; with an Account of Salem Village, and a History of Opinions on Witchcraft and Kindred Subjects*. 1867. 2 vols. New York; Frederick Ungar, n.d.

Vaughan, Alden T. "From White Man to Redskin: Changing Anglo-American Perceptions of the American Indians." *American Historical Review* 87 (October 1982): 917–953.

———. *New England Frontier: Puritans and Indians, 1620–1675*. 1965. 3rd ed. Norman: University of Oklahoma Press, 1995.

Walker, D. P. *Unclean Spirits: Possession and Exorcism in France and England in the Late Sixteenth and Early Seventeenth Centuries*. Philadelphia: University of Pennsylvania Press, 1981.

Walzer, Michael. "Puritanism as a Revolutionary Ideology." *History and Theory* 3 (1963): 59–90.

Watson, Bruce. "Salem's Dark Hour: Did the Devil Make Them Do It?" *Smithsonian* 23 (April 1992): 117–131.

Weinstein, Allen. *Perjury: The Hiss-Chambers Case*. 3rd ed. Stanford, CA: Hoover Institution Press, 2013.

Weisman, Richard. *Witchcraft, Magic, and Religion in 17th-Century Massachusetts*. Amherst: University of Massachusetts Press, 1984.

White, Richard. "Environmentalism and Indian Peoples." In *Earth, Air, Fire, Water: Humanistic Studies of the Environment*, edited by Jill Ker Conway, Kenneth Keniston, and Leo Marx, 125–144. Amherst: University of Massachusetts Press, 1999.

Whitney, Elspeth. "International Trends: The Witch 'She'/The Historian 'He': Gender and the Historiography of the European Witch-Hunts." *Journal of Women's History* 7 (Fall 1995): 77–101.

Willis, William. *The History of Portland, from 1632 to 1864*. 1865. Facsimile reprint. Somersworth, NH: New Hampshire Publishing, and Maine Historical Society, 1972.

Wood, Gordon. "The Bloodiest War." *New York Review of Books*, April 9, 1998.

Woodward, Walter W. *Prospero's America: John Winthrop, Jr., Alchemy, and the Creation of New England Culture, 1606–1676*. Chapel Hill: University of North Carolina Press, 2010.

Worthen, Molly. "Faithless." Review of *The Twilight of the American Enlightenment: The 1950s and the Crisis of Liberal Belief*, by George M. Marsden. *Democracy: A Journal of Ideas*, no. 32 (Spring 2014): 77–85.

Young, Christine Alice. *From "Good Order" to Glorious Revolution: Salem, Massachusetts, 1628–1689*. Ann Arbor: UMI Research Press, 1980.

Young, Martha M. "The Salem Witch Trials 300 Years Later: How Far Has the American Legal System Come? How Much Further Does It Need to Go?" *Tulane Legal Review* 64 (1989–1990): 235–258.

Ziff, Larzer. *Puritanism in America: New Culture in a New World*. 1973. New York: Viking Press, 1974.

Index

Scholarly works on Salem, witch hunting, and related fields appear solely under their authors' names, unless these works occupy pivotal positions in the text.